THE REMAINS OF COMPANY D

The Remains of
COMPANY D

A Story of the Great War

James Carl Nelson

ST. MARTIN'S PRESS ❦ NEW YORK

Book design by Phil Mazzone

Maps by Paul J. Pugliese

Library of Congress Cataloging-in-Publication Data

Nelson, James Carl.
    The remains of Company D : a story of the Great War / James Carl Nelson.—
1st ed.
            p. cm.
    Includes bibliographical references.
    ISBN 978-0-312-55100-1
    1. Nelson, John, 1892–1993.   2. Soldiers—United States—Biography.
    3. United States. Army. Infantry Regiment, 28th.   4. World War,
1914–1918—Personal narratives, American.   5. World War, 1914–1918—
Regimental histories—United States.   6. United States. Army—Military life—
History—20th century.   7. World War, 1914–1918—Psychological
aspects.   8. Cantigny, Battle of, Cantigny, France, 1918.   9. World War,
1914–1918—Campaigns—France—Soissons.   10. Argonne, Battle of the, France,
1918.   I. Title.
    D570.3328th .N45 2009
    940.4'1273092—dc22
    [B]
                                                                2009016931

First Edition: October 2009

10 9 8 7 6 5 4 3 2 1

For my boys, Nathaniel and Ethan

For all the John Nelsons I have known

And for the men of Company D, 28th Infantry Regiment,
United States First Division, in the Great War

CONTENTS

ACKNOWLEDGMENTS

They say it's the journey, not the destination, that matters, and that's true of my own journey in researching and writing this book. Since beginning my search for what remains of Company D, I have crossed paths with dozens of the company's descendants, many of whom shared family materials with me, or, in the equally numerous cases where there was no material to share, at the very least shared their enthusiasm for this project.

There are too many of the above to list here, but I would like to thank the following for their help: first and foremost Hubert M. (Bert) Stainton, Jr., for allowing me access to that box of "stuff" on Marvin Stainton; Linda Matzke, for similarly allowing me to use the material on Rollin Livick; Jason Bronston and Diane Williamson for the letters of, respectively, Lloyd Bronston and Willard Storms; David and Timothy Senay for the great and unexpected gift of Charles T. Senay's unpublished memoir "From Shavetail to Captain"; Margaret Brackett for photos of and material on her great-uncle, Soren C. Sorensen; Dorothy Rinaldo for photos of and letters from her father, William D. Warren; Dorothy Geduldig for material on her uncle Leigh Wilson; Arnold Davis for the story of his family and of his uncle, Paul Davis; and Barbara Babcock for allowing the use of the memoirs of her grandfather, Conrad Stanton Babcock.

I'd like to thank as well Tom Butler, Paul Proulx, Jerre Blythe, Robert Beard, Wray Hall, Emil Eliason, Robert Baucaro, Daniel Newhall, Norma Carns, Carol Corby, George Gahring, and James Underhill for their reminiscences of their doughboy ancestors, and for various family materials that helped flesh out the story of their forebears' unit.

Authors James H. Hallas, Alan Axelrod, Col. Stephen L. Bowman, Edward Lengel, Edward M. Coffman, and Stephen L. Harris were kind enough to read parts of the manuscript and offer their suggestions and corrections; Douglas V. Johnson II was enthusiastic and helpful and kind from the beginning and gave me the encouragement to keep going when all seemed hopeless. Thanks to Andrew Woods, research historian at the Colonel Robert R. McCormick Research Center, and Paul Herbert, executive director of the Cantigny First Division Foundation, for their assistance and insight; thanks also to Ed Burke, executive director of the Society of the First Division, for his help. Also, I want to thank my guides in France—Michel Souquet, who took me to out-of-the-way places around Cantigny, and Frederic Castier, who on a rainy and cold day led me to the top of Hill 240.

A small army of researchers, librarians, and archivists were instrumental in helping me unearth Company D's remains as well: special thanks to Phyllis Goodnow, Mireya Throop, Laurie Miller, Barbara Koski, Ericka Loze at the Donovan Research Library; Tim Nennigan at the U.S. National Archives in College Park, Maryland; and Jerry L. Clark at the National Archives in Washington, D.C.

Thanks also to Rowena Horr in Kansas, R. Garey Hodge in Illinois, Laura Crane in Missouri, Nancy G. Williamson in Wisconsin, Patricia J. Weeks in Mississippi, Michael Brophy in Massachusetts, and Marion Ehrhardt at the Ellenville Public Library and Museum in Ellenville, New York; Lori Berdak Miller of Redbird Research in Missouri, Steve Lyons of Lyons Research, Nancy Stuck in Carlisle, Pennsylvania; and Elizabeth McCall in New York.

Thanks also to my friends Kurt Svenson and Susan Baker, both of whom offered constant encouragement during my lonely quest, as did my siblings, John and Donna, and my mother (thanks, Mom). Special thanks also to my agent, James D. Hornfischer, for his suggestions and enthusiasm for this project, and my editor, Marc Resnick, for making me look good. Thanks also go to copy editor Donald I. Davidson, who asked all the right questions.

Last but by far not least, thanks to my wife, Janet Goodrich, who allowed me to spend the kids' milk money and go the distance in what at times seemed a quixotic effort.

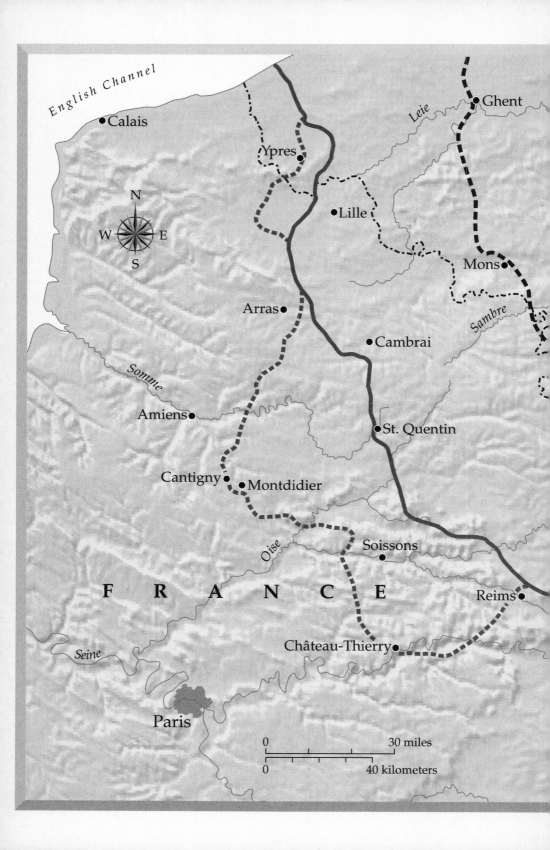

English Channel

Calais

Ypres

Lille

Ghent

Leie

Mons

Sambre

N
W   E
S

Arras

Cambrai

Somme

Amiens

St. Quentin

Cantigny

Montdidier

Soissons

Oise

Reims

F R A N C E

Château-Thierry

Seine

Paris

0   30 miles

0   40 kilometers

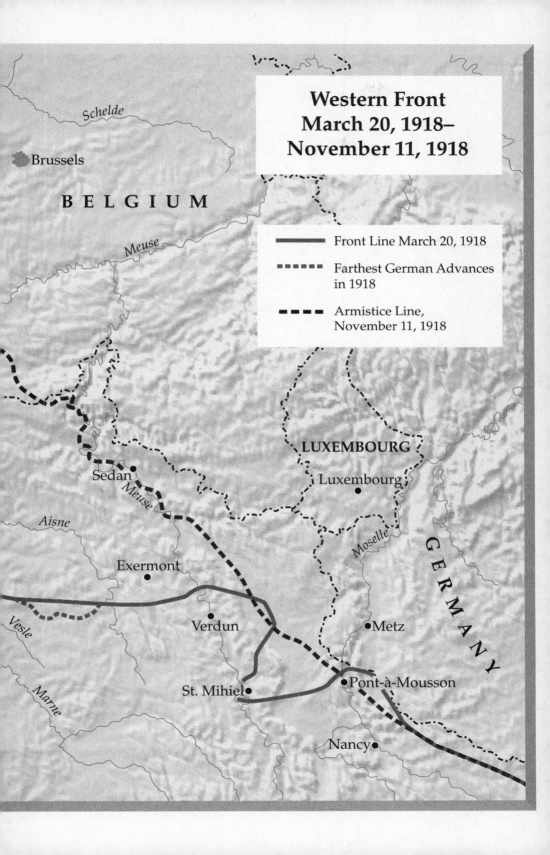

Western Front
March 20, 1918–
November 11, 1918

Schelde

Brussels

BELGIUM

Meuse

Front Line March 20, 1918

Farthest German Advances
in 1918

Armistice Line,
November 11, 1918

LUXEMBOURG

Sedan

Meuse

Luxembourg

Aisne

Moselle

GERMANY

Exermont

Vesle

Verdun

Metz

Marne

St. Mihiel

Pont-à-Mousson

Nancy

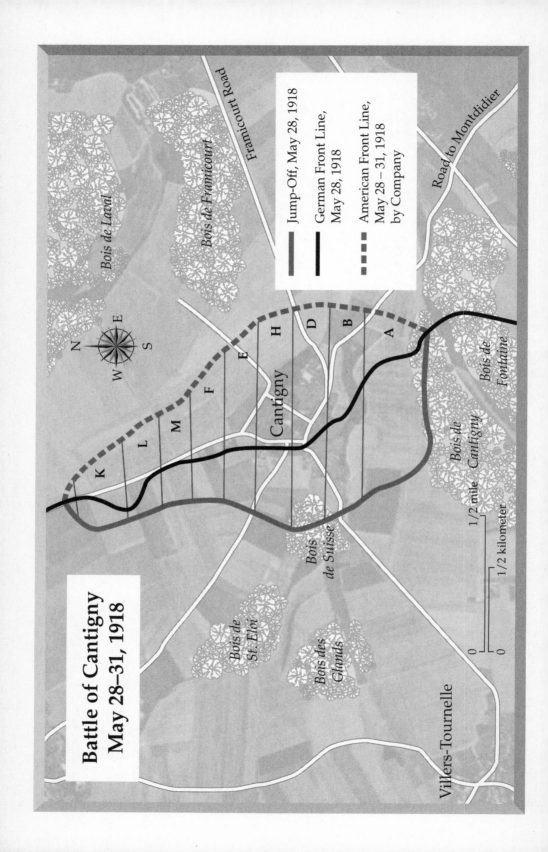

Battle of Cantigny
May 28–31, 1918

Bois de Laval

Bois de Framicourt

Framicourt Road

Road to Montdidier

Jump-Off, May 28, 1918

German Front Line,
May 28, 1918

American Front Line,
May 28 – 31, 1918
by Company

N
E
S
W

K
L
M
F
E
H
D
B
A

Cantigny

Bois de Fontaine

Bois de Cantigny

Bois de Suisse

Bois de St. Éloi

Bois des Glands

Villers-Tournelle

1/2 mile

1/2 kilometer

0

0

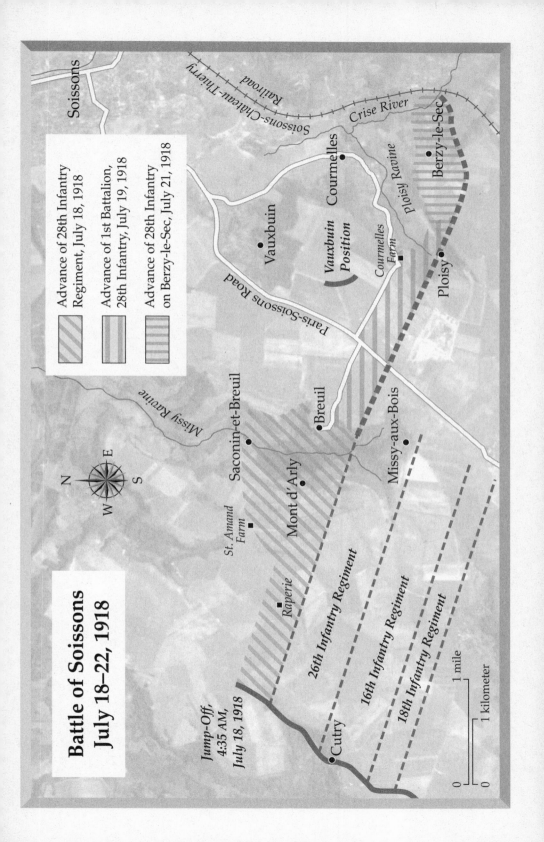

Battle of Soissons
July 18–22, 1918

Soissons

Soissons-Château-Thierry Railroad

Crise River

Berzy-le-Sec

Ploisy Ravine

Courmelles

Vauxbuin

Vauxbuin Position

Courmelles Farm

Ploisy

Paris-Soissons Road

Missy Ravine

Saconin-et-Breuil

Breuil

Mont d'Arly

Missy-aux-Bois

St. Amand Farm

Raperie

26th Infantry Regiment

16th Infantry Regiment

18th Infantry Regiment

Jump-Off,
4:35 AM,
July 18, 1918

Cutry

N E W S

Advance of 28th Infantry Regiment, July 18, 1918

Advance of 1st Battalion, 28th Infantry, July 19, 1918

Advance of 28th Infantry on Berzy-le-Sec, July 21, 1918

1 mile

1 kilometer

0

0

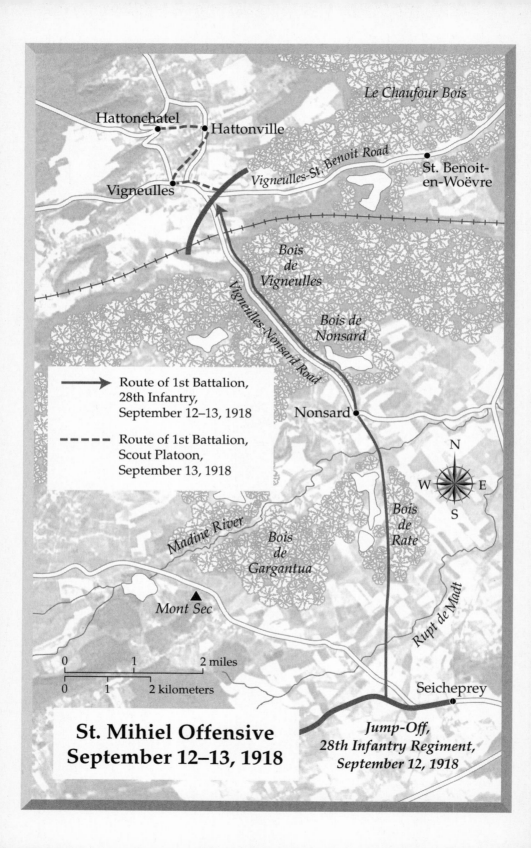

Le Chaufour Bois

Hattonchatel ● Hattonville

Vigneulles-St.-Benoit Road

● St. Benoit-
en-Woëvre

Vigneulles

Bois
de
Vigneulles

Bois de
Nonsard

Route of 1st Battalion,
28th Infantry,
September 12–13, 1918

Route of 1st Battalion,
Scout Platoon,
September 13, 1918

Nonsard ●

N

W ✦ E

S

Bois
de
Rate

Madine River

Bois
de
Gargantua

▲
Mont Sec

Rupt de Madt

0   1   2 miles

0   1   2 kilometers

Seicheprey ●

**St. Mihiel Offensive
September 12–13, 1918**

*Jump-Off,
28th Infantry Regiment,
September 12, 1918*

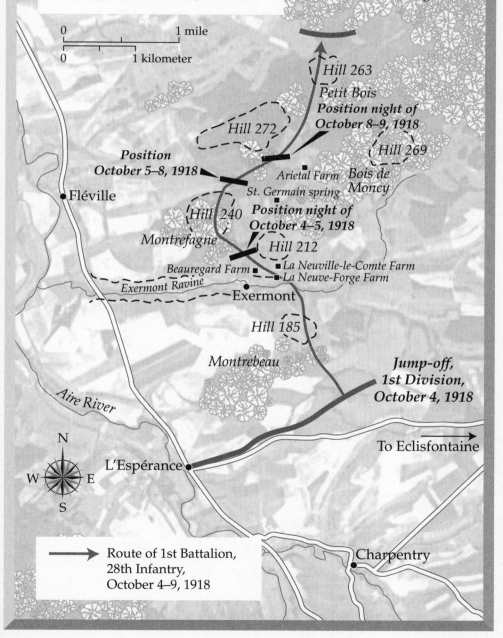

Battle of the Meuse-Argonne
Second Phase
October 1–12, 1918

0   1 mile

0   1 kilometer

Bois de Romagne

Hill 263

Petit Bois

**Position night of
October 8–9, 1918**

Hill 272

Hill 269

**Position
October 5–8, 1918**

Arietal Farm

*Bois de
Moncy*

St. Germain spring

Fléville

Hill 240

**Position night of
October 4–5, 1918**

Montrefagne

Hill 212

Beauregard Farm

La Neuville-le-Comte Farm

La Neuve-Forge Farm

Exermont Ravine

Exermont

Hill 185

**Jump-off,
1st Division,
October 4, 1918**

Montrebeau

Aire River

To Eclisfontaine

N
W   E
S

L'Espérance

Charpentry

→ Route of 1st Battalion,
28th Infantry,
October 4–9, 1918

THE REMAINS OF COMPANY D

PRELUDE

Soissons, France
July 19, 1918

And the bullets so thick now they split the wheat chaff swirling and twirling and flitting before drifting languidly to earth like a shower of gold, down, down over his head, on to his body where he presses his face into the wheat and prays, Jesus Christ, oh Jesus Christ . . .

Snipers in the trees, in the tall pleasant green poplars at the edge of the road; and sharply angling missiles from the machine guns spear the air and then plummet, kicking up tiny black tornadoes of earth and spouting quiet crimson geysers when they catch one of the poor dumb sonsabitches lying here next to him, waiting for the thing, waiting to go over . . .

Just overhead and impossibly close the staccato hum of a blood-red Hun plane, a raptor seeking its prey, looking for movement among the brown forms hugging the wheat, and then the oncoming cowling, winking, becoming larger, and the sharp puffs of dirt and chaff . . .

Then a shadow, and Sorensen's standing over him, and oh, Jesus Christ, a whistle, shrill and piercing. "Get up you sonsabitches, you bastards. Get up and move out. We're going over," and this is it and can he stand and can he move and then a roar, cackling and dry, from scores of parched throats, quickly drowned out in the rising pup-pup-pup of the machine guns and the thing is on . . .

And he runs now, left foot right foot, through the dangling yellow golden stalks, chasing his own shadow, longer now in the late afternoon's glow, and he can make out the long dark tip of his bayonet hovering over his left shoulder as he chases it east . . . and running now double-timing and from the corner of his right eye he can just make out the dark form of one of the boys and then suddenly he's just gone . . . and in the dazzling light something shiny and glimmering and glinting over there on the left and oh, Jesus Christ, the machine guns . . .

He's at the road now, and he's climbing up and over and stumbling atop the bodies of the poor doughboys killed that morning, the bodies swelling already in the hot July sun, and he stumbles for a moment and then slides headfirst to the other side, into the ditch, and then up again, panting, and he chokes once on the dust in his throat and the sweat coursing through his clothing and panting his heart pounding and he can see the boys spreading over the dry plain beginning to glow like cheap red wine in the setting sun and he tries to follow, tries to catch them and . . .

1

A Doughboy

Hᴇ ɴᴇᴠᴇʀ ᴍᴀᴅᴇ ɪᴛ to Berzy. Hell, he never even made it to Ploisy.

He went lights-out somewhere just beyond the Paris-Soissons Road, while the air rained bullets and his company—the survivors, anyway—rolled on through the German line, shooting and yelling and swearing and falling, and disappeared into the smoke and dust and fading evening light of a hot July day.

He took his last look at them, at their sweat-stained, khaki-clad backs and their tin hats, as the shadows began to lengthen across the wheat, as the *pup-pup-pup* of the machine guns rose to a ghastly cacophony, as the rolling barrage he was chasing raced farther out of reach, like a carrot on a stick, and as a single machine-gun bullet pierced his blouse just above his left pelvic brim, bounced off his spine, rattled through his intestines, and then exited above his right hip.

And it was then, as he would tell some insurance clerk in 1919, he fell unconscious in the wheat, as his "unit"—to which he'd belonged for just a month—stepped over him and continued its advance down the sloping, deadly vale into the village of Ploisy, and slightly beyond.

He would awake hours later to the sound of—what? "Intermittent machine gun fire," one report says. To the sounds of a blubbering confession, my father would tell me many years later, as another from his company who lay paralyzed, too, there in the wheat poured out to the Old Man his confessions to having performed every kind of criminal perversion, rape and murder and God knows what.

In the morning, as the sounds of battle rose steadily with the sun, John Nelson had been roughly kicked by an Algerian stretcher-bearer searching for life among the brown clumps of young Americans in the wheat, and he had groaned, and achieved his random salvation on, and his escape from, that terrible battlefield, the one just south of Soissons, where the tide of war was turning in the Allies' favor even as he was being hustled to the back lines.

He was carried to a field station in a cave at Missy-aux-Bois, and then trucked to Field Hospital No. 12, in the village of Pierrefonds-les-Bains, where blood-spattered, exhausted surgeons plied their scalpels and bone saws in an old hotel and, before the battle was done, on tables spilled into the streets.

Once he had been patched together, there ensued an odyssey through hospitals in France as well as the United States, and on April 1, 1919, the army deemed him okay, and handed him $60 and an honorable discharge, and a swift kick out of the gates of Camp Grant.

He returned to his $32-a-week job as a painter in Chicago, to which he'd first traveled in 1911, after leaving Sweden and hopping the *Lusitania* from England to the gates at Ellis Island. And he would live long enough to send his own son into another, second, world war, and to wear lime-green pants with white shoes and to watch men walk on the moon, and to have six grandchildren, of which I was the last.

But in all the days I knew him, he never talked about them, never mentioned his fellow Swede, Swanson, whose body wasn't found until 1933, just a collection of bare bones by then, wrapped in burlap and scattered with three unknowns in a shallow grave in Berzy-le-Sec.

He never mentioned the Norwegian, Eidsvik, whose body went home by boat though the fjords in 1922, nor did he talk of Ralph Pol or Orville Ballard, or any of those with whom he had crossed the Paris-Soissons Road that day and who had also lived—Baucaro and Bronston and Vedral, the tough Bohemian sergeant. He talked a little about that day over the years, but words weren't his currency, and so he had left us with the happy ending, and no beginning or middle, and kept the seamy part, the details of that day, to himself.

On the day he turned one hundred years old I surprised him, and found the ancient doughboy daydreaming in his tiny cell at the retirement home. He was stretched out on his bed, hands behind his head, staring at the ceiling when I walked in. He had never weighed more than 150 pounds, and he was shrunken now with great age, his body a tiny island in the sea of his bed, and lost as well in the blue wool sweater he always wore, no matter the season.

His senses were shot, his eyesight blurred with cataracts, but his mind was still sharp, and he knew someone was there. He startled and sat up as if he'd been caught doing something wrong, and directed me with a wave of his hand to a chair, on which sat a box full of cards and letters. "Read them to me," he said.

There were cards from the few old Swedes back in Chicago who hadn't yet faded away, some from old neighbors, some from God knows who, and it struck me for the first time that he'd lived a whole life I knew little of, though I'd known him thirty-six years by then.

All of those names, all of those unknown well-wishers, added up to a map of where he'd been, touchstones gathered over a century, remnants of his small immigrant drama, people who'd somehow been touched by him enough to remember a birthday and buy a card and walk it down to the post office and acknowledge an old man imprisoned by time, and by his memories.

And now that I know some of the story, more than he ever let on, I wonder what it was he'd been thinking of when I walked into his room, just a few hours before the little party, with coffee, and cake, and balloons, and all the family, even his wife of seventy years, Karin, who was mostly confined to a separate, darker wing of the home since a series of strokes had taken most of her memory.

I wonder now if he'd been thinking of them, the others, the ones who hadn't ever figured in his short, sweet story of near death and salvation on a foreign battlefield long ago; I wonder if he was conjuring the faces of the other boys and all that he saw at the Paris-Soissons Road, images caught from the corner of the eye while running headlong to oblivion: the dead ones, the wounded, the dying horses, and perhaps a broken, smoldering tank.

And I wonder if he was retracing his last few steps, going over his tracks in the wheat, following a wave of khaki soldiers stretched out from north to south in front of him, some stumbling, some toppling, some staggering back with hands to their throats, others on their knees, bleeding.

I wonder now if his one hundred years had been condensed into those few terrifying snapshots, images he'd tamped down over the years into his subconscious, demons let loose like a creeping barrage only in moments of weakness, of which I believe he had very few, though I know now that he had some.

I wonder if he was thinking of these things that day, of the other boys, of Misiewicz and Ballard and Cole, and of the great turn that had been made in his fate, and of how strange and wonderful it had been that he had made it through. I wonder if he was thinking of these things, but of course now I'll never know.

My outfit started advancing on July 18 and moved forward several miles in the first two days. About six o'clock on the 19th I was struck by machine gun fire from our flank, was knocked unconscious and did not come to until about midnight. Was picked up by stretcher bearers in the morning and taken to a first-aid station.

What was left of John Nelson's division, the 1st, was home and parading in Washington on the day he told the above brief story of woe and near disaster to a clerk with the department of war-risk insurance.

Broken, and still hobbling on that day in 1919, he'd come to seek recompense for having crossed the Paris-Soissons Road and seen the things he saw, and for having spent that long night in the wheat among the dead and dying. It wasn't until after he died that I found the record, and it struck me how little the story had changed, how so very little had been added to it, in the seventy-five years he'd had to tell it, again and again.

He had never shown much weakness, even for life, always displaying just the tough crust developed in another century, another millennium, enveloping layers that had their start in childhood, on a small farm in southern

Sweden, where he was born on March 15, 1892, the sixth of eleven children sired by Nils Jonsson, who in maddening Scandinavian symmetry was the son of Jon Nilsson, who was the son of Nils Jonsson, who was the son of yet another Jon Nilsson, the son of a Nils whose last name is lost to history, all of whom had labored on a small patch of ground called Kangsleboda, outside of the flyspeck village of Langhult.

This had gone on for generations, at least since 1735, when John Nelson's great-great-grandfather and namesake had been born at Langhult. All I know of this Jon Nilsson was that he lived to be eighty years old and that when he died in 1815 he had amassed a fortune consisting of twenty-four clay pots, no cash, no silver, fourteen animals, a smattering of copper, brass, and iron tools, and two books—one, no doubt, being a Bible.

The local church records say that it all went to his wife, Ingeborg, and his son Nils and daughter Sophia. "Widow to keep all except husband's clothes that now belong to the folks to auction off," his will said, and someone had added the note: "Sophia is lame. She cannot take care of herself. Nils has decided to take care of her and her property as well as he can. If not some other relative to do so."

Hard times hadn't softened much by the time Kangsleboda was passed to Nils Jonsson, my great-grandfather, in the 1870s. He had by then married Ingrid Kristin Bengtsdotter, who was the daughter of Bengt Jonsson, who of course was the son of Jon Bengtsson, son of Bengt Jonsson.

The couple's firstborn, Pelle August, arrived in 1876, and lived just two years. Bengt—who else?—followed, as did Pelle Johan, Axel, Amanda, Olivia, Jon, Carl Olaf, Viktor, Ernest, and lastly Sven Alfred, spit out when the well-worn Ingrid was forty-six years old and Nils was fifty-three.

At the age of twelve, Jon Nilsson's parents obtained an apprenticeship for him with a local painter, and so he began his life's work, and it was while engaged as a house painter that he saw his first automobile, a rare, shared memory which always brought a guffaw and the line, "I nearly fell off my ladder."

By nineteen a journeyman painter, and with his older brother Axel already having left for America to lumberjack in the Northwest, Jon Nilsson decided it was time to seek his own fortune. He sailed for London and then for the United States, and walked up the dock at Ellis Island on May 5, 1911.

And before too long, and for peculiarly American reasons, Jon Nilsson became John Nelson, alien resident of the United States of America. He traveled first to Chicago, where there was a friend of a friend with whom to stay, and at some point, in 1914 or so, he moved to Denver and hung flocked wallpaper in saloons and boardinghouses for fifty cents an hour.

But when he heard he could earn an extra nickel an hour back in Chicago, he returned to the Windy City—which is where the draft caught up with him in October 1917. And so it was that he became a doughboy—and it was from such origins that so many doughboys came—and was trained at Camp Grant, in northern Illinois, and then shipped to France, and patriotically took his bullet, and was left for dead, as a battle raged over and beyond him, on the second day of the Allied offensive that turned the tide of the war.

He was taciturn, almost silent, a five foot eight inch tower of measured indifference, and as a child I feared him as much as I wondered at the few relics that suggested his story—the army-surplus grenade on the mantel we all wanted to believe had come from his war; the Purple Heart hanging in his den over a picture of Lady Liberty and a kneeling doughboy I was certain was him; and the queer, circular dog tags, with his ridiculously simple name and the numbers 2061839 etched in the silver.

And for many years it was those few things, and his few words about Soissons, that seemed the sum of his great, long-ago adventure.

But I know now there was much more to the story than he'd ever let on, that it loomed in his consciousness throughout each year, throughout all of his many years, and that it was most certainly there every July 19, when Karin would arrange for someone else to watch the kids, and she and her husband would take the day to be alone, to go for a drive in the country, maybe to picnic, maybe sit by a river and just be, just breathe, watch the clouds, and listen to the humming mosquitoes, no words of that day spoken, and none needed.

I didn't know that they did this until I was in my midtwenties, when my grandmother casually mentioned it in a note of thanks for a book on the First World War I'd sent to John Nelson, and it struck me as so odd, yet so pure, such a lifting of a veil.

And I was stunned, and pleased, somehow, to discover that John Nelson kept a rite, a personal Easter—and I was just as happy to find that the heart of a sentimentalist beat somewhere deep down beneath that hard crust.

And thinking now of that small anniversary he kept, that second birthday, I like to think he kept it as well for the others, that maybe he said a few words to himself those July nineteenths when he rose, and thought of a face, or half a name, and of what had happened as they crossed the Paris-Soissons Road. I like to think that keeping July nineteenth sacred was as much for them as it was for himself, but of course I'll never know.

John Nelson lived to be one hundred and one, dying on a cold December day in 1993, with no stretcher bearers around to save him this time, not even a pallbearer to lift his frail form and lay him down to the sound of taps. Instead they shipped his body to Chicago, where he was buried without ceremony.

When he died, I inherited his dog tags. His story, as well, passed to me. It was mine to do with as I wished, to improve upon and maybe finish, or to just let alone. But for reasons I still can hardly articulate, the image of him there in the wheat has haunted my own life, as it certainly haunted his.

Though as a child I'd repeated his tale by rote to anyone who would listen, and often on hot, restless nights when sleep wouldn't come thought of him lying there, it took years, and my own ascent into manhood, and the birth of my own children, to finally grasp the import of the story, and how it had shadowed his seemingly endless days afterward, and how my family's otherwise banal immigrant saga had been interrupted, and almost curtailed, at a place called Soissons.

But it wasn't until he died and let go his ownership of the experience that I felt free to pursue the story. And it was while pursuing it that I stumbled upon the names of the others, and realized I had perhaps stumbled upon the rest of his story, and some of the things he would not, or could not, articulate about what had happened to him there, in the wheat, on that hot July day.

The names had come from a museum, and were there on a muster roll for Company D of the 28th Infantry Regiment, 1st Division, dated August 1,

1918. The Old Man was there, listed as "Missing since recent operations," but his was just one of scores and scores of names who'd gone missing, and the roll, with its names typed so neatly in black ink on white paper, said more about that day, and the next few days, than the Old Man had ever been able.

Livick, Maine, Meyers, Michaud, Manitu, Misiewicz, Moore, McIntyre, Miller, Nichyporek, Nonortovage, Olencak, Orlich, Pate, Person, and Pol had all gone missing, and their names filled just half a page on the roll. There were others—Pringle and Robbins and Rothbart, Adams and Ayer and Ballard and Baucaro—all lying out there in the wheat somewhere. The ink was bold and seemed fresh, and for a minute I thought they might be there still; but I caught myself, and reconsidered, and realized all the time that had passed, and I knew that they must have all passed on, as had the Old Man.

I wondered, though, who among them had known him, and who among them had perhaps seen him there, seen him fall that day, and maybe even stepped over his body as Company D pushed on to Ploisy. I wondered who, if any, among them might be able to finally tell me what had happened that day, and on the days before and the days that were to come, in that long-ago war.

I wondered about these doughboys, and what to do with their war, and with them, those other boys who were sent off to save the world and who did that, for a while, until their sons and nephews had to go back to finish a fight that began in a storm of shells at Cantigny and petered out at the gates of Sedan when the world said, finally, Enough; that's enough for now.

And it was while perusing the list of names that I resolved to finish his story if I could, and find them, the others, who perhaps still lay in the wheat at Soissons, or in the hills of the Argonne where they died in the mud and the rain, or at Cantigny, where their young bodies were pummeled and pounded deep into the earth. I resolved to find what remained of Company D, for him, and for them, and for myself, as well, and complete a story begun on a hot July day so long ago, when young men raced across open fields toward machine guns and disappeared into history.

2

War Fever

ROLLIN LIVICK WAS AT that road, on that day, and he may have seen him, may have seen John Nelson fall headfirst into the wheat to lie still and bleeding in a dreamless sleep as the boys and the war rolled over him and continued on, on to the east, on to Ploisy.

Rollin Livick might have seen some of this as he raced across that road, but of course I'll never know, because Rollin Livick just days later was to become one of those boys who quite literally disappeared, to enter the nebulous world of those eternally "missing," his unknown fate to haunt not just his immediate family but generations of Livicks, who ninety years on continue to wonder what might have become of him.

They say Rollin Livick was one of the nicest boys in town, the town being Edgerton, Wisconsin, a bucolic oasis in the state's verdant and prosperous tobacco belt south of the capital of Madison. They say Rollin was steadfast and true, at just five foot three and 133 pounds small in stature but large of heart, an all-American who despite his size had quarterbacked the high school football team and excelled at basketball and baseball; and had been vice president of his junior class in 1914–1915, acted in the class play,

and edited the sports page in the *Crimson*, the school newspaper, in his senior term.

And they say as well that Rollin Livick was one of the first to appreciate
the "German menace," that he had "the stuff that heroes are made of," a
"fighting spirit, a spirit which chafed at the thot of the wrongs which the
Hun was visiting on the world."

My search for Company D had, by coincidence or serendipity, brought
me first to the strange and unsettling story of Rollin Livick, whose name
sat nineteen lines above that of John Nelson on that August 1918 roll, on
which Rollin, too, had gone "missing since recent operations."

I had zeroed in on Rollin Livick because of his unusual surname—I
didn't think I'd get too far beginning my search with Charles Johnson or
George Smith—and I found him in the ponderous three volumes of *Soldiers of the Great War*, a meticulous and macabre but strangely moving list
of the 100,000-odd American war dead and their home towns, which was
compiled by W. M. Haulsee, F. G. Howe, and A. C. Doyle in 1920 and organized according to the manner of death—killed in action, died of wounds
or of accident or disease.

A quick search of the phone directory turned up several Livicks still living in Edgerton, and the first of these I tried was a Gary Livick, who when
I called him one day in the middle of April 2003 and explained something
of my quest, and asked whether he had any information on a Rollin Livick
who had served in the First World War, quickly replied: "Do you mean
Uncle Rollie?"

And it would turn out that by dumb luck much remained of Private
Rollin Livick, in the form of papers and clippings and a lode of letters he'd
penned from Camp MacArthur in Texas and from France.

But they were all the family was to have of Private First Class Rollin
Livick after he marched off to war in April 1917, his flesh replaced by a
fruitless and desperate search to find out what had become of him after he,
too, had crossed the Paris-Soissons Road—and a rumor that he had been
seen making his way to the back lines for medical treatment was to remain
just that, as his letters stopped coming, as the family's letters to him were
returned, marked "Wounded," and as an enveloping shroud of sadness de-

scended over his parents, Emily and Robert Livick—a farmer and part owner of a local hardware store—and left them almost insane from grief.

Just as I had first heard John Nelson's small war story at a young age, Gary and his sister, Linda Matzke, had grown up with the legend of Rollin Livick, the great-uncle whom they'd never known, and it was Linda who had become the curator of Rollin's paper remains, at one point rescuing a box of letters and other material that had been casually and perilously stored in the corner of the barn of her recently deceased grandfather, James Livick, Rollin's younger brother.

That box held the strange and fascinating tale of Rollin Livick, who by some accounts was wounded on July 19, 1918, and, for all I know, was in John Nelson's line of sight or perhaps right next to him as Company D chased across that goddamn road, at which one would have stopped to lend a hand to a fallen comrade only at his own peril, and which for many marked the divide between life and death on that terrible day.

The evening I called, Linda began scanning and e-mailing some of the story of Rollin Livick to me, and as I opened the first attachment I was dumbfounded to find a browned and yellowed image of a letter dated April 25, 1919, containing snippets from Rollin's original diagnosis tag from the aid station at Missy-aux-Bois—"gunshot wound, lower jaw, battle, first aid 1/2 grain morphine"—and an account on the same document of the by-then deepening mystery of Rollin Livick: "No one in his company seems to have seen him at any time after he was given first aid. Several of them saw him on his way to first aid, and there has been a rumor . . . to the effect that Rollie was placed in a hospital where they were building up a lower jaw."

So here was evidence of his remains, of their remains, some inkling of what had happened at the Paris-Soissons Road on that hot July day; and just a few days later I received more evidence when Linda sent me the con- tents of that box, which had nearly been tossed away as trash, the story of a great-uncle who'd eagerly gone off to save the world only to become lost, forever "missing since recent operations," and whose loss and unknown fate continues to perplex and beguile the Livicks of Edgerton, Wisconsin.

In the summer of 1914, Rollin had played baseball for the Edgerton Cubs, and the team photo shows him smiling winsomely in the front row, bottom left, in the company of Clumsy Schumacher and Chubby Thomas and Severt Amundson. But it was even as he posed for the camera that events were unfolding that would take Rollin four years later to the Paris-Soissons Road, and to another field, and to an unknown fate.

In July of 1914 the world kicked off its own sport, this one for blood, after a Serbian separatist assassinated the Archduke Ferdinand and his wife at point-blank range in Sarajevo. Several weeks of saber rattling ensued, and then the serial mobilizations of empires and countries on a continent primed for a bloodletting.

There were hopes for a quick war, just a summer's exercise, as the Russians headed west to be sliced apart in the forests and marshes of East Prussia, the Austro-Hungarians to the south to thrust into Serbia, and the Germans west to violate Belgian neutrality and hammer across France to the Marne, only to be stopped at the last moment, at the gates of Paris, by a cavalcade of French soldiers brought to the front in taxis.

By late fall of 1914 France had been divided, from Switzerland to the Channel, by a zigzagging network of trenches, and the bloody stalemate had begun, one that would endure until Rollin and his mates landed in France three and a half years later.

In between came the ensuing slaughters, the mechanization and industrialization of the killing, 50,000 casualties on the first day alone at the Somme in July 1916; the bloody standoff at Verdun, where the French barely held on against assault after German assault, and a generation of men on either side was left bleeding into the ground; the thousands upon thousands of lives thrown stupidly and like chaff against the machine guns and the pounding artillery which entombed men of all nationalities in their vile and inhuman trenches.

For several years the United States had managed to steer clear of becoming engulfed in this war and President Woodrow Wilson had even been reelected in 1916 on the promise that he would continue to keep the country out of it.

But bit by bit, year by year, the war had seemed almost to "will itself" across the Atlantic, as Frederick Palmer, the war correspondent, would put it, and into the parlors of every home, including that of the Livicks out on Route 2 in Edgerton, where the plight of our English cousins, and their brave sacrifices at the Somme and Passchendaele, Amiens and Loos, surely were the source of much dinner-table discussion led by the Canadian-born Robert Livick, and his English wife Emily, scions of the Empire.

For those several years many ghastly tales of Hun barbarism had flooded newspapers from coast to coast, some real, some cooked up by brilliant and mischievous British propagandists, who became the only source of war news in the United States once the Brits had cut Germany's overseas cable.

Over morning coffee one could read about German soldiers stumbling about Belgium with bags full of ears—*ears!*—sadistically chopped from the heads of innocent and peaceful peasants; or about the rape of Louvain, or the firing-squad death of the brave nurse Edith Cavell; about Huns hoisting babies on their bayonets; and about reprisals and violations of bodies and of neutralities; until it seemed as if the whole world should fall under the brute heel of the slavering and inhuman Teutons.

And how many adolescent hearts beat a little faster as more tales of "German inhumanity" appeared in the newspapers, such as the following passed on in a letter by a Nebraskan named Duffy Knobles, whose infuriating account of Hun brutality was carried by a small-town Kansas newspaper: "He says a young Nebraskan soldier who went to France was captured by the Germans, who cut off his ears. From a letter the young man wrote to his sweetheart, the Germans learned her address, and placed his ears in a little tin box and sent them to the young woman. Knobles writes his mother that he saw the tin box and the young man's ears."

And that is bad stuff indeed, but no match for the following, the eyewitness a Scottish Highlander named Sergeant A. Goad, who in a wire story duly reported a scene of "indescribable brutality" found in one home after the liberation of a small French village from the Hun: "Against one wall was the dead body of a woman, her hands crossed above her head and nailed to the wall by a spike. Opposite her, against the other wall, was a little three-year-old child, with its head impaled on a sharp hook and its limp little body hanging down. The two had doubtless been crucified at the same time and left alone to watch each other's death agonies."

On top of this came the sinking of the *Lusitania*, torpedoed by a German submarine off the coast of Ireland in May 1915, taking with her 139

Americans; and later the release of the Zimmerman telegram, which was revealed to the world in early 1917, and by which Germany offered to help Mexico regain the territory it had lost to the United States some seventy years before if only it would stir up enough trouble along the border to pin down the United States should it declare war following a resumption of the Germans' submarine campaign.

It had been from this last revelation of German treachery, plus the renewal of the Huns' campaign of unrestricted submarine warfare in a last-ditch effort to starve Britain of food and war matériel, that the march to war accelerated, until finally, on April 6, 1917, the U.S. Senate at Wilson's urging put in for war.

So it was that America weighed in, and everyone ran around talking about Sir Galahad, and about how our boys were to be like knights-errant to save the world from the "Hunnish onslaught" and from itself. And there was ominous talk, as well, of what might happen if they didn't, if the Hun was allowed to overrun Europe while the United States sat idle. Secretary of State Robert Lansing painted this dark picture in one speech: "Imagine Germany victorious in Europe because the United States remained neutral. Who, then, think you would be the next victim of those who are seeking to be masters of the whole earth? Would not this country with its enormous wealth arouse the cupidity of an impoverished though triumphant Germany? Would not this democracy be the only obstacle between the autocratic rulers of Germany and their supreme ambition?"

It was under such a cloud of fight-'em-there or fight-'em-here that America's youth went, that Rollin Livick went, because they had to, because in fourteen hundred and ninety-two Columbus had sailed the ocean blue, because boys will be boys and nobody likes bullies pushing the little guy around, because some of them were brave and true and others like John Nelson were simply drafted, and because who wants to stay home when everyone else is going Over There?

Rollin Livick, at the age of nineteen as noble and steadfast a believer in the Cause as any of them, had "chafed at the thot of the wrongs which the Hun was visiting on the world," the 1919 Edgerton High School yearbook would note, and quickly answered the call to arms, on April 20 enlisting in the local militia, the Edgerton Company—turning up, one can assume, with the same spirit, patriotic ardor, and sense of mission with which later generations of nineteen-year-olds would show up at recruiting centers on December 8, 1941, and September 12, 2001.

The local newspaper would one day report in the funereal and patriotic rot and hyperbole of the day that teachers, students, and Edgerton's businessmen remembered Rollie as "the cleanest of the clean and the bravest of the brave," and he may have been all of that, but it's just as likely that he was (with apologies to Willa Cather) just one of ours, just a kid, a good kid, a kid looking for a little adventure and a Cause and a ticket out of Palookaville, Wisconsin, or Laurel, Mississippi, or Altoona, Pennsylvania.

In fact, it was with some trepidation, some prescience, about what lay in store for him Over There, that Rollin Livick joined the colors. Before leaving home, he would, perhaps as a joke and perhaps not, tell his cousin Frank Devine that if he were badly disfigured in the war, "he would never show up back home" again—words that would haunt Devine for the rest of his life.

Rollin Livick's story quickly haunted me as well, but I took his ill fate, whatever it was, as an omen that perhaps what I was looking for was to be found out there, somewhere, that the remains of those who had been at the Paris-Soissons Road, and at Cantigny, and then at Hill 263, lay in some neglected box on a closet shelf or were hidden away in the corner of some dusty barn or musty and obscure archive, these ghosts, these mostly ordinary boys who been drafted or signed on during a bout of war fever, and who through whatever accident of fate had lived or died or entered the nebulous realm of the "missing," to be dropped from the company's rolls as well as history's before war's end.

Despite my hopes, and despite my quick success in encountering the mysterious saga of Pvt. Rollin Livick, I would quickly find it easier to locate those who had been killed than those who had lived through the war, as most of those who'd almost miraculously survived had returned home and disappeared into their lives, few to emerge from the anonymity with which most of us while away our own days—and very few of them indeed had documented their lives or their experiences in the Great War in any form of print, or recordings by tape or video.

And I suppose that's to be expected as, after all, had someone else taken up my quest, and by some miracle been able to trace one of us to our diaspora in Minnesota or Wisconsin, and had come knocking and looking for what remained of John Nelson's story, what could we have said? That he was shot, somewhere in France, and that he had earned a Purple Heart. That the Old Man had been rescued by a couple of Algerian stretcher-bearers. That he had lived to be 101. *Period.*

When I told friends of my quest, many said that their grandfathers, too, had fought in the First World War, and then they would furrow their brows in puzzlement and quickly add that they had no idea of where or how or in what unit or regiment or division these ancestors had served, or what their experiences had been, one friend telling me: "I think he was in the cavalry."

Many times, too many times, and often after spending days or weeks or months or even years trying to find the descendants of one of Company D's men—George D. Miller, Zygmunt Misiewicz, Huckleberry Shell—I would of course find that I was many years too late, that Grandpa or Uncle Joe had not kept a diary, had never written a word about the war, his letters had neither been saved nor had run in the local newspaper, and my best efforts to get something, anything, from the survivors were rebuffed almost by rote with a "He just never talked about it," or "He just said it was bad—it was real bad, that's all," as Robert Baucaro, son of Company D's Private Benjamin Baucaro, wounded at Soissons and in the Argonne, would tell me.

The dead, though, had left something behind, and I discovered early on that it was the dead who would guide my quest, as is perhaps apt, what with their sacrifices the ultimate in that war, and the accounts of those sacrifices the most urgent, the most necessary, and the most emblematic of the story of Company D.

The names of Company D's dead can be found scattered through *Soldiers of the Great War,* but more easily on the company's Honor Roll on page 316 of the *History of the First Division During the World War, 1917–1919,* though it would turn out that a few of those ninety-seven names did not actually serve with Company D. It would also become evident that several of them had indeed survived the war, and news of their demise had been greatly exaggerated, at least at the time the book was written.

But each—except for one glaring omission—has a burial file in Record

Group 92 at the National Archives, many rife with letters from a mother or father or brother or sister to the government regarding the location of their soldier boy's remains, or seeking claim to the $57.50 per month war-risk insurance for which many of the boys signed up.

Many of the files also contain simple accounts from other soldiers of how the deceased had come to that sorry state, that this one had been drilled in the head by a machine-gun bullet at Cantigny, that one shot all to pieces at the very edge of Berzy-le-Sec, that another had crawled away, wounded and unseen, into the brambles and mud of the Argonne.

As a body these files are an epic of ineffable sadness, the backstory to the victory parades and the flag-waving and to the almost ridiculous ease with which we sent two million of the boys to France, surely knowing what awaited many of them, but not knowing, really, what the point of it all was, the question still remaining, ninety years later, What difference would it have made if the Germans had taken Paris in August 1914 or in the spring of 1918?

Looking back now, it's just as easy to see how close John Nelson came, a fraction of a fraction of an inch, to finding his final resting place in a box at the National Archives, with his epitaph coming from one of Company D's men, and reading, perhaps, that *Pfc. John Nelson was shot in the stomach at Soissons on the 19th of July, 1918. He was taken to an aid station, where he died. He was buried by Father O'Flaherty with 100 others who died in that vicinity.*

And it would be easy now to ask, For what? But these things have to run their course, as always, as they did in that spring and summer and fall of 1917, and on through the following November, all human activities moving in their own time, and with all of the information and passions available at that time, and so it was that even as Rollin Livick was packing his few things and moving into the Edgerton armory, others were responding to the lure of adventure and their youthful pugnacity, all that talk of saving the world and licking Kaiser Wilhelm II igniting a fire in the hearts of young men across the country—including the sturdy one that beat within the chest of Jason Lloyd Bronston, an ambitious, smart, small-town real-estate man from Garnett, Kansas.

Lloyd Bronston was old enough to have skipped the war, clocking in at the age of thirty-one when war was declared; and with the draft age set at twenty-one to thirty, and with a wife and a year-old baby, Jason, Lloyd perhaps should have passed, considering all of the ways in which he could have died in the ensuing two years.

But Lloyd, a burly and jocular two-fisted brawler who as a younger man had had part of an ear bitten off in barroom fight, up and left his little family back in Garnett in April of 1917, and was in command of Rollin Livick's platoon at the Paris-Soissons Road, a bit of information that came my way via one of Rollin's letters, on which Lloyd had scrawled after censoring his mail, *OK—J. L. Bronston, 2nd Lt 28th Inf.*

Lloyd was the grandson of pioneers on the eastern Kansas prairie, emigrants from Kentucky who first appeared in Topeka in 1858, and who had settled in Garnett in 1868. In 1870, prosperity chugged into Garnett with the arrival of the railroad, and Lloyd's father, Jacob Wood Bronston, quickly adjusted to the possibilities of town life, operating a restaurant, followed by a general store, and, later, a real estate business.

Upon reaching adulthood, Lloyd, too, had found real estate coursing through his veins, and by 1910, when just twenty-four years old, he had become a successful developer. The local paper reported on March 11 of that year: "Lloyd Bronston has purchased the tract just west of town known as the Driving Park Association. The entire forty-two and one-half acres will be platted under the name of Bronston Heights and sold at auction."

In December of that year, Lloyd married an Illinois girl, Cecile Stewart, and the happy couple settled into a home in Garnett. Baby Jason came along in March 1916—and the war one year later. After Lloyd had quickly signed on for the great adventure—and only God and the proverbial fly on the wall will ever know the exact nature of Cecile's reaction to his enlistment—the local newspaper would report that he did so for "purely patriotic reasons"; his grandson Jason Bronston would tell me that his grandfather "just liked a good fight."

But the pugnacious Lloyd Bronston would seek to lead, not follow. He applied for officers training, and was accepted for the Second Reserve Officers Training Camp at Fort Sheridan, north of Chicago, the first session having been filled mainly with the best and the brightest from Midwestern universities, and those with previous military experience.

Lloyd was one of 4,000 chosen out of the 20,000 who had applied, the examiners having been instructed to "select men on the basis of merit only," according to camp's history, which further relates that those overseeing the officers camp "were to choose men who were physically fit, men of experience who had already won places of responsibility in civil life."

These, it added, would include "Congressmen, bankers and brokers, business leaders, professional leaders, deans of universities, clergymen, mechanics, golf champions and hurdle champions, actors, playwrights, musical critics, farmers, ranchers, miners, students."

The man who had developed Bronston Heights turned out with the other thousands of candidates when the second session at Fort Sheridan began on August 23, and by the camp's eighth week, the brawny Kansan was into it deep, putting in long hours in the mock trenches on the fort's grounds.

"Each company was in the trenches for thirty-six hours at a stretch, eating, sleeping and living exactly as they expect to live later on in the European battlefields," the camp's history relates. "Amid the crash and roar of artillery and the fusillade of rifle shots every man was on the alert. The wide expanse of No Man's Land at night was lit up by the fitful radiance of the flares and the red and white rockets which were signals for barrage fire to break up attacking raids.

"The grim determination of the men and their alertness in the face of driving rains and raw night winds excited the admiration of their commanders."

Two more Kansans would leap with Lloyd Bronston into the makings of Company D, one to storm the Paris-Soissons Road alongside him as a sergeant, the other to lead a platoon at Cantigny and a battalion at Hill 263, the former being Willard Sidney Storms, a self-employed "chauffeur & repair man"—so his draft card says—who in 1907 had moved from Missouri to the tiny town of Dwight, Kansas, with his family.

There Willard P. Storms had scratched out a living as a farmer and small merchant until he died on March 14, 1917, even as his son and namesake considered a switch in careers. Just a month after his father's death, Willard S. made his first stab at enlisting in the army, but because of some undisclosed medical condition, the army wouldn't take him.

Seeking help for his problem at St. Francis Hospital in Topeka (where he would become smitten with a pretty nurse named Willa May Estus), Willard—tall and gangly, with boyish good looks that belied his twenty-nine years—underwent an operation. On June 4, he was accepted into the army, and given his choice of joining the 28th Regiment at El Paso, or the 10th Regiment at Fort Benjamin Harrison in Indianapolis. He took "the east."

"I'm into it now and going to give all I have in me to whip the Kaiser," Storms would write Willa that summer (with what was for him uncharacteristic grandiosity, no doubt hoping to tug on the heartstrings of his new sweetheart). "I don't expect to come back from the front if I ever go, but I'll know at the last that I've done something for my Country, and Humanity."

His mother, Jessie—"a plucky little woman"—had these last words to her departing soldier son: "Goodbye, son. Be a man, and do a man's duty."

Twenty-five-year-old George E. Butler had also jumped, enrolling, as had Lloyd Bronston, in officers candidate school. The son of a rural mail carrier in Arkansas City, Kansas, Butler had graduated from Wesleyan University, and by the time war was declared the strikingly handsome, strapping, and single six-foot-four, 200-pound Butler was working as an attorney in Indianapolis, where he also threw around his considerable weight—for that time—playing semiprofessional football.

Handily, Butler's assignment kept him in town, he being assigned to the school at nearby Fort Benjamin Harrison, at which the nucleus of Company D would be formed.

That company's core would also include the small and wiry twenty-four-year-old Whitelaw Reid Carns—named so by a mother who held in high regard the newspaper editor and politician Whitelaw Reid—who was born in the famous coal town of Matewan, West Virginia, in 1892; and who was the grandson of Captain William Carroll Carns, who had been captured while fighting with the 2nd Tennessee Volunteers at Rogersville, Tennessee, in 1863; and whose father, Levi, was a blacksmith; and who up and left a troubled marriage and two young daughters and his job as a "shot fireman" at the Consolidated Coal Company in McRoberts, Kentucky to enlist, and to be at Cantigny, and at the Paris-Soissons Road, and two days after that at Berzy-le-Sec, where he would have a thigh bone shattered in two, leaving him considerably shorter than the barely five-foot frame he sported upon enlisting.

There were others jumping in that spring: Orville Ballard, twenty-one, the son of a horse trader in Waupaca, Wisconsin, would be at that road; Otto Beard of Leakesville, Mississippi, just twenty and also the grandson of a Confederate soldier, would join on April 19 to be at Cantigny and at that road; and Jerome Angell, twenty-five, of Kalamazoo, Michigan, who was accepted by the army on his fifth stab at enlistment, his fifth try to get out of his drab job at a paper mill and into glorious khaki, would be there to die when Company D charged Cantigny.

Arza Earl Underwood—"Arzy"—a twenty-one-year-old oil driller from Ralph's Run, West Virginia, would enlist on May 29 and exactly one year later be at Cantigny, and later at that road near Soissons and at that hill in the Argonne, and come out alive with a Silver Star and a piece of shrapnel embedded near his heart; but what the Boche couldn't do, his fourteen-year-old daughter would, on September 12, 1931 when, after an evening spent sipping too much moonshine, Arzy drunkenly tore off all of young Audrey Underwood's clothing "except a brassiere," and then suffered an attack of self-loathing and shame and told Audrey to *Go get the gun and shoot me!* Which she would, killing the former doughboy to "protect her honor," the local paper would dutifully report.

In Janesville, Wisconsin, the declaration of war brought with it an almost delirious joy, at least among those who had no hope or intention of joining up and risking life and limb, among these the mayor, James A. Feathers, who immediately issued a proclamation calling upon all to "Rally Round the Flag," urgently telling the local paper, *The Janesville Daily Gazette:* "The Second Separate Company of Janesville needs more members at once. Therefore I would enjoin upon the young men to rally to the colors by enlistment, rather than await the act of conscription."

For Feathers and his fellow town fathers, the declaration of war brought with it a chance to add to Janesville's proud, if perhaps overblown, military history, it having sent its own boys and many others from surrounding Rock County into the Civil War, one of whom, Private James E. Croft, had won the Medal of Honor while helping drive off the Confederates at Altoona, Georgia, in October 1864.

Yet another bunch, the Janesville Light Guards, had entered the war late, as Company E of the 5th Wisconsin Volunteer Infantry. In December 1864 those Janesville boys entered the trenches around Petersburg, Virginia, and took part in the successful assault on Robert E. Lee's forces the following April, and were in the lines surrounding Appomattox Court House when Lee surrendered on April 9, 1865.

Exactly fifty-two years later, Janesville was rallying around the flag again, and its civic fathers were not going to take no for an answer to their pleas for recruits.

The *Daily Gazette* provided space just days after the declaration to a sixty-four-year-old promoter-journalist-advertising man, Ellis B. Usher, who in an article titled "Hang Out the Flag, America Is at War," rebuked all who pushed for peace, and almost gleefully presaged the crippling and draconian censorship and curtailment of civil liberties which America's war effort would shortly bring: "Hang out the flag! It is war! The decision has been made and there is no place longer under the heaven born flag of liberty for any but freemen. To denounce the president or the government he leads is no longer a liberty of free speech. It is treason. No true American will listen to or tolerate such criticism, much less take part in it."

While Usher wrote, the local militia tried to drum up business, its commander, Captain Edgar N. Caldwell, a Kentuckian and former regular army officer and veteran of the border war with Mexico, turning to the pliable local paper for help in pumping the company's membership from sixty-odd men to a mandated 175 soldiers.

"Enlist in the local company of the national guard and escape the drafting system is the slogan," Caldwell told the *Daily Gazette* on April 9. "Some men have been holding back to see what was 'really going to happen.' It has happened; the company has called for men. It must be recruited to full war strength. Let it be a real Janesville company, so join now."

Embracing the cause, the paper over the next months would breathlessly report the enlistment of each new recruit—many of whom would be transferred to the 1st Division, and to Company D, upon their arrival in France, many to die, and most of the rest be wounded. But unhappy endings seemed not to be on the radar that spring as the company—renamed Company M of the Wisconsin National Guard—drilled at the local assembly hall and in the streets around town.

By June 4, Company M had extracted 173 enlistees from the town and surrounding area. In an article that brings to mind the parading rubes on the old *Andy Griffith Show*, the *Daily Gazette* gave notice that on the following day the company's men were to "report for duty in their uniforms at half past one . . . and will march to Park street, where they will take part in the big Loyalty parade. Following the exercises in the Court House Park, the company will give an exhibition drill on Main street."

Even as the boys paraded through the otherwise quiet streets of Janesville with patriotic splendor, other young men wrestled with their futures, the call to colors—as ever—not always involving a passion for patriotism and fair play, or the simple joy of a good fight, or even wanderlust.

In at least one case, that of Thomas Dewey Slinker, an eighteen-year-old Choctaw Indian from Oklahoma, the impetus to join the army seems to have simply been a matter of spite.

I would find Thomas Slinker at the National Archives, but not in some grim burial file; Thomas would survive Company D's trials, and become the "best bugler in the 28th Regiment," George Butler himself would say after the war. But I would find little trace of his postwar life, in fact not much outside of the 1930 census, which put him in Flint, Michigan, working at an auto plant.

But I found something of him in the records of the Carlisle Indian School, and I can't help but include his story, perhaps just as antidote to the tragedies that would unfold at Cantigny, at the Paris-Soissons Road, and Hill 263, Thomas's story bringing to mind a *Doonesbury* cartoon from years ago, in which the character B.D. joins the army just to get out of having to take a college exam—and winds up fighting for his life in the rice paddies of Vietnam.

Thomas had bounced around a few schools, leaving the Armstrong Academy in 1913 because of smallpox and a school called Good Land because he simply "Didn't like the school." Assigned a guardian, an Oklahoma justice of the peace named Albert Neely, Thomas enrolled at the famed Carlisle school in Pennsylvania—from which Jim Thorpe had shot to Olympic fame—in the fall of 1916. An able student, he earned scores in the 80s in such subjects as history, English, geography, and "physiology and hygiene."

But Slinker had a restless soul and quickly became bored with school and homesick for his family in Calera, Oklahoma, and it wasn't long before he tried to inveigle his way home.

Late in 1916 he complained about his health, making as strong a case for tuberculosis as he was able. And as winter turned to spring, Slinker pressed Neely for money and a ticket home for the summer. On April 13, 1917—just a week after war was declared—Neely wrote to the school's superintendent to say he was denying Slinker's request.

"I will say to you that the environments at his home are such that I think he should be kept where he is," Neely wrote. "He has made wonderful progress so far as I am able to judge and I want him to remain where he is; were he to come home we would never get him back."

Neely's letter urging the school to keep Thomas over the summer brought a strong reply from Slinker to Neely on May 1: "I'm sorry that you want me to stay here at Carlisle you will see me before long. I thought you were man enough to let me come home like a gentleman. But as it is I will have to do the best I can. You can just look for me."

And things might have remained at a standoff had Thomas not received a letter from home later that May. Written by a sister, it told a tale of woe involving his mother, Lizzie, and other family members back on the farm in Calera: "We have all been sick until I couldn't get time to write. Pauline is just able to be up, Edward is sick and sure looks bad if Lizzie don't take good care of him he will never get through the summer cutting teeth. Tom you must come home and help Lizzie she has sure had a hard time. Did you ever see times so hard I never did."

Unable to pay his way home, Slinker nevertheless had enough money to journey to Columbus, Ohio. And it was there that on June 5, 1917, Thomas and a handful of Carlisle buddies—among them the Oklahoma Cherokee Huckleberry Shell and the Wisconsin Menominee Earl Wilber, both of whom would serve with Thomas in Company D—joined the army.

Placed with the 10th Infantry Regiment, Slinker wrote to the school's new superintendent, John Francis, on June 6 and asked for the twenty-five dollars remaining in his school account.

Superintendent Francis sent him his money, and told Slinker: "Remember that you boys represent Carlisle. If you go wrong you will disgrace the school; if you do your duty, as I know you will, you will reflect on the school and make us prouder of you."

Slinker also wrote a goading letter to Albert Neely, leaving his sponsor outraged: "Well Mr. Neely," he wrote, "I'm in the Army now and working for Uncle Sam." Neely in turn quickly fired off a letter to Francis, and asked him about Slinker's alleged enlistment.

Francis replied on June 28: "I have to advise that Thomas left here on the 4th of June to enlist in the Army. Thomas was very much unsettled because he was not permitted to return home and while the war fever struck the school, enlisted without consulting me. Under the law, of course, he had a perfect right to do so."

So it was that Thomas Slinker became a doughboy, to blow reveille and the call to battle on his golden horn, and taps as well for those boys of Company D, 28th Infantry Regiment, United States 1st Division, who would go no farther than that ruined village, or that road, or that hill, at which the Fates were already gathering, but which lay then like a hazy dream across what seemed to be a wide, wide ocean.

3

What Are You Going to Do Now, Young Man?

AND ON WHAT SHELF do we put their war, his war, their suffering and sacrifice and their cause, their lingo, these doughboys who ate "monkey meat" and corn willie, who called their enemy the Hun and Fritz and Jerry and Heinie and Boche, who walked on duckboards in the trenches and dodged "G.I. cans" and who "went west," many of them, more than 100,000 of them in combat and from disease, all in the name of "making the world safe for democracy"?

Perhaps it's the same shelf on which Marvin Everett Stainton slept for decades, Lieutenant Marvin Stainton who pined to go Over There, and who finally went, and who was too late to be at that road but was at that hill, and in fact died on that hill and was buried there, his bones left for the ages to digest as his country moved on to the Roaring Twenties, on to the business of living, and pushed his war and whatever pain it had caused into the closet, into the dustbin of history, and toward irrelevance.

Marvin's story, too painful to touch, would be pushed as well into a closet, and linger there in a box, on some shelf, for decades, its pages turning stiff and brown with age, Marvin's voice receding in that dark place next to the linens, until he would be roused, and his remains and his story disinterred, by my quest.

As with Rollin Livick, I would find Marvin Stainton of Laurel, Mississippi, waiting for me in the last volume of *Soldiers of the Great War*. A dozen phone calls to just about every Stainton in Mississippi brought me finally to Marvin's nephew Irvin McArthur of Denver, Colorado, and Irvin, finally, after telling me that he thought there might be some "papers" regarding Marvin Stainton, pointed me to another of Marvin's nephews, Bert Stainton, who lived not in Mississippi, but in Miami, and who after I sent an inquiry responded in an e-mail:

"I have a box of 'stuff' that belonged to Uncle Fred. I received it after he passed away a couple of years back. I have never gone through the contents of the box but I do know that in it are numerous letters from Marvin to his Mom. I'm a little strapped for time right now but next week I'll dig into the box and see what I can find."

By coincidence a business trip soon carried me to Miami and to Bert's home, where when I arrived and knocked I found Bert, a ponytailed, retired Miami-Dade firefighter and Vietnam vet, seated at his kitchen table, poring over an avalanche of browned and ancient letters and newspaper clippings that had been saved by Marvin's doting mother, Mary.

Mary Stainton had been as meticulous in preserving Marvin's literary remains as had Robert and Emily Livick with Rollin's, there being little else by which to remember a boy lost to war; and I would find that every scrap, every note from or about or to Marvin, had somehow made it through the twenty-three years that would intervene between Marvin's death and Mary Stainton's own in 1941.

Marvin's remains had made it as well through decades of south Florida's stifling heat and humidity in the possession of Marvin's younger brother, Fred Stainton, who when he died in 1978 left them to his nephew Bert, who held "the box" on a shelf for twenty-five years, and who until my inquiry had never peeked inside, and in fact knew little about his war-hero uncle.

It may have been that Bert was tired of war and even talk of war by the time Uncle Fred died. He had kept his own diary and paraphernalia from his Vietnam sojourn until, one day, "I told my wife to just get rid of all that stuff. I didn't want anything around that reminded me of Vietnam"—an act he now regrets.

Marvin's family, too, seemed to have avoided the painful subject of Marvin's passing, shoving his paper remains into a corner of a closet and trying to forget about them—although one can imagine Mary Stainton through the 1920s and 1930s retrieving them on occasion to perhaps lovingly read and reread Marvin's letters, to hear in her mind his voice, and to remember a roving and passionate and perhaps favorite son taken from her, ripped from the world, long before his time.

Otherwise, "Nobody talked of it, nobody spoke of it," Bert told me as we dug into Marvin's remains, quietly and reverently tracking the short life of a small-town boy who was swept up by a world event beyond his ken and carried to a dark and dangerous forest in a foreign land, where fate awaited him on a lonely hilltop, just as a different fate had awaited John Nelson at the Paris-Soissons Road in the summer of 1918.

It was a mixture of accident and providence—destiny, maybe—that had brought Marvin, the eighth of eleven children born to Lafayette and Mary Hasseltine Salter Stainton, to that hill, Marvin early on displaying a deep restlessness and boundless but unfocused energy that would interrupt his schooling and no doubt become a cause of concern to a worried mother and accomplished father.

Lafayette Stainton, born in 1852 near Monroe, Alabama, had traveled west with his family to Mississippi in the great land rush opened by the removal of the Choctaw and Chickasaw Indians to Oklahoma Territory. His own father, David Timms Stainton, had himself marched off to war on the losing side of a civil war, manning posts at Fort Morgan and in Mobile.

Before his 1916 death the busy and ambitious Lafayette Stainton over the years built quite a varied résumé, as teacher, editor and publisher of *The Neshoba Democrat*, superintendent of schools, postmaster, state representative, mayor of Laurel from 1899 to 1903, and, finally, U.S. congressman.

Unlike his esteemed father, Marvin's ambitions remained unclear. As raw and restless as the country to which he'd been born, he left high school in 1912 at the age of seventeen to roam and take odd jobs for a buck or two a day in farms and factories from New Orleans to San Francisco and all the way over to Montana and Missouri, sending home a stack of letters and postcards wondering at the sights he saw, and the experiences that befell him.

With a few dollars in his pocket he had pushed west for New Orleans, thence to San Antonio and Santa Fe, New Mexico—from which he wrote home in late January 1913 to say: "This sure is dry country here. Sand, sand, sand!"

His parents and his bemused older sisters, Alda and Ruby, tried in vain to keep up with his meanderings, sending ten-dollar money orders that always arrived a week or two behind the fast-rambling Marvin, who in early March 1913 found himself in Globe, Arizona.

"Have been working in restaurants here," he reported home. "Pay pretty good. I am getting along fine working in one place and then another." By April he was in San Bernardino, California—and then it was up to San Francisco and beyond, all the way north to Weed, on the slopes of Mount Shasta. "I could not go to work because the place I had to work at was too cold 6000 ft high on top of mountain," Marvin reported.

Early May found him in Portland, Oregon. "Certainly have been seeing some fine sights out here," he wrote. "Saw a whale near Los Angeles. He was 48 ft long." The middle of the month found Marvin in Paradise, Montana. "I got $2 a day + Sunday I got $3," he wrote to tell his mother. "Had to pay $1 a day board though."

June found him in Pocatello, Idaho: "It's just like the moving pictures to see the cowboys and Indians out here. The old Indians wear blankets wrapted around them and feathers in their hair."

Such descriptions excited the imaginations of the stay-at-homes back in Laurel. His sister Alda wrote to him in May to say: "How I should love to see a real cow-boy or even a cow-boy-girl. If you find a cow-boy for sale please crate him up and send him C.O.D."

By mid-July 1913, his wanderlust satisfied for the time being and his eighteenth birthday coming on, Marvin felt the pangs of homesickness and headed east again toward Mississippi. March 1915 found Marvin back in Laurel, "still working at the grocery store yet at 5 a week," he wrote his older brother, Edwin.

He had indulged an interest and talent for cartooning by taking correspondence courses with the W. L. Evans School of Cartooning in Cleveland, Ohio, and some of his drawings had even run in *The Laurel Argus-Leader*.

But by 1915 Marvin's passion for drawing had ebbed, and he let his lessons lapse. In a letter dated March 1, 1915, Marvin told his brother: "Well Edwin I have nearly quit drawing lately. I just can't draw until the spirit moves me—I am a little like the poet you see but I just can't help it. When I begin to feel blue there's no use in trying to draw or do anything else because I just can't do anything."

In the same letter, Marvin referred almost innocently to the war then raging in Europe—and to the assembling and spreading storm which, though he couldn't then know it, would put Marvin on a lonely hill in the Argonne Forest just three and a half years later: "I tell you things are beginning to get complicated. I see in today's paper that England & France has refused to except Wilsons plan for the protection of neutral ships. I hope that Wilson will place an embargo on food to any of the belligerents now."

By 1916 the job at the grocery had dulled. So Marvin cut it loose and joined the Mississippi National Guard as it mobilized to head south for the Mexican border, where Pancho Villa's raids and generally intransigent activities were straining the nerves of the Texans and New Mexicans along the Rio Grande.

Villa strained as well the abilities of the small U.S. Army that chased him hither and yon across that arid land, where its soldiers quickly became caked with powdery desert dust to such a degree that they would be rechristened "adobes," thence "dobies," and finally, as the veterans of the border campaign were rerouted to France, "doughboys." (That, at least, is one explanation of the term's origin.)

Stationed for a long while in Jackson, Mississippi, Marvin impatiently awaited his unit's call to action. "I am to be put into a new uniform, new shoes, hat, gun and all today," he wrote home on June 28, 1916. "I expect that we'll leave for the border without training this week but of course I cannot tell."

That summer, his National Guard unit was federalized, a move that put it under the sway of the U.S. Army. By fall, Marvin was at Fort Sam Houston in San Antonio, but that's apparently as close as he got to the action. Still with the guard in mid-February 1917, Marvin was certain of an imminent end to his military career. "Everything seems to give the impression that we are to be mustered out before the middle of March," he wrote to tell his mother. "All of the boys are anxious to be home again."

But there was to be no return to Laurel for Marvin, as the war was to catch up with him mere minutes before his longed-for return to civilian pursuits; that same month, the Germans resumed unrestricted submarine warfare. As well, the Zimmerman telegram was made public in late February and caused an immediate uproar.

Within weeks, the last few steps in the march to war had been taken, and there was no stopping it, the United States showing none of the restraint it had displayed after the sinking of the *Lusitania* less than two years before.

And it was a little more than a week before the declaration of war on Germany that new orders reached the Mississippi National Guard, just as its soldiers were about to be mustered out to head to their widely scattered homes from Jackson, Mississippi; and it was at that moment that whatever it was that Marvin was going to become, a cartoonist, maybe, or perhaps like his father an educator or editor, dissipated into the murky unknowns of history.

Caught in the impending war's web, Marvin Stainton on March 28, 1917, wrote to his mother to give her the bad news: "I don't think I have ever been more badly disappointed in my life as I was yesterday afternoon. We had been rushing to get ready to go home and we left camp for the train and was getting ready to go aboard when the news come that we had been recalled. If the news had been five minutes later it would have been too late because then we would have been on our way. It will take a long time to get over it."

At that moment war seemed certain; still, America's—and Marvin's—role in the coming crusade was less assured. For several weeks after war was declared there was some thought that America's gift to the cause might entail little more than foodstuffs and machinery. But the Allies were quick to make no bones about what they wanted and what they needed: men, and plenty of them.

On the cusp of its entry into a world war, the U.S. Army was capable of little more than home defense, its rolls containing just 5,791 officers and

121,797 enlisted men, a force supplemented by some 80,000 National
Guardsmen under federal sway and another 100,000 controlled by the
states. The National Defense Act of 1916 had authorized an expansion to
223,000 regulars and 427,000 National Guardsmen in what was then peace-
time, but the army was not the first choice of employment for many, and, as
Frederick Palmer would later note, the economy was humming and "there
was no temptation to leave good jobs in boom times."

In the War Department it was quickly decided that 500,000, and then
estimated that one million, men would be needed to bring the Hun to heel.
But even after war was declared, there came no flood of recruits.

A few noble hearts—Willard Storms, Rollin Livick, George Butler—
had leaped into the great unknown, but they didn't come in numbers anywhere near what was required, despite the best efforts of the editorialists
and government men who cajoled and prodded and tried to guilt America's youth into joining the regulars or the National Guard with such en-
treaties as this, from a Kansas newspaper: "What are you going to do,
young men? You have one of three things to do: Enlist with Company K,
wait and take your chance with the draft, or stay at home. Suppose you
stay home, and your friend goes to the front? What will you think of
yourself? What will your friend think who is patriotic to do his duty?
Don't wait for your friend to enlist. Be that friend—be a friend to yourself. Enlist today."

But there was one thing that the government men and saber-rattling
civilians such as Ellis Usher had overlooked. While Rollin Livick had understood the peril that awaited him in France and enlisted anyway, other
young men who read the accounts of the ongoing great battles Over There
came away only with a keener sense of self-preservation.

As Frederick Palmer noted, Americans for almost three years had read
of the "agony" of the trenches, knew untold thousands had died, and had
seen pictures of maimed soldiers and rich farmland that had become
"threshed seas of shell craters. What adventure was there in submitting
human flesh to this machine destruction that mashed brick and stone?
Who would ask for it as a privilege? The unspoken reply of the masses of
youth was: 'Come and get me if you want me to face all that.'"

And what horrors lurked Over There: The machine gun had changed the very nature of battle, the implement amounting to "concentrated essence of infantry," as the military historian J. F. C. Fuller would write, by which one man could wield the destructive power of forty riflemen, his weapon firing six hundred rounds per minute, and still the general officers on all sides would homicidally insist that their men go forward against the guns at Ypres and Verdun and Loos, thousands falling amid their scything spray.

As well, bombardments with high explosives lasting days and even weeks stunned men and sent them underground to live like moles and rats. The 1st Division's assistant chief of staff, George C. Marshall, would report later from firsthand experience: "A 3-inch shell will temporarily scare or deter a man; a 6-inch shell will shock him; but an 8-inch shell, such as these 210-mm. ones, rip up the nervous system of everyone within a hundred yards of the explosion."

The British army employed 1.5 million such shells to blast away at the German positions along the Somme in the weeks prior to its July 1, 1916, attack—only to find their enemy hustling up from their deep dugouts to man their positions, and their machine guns, and slaughter the advancing soldiers.

And of course there was gas—chlorine, phosgene, and, eventually, mustard—which had industrialized the war even further. First used by the Germans on April 22, 1915, on two French and one Canadian divisions along a four-mile front, the chlorine was released from four thousand cylinders and wafted across No Man's Land in sinister and quiet clouds. Hundreds of men died, the linings of their lungs burning as if on fire, while a French division fled in terror, leaving a wide gap in the lines.

The government tried to put a bright spin on the carnage. Statistician Roger Babson pored through the Allied casualty figures and assured the worried would-be soldiers and their families: "Fourteen men out of every fifteen have been safe so far. Only one man in five hundred loses a limb—a chance no greater than in hazardous conditions at home. Most of the wounds sustained in the trenches are clean cut and of a nature that a few weeks in the hospital makes the subject as fit as ever."

But it only took one bullet to leave a man as dead as ever, as even Babson allowed: "Practically speaking, a wound is either fatal or slight, with few in between these two extremes. Of course, the whole thing is horrible enough as it is. But I wish to tell the fathers and mothers left behind the boys that, looking at the matter in the light of cold-blooded statistics, these boys are not going into anywhere near the danger the folks at home imagine."

By the time Babson's cheery assurances ran in the newspapers in the summer of 1917, the issue of where the United States would get its army was moot. For the first time since the Civil War, the government had, as Palmer wrote, gone out and gotten them, as conscription was introduced, though in a nod to the riots which had broken out in several northern cities some fifty years before, it was prudently decided that local officials, and not the men in khaki, would glad-hand and register their neighbors on June 5, 1917.

All men between the ages of twenty-one and thirty who were residing in the United States on that date were required to register, and in an almost shocking display of civic duty, and without riots or bust-ups, nine and a half million men did come out that day and decamp to their local precinct stations to register for the draft.

And it was from this massive outpouring of lumberjacks, clerks, idlers, coal miners, farmers' sons, teamsters, factory workers, polishers, painters, and every other conceivable occupation and inoccupation that Company D—and the American Expeditionary Force—was born.

Some whose paths would lead to Company D turned out to register but wound up enlisting instead, among them Tempton Corwin Hall, son of a blacksmith from Crosstimber, Missouri. Picking strawberries for a Mr. G. P. Dobbs that early June, the twenty-two-year-old Hall and two buddies were seized with a sudden desire to escape their monotonous plight—and promptly signed on at Anderson, Missouri.

From the dim shadows of Minnesota's north woods, a tough, muscled brawler named James Whalen turned up at a recruiting station on the eve of registration day. Born John Turner in Missouri, he had fought with the army in the Spanish-American War under that name, but had gone AWOL after his return to garrison life—too boring, he'd said—and retreated into the north woods to work as a lumberjack.

It took some time for news of the declaration of war to reach John

Turner, but when it finally did, his reaction was swift. "He said, 'When I heard that, I just leaned my axe up against a tree and walked away,' and he went down and reenlisted under the name of James Whalen, which he said he picked because it was a 'good Irish name,'" his grandson, Michael Whalen, told me.

Of course the Old Man, John Nelson, dutifully turned out at his local precinct station on Chicago's north side on that Tuesday, to stand in line with hundreds of other draft eligibles, and perhaps curse the loss of a morning's wages.

Just twenty-five years old, with eyes of blue and "light" hair, according to his draft card, he was living at the time at 916 Roscoe Street in Chicago, and was a painter, employed by a Swede, of course, Alfred Olson of North Clark Street; and I can only wonder at his thoughts on that day, as he signed his new and Americanized name to the register, and whether a doubt tickled the back of his brain or whether he had any inkling, as had Rollin Livick, of the fate that might await him across the sea.

The Old Man's lucky number came up on July 6 of that summer as the draft lottery commenced, and on October 6 he entrained for Camp Grant, one of thirty-two training camps being hastily constructed for the war effort. The next day, he found himself in the army now, a doughboy, and taking the first steps toward Company D, and France, and the Paris-Soissons Road, and the destiny that awaited him there.

(An innate talent for marksmanship, my father would tell me, would lead to John Nelson's being promoted to private first class—but there was at least one blemish on his short and inglorious military career: On March 19, 1918, the Old Man was found sleeping while on guard duty while still at Camp Grant and "in a time of war."

(Awakening only as his accuser, Captain John Diller of the 344th Regiment, approached, he "got up to his feet and said, 'Halt,' in a very faint voice and then presented arms," Diller would write in his report of the incident. What, if any, punishment John Nelson received remains unknown.)

Even as the Old Man went through the basics at Camp Grant, many of those who would be with him at that road were in training, forming the nucleus of Company D at Fort Benjamin Harrison, where T. C. Hall, Willard Storms, Whitelaw Carns, and Thomas Dewey Slinker and his Carlisle pals were putting in long hours at the rifle range and in the mock trenches dug for training.

There, the rolls swelled with the likes of Lieutenant Max C. Buchanan, who at thirty-seven was something of a rarity, a nineteen-year veteran of the army who had seen action in the Philippines and served on the Mexican border; and Angus Jimmerson, twenty-one, whose father, Doctor Reuben Gideon Jimmerson, was not a doctor but a farmer and a roving and fiery Sunday preacher at churches throughout East Texas, and who "had hens all over his barn and a yellow mule named Dixie that all the children rode," one account of his life says.

As well there was Ralph Pol, twenty-two, a.k.a. Raphael Eppoleto, who at the age of eleven had left his native Argentina with a younger brother, Sam, to live with his father in Chester, West Virginia, but who with Sam had been quickly turned out by his father's live-in lover and put into a children's home, and whose hard-luck story would come to an end just beyond the road that awaited him south of Soissons.

On June 21, 1917, Thomas Slinker wrote from the post to tell Carlisle's John Francis that he, Huckleberry Shell, and Earl Wilber were enjoying their new lives: "We are getting plenty of drill. We drill I guess 7 hours every day. We have reached as far as Instructors and Corporals. The Capt said he never had better boys than the Indian boys. We will be sergeants before 2 months is gone."

Francis replied: "You are up against the real thing and it will be hard at times to do some of the things that you will be required to do, but just remember that you have the stuff to make good on in you and go to it, don't be a quitter."

Willard Storms, meanwhile, had been promoted to corporal. "I'm now known as Corporal Storms, Co. J 10th Inf.," he wrote to his girlfriend, Willa Estus. "Doesn't that sound warlike?"

By mid-June, a real American division—the 1st, cobbled together from the 16th, 18th, 26th, and 28th Infantry Regiments plus adjunct artillery, engineer, and other units—was already on its way to France.

Embarking from Hoboken, New Jersey, and following in the wake of American Expeditionary Force commander General John J. Pershing, the division's men and matériel were loaded onto four transports on June 14 and headed into the perilous submarine-infested waters of the Atlantic.

With an eye to the slaughter of the previous three years, the *Chicago Tribune* noted what awaited the American vanguard—and subsequent shiploads of men of every stripe—on the Western Front: "It is the last expedition for most of them. Pershing's casualty lists will be the first rap of the hand of fate on the American door, and fate will come later with equal foot to the door of the rich and the door of the poor."

In France, the 1st Division would become the model on which subsequent American divisions would be based. With 28,500 men, it was double the size of its Allied and German counterparts, comprising a "square" formation of two brigades of two regiments each. At full strength, each regiment had roughly 3,800 infantrymen—three battalions made up of four 250-man companies each, plus four machine-gun companies. The 16th and 18th Regiments made up the 1st Brigade, the 26th and 28th Regiments the second.

Upon sailing for France, the 28th Infantry carried 65 officers and 2,414 men, and at that early stage of the game was a mix of seasoned professional soldiers and bright-eyed recruits—and some who fell in between. Among that number was Charles T. Senay, destined to command the 28th Regiment's Company C—which would fight in close alliance with Company D in the battles to come.

Just five foot six and 130 pounds, the twenty-five-year-old Senay had been raised by an aunt in rural Connecticut after his mother divorced his father "because he had venereal disease," Senay would write years later.

Impish, precocious, and exceedingly tough for his size, the baby-faced Senay had attended Trinity College and played football at the University of Illinois before joining the army in November 1916 and gaining a commission just prior to the declaration of war on Germany.

Attached initially to the 28th Regiment's Company I, Senay sailed to France aboard the transport *Tenadores*. "There was a leaven of men with years of service," he wrote of that first contingent, "but the great majority were college men, hillbillies, farmers and boys from the cities.

"When the First Division landed in France, it contained some boys of fourteen and fifteen. These kids would invariably poop out during the training and someone else would have to tote their pack. They were soon discovered and discharged for return to their homes."

French officers greeted America's vanguard as it sailed into St. Nazaire on June 25. "There was an air of grimness and sadness among the onlookers," Senay would remember. "The garb was universally black, for everyone had lost relatives. Also, there was despondency because of the bad situation at the front."

After several weeks of patrolling the city's many houses of ill repute as military police—"We did the rounds of the whorehouses and put all but three out of business"—Senay and his company rejoined the 28th Regiment on July 11.

Soon they were rolling across the French countryside in boxcars stenciled with the words QUARANTE HOMMES ET HUIT CHEVAUX—forty men or eight horses; "forty-and-eights," the doughboys would call them—headed for training in a quiet sector at Gondrecourt, twenty-five miles south of St. Mihiel in northeast France.

Accommodations upon arrival were far from luxurious, the men for the most part finding billets in stables and barns in French villages. "Those who could not be crowded into the lofts, with their rickety ladders that served as stairways, were sheltered in Adrian portable barracks, which the troops erected in vacant lots or in the fields adjacent to the towns," the 1st Division's history says.

Under the watchful eyes of their French instructors—the 52nd Battalion of the French Alpine Chasseurs, veteran soldiers also known as the "Blue Devils," and known as well, the 28th's history says, "for their dash and go"—training in the ways of war on the Western Front began.

"They taught us the fine points of trench warfare," Senay wrote, "digging trenches, extending verticals (saps) from them to later be interconnected into new front lines, tunneling, mining, reinforcing with revetments, digging dugouts and knowing how to use the earth for protection."

The finer points of erecting barbed wire, using bangalore torpedoes to cut enemy wire, sticking a bayonet in an enemy's belly, and tossing a grenade were also imparted by the "stocky, tough old timers" of the Alpine

Chasseurs, Senay wrote. As well, "There were long marches and maneuvers."

But while off duty, the red-blooded American boys couldn't help but act like red-blooded American boys. Sex was always on their minds, Senay wrote, and he would remember that an almost Rabelaisian atmosphere surrounded the mixing of cultures and genders around Gondrecourt: "One night, some of our hot-blooded subalterns were horny and decided to go after some tail. The old village priest had been drinking with them and volunteered guidance, but he had become unseaworthy. The youngsters obtained a stretcher and bore him about the village in quest of young ladies of easy virtue."

As well, he wrote, the soldiers were eager to learn French, "not only for practical reasons, but also so they could flirt with the French 'mamselles.' Many a Yank became quite versatile in the strange tongue, particularly with the aid of a 'long-haired dictionary.'"

The doughboys, in turn, imparted a working knowledge of English to their new French friends. "There was a sturdy French girl in the household where I was billeted," Senay recalled. "She was the sugar that drew soldiers like flies. She was eager to speak Americaine.

"One morning, our portly, dignified mayor came strolling down the one main street. She greeted him with a winsome smile saying, 'Oh, shit! Good morning, you son of a bitch!' There was an appreciative doughboy audience lurking in the background."

Doughboy and Frenchman learned to live with each other, but there was a learning curve. "At first the natives knew nothing of American money," Senay wrote. "Our astute doughboys for a few days were buying wine and cognac with the labels from tin cans. This currency had a very brief duration."

As these Americans negotiated their new surroundings, training continued at Fort Benjamin Harrison, Camp Grant, and other installations. War games employed wax balls instead of artillery, and in some camps the men trained with sticks, there not being enough weapons to go around for the sudden army.

In a letter to Carlisle's superintendent in the fall, Thomas Slinker described a war-games exercise his unit—now renamed the 1st Company of the 28th Infantry Training Battalion—had experienced in the perilous trenches at Fort Harrison.

"We fought for 48 hours there were several injured by wax balls," Slinker wrote. "We captured several lines of trenches and the worst of all it rained on us and every body has got a cold. One man died from cold he was captured and tied up in a trench. It rained on him he took cold and died."

Slinker would add that the experience taught him that "war is certainly h---. Like all my fellow soldiers said I can say every one had the spirit of the truest Americans. They all said they wish the enemy were real Germans we would be fighting until yet."

Corporal Willard Storms spent his days at Fort Harrison's target range, trying to teach draftees how to use a rifle. "There are a lot of Wops and city fellows who never shot a gun and imagine that the gun is going to kick the daylights out of them, and a bunch who think they know it all," he wrote Willa May Estus on September 10.

Storms would note of the draftees coming into the camp that fall: "Gee but they are a rough looking lot. I'm glad I don't have to have a bunch of them in my squad. The most of them seem to be the hoboes, while there are lots of white-faced boys from towns with them, who will have a hard time for a few weeks. They haven't been able to get clothes enough for them so they are still in their civilian clothes."

At another post, Marvin Stainton by that summer had accepted his fate. Though a corporal when war was declared, he had applied for officers training—"and without the advantage of a high school education, which it was supposed at that time candidates must possess, he was accepted," notes a family history; a subsequent commission as a lieutenant took some of the sting out of his disappointment over being kept on in the service.

In the few months since he watched one version of his life chug down the tracks without him, Marvin's views of the war had evolved as well. A more serious Marvin came to see his small role in the Mexican affair as a boyish lark, and he began to appreciate, as rich man shouldered up against poor in the trenches of Fort Logan Roots at Little Rock, Arkansas, the democratic groundswell that was mobilizing for what he began to see as a good, and just, cause.

"We all of us have so much more to think about than we did then," Marvin wrote on June 5, 1917. "It was just a bunch of boys then thinking they were going to get into some kind of adventure. Everybody is in this now, married men and all.

"This is the biggest thing that has ever happened for this old country of ours and I am beginning to think the BEST thing for it unites us all and makes the individual give for the benifit of the rest. It puts the rich with the poor, the working man with the business man, the aristocrats with the men whom he had begun to think was his inferior."

The unification cut across not only classes, but races. Marvin wrote that the black troops "seem to be turning out as good soldiers, they have their prayer meetings and sing and 'go on' until they have to quit at taps every night. They sing 'I don't want to be no slacker in my heart' to the tune of 'glory glory Halleluh-a' and 'We'll hang Kaiser Bill to the sour apple tree as we go marching on.'

"And then all the 'hollering' and shouting you ever heard wouldent compare with theirs on the day they leave for the port of embarkation. When their trains pull out you can hear them for a mile, singing and bugles blowing and everything."

The Janesville boys and the rest of what was by then the Wisconsin National Guard meanwhile prepared to move from their small-town armories to sprawling Camp Douglas, near Madison.

In mid-July, the War Department attached the Wisconsin and Michigan National Guards to the 32nd Division, and Company M entered federal service in the 128th Regiment. The first order of business was a ban on alcohol, the *Janesville Daily Gazette* reported on July 16, and "promptly at nine o'clock," the company "went on the water wagon en masse. Absolute enforcement of the government's bone dry regulation for its fighting men will be made by Captain Caldwell, and any saloon owner permitting a member of the company to enter his place will be prosecuted to the full extent of the law."

On August 2, all of Janesville turned out to say farewell to the company as it boarded a train bound for Camp Douglas. The *Daily Gazette* reported that as the soldiers crowded to the windows, "the people surged up to say their last farewells.

"For the sweethearts and families, there was no crowd; their whole life for the moment was centered in one khaki clad boy, smiling bravely as the tears welled up his eyes. There was not a dry eye in the crowd as the boys left. What awaits the boys, no one knows; where their destinies will lie, no one can say; the great fact is that they have gone. Janesville has made its first sacrifice."

Rollin Livick and his company from Edgerton also left for Camp Douglas. Arriving at the depot with his older sister, Gertrude, Rollin couldn't help having some fun, saying adieu to Gertrude with a passionate embrace as the other boys wondered at the identity of the dish seeing him off. Rollin later wrote: "The fellows all thot she was a girlfriend of mine. Guess they thot we were pretty familiar with our embrace. I didn't tell them the difference."

Upon arrival at Camp Douglas, Rollie and his mates were sent hopping. "Got in yesterday morning just in time to take 'morning exercises' and limber up for breakfast, and our six mile hike which proceeded breakfast," Rollin wrote of his initiation into real army life. "I thot my legs were going to cave before we got back from the hike, but I managed to stick it out."

By September, the camp had swelled with the addition of other troops from around the state and Michigan. But by the third week of the month, the population pressures began to ease with the first shipments of the division's soldiers to Camp MacArthur, near Waco, Texas.

Another college boy who'd interrupted his studies to enlist was writing home as his own trip to Texas approached to give some sense of army life. Wilbert Murphy, a nineteen-year-old from the tiny town of Brodhead, in southern Wisconsin, now training with Rollin Livick and "the Edgerton boys," had left Lawrence University in Appleton, Wisconsin, after his freshman year.

Murphy had hoped to see his family one last time. "To night the captain told us that no more furloughs or passes would be issued in our regiment," Murphy wrote to his parents. "That means of course that I won't be able to get home before we go to Texas. I had hoped to come home this week but I guess it's all off now."

By early October, the guard had arrived at Camp MacArthur, and imminent reorganization loomed. Wilbert Murphy and Rollin Livick would find themselves reassigned to Company M, filling out a unit that until then had been reserved for the Janesville boys, and putting both a step closer to the Paris-Soissons Road.

At Fort Benjamin Harrison, the fall brought with it whispers of an impending voyage. "We had orders to be ready to move Aug 6th but then it was changed to 20th, so don't know whether we'll be here very much longer," Willard Storms wrote on August 8. "There are so many rumors as to our destination."

By late August, Fort Harrison buzzed with talk of a voyage to France. Thomas Slinker on September 1 wrote to Carlisle's John Francis to say he would "soon be fighting for Uncle Sam over in No Man's Land, and if there is any thing Carlisle wants from the Kaiser the Indian boys will bring it back. Because we are not going to stop we are going to Berlin and when we get there we are going to sing."

"I am hoping it may never be necessary for you to go to Berlin except as tourists later on when you have made your fortune," Francis replied, "but if you do have to go I am sure that you will remember Carlisle, your race and your country, and acquit yourself like men."

In mid-October, the four 185-man companies of the 28th Infantry Training Battalion headed for Hoboken's docks to board the transport *Mount Vernon*. Just before sailing, Lieutenant Buchanan, the veteran of the Philippine and Mexico affairs, wrote to his father, William, back in his hometown of Brockton, Massachusetts, to rue that he wouldn't be able to visit his family—which included an older brother, Harley—before heading for France.

"They say we are to go right on board the transports, so will have to go without seeing you or mother and Harley," Buchanan wrote. "I had hoped that I could be able to, just for a short time. Dad if I leave here without seeing you just remember I am going over with but one regret—not being able to shake 'paws' with you and mother and my brother Harley, who I haven't seen for about 15 years."

Buchanan added: "I have always been lucky in putting through the little expeditions and feel as though my chances are good in this, the greatest.

Tell all my old friends that I am on my way in good spirits for the big game and not for the grandstand or bleachers but right over the diamond."

Others were less assured of their prospects for "putting through," among that number the eighteen-year-old private James de Armond Golladay, who had left his job as a newspaper pressman to enlist. On the eve of departure, Golladay wrote to his pastor, Rev. N. McClain, back home in Kokomo, Indiana, about his forebodings.

"Since I've enlisted I've felt and enjoyed greatly but now I am under conviction," Golladay wrote. "You know we will soon leave for France, and although I am not afraid, I think it best, if I'm never coming back, to be prepared, don't you?

"I want you to pray for me with all the might and faith you have."

On Halloween, *Mount Vernon* began its long trek eastward, passing the Statue of Liberty on its way out of harbor. The soldiers had not been told where they were headed, but of course all assumed it was France—and foremost in the minds of all was the possibility of being sunk by a German submarine.

But the worst the men encountered during the thirteen-day journey were seasickness and an alert when two ships collided. Harry Martin, twenty-five, a freshly commissioned lieutenant from Emporia, Kansas, who had left his studies at Purdue University to enlist in the 2nd Company of the training battalion, sent home this account of the November 10 near disaster:

"We were down in my room, I had my putties off, and had started to take my shoes off, when the *Agamemnon* blew a short blast, and our ship blew a long one. The first thing that came to mind was a torpedo, so we ran up to the upper deck on the port side, and saw the *Aggie*, all lighted up, the *Von Steuban* near her, and the cruisers playing searchlights on both vessels.

"General quarters was blown on our ship, and we officers went to our respective troop places. That night during my watch, I found out that the *Von Steuban* had rammed the *Agamemnon*, splitting the *Von* low, and breaking three lifeboats on the *Aggie*."

On November 12, Martin awoke to find "two aeroplanes, eight destroyers, and thirty or thirty-five mine sweepers" accompanying the flotilla—and the coast of France soon came into view.

And on November 13, 1917, the 185 men of the 1st Company of the 28th Infantry Training Battalion, each one alive and marveling at the wonders of France, marched off to a forty-and-eight, their breaths mingling in clouds and dissipating in the cool autumn air.

4

The Armies in Heaven

W HO TO LEAD COMPANY D at that ruined village, and at that road, and toward that hill; who to kick John Nelson and the others from their places in the wheat and send them toward the machine guns lining the Paris-Soissons Road, who to, above all else, display courage and energy, to cajole and threaten and bust and praise and lead men against their better judgment over the top, and to be out front as they entered the gates of Hell itself there at Cantigny, and Soissons, and the Argonne?

In John Nelson's case, in Rollin Livick's case, that would be the man whose name sat almost atop that August 1918 roll, and whose story would evade and elude me for years, though I would catch tantalizing glimpses of Soren C. Sorensen here and there—in the Distinguished Service Cross and the Croix de Guerre for his work at Cantigny, in his short report on that battle in the 1st Division's records, in a letter he would write to Rollin Livick's parents in 1919, in the mention in a brigade commander's memoirs of Soissons, and, as well, in the few and almost comical lines in the 1st Division's records from the same battle, him "completely lost" as he stumbled through the darkness, Company D in tow, looking for the action, for the jumping-off trench.

He had left as his emergency contact a "Mrs. S. C. Sorensen," of Grand Island, Nebraska; his DSC citation mentioned that he'd entered the service from the Black Hills mining town of Lead, South Dakota; a letter in his burial file mentioned a mother, Christine Christensen, of Long Beach, California; the same letter gave the name of a brother, G. P. Sorensen, of Hollywood; immigration records had him arriving in New York harbor on the Norwegian steamer *State of Indiana* on July 2, 1885, just two years old and toddling down the gangplank after his mother, Kristen, and father, Andrew, both twenty-nine years old, two Danes come to seek their fortune in the New World.

And I don't know why, but I remember wanting him to live; as I pursued his ghost, I wanted him to have survived the war and to have returned to his Mrs. S. C. Sorensen at 421 East 13th Street in Grand Island, and I was dismayed when I learned he hadn't, that he had died in a motorcycle accident during the A.E.F.'s occupation of the Rhine.

The mystery of Soren C. Sorensen only deepened when, after laboriously negotiating the twists and turns of his family's American diaspora, I located in Texas a distant relative of his wife, who told me, No, it had been no accident, that my heroic captain had been decapitated by a wire strung across the road outside of Coblenz, perhaps the work of German diehards, perhaps not.

Long months of searching brought me to a great-niece in California, Margaret Brackett, who knew little, but who had been handed down a German Luger that had been among Sorensen's effects, as well as her great-uncle's DSC, and pictures of the handsome and steely-eyed commander of Company D, one a typical and formal studio doughboy portrait, others of him in an army uniform and posing stiffly on Alcatraz Island in San Francisco Bay, the photos undated but certainly prewar, he in the company of two fine ladies, corseted and clad in long, flowing dresses, with feathers in their Sunday bonnets, but the story behind the images seemingly gone to dust.

On a trip to Washington, D.C., in 2006 I made a pilgrimage to his grave at Arlington National Cemetery, stumbling along Grant Drive past dead generals and admirals, past the Tomb of the Unknowns, with my own boys, Ethan and Nathaniel, in tow and not understanding why, even though I kept telling them, "He was your great-grandfather's company commander!"

and they hot and tired and shrugging their shoulders, *What-evurrr*, crazy Dad, as if such a remote connection could mean something to eleven-year-old boys.

But my boy Ethan did spot it at last, the tomb of a known but seemingly unknowable, in which he'd been laid to rest in the presence of the grieving Mrs. S. C. Sorensen on the thirtieth of July 1920, only two years after he'd led John Nelson and Company D across the Paris-Soissons Road.

And it was a fine memorial under which he'd slept by then for eighty-six years, a three-by-five-foot shiny granite marker on which a quotation from Revelations—personally picked by the widow—was inscribed:

AND THE ARMIES WHICH WERE IN HEAVEN FOLLOWED HIM UPON WHITE
HORSES, CLOTHED IN FINE LINEN, WHITE AND CLEAN

But who was he? At that point I couldn't really tell, but there was something in the few clues I had, something in the stylized and serene portrait of him that Margaret Brackett had sent, something in the kind and measured few lines he had sent Robert Livick regarding his own lost son in early 1919, that suggested Soren C. Sorensen was a refined and educated man, and perhaps not unlike all of those college boys from fine and upstanding families whom the A.E.F. would snap up for subalterns.

After enough looking, however, and soon after visiting his grave, I was finally able to put some flesh on Soren C. Sorensen, and turn him from the dead and enigmatic and heroic leader of heaven's white-clad and pure armies into a man, an "exceptionally fearless" man, as Wilbert Murphy would write, "courageous and energetic," as one regimental commander would chip in, but a man nonetheless—a gambler and, perhaps, a ladies' man and restless raconteur, a streetwise and tough-talking immigrant who'd absorbed his hard knocks on the streets of Omaha, of all places, and who'd come out unflinching and as a natural leader of men in mortal combat, and a leader now, so his tombstone says, even of the hosts of heaven in perpetuity.

A hunch had led me to the prewar army records at the National Archives, and it was there I found my Soren Sorensen, and the story of the inauspicious beginning of his army career, which started at the age of twenty-one when he enlisted off the rag-tag immigrant streets of Omaha to begin a journey that would take him first to the Philippines, thence to the murderous trenches at Cantigny and across the Paris-Soissons Road, and finally to an untimely and ridiculously unheroic death, after which he would be laid to rest as the hero he was, but with little notice or ado.

Born in Lina, Denmark in April 1883, Sorensen was only two years old when his parents left for the United States. Raised in Omaha, he was working as a laborer when on February 21, 1905, he enlisted in Company H of the 16th Infantry Regiment (which would be folded into the 1st Division in 1917).

Upon his induction, an army physician would note a myriad of scars on his arms, face, back, and legs and a missing left digit on his left pinkie, totems, perhaps, of a rough upbringing on the backstreets of Omaha; before long, Sorensen would add two tattoos, the initials SCS on his right forearm and a "bust of a woman" on the left.

Sorensen was sent to Fort McPherson, Georgia, and in 1906 his unit was shipped to the Philippines, where it helped put down the last gasps of the native rebellion. Through some battlefield act now lost to history, Sorensen was commended for bravery and promoted to corporal. He left the army in 1908 when his three years were up, only to reenlist at Minnesota's Fort Snelling in October 1909, listing his occupation at the time as bookkeeper and asking to be sent to the military brig on Alcatraz Island, where his younger brother, George Peter, was running the commissary.

He reenlisted again in 1912 and was promoted to mess sergeant. In 1914, he married the Omaha divorcee Laura Evelyn Hall, a woman six years his senior, whose parents had traveled overland from New York to settle the prairie near Grand Island, Nebraska.

Sorensen brought Mrs. S. C. Sorensen to San Francisco, and that same year he landed in hot water when he was accused of taking kickbacks from Mecchi & Co., a San Francisco food wholesaler and army contractor, accusations which ironically were brought to the attention of the War Department by Sorensen's new bride, who wrote in an indignant letter on December 7, 1914: "I wish to inform the secretary of war that my husband made application for discharge from the Army, on November 18th 1914, and for some reason, I am sure it is unjust, the Commanding Officer will not forward it. My husband has an excellent record and I have asked him to write you, but he will not. He said he has no 'right' to do so."

Sorensen's application for discharge was held up while the army investigated, and it was through the meticulous records of that probe, and its word-for-word transcripts and depositions, that Soren Sorensen finally spoke to me, finally gave some sense of who he really was, and from where it was he'd come.

And the records paint a picture of a man, perhaps not ordinary but certainly not perfect, either, just one of the few thousands who'd found refuge in the small prewar army, a man who was perhaps more fit for leading a company against machine-gun nests or a horde of machete-wielding Filipinos than dealing with the tedium of everyday civilian life or the back-post monotony he'd found on Alcatraz, where as a mess sergeant his main preoccupation seems to have been dealing with his loser subordinates, cooks, who never missed an opportunity to fill up in the saloons of San Francisco during their off hours.

And, in fact, it was his men's love for tying one on, Sorensen's own superior officer noted during the course of the investigation, that had caused bad blood to run between Sorensen and the men under him: "Several times he came up to me at night and reported the non-performance of duty by kitchen police and cooks who returned more or less intoxicated from the city; in several instances I know that Sergeant Sorensen did not bring this matter of intoxication by the cooks to me until they had repeated it several times and until he had finally gotten tired of the business.

"The cooks in the mess were, at different times, very bitter against Sergeant Sorensen and I have overheard some pretty strong language between the cooks and Sergeant Sorensen because Sergeant Sorensen had reported them to me as mess officer for certain things which happened in the general mess . . . [this] caused a great deal of hard feeling between the other enlisted men and Sergeant Sorensen."

Sorensen himself testified: "I had read the law to these four new cooks that came in. I said, 'The first man who ever brings booze in this kitchen is going to go out.' I said, 'There was too much of that before: it stops from now on.'

"In a short time Cook Sweeting goes to town and comes back about noon. He was drunk and walks up to me and says, 'Have a drink, Sergeant'—fine fellow and all that—and pulled out a big bottle, and I says, 'All right'; all I wanted was to get hold of the bottle, and I got hold of the bottle and took it to his company commander. I just made an example of him to the rest and he was relieved."

Besides charging that Sorensen was taking kickbacks, the cooks claimed he was lifting food from the kitchen, and that he mysteriously seemed to have plenty of money to gamble away. One cook, Benjamin Doerr, said of Sorensen: "He was always talking about what pay he was drawing. I do not know whether he was joking or not, because I never put much confidence in his conversation; I just passed him up as a joker, or 'bull': that is what I would call him. He would go to town often and come back and tell us about what a great time he had—stopping at the Palace, etc."

Sorensen didn't help himself by joking about taking kickbacks from Mecchi, saying at his hearing: "I was playing and went broke in a game and went over to town and borrowed some money; I came back that day, changed my civilian clothes and laid down on the bed, and one of the cooks said, 'Gee! I wish I was a mess sergeant.' And I said, 'Why?' 'Oh,' he said, 'the mess sergeant is never broke.' I said, 'Oh, yes, I am broke lots of times'; and so I made a remark that if a mess sergeant cannot be a mess sergeant and have money he better not be one, and I laughed and made it as a joke that way."

And if you like your heroes to be angels, you can have the tortured and conscientious and clean-living Alvin York of *Sergeant York;* if you like them to be of flesh and blood and have a lust for life and even sin, you'll take Buzz Rickson in *The War Lover,* and you'll take Sorey Sorensen, who beat the silly and picayune charges against him, his inquisitors coming to believe that he had been set up by his spiteful subordinates.

By the conclusion of the inquiry in February 1915 Sorensen had had enough of the army, and reapplied for his discharge, and he and Laura Evelyn soon headed home to Omaha, and thence to the Black Hills of South Dakota, where he managed the telephone exchanges for Deadwood and the nearby mining town of Lead.

After war was declared, Sorensen, the local paper would report, "took his preliminary examination for admission to the officers training camp before Captain Everington at Crawford, Neb. At that time his qualifications seemed to be so unquestioned, that he was advised to resign immediately his position with the Telephone company."

However, it wasn't until June 5, 1917, that Soren C. Sorensen, leaving behind Mrs. S. C. Sorensen, headed once more to arms "on the Northwestern," the *Lead Daily Call* would report, and enter officers training at Minnesota's Fort Snelling. By September, First Lieutenant Soren Sorensen was in France, awaiting the arrival of the *Mount Vernon*, and George Butler and Willard Storms and the rest, those boys he would lead at Cantigny and across the Paris-Soissons Road and almost to the slopes of Hill 263.

It was even while Sorensen was waiting, biding his time, a leader with no followers, that the 1st Division's men began dying, the first three—the first Americans to die in combat in the war—expiring in a trench in what was supposed to be the "quiet" Sommerviller sector in Lorraine, about six miles northeast of Nancy, into which the 1st Battalions of each of the infantry regiments had grimly marched in a cold, steady rain on October 21, 1917, for some "seasoning."

Except for a small raid undertaken by the 26th Regiment, the eleven days and nights had indeed passed fairly quietly. "We learned to distinguish the difference between the exploding sound of a gas shell and high explosives," Charles Senay wrote. "There was some shrapnel and the intermittent rattle of machine guns."

And there were rats—"myriads of brown rats," Senay added. "My dugout was deep and shored and lined with wood. They would run along the woodwork and sometimes bounce from one's body when they descended to the floor, where they would scramble over each other, fighting and squealing."

On the night of November 2–November 3, the 1st Division found itself facing a more lethal pest. That night, the 1st Battalions scurried out of their muddy holes and into the inky night while the 2nd Battalions went in to get their own taste of what America's youth had been missing for three years. Within a few hours, they found it when a violent barrage isolated part of the front, and shadowy forms emerged and picked their way across no-man's land from the German lines.

"At half past twelve the sky on the enemy lines turned a blood red," Corporal Ruben Nelson of Company G, 18th Regiment, remembered. "Long before the report of the big guns sounded we knew what was up. We had never been in it before, but we had the idea of how these things came."

Shells began exploding furiously around Nelson's position, then crept past Company G's lines to the rear, cutting off the support companies.

"The only thing we could do was flank the boxed sector with machine gun fire," Nelson wrote. "At about half past one we could see about 300 [Germans] making for our lines. We knew what was coming. Three hundred against thirty."

The barrage isolated the frontline position of the 16th Regiment's Company F, preventing the unit's support from moving up as the Germans entered the front lines. Making his way down one zigzagging trench, a German confronted Corporal James Gresham as he stood guard over his platoon leader's dugout. Supposing the figure to be an American, Gresham had called out: "Don't shoot—I am an American!"

But the figure had replied in a thick accent: "I am shooting all Americans!" and shot Gresham dead with an automatic pistol. Two more—privates Merle Hay and Thomas Enright—were slain during the fierce hand-to-hand fighting on that dark night, five more were wounded, and another eleven were hustled to the German lines as prisoners.

They buried Gresham, Enright, and Hay not too far from where they fell, with pomp and circumstance and in the presence of soliloquizing French officers, who hid their happiness behind solemn faces, happy not because three Americans had died but because now America was a blood brother, now it had invested something real in the cause, now it had its own deaths to avenge.

One veteran would remember that the names of the fallen sped "like wildfire" across the American front, where the 2nd, 3rd, and 26th Divisions were also trying to get up to speed. But if the news made it to the dry and dusty plains around Camp MacArthur, it went without mention.

The Janesville boys, who now included among their number Rollin Livick, were stuck in Texas, some of them having endured seven full months of training, of sticking it to the ribs and twisting and pulling it out and then doing it again; seven months of marching, of living in tents whose sides shuddered and shook in the frigid blasts of the Blue Northers; seven months of wondering when the army was going to let them have at them, so they could see, or maybe prove, finally, just what it was they were made of.

As worlds turned in the American trenches, camp drudgery ruled in the States. Boneheaded soldier's arguments filled the few idle hours, noted the now Private First Class Rollin Livick, who while writing home to Edgerton to say he'd been hospitalized with a suspected case of measles mentioned one such tiff: "The other morning we were discussing the war, and an Irishman said the only thing he regretted was the U.S. being allied with Eng. Some German sided with him of course. I gave them hell. It's no use arguing with them, because they didn't know any thing about it anyway. It beats all how many ignorant and disloyal people one will find in the army."

At Camp MacArthur the training was intensified. Rollin that fall would send home "films" of British bayonet and French bombing instructors, the Brits appearing casual and jaunty and dapper and relaxed, each of the five holding a walking stick in an *eh-wot* sort of way, the mustachioed French looking *très serieux*, some of them dour, impatient with these dallying Americans, what with France split in two by a great ditch and the Hun prying at the locks to the gates of Paris.

Rollin and the rest took their place at the rifle range and practiced digging and manning trenches, sometimes all night, none of which dampened his ardor for the coming trials, but did seem to reinforce his feelings of foreboding.

His cousin Frank Devine, training as well with Company M, remembered years later that one night on the way back from an off-post musical show Rollin "took our ticket stubs and tore them in two cornerwise. Then he handed me one half of the stubs and said that if anything should happen to either of us and it was required for identification the pieces could be matched up for that purpose. I didn't think much about it at the time but later I had a long, long period of years to consider the significance of it."

Rollin chose not to share any feelings of dread with his family. Instead, he mostly described the intensive, nonstop training. "For two days we dug trenches, and one day (Sunday) we lived in them, slept, ate, and worked in them. It sure was some experience," he wrote in one letter. "I worked harder that day than any day since I've been in the Army.

"Last week we donned masks and visited the gas house. We went thru three kinds first with masks on, and then with it off and there sure was some difference."

The nicest boy in Edgerton was no pawn and no fool. While many of his young comrades may have endured the grinding monotony of camp life as if they were little more than draft animals or cannon fodder, he seemed always to understood the big picture, and his role in it.

On January 18, 1918—three days after his twentieth birthday—Rollin wrote to his older and married brother Roy, imparting a worldly knowledge of the situation in Europe, and some advice should Roy be drafted: "Don't go in with the idea that you are going to have a good time, if you do by god you are due for a jolt. It's a joke to hear a lot of soldiers talk. They all say one big drive in the spring, and it will be all over. There isn't one soldier in ten who has an intelligent view about this war. Personally I don't see how it can end inside a couple of years if the people in Germany stick together."

Few who were then leading American troops in France—by the first months of 1918 only 175,000 U.S. troops had embarked for Europe—would have disputed his assessment. As the country continued to build an army almost from scratch, and faced the difficult problems of training it and transporting it overseas, even the most optimistic among the Allies did not believe victory was possible in 1918.

In fact, there was a larger concern among the French and British that despite the first American deaths in battle, the effort was coming too late, and the war would end before the United States could train and send over meaningful numbers of men.

For the French and British, the year 1917 had been unproductive, and wasteful. As American combat troops began to arrive in dribs and drabs through the summer and fall of 1917, a British offensive at Passchendaele was winding down, at the cost of 62,000 dead and 164,000 wounded in a four-and-a-half-mile advance since July.

An equally disastrous French offensive in April 1917 began with the aim of gaining six miles, and was halted at the cost of 100,000 casualties after inching just six hundred yards. The enormous slaughter—by the end of 1917, 2.6 million French had been killed, captured, or permanently disabled—led some French units to mutiny that summer, three years of hardship and death having sucked out of the poilus the will to fight even as their fresh-faced and energetic American counterparts began to land in France.

Germany, meanwhile, abandoned the offensive through much of the year, instead straightening its lines and reducing the territory it had to defend on the Western Front by pulling back to a new fortified position called the Hindenburg Line. Germany, too, had been bled almost dry, but turmoil in Russia, where the Bolshevik revolution was under way, promised to take that eastern ally out of the war by the end of the year. German divisions that had confronted the Russians would be moved west once Russia formally withdrew and as the American buildup continued, the German high command laid plans for an all-out offensive to begin in the spring of 1918 with the hope of winning the war before the Americans could arrive in numbers large enough to tilt the balance.

The prospect of a massive German offensive led the French and British to press General Pershing to parcel out arriving U.S. troops to the Allies. But Pershing through the last half of 1917 and the winter of 1918 insisted on keeping his army intact for a variety of reasons—including a perceived need to train officers to American standards, and cultural resistance "among our population of varied origins," wrote James Harbord, who would command the 2nd Division at Belleau Wood and Soissons.

Harbord acknowledged that the U.S. stance carried severe risks. "I know of no greater responsibility ever placed on an American Commander than that which now rested on Pershing. He risked the chance of being cursed to the latest generation if, through his failure to co-operate, the War were lost."

Pershing's intransigence over where, and in what manner, American troops would be used would continue until events forced his hand in the spring of 1918; in the meantime, American troops continued to land in France—among them George Butler, Thomas Slinker, Willard Storms, and the rest of the Fort Harrison boys, who walked down the gangplank of the *Mount Vernon* and into a world war on November 13, 1917.

Blissfully ignorant of the deaths of Gresham, Hay, and Enright after two weeks at sea, the men of the 1st Company, 28th Infantry Training Battalion boarded a forty-and-eight and entrained for Trevary, where they were folded into the 28th Regiment, and their unit renamed Company

D. George Butler would take note of the change—and of his small delight in ranking another officer—in a letter to his mother. "I am still with the same company, but we are now called 'D' company, 28th regiment, as we are with the whole regiment now. I also have a nice room with another Lieutenant, who belongs to Company 'D.' The room has an old fashioned high bed which I use and make the Lieutenant use his field cot for I rank him so I get my choice and he gets what is left."

In late November, in a letter to his mother, Willard Storms mentioned the Thanksgiving feast the army had served—one of the few pleasures of home the men would receive that winter—and his first impressions of France: "We are in a very beautiful country as far as the scenery goes and the climate so far is mild but rainy, the people are mostly of the peasant class, very poor and very queerly dressed.

"Wooden shoes seem to be the style. Most of the work is done by the women, or old and crippled men, the young men are at the front. Have seen a good many Germans but they were in prison camps. Expect to see enough of them before long."

In anticipation of the great battles to come, units were quickly shuffled and reshuffled, veteran noncoms and privates from Companies A, B, and C being reassigned to the new Company D to season its ranks. Amid the blowing snows and cold rain of winter, the Fort Harrison boys began training in the area around Gondrecourt.

Billets were found in ramshackle barns. "There were mornings when, upon rising, the men would find that snow had blown in and sifted over their bunks and quite often, before one's shoes could be drawn on, it was necessary to thaw them out by burning straw or paper in them," the 28th Regiment's official history says.

Proper footwear was scarce, as well. "When we first came here most of us did not had shoes that his best friend would call worthy of that name," Company D's Sergeant Anthony Vedral, a Bohemian immigrant and former housepainter who had trained at Fort Harrison, recalled.

Now in charge of the 1st Division, General Robert Lee Bullard appreciated the trying conditions in which the men trained. But the work had to go on amid the worst of the winter weather at Gondrecourt, Bullard wrote: "There was nothing for the Americans to do but continue their training no matter what the weather or what the suffering. In the last two weeks of 1917, in cold, hard December weather, the 1st Division were executing manouvres which required camping overnight, sleeping upon the ground, and standing in the open during hours and hours of waiting, chilled by winds after being wet with rain."

Bullard also noted the importance and stature that had been placed upon the 1st Division's men not only by Pershing, but by the Allies: "If they failed the world would say that America would fail. For this reason the drill and training were probably made the hardest that ever American troops were put through.

"It had been decided by General Pershing that the very best officers that could be made available would go to the 1st Division. Therefore this training was made a severe test of officers and non-commissioned officers."

And it was at Gondrecourt that one of those "very best" officers, Soren C. Sorensen, took command of Company D on December 10.

The old regular, Lieutenant Max Buchanan, had led the company for just a few days before the switch, and upon Sorensen's arrival was immediately sent to "sniping school"—on-the-job training in the front lines with a Canadian outfit, by which Buchanan became the first of the Fort Benjamin Harrison boys to get a taste of trench warfare.

Buchanan wrote to a friend in Brockton, Massachusetts, to say he'd had "a most enjoyable Christmas with the Canadian regiment, but I must say it was more like a Fourth of July celebration. It was supposed to be a quiet sector, and I guess it was—to them. However, there were five casualties during that relief from German sniping.

"I had the pleasure of being under shell fire several times and had quite a few close calls but nothing serious resulted. I guess it was a poor day for the Huns."

One of Sorensen's first orders of business was to instill more discipline. Bullard's predecessor had been axed by Pershing for, among other things, running a lax operation, and Bullard quickly made it clear that there was a new sheriff in town.

"I think I've scared 'em all by telling them they'd be 'relieved' without any hesitation on the part of General Pershing if they did not 'deliver the goods,'" Bullard wrote. "They must succeed or they would lose their commands. They are at work; I can vouch for that."

And to the man who'd faced off with a bunch of drunken, backbiting cooks and carried the day, kicking some spirit and discipline into the unit surely seemed child's play. Company D's brig soon became a busy place, filled with dozens of privates and even noncoms who had sneaked away for a night's fun at a local cafe or bistro and tarried too long, incurring the wrath of the former mess sergeant.

Company D's rolls from early 1918 tell the story:

"Olencak, Ignatius. AWOL fr Jan 6 to 7/18 . . . To perform hard labor with his company for two months.

"Robbins, Fay. AWOL Jan 5 to 9/18. To forfeit five-sixths of his pay per mo for three months.

"Vances, Paul. AWOL fr Dec 31/18 to Jan 10/18. To perform hard labor for three months and to forfeit five-sixths of his pay per Mo for a like period."

Sorensen and the other company commanders would learn other ways of doling out punishment, one lesson coming in the middle of a cold night on which Sorensen found himself answering an urgent "officer's call" to regimental headquarters.

After the 28th Regiment had gone without pay for several months, the paymaster had visited that day—and "some six men per company were missing at bed check," Charles Senay, now in command of Company C, remembered. "It was obvious that our hardened sinners had departed to a nearby town to relieve their pent-up repressions for liquor and women. The colonel was greatly upset."

After a heated discussion on how to punish the many offenders, one major—a transferee from the Canadian Army—suggested "wagon wheel treatment," Senay wrote. As the AWOLs stumbled into camp that night singly and in small groups, they were grabbed, and each was spread-eagled on a wagon wheel "with his ass on the axle and his wrists and ankles lashed to the rim in a quadrant," Senay continued, adding: "There was quite a bit of profanity and obscenity but, in the main, the victims accepted their punishment passively."

Such harsh treatment would not prevent a capital crime from being committed within Company D's ranks. On the morning of February 15, 1918, Private John G. Warren, a mechanic from Cicero, Illinois, was found dead in his bunk with his head split open—a victim, it seems, of murder.

Details are sketchy, but the Graves Registration Service would report after the war that Warren was "found dead in bed—reported that he died of a fractured skull. No mark on his head. Paid off the night before and put to bed by two companions."

Warren, the report added, "had been hit with a brick some months before in a scuffle. Sgt. Storms and his friends were discussing it and thought, that as he was a pale sallow man, his death might have been caused by the night in town."

Sergeant Victor Reese would relate that Warren's murder would remain unsolved. "From examination of the deceased man it was feared that he had received a blow on the back of the head," Reese would say. "Some suspicions were entertained as to who might have been responsible but the man under observation was transferred to another organization (perhaps owing to the pressure of suspicions) and I do not recall any further action taken to fix responsibility of this man's death."

But Private Andrew Jackson Van Dusen would report that the murderer was found. Warren's assailant—"whose name informant can not remember"—was "court-martialed and executed," Van Dusen said.

Who might have murdered the "sallow" John Warren? The only possible suspect within Company D is Private Golladay—the Kokomo, Indiana, teenager who'd had a premonition of death and who had implored his pastor to pray for him prior to leaving for France.

The company's rolls show that Golladay was the next Company D soldier to die, on March 18, by an unexplained "accident" exactly one month after Warren's death. But in a strange omission, Golladay has no burial file in the National Archives, the only deceased member of Company D not to have one.

In fact, Charles Senay would note, there was probably any number of men capable of the deed. "There were violent men in every company," Senay remembered, though Golladay by all measures would not seem to have fit that description. "At one and the same time I had four undetected murderers. I once had two characters who every pay day chased each other with hand axes, bayonets or some other lethal weapon.

"Pay day I established special patrols to cut down this foolishness. We'd subdue the rambunctious ones and confine them until they were safe for their fellow soldiers." (One of those axe-wielding "characters," Senay would note, was Corporal Michael B. Ellis, whose actions in the Argonne would win him the Congressional Medal of Honor.)

Almost ninety years later the cause of Warren's death, and who was to blame for it, hardly matter; still, in light of the coming year, when so many of the company's men would die in battle, it remains ironic that the company's first casualty—and perhaps the second—may have resulted from some rounds of drinks in town, and not a round of artillery in the trenches in which Company D found itself just weeks after Warren's death.

5

"It's Easy to Lick the Kaiser"

A FEW FAR-OFF AND flickering lights from a hilltop village, the drone of an airplane in the darkness, then wire, and *It's a trench!* and they're off into the inky night, racing across a muddy field and laughing, some of them, each one intent on being the first poor, dumb doughboy into that exotic ditch— and then machine-gun fire, and a few desultory rounds of artillery splattering dirt and *so this is war*; and now Rollin Livick and the Janesville boys are beating a hasty retreat, under fire, a lesson learned, no harm, no foul; no harm—not yet.

Their forty-and-eight had stopped in the middle of that black March night, and in the middle of France, interrupting for no apparent reason their Great Adventure and their journey to join "the famous 28th Regiment," as the former Lawrence University student Private Wilbert Murphy would write.

Like schoolboys on a summer lark, fifteen of the naïve recruits set out to explore their new world and to get nearer to the war of which they'd heard so much, with no idea of the dangers surrounding them, no idea even of where they were.

"Expectations, you may be sure, were high," Company M's Private John

Johnston recalled. "While our first train ride in the land of the Frenchman was taken in passenger coaches, of the French sort, this ride was taken in box cars, which had signs on them that when translated means, 'Forty Men or Forty Mules.'"

At eleven P.M., the train lurched to a stop. "The boys did not know the meaning of this," Johnston recalled. "The lieutenant had told us we were going to the front, but we could not believe that we had reached the fighting lines, as we could hear no shooting. But the officer answered: 'What do you want. If we go any further we'll go into the German lines.'"

But the doughboys couldn't "stand the strain of those cars, which we were ordered to remain in all night, and so we sought terra firma," Johnston wrote. "In the distance we could see the lights of a town, situated on a knoll, and we struck for this. Soon we ran into an abandoned trench, and then an old barbed wire entanglement. This considerably startled the exploring party."

The doughboys made a dash—"to try and be the first man of the outfit 'into the trenches,'" Johnston wrote. "Suddenly we heard bombs striking the ground near us, and then machine gun bullets. I'll say we got out of there quick.

"A French sentry let us know before we reached our box car sleeping arrangements that had we reached the town we would have been wiped out, as it was near the German trenches, and it was the Boches who were sending the machine gun bullets towards us."

The Janesville boys and the rest of the 128th Regiment had left Waco in early February, taking five days by rail to get to Camp Merritt, New Jersey, along the way stopping to parade in Birmingham, Alabama—where the boys were "entertained royally," Johnston would write—and another five days at the camp getting ready to sail.

In mid-February, they headed for the Hoboken docks and the *Covington*, a German-built liner that had been seized in U.S. waters upon the declaration of war and turned over to the navy for use as a transport. On February 18, 1918, the ship shoved off for the unknown and to whatever fate might await the Janesville boys—"whatever they had to hand us," Johnston would recall.

Company M's men were "a most happy bunch, who were in the thing to the last drop of the hat," Johnston wrote. And for several days, all was quiet as *Covington* plied the cold North Atlantic, though the fear of German U-boats was a constant companion for each of the Wisconsinites, most of whose experience of deep water came from muddy swimming holes or prairie lakes, or at best a dip in Lake Michigan after a half-day's hot ride.

The *Covington*, Rollin Livick would write, was "a sea worthy vessal, but not very fast. It's poorly ventilated, but our compartments were next to the upper deck so we were real lucky." Seasickness, however, was rampant, Rollin added: "Was sick the second day out, but nothing serious. Some of the fellows were sick for nearly a week."

"I was never so sick in my life," wrote Private Charles Maine, who like Rollin was destined for service in Company D. "Some of the boys just laid in their bunks and wanted the ship to sink, they were so sick."

Midway across the Atlantic, it seemed for a moment that the boys would get their wishes; the periscope of a dreaded U-boat was spotted, and just as quickly the call came for all aboard to head topside. "Everyone on board was shaking, for they were decidedly unaccustomed to this experience," Johnston would remember.

"Then we experienced our first touch of war. Everyone had been given the 'stand to' drill, with life preservers. We had our own regimental band with us, and things were gay. I was standing with a group of men on the deck singing 'It's Easy to Lick the Kaiser.' Every fellow on board was anxious for a look at a submarine, and everybody had his eyes peeled."

Within seconds, and drowning out the band, the battleship *South Carolina* blasted its whistle, followed by two toots from the transport *George Washington*. "Short fiery puffs were coming out of the funnels of the *South Carolina*, which means that she was getting ready for battle," Johnston wrote. "She turned broadside to the 'sub,' to protect us, and turned loose eight shells."

Soon, Johnston added, a periscope was sighted—and fired on. "Our ship was accredited with making the best shot, for one of our gunners actually knocked the barrel off the periscope," Johnston recalled. "Depth bombs were dropped and it was thought that the 'sub' was done away with."

(The apprehension of Johnston—and of all doughboys—over being sunk by a U-boat was not misplaced. *Covington*'s run as a troopship ended on July 1, 1918, when a torpedo from the German submarine U-86 ripped into her port side as she headed back to the United States after having delivered her sixth load of doughboys.

(The blast killed six crewmen, and *Covington* sank the next day about 150 miles off of France. *Mount Vernon*, too, was torpedoed on September 5, 1918, after delivering its ninth complement of doughboys. The ship was repaired and put to work bringing the boys home in February 1919.)

By March 7, *Covington* had docked at Brest, where, still aboard ship, Rollin wrote home to say that despite the scrape with the U-boat he "enjoyed the trip. It surely was a great experience."

Always keen on understanding the big picture, he chafed at his isolation on the ship. "We know nothing about the war or current events. There are all kinds of rumors floating around. Some say Austria has declared separate, and others say the American forces have started a big offensive and etc. I'm not banking very strong on any of them, but wish to hell I could get hold of a news paper."

(Rollin would also add a line that would serve to tantalize his family members—and their descendants—over the ensuing decades: "I am keeping a diary, and will be able to tell you a lot of things that I can't now when I get back.")

The men disembarked from the *Covington* the next day, wondering at their first sight of the enemy—captured German soldiers unloading ships. After several days, Johnston wrote, they were handed three days' rations, loaded their packs with "cheap and abundant" wine, and were put on the move.

"We took train for a small town where we were to locate for training," Johnston recalled. "The people of this section of France were exceedingly gloomy. The Americans were the only cheerful people. Everyone had a hopeless look, and their faces seemed to say louder than if they had expressed it in words, 'You Americans sure are going to have a hard time.'"

In mid-March, word came that the 128th Regiment would be broken up, and its privates, and some of its officers, transferred into the 1st Division to bring it to full strength. The news that he would now lead Company A of the 16th Regiment, and not his beloved Janesville boys, into battle was a bitter pill for Company M's commander, Edgar Caldwell. "When our company commander, Captain Caldwell, left us, he cried," Private John Johnston recalled.

"It was indeed a blow to me to be taken from my company in which I felt such a great pride," Caldwell would bitterly complain in letters home that summer. "I had watched each man develop from a green recruit into a first class fighting man, and each one individually had grown very close to my heart.

"I often think that they themselves little realized how close they were to me, for I suppose to them I was always the drill master and strict disciplinarian. But I loved every one of them and felt a great responsibility to their families and friends left at home. I would gladly make any sacrifice to be able to lead them home each one as I took him away."

The feeling doesn't seem to have been mutual among those privates now headed for the 28th Regiment. No tears were shed in commiseration; instead, a sense of adventure, and a wonder at all of the unknowns to come, overtook the Janesville boys, who soon found themselves rolling in that forty-and-eight across the French countryside, heading toward the 1st Division and making that short, and terrifying, nighttime excursion along the way.

On March 27, the Janesville boys reached the 28th Regiment's lines, bid adieu to each other and were scattered across the four companies—A, B, C, D, and the smaller Machine Gun Company—comprising the regiment's 1st Battalion. Rollin Livick, Wilbert Murphy, and thirty-four other Janesville boys reported for duty with Company D.

"The first battalion had just come out of the trenches for a rest, consequently we heard many stories about the front and what everything up in front was like," Murphy would write.

The 1st Brigade of the 1st Division—the 16th and 18th Regiments— had entered the lines in the Ansauville sector in January, relieving a Moroccan division along a seven-mile front at the base of the St. Mihiel salient, fifteen miles northwest of Toul, as the 2nd Brigade continued to train at Gondrecourt.

On March 9, the 2nd Brigade relieved it—and ten days later Company D for the first time entered the trenches, it not having quite been born when the 28th's 1st Battalion went "in" for a ten-day stint at Sommerviller the previous October.

And when it did, it went under the command of the immigrant Soren Sorensen, the regular Max Buchanan, the Kansan and former Indianapolis attorney George Butler, and two lieutenants new to the company—William Ross Gahring, twenty-four, the son of a drugstore owner in Mount Vernon, Missouri; and John Huston Church, twenty-five, an ironworker's son from Glen Iron, Pennsylvania, who left New York University when war was declared and found life in the army so much to his liking that he remained in it for most of the rest of his life and retired a brigadier general.

The 28th took over a portion of the trenches that ran through the shattered remains of the village of Seicheprey, to the northwest of which loomed the imposing four-hundred-foot Mont Sec and a network of German strongpoints that had been built within the salient over the two previous years, after a furious and costly German offensive had been checked.

"From Mont Sec," the 28th's history notes, "the enemy had excellent observation of the whole American sector and there was not a man in the 28th who did not cherish the ambition that some day they would drive the Germans from that hill."

Just six months later, the 1st Division would return to jump off from these same trenches to cut a swath deep into the St. Mihiel salient, but during March 1918, Seicheprey marked for most of the men an introduction to the deadly peculiarities and frustrations of trench life.

The grim ruins and desolation of war had increased daily as the 28th Regiment marched from Gondrecourt, and surely put a lump in the throats of many of Company D's men as they neared the front lines.

Edgar Caldwell would note that as his own journey to join the 16th Regiment progressed, the vegetation disappeared, forests were reduced to a series of splintered stumps, and "the whole surface of the ground looked like it had been churned up. Graves with little crosses of wood were everywhere as far as you could see—both German and French.

"Many bodies lay bleaching in the open where they had been disinterred by exploding shells. I saw one place where they had dug a trench right through one of these little cemeteries, and packs, boots, pieces of clothes, etc. were sticking out of the trench walls."

The *Collier's* correspondent James Hopper, too, described the gradations of destruction through which the doughboys passed on their way into the battle line. "As you go on, the civilian population decreases and the military increases," Hopper wrote. "Then you get to one in which a few houses are destroyed as though by earthquake. The next village is still queerer. Half the houses are down; all the roofs punctured. Then comes one in which there is no house, only walls, angular and torn and where everyone lives in the cellars. The next village is just one, razed black horror."

For the most part, the Germans and whichever among the Allies happened to occupy the base of the salient seemed happy with the stalemate, and the sector had been fairly quiet since the Germans created the bulge in a failed attempt to break through in 1915.

But "quiet" was relative on the Western Front—and the company would learn much about survival in the next month, the most important being to keep their gas masks handy at all times, lest they be asphyxiated, burned, or temporarily blinded by the variety of colorless and hard-to-detect chemicals the Germans had been busily developing and employing since introducing the noxious weapon in 1915.

While the threat of a full-bore German attack in the sector was unlikely, the Germans' love of gas kept all on edge while in the trenches. The Hun threw over canisters filled with chlorine and phosgene by the bucket load at Seicheprey, but the worst was mustard gas, in reality an oil, first used by the Germans in July 1917 and which between then and October caused more casualties on the Western Front than did all of the other gases combined.

Hard to detect, mustard gas caused chemical burns that rendered its victim practically useless for three to five weeks. As Rexmond C. Cochrane of the U.S. Army Chemical Corps described it, "Its least effect on the eyes was a loss of vision for from three days to three weeks."

The 1st Division's soldiers were issued French and British gas masks, which were difficult to see and breathe through, but at least afforded some protection from the gases, which were usually more debilitating than lethal. Mustard gas would prove to be the most insidious of all; it pooled in the soil and in the bottom of dugouts and found its way into clothing and even food.

"Mustard gas attacks any moist spot on the body," Charles Senay wrote. "One could be badly burned under the arms, around the waist and on the scrotum. Many soldiers packed their sex organs with oil-saturated rags when fearing the gas. It was supposed to cause complete loss of virility."

Because of the insidious nature of mustard gas, Cochrane wrote, orders directed that "anyone passing through a gassed area was to beat and shake his clothes before entering a dugout, and to use soap suds as first aid treatment for liquid mustard on the skin."

The French would eventually counter with mustard gas in the form of yperite, but it remained under development in the spring of 1918. The 1st Division's artillery used other gases, mostly phosgene and cyanogen chloride, but being at the mercy of the French, who supplied the ammunition and artillery from which it was shot, the 1st was limited to an allotment of fewer than a hundred gas rounds per day. Still, division commander Bullard would write, the French gas "was very deadly and the enemy had a wholesome fear of it."

So did the Americans. Colonel Theodore Roosevelt Jr., who commanded the 1st Battalion of the 26th Regiment and was one of four sons the former president Teddy sent to war, recalled an elaborate warning system—"bells, gongs, Klaxon horns, and beautiful rockets"—aimed at alerting the doughboys to the sinister substances sent over into their lines.

"A nervous sentry would be pacing to and fro," he wrote. "It would be wet and lonely and he would think of what unpleasant things he had been told happened to the men who were gassed. A shell would burst near him. 'By George, that smells queer,' he would think. He would sniff again. 'No question about it, that must be gas!' and blam! would go the gas alarm."

Soon, "from one end of the line to the other gongs and horns would sound and green rockets would streak across the sky and platoon after platoon would wearily encase itself in gas masks. One night I stood in the reserve position and watched a celebration of this sort. It looked and sounded like a witches' Sabbath."

Under threat of raids, gas, and shelling, the men labored at night, waist-deep in mud and water, and found what shelter they could during the day in dugouts and holes notched in the sides of the trenches.

"We were billeted in shell-craters some of them full of water and it is needless to say that we were compelled to keep our heads down out of sight during daylight," Company D's Willard Storms wrote. "Our work had to be done at night, likewise our eating. Some could sleep a few hours during the day if their craters permitted. Lots were lying in water from waists down all day."

Pyrotechnics ruled the night. "Fritz usually sent his greetings on 'Creeping Jimmie,' 'Mournful Marys,' 'Whizz Bangs,' G.I. Cans or Rolling Kitchens and a few millions of machine gun bullets," Storms wrote. There was also the gas. "I got a little touch of the latter before I could adjust my mask as the shell struck so close, but it only bothered me a few days."

Storms would add that the volume of shellfire and gas made quick veterans of Company D's men. "Since our first few days up there, we have had what would appear to be a different group of men."

Lieutenant Butler would remember Storms—who would be promoted to sergeant on March 30—being a different type of man from the start. Willard, he noted, volunteered to locate and retrieve a lost patrol on the company's first day in the trenches: "I sent a squad out just before daybreak to inspect our wire entanglements and it lost its direction and was going toward the enemy lines when Willard voluntarily went out into no mans land and guided the Patrol back to our lines. He was fired at twice by an enemy sniper and I saw him wave his arm in derision and keep on going."

Storms would write of his first taste of the front lines: "The excitement of it is like liquor—hard to stay away from."

Others were less steady. Their nerves on edge, boys who just months before had been carpenters and clerks and farmers peered into the black night while on forward duty and imagined Germans coming from every angle.

"Naturally, the men were nervous, and on the alert, and often imagined things, sometimes shooting at a post, mistaking it, or a stump of some shell battered tree for a man out there beyond the trenches," John Johnston, now assigned to the 28th's Company A, wrote.

With the threat of a German raid constant and very real, frontline justice was harsh. It was at Seicheprey, Charles Senay would remember, that on one "rainy, windy night" he was called from his dugout by the military police. "They had four prisoners," Senay wrote. "I was told that these prisoners were to be placed between the lines headed toward the enemy and shot if they tried to return. This was done and I've never learned the fate of these men. They could have been an espionage unit. They could also have been condemned criminals."

Toward the end of its baptism, the 28th Regiment staged a daring raid of its own. On March 29, the 3rd Battalion sent its intelligence officer, Lieutenant George Buchanan Redwood, out on an early-morning raid to secure prisoners, the regiment's first of the war.

Company L's Private Edward Armstrong would remember that, at 1:00 A.M., "the Lieut. asked for volunteers to go and of course we all wanted to go with him. Well he picked four of us to go and the five of us started out and got into 'No-Man's' land about 2 A.M.

"It was very dark and raining a great deal, we had a very hard time finding our way and crawling around shell holes and through barbed-wire. We finally got over and into the German trenches and took our prisoners and got back all right because it was getting daylight."

The exploit would win Redwood, twenty-nine, and his volunteers a write-up in the press, ten-day leaves, and gain them Distinguished Service Crosses from an army eager to make its mark in the war.

Willard Storms wrote home to extol such American verve. "By now you have heard how the Sammies or the 'Amex' as we are called here are fighting. Every time they've 'gone over' they've brought some-thing back that could walk.

" 'Crazy Americaine,' the French say. 'Boo koo fight.' 'Fight, no bon.' They can't understand why we are so anxious to get started. They laugh when the boys sharpen bayonets. But when it comes to 'going over,' we can show 'em all who has the intestinal equipment."

A better chance to show the Germans such intestinal fortitude was even then creeping closer. On March 21, the Germans launched their spring offensive, Operation Michael, a massive assault, fifty miles wide, aimed at separating the main British forces on the northern sector of the front from the French forces to the south.

Preceded by a jarring artillery bombardment, the attack rolled through the British lines at Cambrai and those of the French at St. Quentin, gaining thirty miles of French soil in just two weeks, almost destroying one British army, and taking 90,000 prisoners as well.

In the wake of the success, a huge gun, called Big Bertha, was hauled up behind the advance and began shelling Paris. The assault, Harbord wrote, "seriously lowered Allied morale and correspondingly raised that of their enemy. The Germans demonstrated that they could break through highly organized defenses."

The Germans had beaten Pershing to open warfare.

Facing crisis as the German armies seemed poised to continue south to the gates of Paris, Marshal Ferdinand Foch on March 26 was appointed chief of the Allied armies on the Western Front, in an attempt to unify the commands. His hand forced, Pershing on March 28 personally went to Foch and, abandoning his immediate hopes for an all-American army, told him: "All that we have is yours."

Exactly six days later, Company D and the 1st Division were on the road again, marching to the Bois l'Eveque near Toul, and then boarding trains which carried them to a training area northwest of Paris (the 1st lost 56 officers and men killed and another 277 men wounded or gassed in its two and a half months in the Ansauville Sector; its replacement, the 26th Division, would suffer more than 650 casualties in one *day* when the Germans staged a raid in force on Seicheprey on April 20.)

After a week of training near Paris, the 1st Division hit the road once more, its destination Picardy, about fifty miles north-northeast of the French capital, where a renewal of the great German offensive had temporarily ground to a stop on the eastern outskirts of the tiny village of Cantigny, three kilometers northwest of Montdidier.

"Our way lay through small byroads; sometimes our regiment seemed isolated and lost, the only one, abandoned, marching on to battle—and then, on the top of a far hill we'd see another column," James Hopper wrote of the division's march to Picardy, where a "low rumble" over the horizon marked an ongoing, seesaw battle between the Germans and the French and Moroccans.

Toward the end of the march, he wrote, the troops saw sausage-shaped antiaircraft balloons on the horizon, growing ever larger as the 1st Division approached its destination—"the salient of Montdidier, of now historical Montdidier where the French had broken at length the German advance."

"Gee but it's sure great to be out with a bunch of men so large that one cannot see to the front nor the rear of the column and each man swinging into step with his O.D. Baby (pack) and rifle on his shoulder," Storms would write on April 22. "It makes one know what the outcome of this war will be to see the determined look on each mans face as he marches out toward the sound of the big guns. Then to see them 'out there,' each man settling himself down to make the best of it and quit growling and be ready to get 'Up and Over' if the time comes. It's something to be proud of just to know that I am one of the bunch."

Relieving two French colonial divisions, the 1st Brigade took over several kilometers of the front, just west of the village of Cantigny, which was "perched on the nose of a commanding hill," Charles Senay wrote. "The *boche* could look down our throats. That was SOP with the *boche*."

The miseries of Seicheprey quickly paled once the doughboys got a good look at their new home, around which continual machine-gun and artillery fire rattled and shrieked, and the bloating, fetid corpses of dead Moroccans and Germans carpeted the lush fields of red poppies and unripe wheat.

Corporal Ruben Nelson made a reconnaissance of the new lines on April 23, a day before his Company G of the 18th Regiment moved up to occupy the front line, and decided his chances of surviving had decidedly dimmed. "From where I could see we were in for a merry spell as soon as we entered the lines. I was already carrying $5,000 war risk insurance and when I went back I soon made arrangement for $5,000 more."

On April 24, Nelson's company was ordered into the trenches. They ran into shell fire several miles from the front line but continued on. "I had not gone but a short way when one of my gunmen was struck by shrapnel. Making the relief I lost five men. The loss of the whole Co. amounted to 19 killed."

Nelson's company mate, Private Frank Last, remembered his unit relieving a battalion of Algerians who stumbled, filthy and exhausted, from the front. "They were pretty well worn out. They had been up against a pretty hard fight and had been in the trenches for twenty-three days. We couldn't understand how they could endure it all. They were alive with 'cooties' and left plenty of them behind for us."

The fighting, it was quickly understood, had been hard.

"We were lucky enough to have a few men who could 'compre' and 'Polly' French enough to get along," Last continued. "The 'French Negroes' told us about how many men they had lost and were wounded.

"They had been replaced several times. They left plenty of proof, because there were several pieces of man lying about, and when the wind happened to be in certain directions the air was not very refreshing."

Last and his company settled into its portion of the line before the village of Cantigny and spent a first, sleepless night. "It was raining," Last wrote. "We were soaked to the skin and there was plenty of water and mud in the trench. We didn't sleep any, because things were more lively around there. Fritz furnished amusement enough to keep us awake. He must have known that a relief was made that night."

The first order of business was entrenching the front line—because, as one French officer noted, the area in front of Cantigny was "not a sector but it is a good place to make one."

The front line was a series of shell holes strung together, with little or no wire placed in front to slow down a German assault. Because no communication trenches—perpendicular pathways through which food, men, and orders could more safely be brought up—had yet been dug, frontline units were on their own in daylight.

Captain Edward S. Johnston, who commanded Company E of the 28th Infantry, recalled a "virgin" battleground over which a cascade of shells soared, some heading east, some west, ten thousand per day from the American side alone.

Planes, mostly Hun, put-putted in the skies above while the doughboys dug furiously, consolidating and deepening their trenches. Shells—American and German—ploughed into the chalky soil at all times of the day and on every portion of the sector, turning the green and gold fields white with a film of fine powder.

"The forest patches were writhing into distorted masses," Edward Johnston wrote. "The villages were dissolving slowly into slag heaps; the encircling horizon rang at all hours with the reverberations of cannon, and this vast orchestral accompaniment of war was punctuated at intervals by an obbligato of machine guns, and now and then the rattle of musketry.

"It was an active sector."

Lieutenant Jeremiah Evarts, who led a platoon with Company E of the 18th Infantry, recalled life in the trenches at Cantigny as "the most extraordinary game of life and death ever invented.

"Men lived on their wits, their nerves and that sixth sense which combined all other senses, and were assisted to live once each twenty-four hours—if the chow party was lucky—by a slice of meat, a spoonful of sour mashed potatoes, a canteen of water, a canteen cup of coffee, a half-loaf of bread, a beautiful country and sometimes a sunny sky."

Placed in reserve through the first weeks of May, the 28th bided its time before heading up to the front. Even in the back lines, the stench of death could not be avoided, and was carried on the winds as far as Villers-Tournelle, several kilometers southwest of Cantigny, where Charles Senay set up Company C's command post in a sturdy brick house.

Nearby, a German aviator sat entombed in his crashed Fokker. "His flesh had turned quite black," Senay wrote. "The skin was broken in places and he was breeding countless flies. It became a practice to say hello to him as we passed him mornings, but always from the side away from the wind."

Shelling, Senay added, was nearly constant as the German gunners probed the far rear lines in search of artillery emplacements and reinforcements moving up.

"We would lie on the hillside under the constant drone of shells," Senay wrote. "They gave off different sounds and men named them for various railroads such as the Missouri-Pacific and the Southern. All night long star shells of different kinds rose from the enemy lines."

Sunny weather brought the threat of attack by German planes, so the 2nd Brigade drilled "on cloudy days," Private John Johnston wrote. "We prayed for sunshiney days, but it generally rained, and the harder it rained the harder we drilled."

On one such "sunshiney" day, Willard Storms described his new environs: "Perpetual thunder has become our good night lullaby . . . most men refer to it as Field Music. Sometimes I wonder how it would seem to try to sleep without it, and how land would look without windrows of earth marking the trenches and thousands of strands of barbed wire stretched and looped and tangled in every direction."

On the night of May 3, the Germans launched a massive gas attack on the 18th Regiment's lines, throwing over between 6,000 and 10,000 shells filled with mustard oil and causing between 700 and 900 casualties among the men of the regiment, a number almost equal to an entire battalion.

The attack sparked a warning of reprisal.

"Came reports that the Eighteenth had been wiped out by gas, which later proved true to a large extent," wrote John Johnston. "To say this made us mad is putting it very lightly. So we sent over a balloon with a card attached, informing the Germans that if they sent gas over for one hour more we would retaliate with twenty-four hours of gas. The warning worked."

Soon enough, Johnston and the rest of the 28th's 1st Battalion were told to get ready to take their turn in the front lines and relieve the decimated 18th and the still-intact 16th Regiments.

Such midnight "reliefs" were one of the most dangerous aspects of trench life, as the doughboys were easy prey for prowling German artillery that raked the area of Death Valley, a ravine southwest of Cantigny through which men entered and left the trenches.

Before heading toward the trenches, John Johnston wrote, the men were warned by their officers that "it would be a thousand times more dangerous" than the front at Seicheprey. On the afternoon of May 14, the battalion loaded onto trucks.

"About ten that night we started for the lines," Company D's Private Wilbert Murphy wrote. "At first everything was quiet and we had hopes that Fritz wouldn't do any shooting. We were marching in single file and were about four kilometers from the front line when Fritz began to drop shells on the road. It was my first time under fire and naturally I was a little shaky."

German gunners, sensing that a relief was taking place, increased their volume of fire. Soon, the men found themselves in a race with death as German shells ploughed into the earth around them.

"They come at you with a roar like a locomotive, and this one struck twenty yards in front of me," John Johnston wrote. "I will admit that I buried my nose in the dirt, and everybody else did likewise. It seemed as though I was in a trance. I figured that it was just as safe to go ahead as to go back again over the way we had come, and this was some consolation. And then we struck our trenches and they seemed like home to us after what we had come through."

As Company D moved into the trenches, a high-explosive shell smashed into the position. Caught in a geyser of rock, chalk, dirt, and raking steel splinters, one of the former Janesville boys—Private Richard Ellis—was killed. Two others who had trained at Fort Benjamin Harrison—Private Edward Weil, of Cincinnati, and Corporal Milton Scarborough, from Childs, Maryland—were also left dead.

Another private, Neal Gallagher of Ireland, lay mortally wounded. "A large piece of the shell hit him in the leg, causing his leg to be amputated, from which he died," Corporal Bartley Larkin remembered.

The blast left another half dozen of the company's men wounded, among them Willard Storms. But it was the quick death of Ellis that proved a stark and sobering initiation into the trenches for those who'd left placid Janesville, Wisconsin, the previous September.

The dawn would bring only more vivid reminders of the men's perilous reality, as they peered from their trenches to see a carpet of bloated corpses smothering the fields before Cantigny, which sat like a bombed and battered acropolis atop high ground one mile away.

"The battle ground held horrible sights," John Johnston remembered. "It had been a wheat field, and there was considerable wheat growing there still, with the wrecks of cannon, and dead men scattered about it. We saw a French soldier and two French Moroccans—dead—in a kneeling posture out beyond the trench. There were large numbers of large black buzzards, eating the dead all over the battlefield."

The now-bloodied Company D settled into its trenches for a week of digging, digging, and more nocturnal digging during "soft summer nights of romantic moonlight, but of unalluring labor with pick and shovel," Captain Edward Johnston wrote.

The work went on temporarily without the injured Willard Storms.

"I am among what the French call Petit Blessé—'Assis,' or slightly wounded," he would tell his mother. "I was taken to a Fr Hosp when I came from the field and when I saw the Asses over the ward tent door I wondered if my ears were long enough or if I was to be fed on hay.

"Fritz sure gave us a very warm reception and I am sorry to say that I was not the only one hurt from our company. However, this is just one of the little necessities of war. Thousands have to be wounded and killed to make things decisive."

Now a veteran of trench life, Murphy also wrote home to tell of its miseries: "You know the *Boche* use a lot of gas on us. Well, every night after you have crawled down in your dugout to sleep he opens up on you and cheats you out of your sleep because when you are wearing a gas mask it is hard to sleep.

"That may sound like the 'square heads' make it miserable for us, but for every shell he sends at us we give him a dozen at least."

Having contracted scarlet fever during his first stint in the front lines, Murphy on May 27 penned his parents another letter while in the hospital, and tried his best to make light of the dangers he and Company D faced: "Nothing very exciting, excepting a pay day or the arrival of mail, ever takes place unless one is in the trenches and then there is plenty of excitement. I don't want you to worry about me but just recently we came out of the trenches. There was quite a little excitement at different times."

Isolated from Company D in the regimental hospital, Murphy could have but little idea of the "excitement" then brewing in the back lines of Cantigny—and of the momentous and world-shaking event in which the company would play a starring role on the very next day.

6

Zero Hour

Aɴᴅ ɪ ᴡɪsʜ ʏᴏᴜ could have seen them, seen them there, rolling out of the smoke and dust just to the west of Cantigny, stepping from their trenches toward a brilliant and yellow and rising sun, bayonets gleaming like flame-throwers, singing, they said, singing "It's Easy to Lick the Kaiser" or some such doughboy ditty as they stepped into a world war, American boys, America's sons, Rollin Livick and Thomas Dewey Slinker and James Whalen walking forward, stopping to kneel like knights amid the plumes of rock and dust from the halfhearted German shelling, then rising and plodding on with grim determination, unstoppable, mad with war, with the glory of war and mortal combat, and the satiation of a thirst for combat, for action . . .

I wish you could have seen them fall in among the Hun there in the town, using their long knives, the bayonets, or clubbing a shocked Fritz, swinging rifle butts like baseball bats, throwing grenades "like baseballs," George Butler would say, the poilus at their side squirting yellow and fiery death into the cellars of tumbled-down buildings, piles of bricks and stones; and I wish you could have seen Company D that morning in the full bloom-ing and fury of war, the unleashing of American might, the sons of the prairies and of the towns come to announce their presence and show a fury few could have known lay inside them, come to save civilization, come to avenge the *Lusitania* and Edith Cavell and whatever else you had.

I wish you could have seen them then because you wouldn't have wanted to see them minutes later, certainly wouldn't have wanted to *be* them then, after their grand and glorious assault on Cantigny spilled out onto the plain beyond, toward the German line to the east, and America's first full-scale assault of the war turned ugly and nasty and desperate and profane, a matter of digging furiously and hanging on and clinging precariously to the ground in front of the ruined village, a matter of sheer survival in the face of almost uncontested German shelling and murderous machine-gun fire and counterattacks that would lay twenty-five of Company D's men in the ground, put more than sixty more out of the war with severe wounds, and after three nightmarish days leave the survivors numb and exhausted and mumbling and hollow-eyed but also exultant, reveling and in a state of grace, of wonder.

Company D took its pounding and gave some back at Cantigny, where one-third of the 28th Regiment's men would be killed or wounded, but the attack—the first large-scale American assault of the war—had few significant strategic aims. The Battle of Cantigny was, instead, a simple and brutal announcement of American power, American resolve, a public-relations coup intended to leave Fritz humiliated, and to portend what lay in store for him once the United States really got up to speed, once "We're coming over" became "We're here."

And it was to that end that Company D and the rest of the 28th Regiment would bleed and die for three long days and three almost equally long, cold, dark nights, all for a little PR, a little "in your face," a little what-for.

As well, the operation would determine the future of Pershing's army, and whether he might even be able to continue to call it his, defeat perhaps bringing a lesser, piecemeal role in the war for the A.E.F., and more difficulty in resisting the Allies' demands that his army be divvied up to serve under French and British commanders; success also would allow Pershing to make a stronger case for an eventual all-American army that would hold the lines in or attack from its own sector.

The German position had tempted the American command since the 1st Division took over the lines opposite the village on April 24, and plans began to be laid for the taking of the village soon after. An initial draft, which called for the 18th Regiment to make the assault on May 25, had to be scrapped following the gas attack of May 3, which disabled nearly a third of the 18th.

The 28th Regiment became the next obvious choice for the assault, as many of its noncoms were regulars and its ranks were in any case filled with privates who had trained over the summer and fall of 1917 in the States, and in France in the winter and spring, and learned something of trench life.

So it was that Company D would take its place on the world stage for a few terrible days, bearing the weight of the A.E.F. But it would have, if nothing else, public opinion and adoration on its side, as news-starved correspondents who had chafed under the A.E.F's tight-fisted control were tipped off to the assault by none other than the 1st Division's George C. Marshall and raced to Picardy to be there when the Americans received the ball, advanced all of one mile, and held their lines through three days of bloody combat.

In order to prepare for the assault, the 28th Regiment was pulled out of the trenches on May 23 and sent to the rear for several days of intensive training on terrain similar to that around Cantigny. So that nothing would be left to chance, and every man, from regimental commander to engineer to buck private, would know what he was to do, and where, three rehearsals were carried out, the last a full-scale "dress rehearsal," watched and critiqued by the 1st's brass.

By detailed maps and sand tables "all platoon commanders were shown . . . exact building and strong points in their sector which must be overcome, also line of attack and place of consolidation upon reaching of objective," Company D's Soren Sorensen would write.

The attack was to be carried out in three stages: In the first, the boys would rush the ruined town, which was strongly held with a solid first-line trench dug into its western edge and a dizzying web of machine-gun nests posted throughout, the village, in which Germans lurked in every cellar of every bombed-out building. To help them roust the Boche from their holes, a dozen tanks loaned by the French would complement the attacking infantry and, if nothing else, terrorize the Germans into surrendering.

Once clear of the village, the 28th Regiment's three battalions were in the second phase to advance five hundred yards onto the plain east of Cantigny, dig in, and hold on. For how long, no one knew. The grand finale, the third phase, would be written on the fly.

The 1st Battalion—called "Battalion A," with Company D coded in reports as A3, Company B as A2, Company A as A1, and Company C as A4—was assigned to the southern third of the field. Company D, on the battalion's left flank, would attack through the southern half of Cantigny alongside French poilus carrying flamethrowers; on its right would be Company B, and to Company B's right, Company A would swing from the Cantigny woods and protect the battalion's right flank along the road to Montdidier, three miles east. Company C, meanwhile, was held in reserve.

Battalion B—Companies E, F, G, and H—would assault the northern half of the village, while Battalion C—companies I, K, L, and M—would fan out to positions on Battalion B's left and dig in. A battalion of the 26th Regiment was also available on the right of the 28th in the Cantigny woods, and several companies of the 18th Regiment, in reserve, would see action before the battle was finished.

Holding the town were the German 271st and 272nd Regiments of the 82nd Reserve Division. Though the 1st's intelligence section considered them third-rate—"Kampftruppen 3" on a scale of four—one American commander disputed this, saying that after long service on the eastern front the division had been given good replacements and training, and by the time they entered the lines at Cantigny they were "experienced units," and "by no means inferior and knew their work thoroughly."

The best-laid plans were almost ruined, the production canceled, before opening night. On May 26, just thirty-six hours prior to jump-off, a group of engineers headed into the forward trenches to deposit entrenching tools and ran into a group of Germans. After a fierce fight, the engineers beat it back to their lines, but one young lieutenant was left behind—along with maps of American positions that could have been interpreted by the Germans as a portent of a coming offensive. (The unlucky lieutenant would be found after the war in a shallow grave, his throat cut.)

Following the relief of a battalion of the 18th Regiment by the 2nd Battalion of the 28th Regiment on the night of May 26, the Germans staged a raid in force, perhaps guided by a sense the Americans were up to something. In the early morning hours of May 27, more than fifty *Jagdkommando*—soldiers handpicked for duty in a permanent raiding party—followed a lethal barrage and swooped in on forward positions manned by Company E, intent on taking American prisoners.

The assault was beaten back. "Our men responded with terrific rifle fire and only four of the raiders crawled back to the German trenches," Company C commander Charles Senay wrote. "The German officer was killed and his papers secured. Two prisoners were captured." Still, the raid left twenty-four of Company E's soldiers dead and another thirty-nine wounded, and led to doubts about the operation planned for the next morning.

On the same day, the Germans launched another massive offensive—the third of the spring. Seventeen divisions spilled across the Chemin des Dames toward the Marne, forty miles southeast of Picardy, swallowing the ancient city of Soissons and slicing through the Allied defenses to a depth of thirty miles.

This crisis would affect the Cantigny operation, as the nervous French would pull out their artillery and send it south to face the new threat just as soon as the Americans had passed through Cantigny; over the next three days, the lack of suppressing fire from the French would make itself felt, as the Americans huddled in their shallow trenches under strict orders not to give ground and endured the worst the Germans could throw over.

Despite these several hitches, plans for the assault moved forward, and so it was that Company D and the 28th Regiment prepared for the dough-boys' debut, which was set for a zero hour of 6:45 A.M. on May 28, 1918. And in the early hours of May 28 several thousand Americans began climbing into American trucks, and moving forward to their American jump-off lines, to deliver an all-American punch to the nose of the bullying, baby-hoisting Hun.

Once in their trenches, there was little to do but wait, wait and wonder what awaited out there in the night, how one would hold up and whether one had the will to kill, these boys from sleepy Edgerton, Wisconsin, and Crosstimber, Missouri, and Ralph's Run, West Virginia, and the immigrant streets of Omaha and Chicago; all of them hoping for and yet dreading the moment when the American artillery would open up to soften the German defenses with a creeping barrage.

And so they waited—Rollin Livick waited, Soren Sorensen waited, Whitelaw Carns waited, and George Butler waited, the worst part of it being "the minutes approaching the time to go into action," Butler would later say. "We were anxious to have it over with. It was not fear but a sort of false excitement."

"We sat in those trucks for two hours and fifteen minutes waiting for zero hour to approach," Lieutenant Harry Martin of Company H would later write. "I would look at my watch and when it read another five minutes more, every minute after that seemed an hour."

Finally, at 5:45 A.M. the curtain lifted, and the artillery began its "preparation fire," pounding Cantigny and the German artillery positions, lobbing every caliber of shell in its possession—75 mm, 155 mm, and the huge and ponderous 260 mm shells—toward the German lines. The barrage further pulverized the village, its host of shell-shocked Bavarian defenders cringing and huddling in brick-strewn cellars, praying to *Gott in Himmel* himself and sucking in the flying dust, the earth shaking, ceilings pouring down, and the world itself seeming to collapse in on them.

Lieutenant Stuart D. Campbell, watching from a reserve position behind the jump-off lines with Company E of the 18th Infantry, said the American firestorm was "a sight never to be forgotten . . . the whole village of Cantigny was going skyward, large pieces of stone, shell and brick were thrown into our position by the force of the explosion of the larger shells.

"I have previously seen heavy preparation fire while on the British front but in this case it did not seem possible that the air could contain so many shells coming and going."

The bombardment helped steady the nerves of many. "I had always supposed that the last few hours before going into battle were full of tense excitement," Company L's Lieutenant Richard A. Newhall, a twenty-nine-year-old Harvard Ph.D., would write. "They're not. We had practiced it until each man knew just what he was going to do. Our artillery was pounding the German lines in such a way as to make it seem probable that we would merely walk over and occupy them."

"The air seemed to be clouded with trench mortar shells tumbling through the air into Cantigny," Welcome P. Waltz, waiting to jump off with Company C of the 3rd Machine-Gun Battalion, remembered. "All of us, at once, sensed the power of our own artillery and knew that with that kind of protection the enemy would be helpless.

"The weapons which really brought the awaiting troops to their feet were our large howitzers as their projectiles roared just over our heads onto the front line trenches of the enemy. The results were inspiring."

At 6:43 A.M., the artillery laid down a barrage for the troops, and shortly thereafter a 1st Division pilot flying overhead fired a single rocket; at 6:45 A.M. the thing was on, as Company D and eight other frontline companies from the 28th Regiment and their complement of machine gunners— roughly 2,400 men in all—jumped off into the unknown.

And oh, it was a sight to see, this mass of men, this ocean of gleaming bayonets, all stepping out as one, and leading all, soldiers and civilian observers alike, to afterward wonder at its beauty. "The most beautiful thing I've ever seen," so many would say, and bring to mind Robert E. Lee's famous line, "It is well that war is so terrible, or we should grow too fond of it," made in December 1862 as he watched from the heights above Fredericksburg as Burnside's oh-so-blue Yanks fanned through the town, to approach the deadly slopes before them.

But the approach to Cantigny would not be nearly as costly to the Americans as the assault above Fredericksburg had been to the North; in fact, very few casualties would occur during the attack on the village itself. And if the village had been all these Yanks wanted, the great Battle of Cantigny would have gone down in history as little more than a raid in force, a footnote.

But Bullard, Pershing, and the Allies wanted more. All wanted to blacken the eye of the Hun, to show staying power; and to that end the quick and glorious taking of Cantigny would turn into three days of suffering and endurance that would haunt the lives of the survivors for the rest of their days.

However the boys don't know that yet. All they know is that it's 6:45 A.M. on May 28, 1918, and Sorensen's shrill whistle is blowing through the roar of the cannonade, and so they are scrambling as planned from their trenches one mile directly west of Cantigny, in a patch of woods they call the Bois Suisse.

It's cumbersome to move, because among the things they carry are a shelter half, 220 rounds of ammunition, a rifle, two hand grenades, one rifle grenade, one Bengal flare, four sandbags, two days' reserve rations, two canteens of water, marking panels for the airplanes, and either one heavy pick or one heavy shovel; and they gave them cookies, too, and a couple of lemons each—palate cleansers with which to ward off the coming stink of blood and gunpowder and death.

In seconds the first wave is over, on its way toward what was once a town, artillery rounds screaming overhead, the roar of the guns and the rumble of the tanks deafening, the black exhaust from the newfangled machines filling the eyes and lungs of the men in the second wave. Advancing with them are the flamethrowing poilus, sent in to fry Fritz, sear him in the dank and rubble-strewn cellars in which he lurks with yet another new instrument of industrial death.

And among them are privates Rollie Livick and T. C. Hall, the Choctaw Thomas Slinker and the Menominee Earl Wilber, the diminutive former coal miner corporal Whitelaw Carns, and the tough sergeants Everett E. Adams and John D. Licklider and the brawling Irish James Whalen, who had traded his lumberjack's ax to be a part of this, this mass of men, boys, walking into battle on this fine, sunny Tuesday morning.

They move forward across fields of wheat and blood-red poppies into the choking smoke and flying dust and rock, with Sorensen leading the vanguard, lieutenants George Butler and John H. Church—who as a general some twenty-seven years hence would lead Task Force Church in another assault on the Germans, this one into the Fatherland itself—and Max Buchanan and Ross Gahring walking behind the first wave, ready to kick the weakhearted back into formation, and with the newly commissioned subalterns Edmund Corby and Frank Cooper behind the second wave, leading a stumbling and overburdened carrying party.

They step as one toward the rising sun, and yes, this is a glorious moment, waves of khaki-clad and intent doughboys, soldiers, smoking cigarettes, some of them, and smiling with a youthful bravado meant perhaps more than anything to hide just how scared they are. "The boys went in singing," George Butler would say—singing!—and they keep on, keep going, about to fall upon the shocked Hun.

Far to the right, to the south, Companies A and B are being murdered as they cross a deep and open ravine and are enfiladed with cross-firing machine guns, their laughter and smiles quickly evaporating in a hail of lead and desperate digging; but Company D's men plod straight ahead, east, untouched as they approach Cantigny's western limits, and begin the quick ascent toward that shambles of busted timbers and half-intact buildings, as those behind watch "with abated breath and urging them on with all the mental effort possible," as Stuart Campbell would write.

"There it was, all before me—the most beautiful sight ever mine and ever to be mine," *Collier's* correspondent James Hopper would write.

"The three waves looked one—a thick mass of men stretching all the way across the plateau, the beautiful plateau, a great open regular rectangle, sloping very gently before us, inviting our charge, a clean and virgin No Man's Land untainted yet of the terrible stench of mortal man, carpeted with flowers, with grass, with wheat, with red poppies, yellow buttercups, and purple thistles—the ideal battle field of an ideal battle."

Imbuing his account with the colorful imagery from an earlier crusade, Hopper would add: "Beside the riflemen there were many that carried machine guns, tripods, shovels, crowbars, rods; and these implements—some of humility and of peace, in the singular light, borne upon the shoulders of these men who, as they left me farther behind, took on more and more an aspect of gigantic unreality—became maces, lances, catapults, and flaming swords."

"Occasionally a shell would strike among them and a gap would appear among the pickets, then quickly close," Major Raymond Austin of the 1st Division's 6th Field Artillery would remember. "They walked steadily along behind our barrage accompanied by the tanks which buzzed along with smoke coming out of their exhausts and their guns."

Major George Rozelle, 1st Battalion commander, would recall that "there was absolutely no confusion in the ranks; in fact, the movement forward went along more smoothly than at drill, the men advancing close up under the barrage, kneeling, and moving forward again with each jump of the barrage towards the enemy."

"When zero hour came and the rocket was shot up by the first division airplane I took my men, for the first time, over the top, all smiling and with the determination that all Heaven and hell couldn't beat us," Lieutenant Harry Martin, leading a platoon from Company H on Company D's immediate left, would write.

"All the men were walking with a firm step, rifles with bayonets fixed and at a high port, walking over No Man's Land with worlds of artillery fire over our heads. We spread out as did the first wave and fought in groups wherever was needed. Each man had been told by me that no prisoners were to be taken and my orders were carried out. Finally we reached the town, and then the fighting started."

Within minutes Company D, too, was through the German front line, racing up the slope at the western edge of town, still largely unscathed, maybe even still smiling, their young hearts pounding faster and faster as the chattering *pup-pup-pup* of the machine guns became louder, and they began to see the darting blue-gray forms of the alarmed Hun racing for cover.

Just as quickly, adrenaline and the strong sense of self-survival took over, as the German line of resistance was buried in a mass of khaki forms, a melee of swinging rifle butts, well-aimed shots from pistols and from the French Chauchats some carried, and occasional and individual bayonet duels.

And it was here that Rollin Livick and Arzy Underwood and the rest found for the first time that they did, indeed, have the will and ability to kill. As Captain Senay would write: "New soldiers are bloodthirsty and vindictive. They take everything in stride."

The German line overwhelmed, Company D's men fanned through the southern half of the village, hunters seeking their prey amid splintered and fallen timbers and crushed masonry and rock. Combing the ruins, they rousted recalcitrant Germans with bayonets and pistols and rifles; and when those didn't work they brought up the poilus to fricassee the holdouts with flamethrowers; and when even that didn't work the boys lobbed grenades in and blew them up in the cellars where "about 60 German dead" would later be found in the company's sector, one after-action report would say.

"The infantry advanced in waves through ravines and rushed the ridge entering the streets of the battered village," Butler would write. "The enemy came out of caves and dugouts very much scared. It was a tough-looking bunch of youngsters and old men. There was no fight in them.

"The platoons in the second wave," he added, "did most of the mopping up in the sector which consisted principally of driving the enemy out of his dugouts by means of hand grenades and automatic pistols. In one dugout alone two men of the company found 47 of the enemy and after killing 5 of them the remainder walked out and surrendered."

It was an almost bloodless coup, at least for Company D. Only two privates—the Chicagoan George Dust, whose death would be attributed not to German resistance but to an American artillery round that fell short, and the Iowan Walter Dawe, who took a bullet in the back from a German passed over in the initial advance—would die before reaching Cantigny's eastern edge, where the company's men's paused briefly to consolidate, and to perhaps consider their chances of making it across five hundred yards of naked, level plain that was even then being raked by artillery and machine-gun fire.

As Company D regrouped, life-and-death dramas played out throughout the village and across the battlefield.

"One little incident which happened was this: On our way through the town I saw a German hiking down the street," Lieutenant Martin would write. "I raised my pistol on him and with his left hand in the air yelling 'Kamerad!' I saw him reach with his right for his gun. Fortunately I was a trifle too quick for him and I gave him two bullets."

Sergeant Boleslaw Suchocki of the 1st Engineer Regiment—whose exact ethnicity remains undetermined, but whose phonetic, immigrant prose simply has no match in the doughboy canon—advanced with Martin and the 2nd Battalion, and described another drama that played out as the doughboys moved through a hedge at the east end of town. "A doughboy was chasing another Dutchman but he did'nt shoot at him only was trying to stab him, the Dutchman grasp the doughboys bayonet with one hand and push it a side, bend the bayonet pretty bad right at the handle," Suchocki wrote.

"I look at the struggle it was about ten feet a way from me, so I hollered shoot him but the Dutchman throw his hands up and hollered in German,

'Don't shoot me I will tell you something.' I said to the doughboy holt on, but it was too late, the shot fired and the Dutchman tumble down."

Moving on, Suchocki encountered a camouflaged trench on the other side of the hedge. "I hollered few times 'come rouse' but no one was coming out," he wrote, "so I open fire right at the hole, fired five rounds, then I hear some kind of squiling in the hole. I stepped closer to the trench and pull the top off, there was four men convolsively twisting in the trench."

Stiffer resistance greeted the Americans farther to the north, where Company L's Lieutenant Richard Newhall was struck in his right armpit by a bullet after his platoon had advanced several hundred yards over the plain north of the village.

Knocked over by the blow, he "jumped up and resumed the advance. I had not gone much farther before a second bullet went through my left arm breaking the bone a little above the elbow. That knocked me over again. I think there was a sniper in front of us picking off the officers. In order to make sure of me he fired again as I lay on the ground.

"The bullet struck my left arm at an angle, broke the bone again, flattened, and tore its way out through the muscles of the upper arm leaving a wound about seven inches long and two wide. That dazed me and I lay still."

At the same time, Newhall's good friend and fellow Harvard alumnus, twenty-three-year-old Lieutenant George Guest Haydock, paused to reorganize Company L's first platoon.

"The lieutenant walked from one end of the platoon to the other, cautioning repeatedly, 'Men, keep lower for your own sakes,'" one of the company's men would recall. "They replied, 'Lieutenant, you keep low, they will get you.' The last words he spoke were, 'They can't kill me.'"

Shortly thereafter, the first platoon came under severe machine-gun fire while clearing the German main line. "George rushed out ahead of his men, and alone ran straight for a machine gun trying to kill the crew with his pistol, and he fell riddled with bullets," another of Haydock's pals, the 3rd Machine-Gun Battalion's Lieutenant William O. P. Morgan, wrote despondently after the battle.

"Thank God he probably didn't know it. I can't help but think that his spirit and clean character were too good for *boche* lead."

Julian Dorr, a regimental medic and the son of Rheta Childe Dorr, au-

thor of *A Soldier's Mother in France*, was also among the first Americans to
fall that morning. "I got smacked in the leg with a machine gun bullet when
we had gone about 100 yards," he recalled in an after-battle interview. "I
tried to keep on going, but I had to flop. The fellows all swept on behind
tanks, some even going in front, they were so impatient. I had to lie in No
Man's Land for two hours before I was picked up."

Leading an ammunition-carrying party behind the front waves, Company I's Private Sam Ervin—the future senator and famed Watergate in-
quisitor from North Carolina, who earlier that spring had been busted from
lieutenant to buck private after being found asleep at his post—encountered
a wounded German soldier as he waded through a field of high grass.

Kneeling to tend to his foe's broken arm, Ervin was shot clean through
his left foot by a Boche machine gunner. "Wir sind verdammte Schweine
("We are damned swine") the wounded and apologetic German told Ervin,
who managed to make it to the back lines by walking gingerly on his heel.

On Company L's right, Company M struggled to keep in touch with
the 2nd Battalion's Company F, which lagged behind on the right. Lieutenant Gerald Tyler had instructed Sergeant Carl Sohnke to keep in
contact with Company F, and grew concerned as he noticed the gap between the companies growing larger.

Upon learning that Sohnke had been killed, Tyler sent a runner to
Captain James Anderson, commander of Company F, "to ask him to shift
his men toward the left so as to reestablish connection with us. The runner
soon returned saying that Captain Anderson and all the other officers of
the Company had been killed and that he could not find anybody in command."

With Company L on his left also lagging in the advance, Tyler spread
his platoons into a "fan shaped forward movement which caused me great
alarm, because they were now occupying a frontage ordinarily held by two
or more Companies."

Locating the place he thought was his company's objective, Tyler ordered his men to go to work with their shovels before "a French Captain
who was with the tanks came to me and suggested I move my men about
200 meters farther forward as they could get a much better field of fire
from there."

After some wrangling, the captain insisted that Tyler move his company farther east. "The enemy's shells were now falling among us and there were many calls for first aid men," Tyler recalled. "However, the men silently replaced their packs, picked up their rifles and entrenching tools and moved forward.

"The French captain was enthusiastic about this and told me that it would never have been possible to persuade French soldiers to move forward under fire after they had been ordered to dig in."

On the far left of the advance, Sam Ervin's former University of North Carolina classmate, Lieutenant Samuel I. Parker—who would win the Medal of Honor for his actions at Soissons—led a platoon of Company K from its jump-off trench.

As the doughboys advanced, they "let out a terrible 'rabbit-hunting' yell and began cutting them down with their rifles," Parker would write. "It was great sport then, all the seriousness was over."

Parker added that as he and a party of twelve of his men rushed the German position, "One big burley cuss, with whiskers, thought that he would stay us off. He threw a grenade right between my sergeant and me, but it did not explode until we had rushed past.

"The big brute saw that his grenade did not phase our bunch, that we were coming on after him; so he jumped out of the trench with his hands up yelling 'Camerad.'

"Sergeant said, 'Yes a Hell of a Camerad,' and shot his bayonet clear through him."

Fifteen "square heads" then came running with their hands up.

"I will never forget the expression of one of them," Parker wrote. "He was scared plum to death. His hands were just about as near heaven as he could get them. He cried out in English, 'I have a wife and five children.' I took him prisoner. Didn't have the heart to shoot him."

Their blood up, and acting from hate, or fear, or both, other doughboys had no such qualms. Sergeant Suchocki would claim that, in one instance, only the timely arrival of 2nd Battalion commander Lieutenant Colonel Robert Maxey, who would soon after fall mortally wounded, interrupted a massacre in progress of a group of surrendering Boche. "There rose over twenty Germans, throw their rifles down and stood with their arms up.

The doughboys didnt pay attention only shoot at them and stab them too, one of the doughboys on the run stabb a Dutchman that the bayonet went clear through."

Before long, a group of about "sixty Dutchmen" were milling about with hands up, each one frantically imploring in German that his life be spared. Their luck turned with Maxey's arrival.

"If Col. Maxey didn't come on time we would kill every one of them, but he stopt us from doing it," Suchocki wrote. "He raised his hand and said, 'boys, spare them, take prisoners.'"

Those who managed to surrender without being murdered—somewhere around 250 of them that first morning—were herded back of the lines, where many of the doughboys got their first good look at their foe. Many looked nothing like the *Übermenschen* featured in Allied propaganda—"So many young boys—they looked hardly sixteen," James Hopper would write—while others appeared as hard and cold and heartless as the iron-jawed Teutons featured on recruiting posters back in the States.

"The prisoners were a sad-looking lot—thin and hungry, some of them, and others badly wounded," Major Austin recalled. "Most of them seemed quite young and all were apparently glad to be captured excepting the officers. I took a helmet off of one as they came by and gave him a box of cigarettes which seemed to surprise him."

Other soldiers, too, loaded the prisoners down with "food, tobacco, etc.," Austin added, "forgetting that those same pitiable Boches would gladly stick a knife in them if they had half a chance and would play the customary german trick in battle of pretending to be wounded and then knife a man who goes to help them."

Hopper, who would make headlines for his supposed "capture" of a group of surrendering Germans, remembered being at first amused by the prisoners. "So comically bedraggled and piteous, those warriors whom it has been the great care of their masters to make appear dreadful and terrible—they looked so small, their clothes were so wrinkled, their faces so dirty." Leading each group, he added, "would be a score who held their eyes fixed upon us in attention of our slightest wish, of our slightest gesture, who jerked their hands higher if we but moved to fill our pipes, whose eyes kept traveling fearfully, searching for the most powerful of us, for the one it would pay to most please, for the little Kaiser there might be among us."

But Hopper, like Austin, did not forget they were the enemy—and let his Teuton-phobia run wild in demonizing the "others" who paraded to the back lines that morning, describing them as "big heavy louts with faces incredibly brutal, brutal with a brutality which was not frank as brutality is thought to be, but with a brutality allied to the lowest cunning.

"If we had brought each to a little babe and told him to stick a bayonet into the soft body, each without question would have stuck a bayonet into the soft body—every word, every gesture, every posture advertised the fact."

As the German prisoners went west, the Americans continued east, onto the plateau beyond the wrecked village. Companies A and B encountered devastating fire as they advanced through an unsheltered ravine.

"The further we advanced over No Man's Land the smoke got so thick sometimes that you could hardly see," Company A's Private Ralph Loucks, one of the Janesville boys, would remember. "And the shells would burst and tear holes in the ground big enough to put a threshing machine into, and the machine gun and rifle bullets singing around you."

Reaching the German line, "the Americans bayoneted lots of them before they had a chance to run." Others held fast, firing machine guns—one wounding Loucks and killing one of the Janesville boys, Private Walter Detwiler. "I heard something go through my arm like a red-hot iron. The bullet went through the upper part of my left arm through the muscle. At the same time a Janesville boy about four feet away from me fell shot through the chest. I guess he never knew what hit him; he died a few moments later."

Private John Johnston of the same unit would remember his company mates casually rolling cigarettes as they went over. But the youthful bravado turned quickly to a desperate will to survive as the Boche machine guns played on Company A's advancing line and they were forced to find cover.

"I and some other fellows found a shell hole and we dropped into it," Johnston remembered. "The fact that we found this hole saved my life. A comrade, whose name was Dedweller was killed at my side. We dug while the sun was coming up, and half of the boys dug, and dug frantically, with their helmets."

("I went over the top at Cantigny with a cigarette in my mouth but after that—well, I thought a little more about it," another of the Janesville boys, Company B's Private Leo Gehrke, would recall with a laugh.)

Company C, meanwhile, edged forward and took up positions in support of the 1st Battalion on the eastern edge of Cantigny. "All objectives had been reached by 7:30 A.M. and everyone was digging frantically in the flinty soil," Charles Senay wrote. "When we reached our objective, we sent back the prearranged phrase, 'The Goose hangs high.' For the most part we found shelter in shell holes, some of which were very large."

After pausing at the edge of Cantigny, the men of Company D stumbled east across the plain under a hail of machine-gun bullets, reaching their objective at 7:30 A.M. Dropping their ponderous loads at the direction of Soren Sorensen, they began to dig as the sun came up.

And it was as the sun came up that Company D's men would begin dying, or to suffer terrible wounds, as machine gunners hidden in the fields of wheat that stretched east opened up, and caught man after man in the open.

The attack's plan called for a standing one-hour barrage just east of the consolidation point, to prevent the Germans from immediately launching a counterattack while the doughboys dug in. But a standing barrage is not designed to stop machine-gun bullets, and through the plumes of earth and rock and chaff sent up by the American artillery, the gunners found their marks, spraying the company's ranks.

Then, too, the German artillery hidden in the Bois de Laval and Bois de Framicourt opened up from well-sighted positions to the front and left, finding their marks with the help of spotters in planes high above the doughboys, who now pitched into the French soil, seeking refuge from a whirlwind of hot steel.

And no, you wouldn't have wanted to have been among them there, not on that morning, as the sun rose and Company D's men dug into that chalky soil, burrowing with shovels and tin hats and fingernails, even, the white powder soon covering the poppies and wheat like drifting snow, spotted here and there with the blackening blood of American boys, and no intermission, no dramatic pause, no curtain, no respite, before act two commenced on that terrible plain east of Cantigny.

7

"I Wonder How Deep It Went In"

Leigh Ellsworth Wilson was one of them that day, now racing through the battered and bombed village of Cantigny, through and over the German trench in the middle of town, past the bodies of the dead Boche that lay here and there in their last positions of agony, eyes wide and lifeless, and through the acrid smell of burning Hun flesh, some of them on fire and running from the cellars, reminding one young lieutenant of the time he'd seen rabbits back in Kansas run out of burning haystacks like that, only to keel over, and lie smoking and charred, writhing and doomed.

Leigh Wilson was a mama's boy, and it was better that his mama, Anna, couldn't see him now, better that she was at home in the small town of Janesville, a tree-lined and tiny island amid the lush green pastures of southern Minnesota, where in her bed in the safe night Anna would sometimes awaken and think of Leigh, and wonder where he was, and what might be happening to him, what with him being so far away and far beyond her ability to protect him.

Anna, the daughter of pioneers to the Minnesota River Valley, had hid with her family as a two-year-old, hid out as the Great Sioux Uprising of

1862 burned with murderous fury across the settlements up and down the river, hid out with the other greenhorns, eyes wide with terror, fingers running through their precious scalps, the smoke from their torched neighbors curling into the clean pure air, the bodies of people they knew sprawled lifeless and bloody by the corncrib and at the thresholds of their simple homesteads.

And now her precious son Leigh was out there, running, panting, racing for the thin plumes of dirt and rock out on the plateau east of Cantigny, to circle the wagons, to put to digging, digging while the sun rose, the harsh filtered rays of sunlight streaked and dirty brown amid the roiling of the explosions.

Not even seventeen, Leigh had lit out from Anna's home for the army, enlisting on January 16, 1917; lit out from her tidy kitchen filled with colored glass baubles and jars stacked on the windowsills, and from his sisters, Fannie Ellen, Myrtle Grace, Addie Mabel, Eliza Marie, and Rilla May; lit out as had his father, William, who chose the isolation of his lumber camp in Wisconsin to the home filled with chattering women back in Janesville; lit out as had his older brother, Chauncey Roy, who left for St. Paul, to become a drunk and disappointment to his mother—so Anna's granddaughter Beverly Fuque would tell me—who in turn obsessed over Leigh.

And I can't help but imagine that Anna had pleaded with her youngest son not to go, not to join the army, and that perhaps he had done it on the sly, lying about his age upon his enlistment, and I can't help but believe that after Leigh had left for France with the Fort Harrison boys, Anna had desperately tried to keep track of him, smother him from five thousand miles away, her constant letters not only to Leigh but also to Soren Sorensen no doubt an embarrassment to Leigh, a teenager making his way to manhood in a man's army, my only evidence of this, though, being Leigh's last letter home, posted from the backlines at Seicheprey and dated March 27, 1918: "I wrote you a letter just the other evening and also one to dad but the Co. received a letter that you were worried so I shall write again. It is very warm today but the weather is awful changeable. About two days ago we took a bath in the creek and yesterday morning it snowed a little but [not] to stay on the ground."

Leigh added these reassuring lines: "We are living pretty good now for being in the field and are most always living in billets and getting as good care as possible. Don't worry much about me, as the allies don't worry me at all, so I will close hoping you are all well at home."

And of course Anna must have had nightmares about this day, this morning of May 28, 1918, where on the plain east of Cantigny Company D's men were now digging in behind a standing barrage, trying to hide behind a pounding crescendo of dirt and rock, as Anna and her pioneer family had hid from the Sioux all those years before.

But it was better that she couldn't see this, couldn't see her baby boy now digging, now crawling, as the German machine guns began playing, searching and spraying and looking for Leigh and the men of Company D, and finding their unwilling targets in droves.

Yes, it had been a fine sight to see, just half an hour before, the pomp and glory, the boys smoking and singing, the shocked Bavarians emerging, frightened and wary, with hands up, from seared cellars.

Once on the plateau, and fully exposed on the open ground, the Germans began bringing to bear all they had with machine guns and artillery—one round knocking Lieutenant John Church senseless as he led his platoon to its consolidation point east of Cantigny.

"A 'big one' exploded within a yard of me, blew me ahead about 10 ft.," Church recalled. "God was with me, and was not badly hurt." After coming to, he headed to the rear for aid; recovering, he stumbled forward, overtaking Company D's castaways as they dug in amid plumes of earth and the skipping and pinging of machine-gun bullets.

"The boche machine guns ranged in half a circle began spouting bullets," Lieutenant George Butler would say. "It was like a pack of bumble bees. I felt a tickle along the back. At first I thought it was a 'cootie,' but later I found that my back had been grazed and that I had a bullet in the leg. It seemed like being hit with a rock. The pain was not much worse."

Butler walked off the field under his own power, but Lieutenant Ross Gahring would not be so lucky. A shell tore part of his spine away and spun him around. Stunned, he lay helpless as six machine-gun bullets ripped into his legs.

Dragged from the exposed plain by Sergeant Everett E. Adams, Gahring refused to be evacuated, and "although wounded he remained on duty with his platoon for nine hours, lying in a shell hole and issuing orders to his men," his subsequent Distinguished Service Cross citation says.

"I could still crawl," Gahring himself would say many years later.

Another noncom, Butler wrote, at about that time "took command of the Company and completed the organization of the position and held the ground during the first counter-attack"—that sergeant being John D. Lick-lider, an old vet who'd enlisted from Martinsburg, West Virginia, in 1913, and who would also win a citation for his efforts on that day.

Within minutes, dozens of the company's men fell dead or wounded.

"Most casualties were on reaching objective where we received heavy machine gun fire from wood on our right causing about 30 percent casu-alties," Sorensen recalled. "On reaching objective reports reached me that platoon commanders of the first, second and third platoons were wounded."

Noting "considerable confusion" where the men were digging a for-ward line, Sorensen moved through heavy fire to sort things out, finally establishing a line of resistance "about twenty yards in advance of brick ruins east of Cantigny."

Still trying to consolidate, to get organized out there on that plateau, Sorensen would make no mention of a noncom running things, but he may have been unaware that Licklider was, in effect, commanding a portion of the line for some time, as Gahring lay bleeding and helpless in the bottom of a makeshift and shallow trench.

Because those first minutes were confusing and stressful, to say the least, as machine-gun bullets continued to spray the position, and the Ger-man artillery found its range and opened up as well, and Sorensen ranged up and down the line, trying to get some men into a far forward surveil-lance line, others to the line of resistance nearer to Cantigny, all while dealing with his other subalterns, one of whom, twenty-four-year-old Ed-mund Corby, had been spooked by the sight of his own blood.

"About ten minutes after reaching objective Lt Corby reported to me that he had been wounded, and he said 'In the arm and was weak on ac-count of loss of blood,'" Sorensen wrote. "I looked at his hand and seeing no blood and the way he used his arm I did not consider it serious enough for him to go to the rear zone, so I ordered him to go forward to line of [surveillance] and see that it was properly consolidated and that connection was made with units on right and left.

"About twenty minutes later Lt Corby reported back that everything was O.K. and I then ordered him back to Aid station, at this time only two officers were on duty with the company, Lt Buchanan and myself, as action had quieted down considerable."

Buchanan in one of his last letters home had expressed optimism at his chances of "putting through" the war, just as he had made it through his Philippine adventure and the three-ring circus on the Mexican border two years earlier. But Buchanan would have no reunion with his older brother, Harley, or a shaking of "paws" with his father, William, back in Brockton, Massachusetts.

Sorensen would remember that not long after he sent the wounded Corby to the rear, "I went over to make an inspection on the left and found it in good condition and was giving orders to Lt Buchanan in regards to action to be taken in case of enemy counter attack, when he was killed by a shell, also another man standing on his left was killed by the same shell. I was also slightly wounded at this time."

Buchanan's death left Sorensen the only Company D officer still standing, and he, too, was wounded. Likewise, in those first terrible minutes on that exposed plateau, one-third of the company's men would be killed or wounded, among them Private Frank Beck, of Fairhope, Pennsylvania, who had been unlucky enough to be standing by Buchanan's side when that shell plopped in, another soldier remembering: "We heard the shell coming, we all dropped down, but the shell hit between Lt Buchanan and Pvt Beck, killing both of them instantly."

(Company C's Charles Senay would paint a more gruesome picture of Buchanan's death, attributing it to the effect of a German 37 mm shell the doughboys called a whiz bang—"it had already passed with a whiz before you heard the bang of the weapon": "One of our officers was talking with one of his lieutenants when a whiz bang decapitated the lieutenant. It not only was nerve wracking, but it left the captain's face with a thick poultice of blood and brains." Beck might have been decapitated by the same shell; upon the disinterment of his body in 1921, a graves searcher would note: "Head missing.")

Sergeant Roy Hockenberry, of East Waterford, Pennsylvania, was hit while digging in, "just after we had reached our objective," Corporal Walter B. Rice remembered. "He was hit by at least five bullets, which pierced his chest and stomach."

And as Roy Hockenberry pawed himself frantically looking for his wound, trying to determine if he was to live or die, he would utter these last words: "I wonder how deep it went in."

Privates Elmer Dunkle of Wrightsville, Pennsylvania, and William Fishette of Bescaccia, Italy, were killed as the company's men furiously burrowed into the earth—Dunkle by "a large caliber shell," Private Leroy Bright recalled, and Fishette "by a machine gun bullet [that] hit him in the forehead, and killed him instantly," according to Private Oscar Roulo.

Others struggled with wounds to the head—"Well, mother, they took a machine gun bullet out of my head," Private Edward Joholski wrote home in wonder—legs, and arms, and dragged themselves or were carried to the rear through the torturous machine-gun fire while other wounded, like Gahring, remained incapacitated in the bottom of their puny holes.

By nine o'clock, the company had nearly consolidated the string of shell holes into something of a line, just in time to beat back the first of several German counterattacks—"a poorly organized attack . . . quickly broken up by the Artillery and small arms fire," Butler would later write.

As the gray wave of German infantry spilled from the Bois de Framicourt, Sorensen noticed a gap between the right of Company D and the left of Company B and quickly called for volunteers to bridge the space.

Into the breach stepped the Irish James Whalen, taking up an automatic rifle and racing into No Man's Land with Privates Ben Beno and John D. Byer (whether they so nobly volunteered or were kicked to the front by Whalen, we will never know) "amid a rain of machine gun bullets and artillery fire to a shell hole about fifty yards in advance of our lines," the Whalen's DSC reads.

And there, as the Germans probed the company's shallow lines, Whalen was quickly wounded, but stuck to his post with Byer and Beno through several more counterattacks, "until the enemy were finally turned back."

Others were proving themselves heroes that morning, one—eighteen-year-old Corporal Philip Danforth Peterson of Hammond, Indiana—also slithering from the company's precarious trench line to a far forward position, the better to cut down the advancing Germans.

Private Earl Wilber remembered: "He had previously captured a German Machine gun, the first one captured by our company and carried [it] up about seventy five yards in advance of our front lines and set it up against the Germans. He was wounded about this time."

During the first counterattack, Sergeant John Pooler, of Johnson City, New York, was cut down—not once, but twice, as he supervised a detail carrying ammunition to the front lines.

"When the Germans started their counter attack we all took cover in shell holes from the German barrage, he was in act of trying to keep the other men down in holes, when he was struck by a machine gun bullet," Corporal Ira Huddleston would relate. "He then started to the rear to have his wound dressed and was hit by another bullet killing him instantly."

Others would die under hazier circumstances, among them Corporal Rufus Durham (and perhaps an entire squad of men under him). Two very different versions of the death of the Big Stone Gap, Virginia, native were chewed over by his mates following the battle.

Willard Storms, who was in the hospital and missed the battle after being wounded on May 14, would remember being told that Durham and his squad had taken cover in a shell crater "when a large shell hit either directly in the crater or so near that the entire squad was either buried or blown to bits. Some of my men were on burying detail there and reported that none of that squad could be found although there were any number of torn and mangled bodies that could not be recognized that were buried in a shell crater."

But Whitelaw Carns would tell graves searchers: "It was while we were advancing toward Cantigny. Durham's squad was in the first wave. A shell burst in the center of the squad and Durham was never found. He couldn't have been captured and he couldn't have run away for he wasn't built that way. Durham was a good fellow."

Another good fellow, George Anslow, of Boston, Massachusetts, fell in midmorning. Accounts of his death from fellow Corporals Joseph Scott and Fred Corsaut say Anslow "was sniping with his helmet just above the parapet. Dropped his head a little. After a while the boys asked him why he did not fire. No answer. Asked him if the Germans were coming over. Then they saw that he was dead, with seven bullet holes in his forehead—sniped by a machine gun."

Private Jerome Angell had written to the editor of his local paper just weeks before to "tell the boys at home to ginger up and give us a lift. The sooner they get here, the sooner the war will be over." Angell would be credited with dropping eight Germans that morning while sniping from the company's thin trench, and be cited for gallantry. But the 1st Division's praise was to be posthumous. By midmorning he was dead, the last drops of his blood oozing from a direct hit by a 37 mm shell.

And so, no, you wouldn't have wanted to be them, not there, not on that morning, alternately scratching the chalk from the soil and then popping your head over the top of that slim trench, to shoot at an enemy unseen in the wheat or woods to your front, as the German planes circled high above like birds of prey, directing the Boche artillery to shorten its range here, lengthen it there, and the heavy, ponderous German shells dropped in, so big you could watch them tumble in, as big as paint cans, and nowhere to run, nowhere to hide.

By midmorning, the French had pulled their heavy artillery out of the lines, and rushed it to the southeast to help counter the Germans' advance toward the Marne. The loss of suppressing fire from the French big guns left the Germans free to shell the Americans at will, and with little fear of retaliation.

A 28th Regiment report would note that once the French guns were withdrawn, "the German Artillery began to bombard our line of resistance." The German artillery fire, it added, "at first was inaccurate," but eight German planes set the guns straight, flying and strafing over the American lines "and correcting the artillery until they had the exact range."

Machine gunner Welcome Waltz remembered "large 10 inch ashcans or mortar shells" descending through the air, "flopping lazily" and "whistling a very unwelcome tune" as they careered out of the morning sky.

"They came over so low that one, in looking up at them in an endeavor to gauge their line of drift, had too much time for reflection and this condition made their presence very undesirable. One of these bombs dropped exceedingly close to my hole and the concussion seemed to create a vacuum in the hole."

The explosion, he added, "pulled all the air out of my lungs and I had to stand up, lean over and gasp for my breath. My heart ached for sometime after that. The terrific concussion had almost finished me."

What's more, the German planes high above ranged almost at will. Waltz, who took up a position on slightly higher ground to the rear of the link between the 2nd and 3rd Battalions, watched a single American plane "with red streamers flying on the end of each wing" swoop over the battlefield shortly after consolidation, the lonesome aviator no match for the German planes he soon attracted.

"It shot low over us and cut figure eights around us. The observer would lean out and wave his arms. It was a wonder that an enemy shell didn't get him as he swooped low, right into the path of their trajectories.

"The enemy had about eight planes circling over our heads while our one lone plane would have to dart in among them now and then, when they would be over their own lines . . . there is hardly anything so depressing to troops as to see the sky filled with enemy planes and none of yours in sight."

Waltz remembered that the German planes remained "content with observing and spotting for their artillery" that morning. But by the afternoon "business began to pick up," and death from above by strafing was added to the miseries suffered in that exposed position.

"The planes came lower and out of one group swooped a fast plane onto our strongpoint," Waltz wrote. "His forward guns were pouring it into us from the second he tilted for our position. He kept on coming and it looked as though he was going to bury himself in the first fox hole on our left flank.

"The riflemen were shooting at him and couldn't help hitting him, he was so low. But our first hits on him showed us that his vital parts were metal-covered for we could see sparks fly as our bullets glanced off his metal sides."

It wasn't until early in the afternoon of May 28 that some sense of what was actually happening in the front lines began drifting back to the battalion, regimental, and division brass.

John Church had reported that the company's line was "established and dug in about 3 feet along line of Fontain Sous Montdidier," the regimental adjutant, Captain William Livesay, passed up the chain of command. "Most of the officers in D company have been wounded by shell and machine guns."

And in a message to the 28th, Sorensen said of his situation: "All officers of Company wounded including my self. Lieut. Buchanan killed. Will reorganize after dark and move to left."

The plight of Company D—A3—was laid out in more detail in a message sent by Rozelle to the 28th's commander, Colonel Hanson Ely: "Sorensen reports about 30 percent casualties in A3, including all his officers and about 4 sergeants. A3 has a number of wounded who will have to be evacuated as soon as possible by party from rear. A2 and A3 will have to be reinforced or be relieved."

Things were no better on Sorensen's immediate left, where Captain Clarence Huebner had taken over the 2nd Battalion for Colonel Robert Maxey, who fell mortally wounded during the advance through the village.

At one o'clock the worried Huebner said in a message to Ely: "The battalion has had three officer[s] killed and 2 wounded and about 80 killed, wounded, or missing. I think it would be advisable to call off raid as there are a great many wounded and killed to be evacuated tonight."

But their orders on this day, as over the next two, were to hold, and it didn't matter that by late afternoon the American position was "well known and the range certain" for the Germans' artillery, as Stuart Wilder would write, and the doughboys just stationary targets, blobs of mud- and blood-stained khaki huddled at the bottom of a three-foot ditch in an open field, and it didn't take a master gunner to find them where they huddled, and take them out one by one—Jerome Angell and William Oliver Phillips, Omey Olson, Frank Beck, and Max Buchanan.

The intense fire prevented many wounded from being evacuated—among those Company L's Lieutenant Newhall who, after being hit three times by sniper fire in the morning's advance, managed to find refuge in a trench where he lay all day "longing for unconsciousness" that never came.

"The enemy began to shell us pretty heavily," Newhall wrote. "There was nothing for me to do but lie still with my helmet over my face . . . hoping that if I got hit I would be killed and not merely badly wounded. One shell did hit the little trench next to me and killed a corporal.

"I was repeatedly showered with loose dirt. A stone thrown out by one shell hit me in the left shoulder and I tho't broke the collar bone. Another time a tiny splinter hit me in the head but it was spent and merely dazed me for a minute."

Soon, a rumor spread "man to man" along the line held by Companies K and L that the entire 3rd Battalion was to be withdrawn. Newhall remembered a sergeant crawling to him to tell him the company had "fallen back to the old line and the Germans are forming for a counter-attack." Newhall was stuck, having nearly fainted from pain when one of his men tried to lift him from the trench earlier that day. He told his sergeant to leave him and fall back with the others.

"The sergeant, a Pole, bade me quite an affectionate farewell, kissed my hand twice, and assured me he would come out for me that night," Newhall wrote. "He was wounded later in the day, I have since learned. I now expected to be taken prisoner (it never occurred to me that since a battle was going on I was much more likely to be bayoneted where I lay). But the German counter-attack never got to me."

Battalion commander Major Jesse Cullison would report that the two companies "withdrew in an orderly manner, by echelon" to their original jump-off positions, forcing him to send forward Company I, which had been in reserve, as well as Company G of the 18th Regiment.

Lieutenant Herman Dacus of Company I remembered being commanded to "Go forward until you meet enemy fire, then stop and dig in!" He added: "My platoon sergeant was a former miner from Pittsburgh, so he and I made the dirt fly."

The 3rd Battalion's intelligence officer, Lieutenant George B. Redwood, who had led the 28th Regiment's first successful raid on the German lines at Seicheprey in March, lost his life while trying to stem the retreat. Lieutenant Tyler of Company M remembered Redwood crawling to his shell hole and asking "how things were going. I gave him what information I could and advised him to get under cover because the area was being subjected to heavy machine gun fire," Tyler would write.

"I noticed that he was holding his right hand up to his chest at this time. He replied that he had already been wounded and intended to proceed at once to Bn. Headquarters to make his report. A few minutes after this, word was passed to me that he had been killed by shell fire."

Redwood had stopped to give aid to Company M's Sergeant Max Rosenbaum, who remembered that Redwood had "regardless of his own safety carried me thru intense machine gun and intense artillery fire" to the rear.

"While assisting me he was severely wounded, and instead of receiving first aid treatment as I asked him to, he attempted to reach the lines again, in order to lead a retreating company (Comp. K) up to their line of resistance," Rosenbaum would tell Redwood's mother. "While doing so a high explosive shell burst near him killing him instantly. You can imagine my sorrow to see the man killed, who a few moments before had saved my life."

Captain Stuart Wilder, whose Company M, 16th Regiment, would help relieve the 28th's 3rd Battalion two nights later, disputed Cullison's characterization of the retreat from the front lines. "The company commander had been killed and the men escaped from the lieutenants due to the difficulty of control under the heavy fire. An order to withdraw, of unknown origins, is alleged. The right of L (the right) Company became involved and also fell back."

The stampede was finally stopped in the Bois St. Eloi, and the retreating men were sent forward to their original jump-off line. "The withdrawal," Wilder would write, "was not, as described by the battalion commander, 'in an orderly manner, by echelon' but a disorganized retreat."

George C. Marshall witnessed the day's confusion as panicked, wildeyed, and shell-shocked soldiers made their way to battalion and regimental posts behind the lines. There, optimism ruled the day, even though the telephone lines had been cut by the German shelling, runners were unable to move because of the constant, streaming machine-gun fire, and American aviators could not see through the clouds of dust and smoke covering the battlefield.

"Frequent reports, highly alarming and often unjustified, poured into Division Headquarters," Marshall remembered. "A few men made their way back with clothing in tatters and reported themselves as sole survivors in their companies. To these, we gave hot coffee and food and then sent them back to the fight with renewed courage and less exaggerated ideas as to the extent of the losses."

But the perils facing Company D and the rest of the 28th Regiment were by no means exaggerated. Having been pounded throughout the day by German artillery, and beset by a relentless swarm of machine guns hidden in the wheat and dark woods to the front, Soren Sorensen at 4:45 P.M. ordered his forward line of surveillance to be abandoned "on account of being untenable by machine gun fire."

Just as Sorensen was pulling back his forward line, the Germans launched their second counterattack. Stepping out of the Bois de Framicourt tentatively, almost reluctantly, the line "was caught under heavy artillery and small arms fire and was quickly broken up," George Butler wrote.

Sorensen would recall that as the first day wore on, the enemy's uncertain aims and his tactics—sending men toward the Americans on the pretext of surrendering, or snaking stealthily through the wheat unseen to take potshots and man hidden machine-gun nests—led his men to fire first and ask questions later.

At 6:30 P.M., "about sixteen to twenty Germans came marching up in column of fours on road thru my left flank holding up their hands in sign of surrender," Sorensen wrote. "I ordered the automatic rifles to be trained upon them and no one to fire except by my orders."

At that moment, "A soldier sprang out of the trenches on my extreme left and ran down the road to meet them, but a machine gun from the company on my left opened fire on them and caused my man to hit the ground. This caused the Germans to disperse and retreat and result none captured."

After a brief lull, heavy artillery fire once more blanketed the dough-

boys' lines, and at 6:45 P.M. the Boche came rolling from their wooded retreat and through the American counterbarrage. Some managed to reach
the lines of Companies B, D, and H, where the men, by Butler's account,
"stood up in their shallow trenches and with deliberately aimed fire picked
off all the enemy who had managed to get inside the barrage."

For the country boys—Arzy Underwood, Whitelaw Carns, T. C.
Hall—who'd grown up with squirrel rifles in their hands, the gray forms
emerging tentatively into the failing sunlight made easy pickings, the best
shots squeezing off at a range of two hundred yards and leaving hundreds
of Boche piled in gray heaps before their trenches.

The attacking Germans, battalion commander Rozelle would note, "at
first seemed to expose himself in a reckless manner and we were led to
believe that he was unaccustomed to receiving effective rifle fire at that
range."

The pickings were just as good on the regiment's left. Company M's
Lieutenant Rudolph Koubsky remembered that at dusk on May 28, a wave
of Germans edged out of the Bois de Laval only to be "beaten off with
heavy losses, by our rifle and auto rifle fire which lasted until dark."

By nightfall, an estimated 275 to 300 Germans lay piled up in front of the
regiment's lines. But losses on the American side had been horrendous, too,
as the German artillery continued to prowl the line with heavy shells, and
machine guns from the wheat and the Framicourt Woods took their toll.

As the long day edged toward an uncertain and menacing night, a cho-
rus of traumatized officers asked for relief from their plight. "My company
is practically wiped out," Captain Francis Van Natter would say of Company L in a message to Ely at about seven o'clock. "I have lost Lieut. Haydock killed, and Lieut. Newhall and Lieut. Hook wounded. M.G. fire has
raised havoc. I have grouped about a dozen men which I am covering the
ravine and north of ravine. Practically all of my noncommissioned officers
are wounded."

That message went ignored, so at about eight o'clock Van Natter sent
another, this one amounting to a tremulous and obsequious plea for mercy:
"I have thought this over very carefully for the past hour—I feel I should
not ask it, but I believe I owe it to the men. My men have fought hard hand

to hand all day long with the enemy, they have suffered heavy losses, no rest or sleep and little time to eat. What I should like is to have them relieved.

"Losses 60 to 70 per cent killed or wounded. Capt. Hawkinson's platoon held out until all their ammunition was gone and then took German rifles and ammunition to fight with. If you can effect this relief it will be appreciated."

Having suffered similar losses in his 1st Battalion, Rozelle seconded the request for his own men: "Account shortage of officers and men this Battalion should be relieved at once. Practically all officers excepting Oliver and McKenzie are out of commission in A-2, A-3, and A-4."

Meanwhile, 1st Division commander Bullard and his staff blamed the losses on the sheer numbers of men being crammed together on the cramped front, making easy pickings for German artillery and machine guns.

Bullard also remained concerned about the activity on his far right, where the Germans were pouring toward the Marne from the Chemin des Dames, and he did not want to commit his reserves to Cantigny as long as a threat of attack from the south remained.

As well, the limited and set-piece attack on Cantigny had drawn the intense interest of John Pershing. Just as Rozelle was asking Hanson Ely for the 1st Battalion to be relieved, Bullard was telling 2nd Brigade commander General Beaumont Buck that there would be no relief—and no retreat, on Pershing's specific orders.

Pershing had remained long enough at Cantigny to watch the 28th Regiment roll through town and establish its forward positions, but he did not at first seem particularly impressed with the action, regarding it as "a simple affair," Bullard would write.

But several hours after leaving the scene, Pershing fired off orders that the position was to be held at all costs, Bullard remembered: "I think he must, after leaving me, have encountered some of our Allies and heard them express doubt of our ability to hold what we had won. He meant to show them that we could and would."

And so in response to the urgent pleas for relief passed on from Ely, Bullard would retort in a message sent at 7:35 P.M. and repeated at 8:27

P.M.: "Inform Ely as follows: Try tonight if practicable to adhere to original plans by withdrawing some units for counterattack thus thinning lines and reducing losses. The position must be held. The C of C expects it."

But the losses continued to appall and concern Ely, who at 8:40 P.M. notified Buck of the dire situation in the front lines: "All men in one Co. gone but 12. He will stay but should be allowed to reinforce. Rozelle reports his Bn. has suffered such losses it should be relieved at once." (Just who "He" is no longer known.)

Despite the losses, despite being left on their own and in the open as little more than target practice for the Germans, and despite repeated requests from Ely that the 28th be relieved by the 18th Regiment or withdrawn to the positions from which they had jumped off that morning, the men of the 28th were ordered to stay.

But by 9:02 P.M., Ely's pleadings for relief gained momentum, and the 1st Battalion of the 26th Infantry Regiment was allowed to relieve Company A on the far right of the battlefield. Ely then ordered Charles Senay to move Company C forward and fortify the frontline position between Company D and Company H, a mission accomplished at about 10:30 P.M.

Through it all, wounded men lay in agony in the regiment's forward positions as the first day's drama closed. Newhall recalled that in the deepening night of May 28, "Everything was quiet except an occasional burst from a machine-gun fired into the dark at random. I lay still, afraid to move for fear the searchers would miss me. Nobody ever came."

In the black night—somehow darker in France than anywhere else he had seen, Welcome Waltz would write—the cold air descended into the bottom of the makeshift trenches where Company D's wounded lay, their khaki tunics stiff with blood, mouths dry, shivering, as medic Fred L. Gunn tended to them as best he could, though with few medical supplies at hand, and certainly not enough for the dozens who lined those holes on that plain.

And among them was Leigh Ellsworth Wilson, just eighteen and his life's blood draining into the earth, his mother Anna long up by now and perhaps writing him again, writing to make sure he's okay, and then walking the few blocks to downtown Janesville, Minnesota to post the letter, post yet another letter to Pvt. Leigh E. Wilson, Company D, 28th Infantry, APO, Tours, France, and walk back home and wait for word from him, wait for word and try not to think of all the things that could happen to the boy who'd left home against her will, to get out of that house with all of those women.

8

"They Thought We Were Only Children"

They say she collapsed, just fainted dead away, when she received the news over the telephone from the railroad station; they say Dr. Hartvigsen rushed out to the Gittins place with his medical kit and worked over Eliza Davis for "two or three hours" before she regained consciousness, as ten-year-old Ernie Davis raced off to find Pa, and as word spread and the "whole town and surrounding community" went into mourning.

They say Eliza had been expecting good news on the afternoon of June 27, 1918, when she'd been summoned to the home of Edwin Gittins, who owned the nearest telephone; but the news was anything but good, and shock had set in quickly as the lines from the telegram were read to her, the words "deeply regret to inform you" rolling into the worse and dreaded "officially reported killed in action."

And it was on hearing those last words that Eliza Davis dropped the receiver and collapsed in the Gittinses' parlor, and young Ernie set off at a run for home, to relay two bits of bad news to his father, James Hyrum Davis, the first being that James Davis's eldest son was dead, the second that Ma had passed out on the Gittinses' floor and he couldn't wake her up.

They say Eliza Davis even upon awaking did not recognize her husband, or even her children, for some time, and that she spent the next week at the Gittinses', bedridden, before she felt well enough to return to the family farm outside of McCammon, Idaho. And they say that even upon her return home she could not sleep for many weeks, until one night her son appeared at the foot of her bed, and Private Paul William Davis of Company D of the 28th Infantry Regiment told his mother, "All is well— do not grieve for me anymore." And they say it was then that Eliza Davis finally began to feel some peace.

Twenty-two-year-old Paul Davis had been another one of them that day, May 28, jumping off beside Rollin Livick and Leigh Wilson and the rest, taking his place in one of the waves as Company D rolled through Cantigny. He was another farmer's son, born at West Kaysville, Utah, on the edge of the Great Salt Lake, where his father—though left lame in one leg by a bout with typhoid fever—scratched a living from the briny soil. Strapping for his time, the five-foot-nine, 155-pound Paul Davis would have dwarfed Rollie Livick and Whitelaw Carns and many others, his life of hard, outdoor labor producing a thick trunk and broad shoulders.

He'd worked that farm until he was a teen, until one spring the waters of Great Salt Lake had risen higher than usual, taking when they receded "a large part of the farm" with them, a family history says. The next year, 1913, Paul Davis had helped an uncle work a plot near McCammon, and it was while working that land that Paul came upon an eighty-acre section for sale that looked promising.

The following spring, Paul loaded "their plow, harrow, and what little farm equipment they had" into a wagon, and went up to Idaho on his own to begin putting in a crop. By fall, Eliza and James and their other children— Mable, Viola, Beulah, Linn, and Ernest—had left the stead on Great Salt Lake and set up housekeeping in the scrublands of southeastern Idaho, where the roof of their home consisted of straw and dirt, but where the threat of flood was nil and where, "by the time they had it all cleaned, the inside whitewashed and James had added more straw and dirt to the roof, it seemed a lot better," the family account says.

Though she could barely read or write herself, forty-six-year-old Eliza had loved to listen as her father, Joseph Smith Marston, read from the Book of Mormon on winter evenings. Despite a hard childhood filled with illnesses, she developed "a pleasing personality and one could listen to her tell stories, experiences, or explain the gospel principles for a long time without becoming tired."

Following her March 1889 marriage to the hard-luck James Hyrum Davis, the son of English immigrants to the Mormon community at Kaysville, Eliza lost her first-born, Joseph, at the age of seven months. More children came, but with each pregnancy and birth she suffered from a recurring and painful swelling of the femoral artery—"child bed fever also called milk-leg and was confined to her bed for a long time," according to the family history.

In 1904 Eliza became pregnant again, but for reasons unknown, the pregnancy did not bring with it the suffering the others had. Her second son, Linn, was born on April 1, 1905, and because of the ease with which she produced him Eliza "felt she was going to have an exceptional child, but he resented her teachings as a child and was not any easier to teach than were her others."

Ernest, her last child, arrived in 1907. The family history says young Ernie "cried almost continuously from the time he was born until he was blessed when he was five months old. The older girls were afraid he would die he was so quiet."

Paul seemed to have caused few such troubles, and was described as industrious and dependable, "a tall, well-proportioned, handsome young man, loved by his family because of his gentle, loving, thoughtful disposition." But he was not afraid to speak his mind, either, on one famous occasion dressing down with the threat of violence a couple of young men whose crude language offended him: "Paul was in the shop having a haircut when some young men came in using profane language and making vulgar remarks. Paul told them to stop talking in that manner or he would throw them outside if necessary. The young men stopped talking as they were and left the shop."

By the spring of 1917, well settled at McCammon, Paul Davis had a girl, one Annie White, whom he "liked especially well and talked of asking her to marry him as soon as he could get in a financial position to do so."

But the government had other plans for Paul Davis, and after his number came up in the summer of 1917, he found himself in the army, training with the 162nd Regiment of the 41st Division at Fort Lewis, Washington, at the same time and from similar beginnings becoming a doughboy just like John Nelson. "It was a sad day when Paul left for he was his father's main help on the farm and the favorite of all the family," the family history says.

Soon "shisked" off to France with the 162nd, the farmer's son Paul Davis marveled, as did so many farm-bred doughboys, at the ancient villages and communal agricultural methods of the Old World. He wrote home on April 25, 1918, to say he was happy that his unit had moved from one overcrowded camp to another site, "more out in the country," where "everything seems to be more clean and fresh," and noted with some wonder that the French farmers "live in one little group or village, instead of living on their farms like we do. No fences or anything much to divide their places and not many weeds to be found around the edges either.

"There is acre after acre of grapes here, and believe me, they are sure cultivated, too. They must be pretty good kinds, as some of their wines are pretty stout."

There might have been more, more letters, more stories to tell upon his return to that dirt-roofed hovel outside of McCammon, and perhaps while sitting on that porch out at the White place, Annie by his side, more talk of the wonders of France and all that he had seen, and whispers between them of betrothal and marriage, and perhaps of the crops he was going to raise, and how many children might be enough to help him do that; but on the very eve of the A.E.F.'s first offensive, Paul Davis was transferred into Company D, a replacement for one of those who had fallen on May 14.

And just days later Paul Davis was one of those who stepped out to Sorensen's whistle, one of those who went over the top and through Cantigny and onto the plain beyond, perhaps even to survive that first day of shelling and counterattacks, only to fall, the War Department would tell Eliza Davis, on May 29, although Sergeant James Whalen would report that Paul Davis was killed the day before "by a fragment of a large caliber shell" as the company dug in just east of Cantigny.

Paul's younger sister and "constant companion," Beulah, had just such a vision of her brother's death, one night having "a dream telling her how he died in a bomb explosion"; but both accounts contradict the hazy childhood recollection of Paul's nephew, Arnold Davis, Linn's son, who would tell me he remembers hearing from an early age that his uncle had been killed during a vicious and frantic duel with three Germans, two of whom Paul killed before succumbing at bayonet point to the third, information that may have come from some long-lost letter to Eliza Davis from another Company D soldier.

However and whenever he died, Paul Davis became one of those Company D men to be "buried in shell holes in the rear of the front line trench" during those terrible three days, Sergeant Everett E. Adams would tell the Graves Registration Service in 1926, his 155 pounds being lifted with some effort by the company's men to be pushed away like so much offal, the living then turning to face east again on that May 29 and quickly forget the unfamiliar newcomer Paul William Davis amid the chaos of another day of battle, of cascading bombardments and random sheets of machine-gun fire on that plateau east of Cantigny, where dawn was breaking now, the first gray rays of light bringing with them a furious shelling, and soon enough the now-familiar visage of the gray-green Hun infantry rolling through the mist from the dark woods and toward the American trenches.

Once again the artillery opened up, and once again the surviving members of the 28th Regiment, now reinforced by several companies of the 18th Regiment and the 1st Battalion of the 26th Regiment on the far right of the battlefield, stood in their shallow trenches and with Chauchats and rifles cut the Boche down.

"As the smoke cleared away 3 waves could be seen advancing to our front and left front, attempting to envelope our left flank," Company M's Rudolph Koubsky would later report. "They were beaten off with heavy enemy losses again."

Charles Senay got his first kill in the morning's gray light. "I was watching the front very closely," he remembered. "Suddenly an enemy soldier cradling a light machine gun crept crouching toward our lines. My Springfield was cocked and contained a full clip. I fired at his head and nothing happened. I worked my bolt, aiming lower, and missed again.

"The third time I aimed at his feet and took the top of his head off."

During the night, a soldier on duty to the far front of Company B had discovered and captured ten Germans heading for the company's position. Company commander Clarence Oliver reported that in the inky darkness his men also found a machine gun near where the men were captured.

Also during the night, ambulances were ordered forward by Hanson Ely, and by seven o'clock on the morning of May 29, 278 wounded men had passed through the regiment's evacuation hospital. By eleven that night, the count stood at 400 wounded for the two days of battle—"and others to be still coming in," a report to the 1st Division said.

Lights out, the Ford trucks plied the bumpy, shell-pocked roads to the front and back blind, racing and careering in an effort to avoid shellfire, each contortion of their springs producing untold agony for the wounded who lay in back.

"I don't think you have ever known the joy of a ninety K. ride on the upper deck of a pitching ambulance," medic Julian Dorr would write. "It's an experience. I appreciated the sensations of a pup with a tin can tied to his tail."

The dead of both sides, meanwhile, quickly became stinking dross, their lifeless and stiff forms nothing but nuisances to the living. Senay wrote: "German dead littered the ground. We simply rolled them into shell holes. The same thing happened with our own dead except that we covered them with earth and marked their graves with a bayonet often bearing their dog tags."

"All the soldiers that were killed at Cantigny were rolled in the nearest shell hole and covered up to keep down the oder from their bodies," Company D's Sergeant Licklider would write. "Later there was an order from the War Department against this, and they were left where they fell."

The dead would never know, and the survivors couldn't then know it as they hung on into a second day, but the 28th's initiation into battle was causing a sensation back in the States. Newspaper reporters who, like James Hopper, had been tipped off about the assault had flocked to the tiny village, and were sending back rapturous accounts of the battle that made the afternoon papers on May 28.

Wrote Emmet Crozier in his study of the press on the Western Front: "Cantigny! Cantigny! Cables and telegraph wires hummed with the name and all American was learning where it was on the map and trying to pronounce it."

The Associated Press reported: "American troops in their first assault against the Germans in Picardy have scored a brilliant success. Striking the enemy where he had been repulsed the previous day, Gen. Pershing's men advanced their line to a considerable depth on a front of one and one-fourth miles, captured the town of Cantigny, West of Montdidier, and took 300 prisoners. Heavy losses were inflicted on the Germans, while the Americans suffered relatively small casualties."

In one of the many dispatches that would give George Butler his fifteen minutes of fame, the *New York Tribune* reported: "Lieutenant George E. Butler, formerly an attorney in Indianapolis, who was slightly wounded in the leg, said that going over the top was like a manoeuvre in the training camp back home.

"The men were eager for it, he said, and some of them remained up in the trenches all night talking about the approaching adventure with cheerful anticipation."

When another casualty, Lieutenant Albert Billings, was placed in the bed next to Butler's, "they clasped hands and greeted each other like long lost brothers," the paper reported. " 'It was a great show, wasn't it,' " Billings said. " 'Gee, I wish the folks at home could have seen it. I wouldn't have missed it for the world.' "

But Butler and Billings weren't in the front lines on the second day, as the men continued to hang on by their fingernails, and as Companies D, B, and C continued to hold the support and frontline positions of the southern third of the battlefield amid continuing artillery fire and harassing fire from "many light machine guns. These were very annoying," Senay would write in a report.

As well, Senay wrote years later, the Germans during some of the attacks employed flamethrowers, giving back to the doughboys a taste of the medicine doled out by the poilus the previous morning.

"These were simply tanks of combustible fuel strapped on the back of a soldier," Senay wrote. "We would concentrate our fire on the tank. The bearer of the tank was incinerated by his own fuel and would stagger in weakening circles until he collapsed and died in a charred huddle."

Artillery fire also continued to plague the 28th Regiment's men throughout the day. "Such a deluge of shells I never thought would be placed on such a small position," machine gunner Waltz wrote. "The dust created by the bursting shells around our position was so great that it looked like the heaviest London fog. French artillery observers, afterwards, stated that it was the heaviest artillery fire they had ever seen delivered on a small sector in four years of war."

Particularly disturbing were the shells coming from two long-range German guns, Waltz wrote: "These guns were so far back that we could never hear the report of the gun but our first warning of the approaching shells was a great roar as the giants would twist over and then a succession of roars and when it sounded like a mountain was on the point of smashing us, we could look up and see two huge logs bearing down on us, both together.

"The earth seemed to buckle and shimmy around in a crazy manner. This type of stuff is what makes men go insane."

Senay was almost killed by just such a blast that day. "An in-coming shell collapsed the shell hole and I was upended and buried alive with a dead or dying soldier on each side of me. Fortunately, one of my feet was exposed and members of my company dug me out before I could suffocate.

"I regained consciousness, powder blackened and bleeding from my eyes and ears as well as nose, with my second in command kneeling and praying over my bedraggled, but still intact, body. One of the two men buried with me was terribly mangled and had died instantly. The other remained unconscious until he died some twelve hours later."

Almost as bad as the pounding and arbitrary artillery was the constant tension, as every small gathering of Germans across the way seemed to presage a counterattack, and every rumble from the woods to the front was taken as a sign of tanks moving up to the attack.

Sorensen would report that, on May 29, "consolidation continued but was very difficult on account of machine gun fire from enemy in woods on the right." The afternoon would also bring the hair-raising report "that enemy tanks were seen to be approaching on my right, none seen."

As the second day wore on, the Americans seemed to see or imagine German tanks everywhere. "In the afternoon many reports came in of a

German attack forming aided by tanks, opposite Cantigny," a 1st Division report would relate. "Aeroplane observation reported that no tanks were visible, nor were any concentrations of German infantry apparent."

Simple exhaustion may have fueled such hallucinations. Though "German tanks were reported frequently, even by an Artillery colonel," the Germans were "actually demoralized by the French tanks which no one had ever seen before," the 16th Regiment's Stuart Wilder wrote.

But the Germans weren't beyond wild imagining themselves, inventing counterattacks from thin air, according to Wilder. "They dressed up their operations reports with an imaginary attack on the 29th (along our entire front in 'dense waves' which they halted with 'heavy losses.')

"As a matter of fact both sides were exhausted and incapable of further effort. Americans and Germans were glad to settle down to digging in their new positions, while gratifying their feelings by harassing each other with all the available artillery."

The Germans would pour somewhere around six thousand 77 mm and 210 mm shells into the new lines from May 28 to May 30. Under such a pounding, some could no longer sit still and sought to do something—anything—to get out from under it.

Waltz remembered one such group of 2nd Battalion men racing hell-for-leather through his position on the second afternoon, headed for the front line. "Up from the rear, and through heavy fire, a reserve platoon came on the run, up to our position. The officer was wild-eyed and all out of breath, as also were his men. He had his pistol in his hand and it looked like an infantry charge to me. He halted long enough at our place to yell, 'Where are they?' We pointed up ahead and he with his followers disappeared in the trees beyond.

"We never saw him or his platoon again."

At wit's end, an enraged Hanson Ely would on the evening of May 29 once more insist on the relief of his battered regiment, messaging Bullard that he was not going to take the blame for what seemed to be the ruination of the 28th: "Front line pounded to Hell and gone," he wrote, "and entire front line must be relieved tomorrow night and he would not be responsible."

As much as the men suffered physically in the front lines, Ely suffered psychically as he tried to save them from his regimental command post, located in a cave in the Bois de Eloi on Cantigny's northern edge.

By the morning of May 29 Ely "wore a sleepless look," Lieutenant Daniel Sargent, assigned as liaison between the 1st Division artillery and the 28th Regiment, would recall years later of his visit to Ely's lair. Despite his continued demands for relief, Ely also "had a most calming presence, and calming look." While the previous artillery liaison lay exhausted on the floor of Ely's cave, "staring up at the ceiling glassy-eyed," Ely, seated on a horse saddle, ordered Sargent to enter Cantigny and find Major George Rozelle's 1st Battalion command post, located in a cellar dugout in the ruins of the village.

Sargent, who remembered the battalion commander as "Major Roussel," and who remembered as well that Rozelle referred to him always as "Mr. Artilleryman," found Rozelle seated in the cellar of a bombed-out house with five other officers—two French, three American.

Clouds of dust created by the incessant German shelling sifted through the dugout roof, which covered "a room with stone sides, and a vaulted ceiling of brick." The room was about seventy square feet, and at either end of the cellar were large hogsheads filled with cider—a cup of which was offered to the pleased Sargent. "It was a God-send," Sargent wrote, adding, "I don't want to give the impression that we were having a vacation in Cantigny. Being in it was like being in the crater of an active volcano. At any moment a heavy howitzer shell might land on the roof of our cellar and we would be buried alive.

"But more important, there was always the possibility that the Germans might break through and it was a torment to have to listen to the incessant bombardment, now intense, now not so intense, but always continuing."

While Sargent and his cohorts enjoyed their cider in the relative safety and comfort of Rozelle's post, the men in the line faced the uncomfortable prospect of yet another night in their open, shallow, and dead-lined trenches.

As the sun set behind them, coloring the lifeless blue-green forms of the dead Germans before them with in blood-red hues, intermittent and random bursts from machine guns and artillery swept their lines, and the men checked and rechecked the breeches of their rifles and Chauchats, grimly awaiting the next saturation bombing that would presage yet another counterattack.

Another night passed—"second night same as first night," Sorensen would report in blasé fashion; same old chattering of the machine guns, same old battering from the heavy German artillery, same old thirst, hunger, nerves on edge, same old worrying over German sappers snaking through the wheat for a final mad rush in the dark, same old grime and sweat and blood congealing in the "extremely cold" night, as Waltz described it.

Lieutenant Richard Newhall had by then lain bleeding and in pain for forty-two hours in his small refuge near Company L's former front line on the regiment's left, one of those unreachable and seemingly forgotten men amid the shelling and counterattacks of the previous two days.

He spent all of May 29 next to his dead corporal, "slowly thinking out how I would get myself back that night," he later wrote. Under cover of night, "I removed all my equipment and abandoned it, except my gas-mask and helmet. From the trap by which I carried the Very pistol pouch I made a sort of sling for my left arm.

"Then I got to my feet. The effort caused me to faint but I fortunately fell against the parapet and so remained upright. The cold night quickly revived me. Somehow I managed to get out of the trench. Perhaps I fainted again; I'm not sure.

"The only way I could move was upright which was dangerous because of the random machine gun fire, but couldn't be helped."

Painfully making his way the two hundred yards to the American lines, Newhall had to stop over and over so as not to faint. His last hurdle was avoiding being murdered by his own company mates as he approached their lines.

"When I began to make my way through our wire, fortunately not very thick, I was challenged from our trench," he remembered. "They were fearful of me for fear it was some German ruse, but finally allowed me to come in, and as soon as I could tell who I was jumped out and helped me into the trench."

A few hours later, a heavy bombardment of the American lines began once more, and as dawn broke on May 30 German troops probed half-heartedly and futilely out onto the field. Artillery and rifle fire once more sent them packing, and through most of the day the usual desultory firing back and forth ruled.

Late in the afternoon, however, the German bombardment again grew heavier, and Sorensen worried that the Germans might be making one last push against his position. The company suffered eight more casualties from the bombardment and from machine-gun fire, and, Sorensen wrote, "I was sure an attack would follow immediately and passed word down the line as soon as barrage lifted for everyone to man the trench."

Ironically, on the other side of the battlefield, the Germans were just as worried about American intentions. Stuart Wilder would write that a German pilot had messaged that he saw the doughboys massing for an attack, and the Hun subsequently placed "annihilation fire" to prevent its development.

In fact, the mass of doughboys was Stuart Campbell's Company E of the 18th Regiment. The late-afternoon bombardment had led a nervous George Rozelle to bring Campbell's unit forward to reinforce Company D's position, and Campbell was more than happy to get into the fight after three days of waiting helplessly in reserve.

"Our men were only too anxious to get into it as anything was better than taking the pounding we were being subjected to without any means of retaliation," Campbell wrote. "Although heavily shelled while crossing the valley, we did not lose a man having taken advantage of the terrain consequently the machine guns were shooting well over our heads."

Just before Campbell and his men began their race for Sorensen's position, Rozelle ordered him to "take what cover could be found and await developments. As could be expected little cover could be found and shells were ploughing up the earth in all directions. It was only by the grace of God that we did not have heavy losses at this point."

The late-afternoon attack on May 30 was quickly broken up by the 1st's artillery—"and the Germans had now had enough," Charles Senay wrote. The Boche withdrew and "vented their spite by intermittent artillery fire."

The failed assault was the last act of the great drama; that evening, patrols from the 16th Regiment quietly moved up in the dark to mark the routes for their relief of the 28th Regiment. At 2:30 A.M. on May 31, what was left of Company D and the 28th Regiment stumbled, exhausted and "hollow-eyed," as Ely would remember, from its improvised trenches.

The 28th had suffered, but the Germans had indeed had their eyes blackened severely. During the three days of sending out futile counterattacks, the 271st and 272nd Reserve Regiments would squander 48 officers and 1,290 enlisted men. Another 29 became casualties on May 31—even as yet another counterattack by the 270th Regiment on the American positions was planned and then nixed, "thereby avoiding another fruitless slaughter of men who from the start never had a chance," Wilder would write, adding: "The 82nd Reserve Division was through."

The 28th Regiment was not quite "through," but Cantigny had bled it, causing casualties equal to a full-strength battalion. Thirteen officers were killed, as were 185 enlisted men. Another 32 officers were wounded or missing, as were 837 men.

Company D had only barely survived its baptism under fire. An accounting shortly after the battle would put in stark, black-and-white terms the damage Company D had incurred, frightful losses even when compared to the other units in the 1st Battalion:

PRESENT EFFECTIVE STRENGTH

	OFFICERS	MEN
Company A	1	182
Company B	5	184
Company C	6	205
Company D	1	120
Machine Gun Company	9	159

According to the company's morning reports—a day-by-day accounting of Company D's strength—Sorensen had led 6 officers and 206 noncoms and privates into battle on May 28. Twenty-five of these were killed in action, gone forever missing, or would die within a month of their wounds, while more than sixty were wounded, many of them badly enough to require hospitalization and a transfer from the company rolls to the limbo of a "replacement organization." For many of these, the war was over, their bodies too broken to continue in active service. Among them were lieutenants Ross Gahring and Frank Cooper.

The Americans had taken Cantigny. They had even held Cantigny through three murderous days. But had it been worth it? Had the taking and holding of the blip in the lines around Cantigny had any military justification?

Hanson Ely's immediate answer to that question "verged on the insubordinate," according to the historians Meirion and Susie Harries, and in stark terms pointed out the absurdity of keeping exhausted and battered men in such an exposed and perilous position for three days.

Ely wrote in his report of the operation on June 2: "The great strain of men holding a front line trench or being practically without sleep for three or four days and nights seriously weakens them; and when there is added to this casualties amounting in some companies to as high as 40%, with casualties among Company Officers of Infantry Companies of from 33% to 100%, it is believed that as soon as a force has gained and fairly consolidated its objective, having suffered any such losses that it should be relieved by fresh troops, as any enemy's attack after H plus 48 hours will probably be made by entirely fresh troops."

The Americans had advanced a little more than one mile along a one-and-a-half-mile front, and held their ground for three days; to keep things in perspective, by the end of that May 28 the German offensive launched the day before had advanced fifteen miles along a forty-mile front, and its vanguard was only forty miles from Paris.

But the Battle of Cantigny had achieved its aim—that of displaying the American military's toughness and resolve. And in that sense, Cantigny would certainly be seen as a huge opening-night success.

George Butler summed up those feelings, noting that the action at Cantigny, though holding no "tactical or strategical advantages," paved the way for the Americans' further use in the furious fighting at Belleau Wood and Château-Thierry just days later. "More important than any local tactical gain was the fact that at last the American Army was ready and able to take a portion of the burden from the shoulders of the Allied Armies."

Captain Edward Johnston of Company E, 28th Regiment, was even more forthright. "If every man of the 1st Division had had to die on the plateau of Cantigny, the sacrifice would have been justifiable. The probable consequences of failure were so momentous that success must have been attained at any cost."

Even Hanson Ely, who had watched in horror as his regiment melted away, developed an appreciation of the battle's import, writing twenty years later: "The result of the taking of the village of Cantigny was to harden the English and French, raise their morale and place a scare into the German armies. To my mind the engagement at Cantigny was a cloud upon the German's horizon that later meant defeat to their cause."

To George Marshall, the battle also represented an eastward tentacle of America's democratic Manifest Destiny. "This little village marks a cycle in the history of America," Marshall wrote. "Quitting the soil of Europe to escape oppression and loss of personal liberties, the early settlers in America laid the foundations of a government based on equality, personal liberty, and justice.

"Three hundred years later their descendants returned to Europe and on May 28, 1918, launched their first attack on the remaining forces of autocracy to secure these same principles for the people of the Old World."

As for the boys who'd fought and bled?

Hell, they were just happy to be alive.

In the days to come, the 28th's men would be toasted as heroes and gain the nickname "Black Lions." But in the early morning hours of May 31, 1918 they just wanted some sleep.

Harry Martin probably summed up the feelings of all who had endured those three days, writing just hours after being relieved: "I have my first boche and let me tell you I didn't hesitate when I saw them. My .45 automatic and my hand grenades were working in fine condition. We all did our share, and the American soldiers deserve a world of credit. They are surely some fighters.

"I am awfully glad that I was in it and wouldn't have missed it for anything, but I'm not overly enthusiastic about 'over the tops.' They all sound fine on paper but actually it is a mean thing. You can't tell when you are going to get yours and it is one mean sensation, too, men falling dead or wounded on all sides of you. Thank goodness I am alive, safe and sound, although awfully tired."

Lieutenant Samuel I. Parker would claim that his platoon of Company K "can easily account for 350 of the enemy," and added: "If they get me now I can 'turn in' with the satisfaction of knowing that I have done as much as the average officer to put an end to Prussianism."

Parker would also claim that just eleven men from his platoon had survived the ordeal, while the rest gladly sacrificed their lives.

"Those that gave the 'last full measure of devotion' did it without a groan or complaint," he wrote shortly after the battle. "I had several call out to me in a perfectly cheerful voice 'Lieutenant they got me.'

"The men that died, died happy. I have never seen such spirit, and if I live to be a thousand years old and am in battle every day of it, I never expect to see better spirit."

Company D's survivors were also writing home. Under the strict rules of wartime censorship, they couldn't dwell on military details, but they could express their feelings about the American debut. Private William Schindler, one of the Janesville boys, wrote in a letter to his parents: "You know I have been in the fighting lines several times and returned safe to our resting places. I can say we did have some fun by getting the best of Kaiser Bill and his men."

Schindler added: "They thought we were only children, but they found out that we are better and harder than they are."

George Butler wrote home to Arkansas City in early June to say he was okay—and to disparage the Germans' fighting abilities. The letter to his sister ran under the banner front-page headline "Lieutenant Butler Says the Boche Are Yellow" in the local paper, and read in part: "Rest assured we have been showing the Boche how to fight. I have been surprised by the fact that unless they have about 10 men to one the Boche will stick his hands a mile in the air and holler 'Kommerad' as loud as a sick mule.

"They are physical cowards when it comes to fighting man to man.

In fact they won't fight that way at all, but then as the British say, 'When they stick up their hands it makes their belly a better target for a bayonet.'"

Others wrote home to express their amazement at having survived. "Well, mother dear, I am in the hospital laying with a bullet wound in my head," Private Edward Joholski, another of the Janesville boys, would matter-of-factly tell his perhaps mortified mother. "Gee, mother, we sure had some battle and we won it, but we had an awful hard fight and a lot of the boys got killed and wounded, but there was more wounded than killed.

"I got hit at 8:30 in the morning and walked back to our line to the hospital. Am feeling good and will be out of the hospital in a short time. Tell father I got lots of Germans and they won't bother anyone again."

Joholski had survived, but what of those in the nebulous otherworld, those nine who would be listing as missing on the company's June rolls?

No one could say where they lay, and in some cases no one could say even what had happened to them, but the best guess as to the disposition of their remains may lie in the testimony of John R. D. Wallace, who served under Stuart Wilder when Company M of the 16th Regiment took over a portion of the trenches from the 28th Regiment on May 31. During his time in the front lines, he wrote, he helped bury "a number of bodies there that were in such condition as to make it impossible to identify them. We buried bodies in a shell hole, say one night, and the next night we would bury another bunch in the same hole.

"There are shell holes near Cantigny that I know had four layers of bodies buried in them and no markers were put up to show who or how many were buried there."

It wasn't until May 1927 that one small trace of the missing emerged from the quiet fields at Cantigny. Walking the battlefield one day, a souvenir hunter found two small silver discs near the 1st Division monument, and turned them over to Lew Hoyt, a major with the U.S. Marines who happened also to be walking the battlefield that day. Two years later, Hoyt passed them on to the Graves Registration Service.

They remain today sealed in a burial file at the National Archives devoted to one of those doughboys who fell at Cantigny. And inscribed on each of the identification tags is the name and unit of the fallen.

The tags read:

PAUL DAVIS
CO D 28 INF

9

No Man's Land

Emil Eliason would never forget the sight, the vision of a soldier, something like the tin ones he played with on the stoop in front of his home at 8015 South Throop Avenue in Chicago, though this one was clad in a long brown overcoat and puttees, walking with long strides toward six-year-old Emil, coming ever closer and seemingly headed right toward Emil's house, which caused him to race inside and shout to his mother, "A soldier is coming! A soldier is coming!" But when Signe Eliason came to the door and saw the figure she just smiled and told her son, "Why Emil, that's your Uncle August."

Twenty-eight-year-old August Adolph Hedblom hadn't wanted this, hadn't wanted to be in this uniform, marching as to war, with just a quick stopover at his sister's home in Chicago before heading on with John Nelson and a contingent of Camp Grant replacements, their destination France; August Hedblom would have much preferred to stay back on the farm near Rice Lake, Wisconsin, where his Swedish parents, Lars and Julia, had found their American dream amid the cold winters and tall timbers of northwestern Wisconsin.

Lars and Julia had seven children, two of whom—Herbert and Edwin—

had up and left the farm to join the army in the spring of 1917, while August tarried, hoping against hope his number wouldn't come up. He seems not to have understood what all the fuss was about, nor why he should want to go Over There when there was so much work to do here, in his father's pastures, and in fact August had tried his best to avoid the war, writing on his draft-registration card on June 5, 1917, that he didn't feel he'd be much help in licking the Kaiser, as he was at the time "layed up on account of lame arm."

The local draft board, though, had nonetheless deemed him well enough to stop a bullet, and so over his own objections and the objections of a father now left to run things with his two remaining boys—fifteen-year-old Arthur and three-year-old Walter—August had joined John Nelson at Camp Grant that fall.

And he would be with John Nelson as the contingent steamed east to France, and as the men climbed aboard a forty-and-eight for the rumbling ride to the lines at Cantigny, to become replacements, curiosities to the likes of the veterans Rollie Livick and Whitelaw Reid Carns and James Whalen and the rest of Company D's boys, who'd held their ground and somehow survived those three terrible days in front of that ruined village.

And as their train headed east, ever east, the Swedish immigrants August Hedblom and John Nelson came ever closer to the Paris-Soissons Road, where each had an appointment, though they couldn't know it, as did some of those with them, the boys of the 344th Regiment, which was on the verge of being separated and dished out to the 1st Division, new blood and new bodies to replace some of those wounded and all of those dead and missing at Cantigny, the likes of George Anslow and John Pooler, Rufus Durham and Paul Davis, and Elmer Dunkle and Jerome Angell, young boys gone to dust during that simple "straightening of the lines," as the *Chicago Daily News* characterized the operation.

And I wonder now if as that train chugged toward Cantigny these two Swedes, these accidental soldiers, found common ground in their native language and in their newly dire circumstances, watching with perhaps concern as well as wonder as their destination beyond the poppied fields of Picardy came into view, and with it the dim outline of a tumbled-down and ruined village set below barrage balloons, while the ever nearer thudding of artillery raked the air around those lines won just two weeks before at such a price.

I can now picture John Nelson rolling toward such a scene, but for much of my life, and certainly for all of the years I knew him, I'd mixed up the twin pillars at the core of John Nelson's long life, the first being that he had emigrated to the United States from Sweden at the age of nineteen, and the second that he had been shot in France, which for many years left me under the impression that he had been serving in the Swedish army when this occurred, an idea that now makes me laugh, now that I know so much more of the story.

But we were all confused, and the exact manner in which and in what locale and even why John Nelson had been shot was the source of numerous conversations at the dinner table, the facts not even fuzzy or indistinct but nonexistent, beyond the actual wound and the slightly hunched and teetering gait with which he'd been left, and his race to the bathroom after every meal to empty intestines abbreviated by surgery in a Red Cross hospital in Paris.

My father had even once insisted that the Old Man had been shot while in an onion patch, into which he'd supposedly crawled for a meal, a version which I now know was meant to take some of the glory, some of the daring, some of the sheer bravery from the act, and which was indicative more of the ambiguous and distant relationship John Nelson shared with his only son than any battlefield reality.

The Old Man was tough, too tough, and I wouldn't have wanted to have been his son, and have had to try to measure up to him, have had to try to match his simple drive to survive, his immigrant psalm, and that night in the wheat and the nightmares and knowledge he'd gained there at the Paris-Soissons Road, which combined with those lean years at Kangsleboda had left him with the understanding that life was hard, that only the hard survive, and perhaps maybe that only fools could find joy in the simple reality of existing, in which he indulged himself only once a year, every July 19, when he allowed himself to exult in breathing, and then on the twentieth it was back to work, back to the grim work of surviving, enough foolishness for one year.

"I *think* he loved me," my father would many say years later, after the

Old Man was gone, and not too long before he passed on himself. And wasn't that a sad thing to have to wonder, at the age of seventy-seven, with no hope of reconciliation, and then to die at the age of eighty-one still wondering, still the abandoned son, still pondering the unanswerable question of a lifetime, still looking for a father's approval, and love, forever unattainable but perhaps always there at the same time and just unspoken.

As a grandfather John Nelson was almost as remote, and as hard, as he had been as a father, not the spoiling type, not a doter, his lap not a place where a kid could find much solace or fuzzy warmth. He did not spread candy around, or dollar bills, or love, really, though I remember once he bought me a toy horse, a small and spontaneous gift from some dime store, the only token of affection, or whatever it was meant to be, that I ever received from him.

But John Nelson had left his son, and all of us, a greater gift, maybe all he had to give, and perhaps that has to be enough, perhaps that is enough. He had crossed the Paris-Soissons Road and endured that night in the wheat and returned to give us all life, and he had given us America, his America. He had by sheer determination put us in the New World, and I can't help but think now that as John Nelson's forty-and-eight rolled across the French countryside in early June 1918, past half-destroyed cottages made of stone and sticks and straw, and past old women, bent and careworn and adorned in black, their faces deeply etched with the lines brought by a hard life and a harder war, that to John Nelson it all looked too familiar, and that he must have thought he'd died and gone to hell.

He'd held no sentiment for this world, this old one, and instead was captivated by the promise of America, of the American Dream, which for him was embodied in a membership in Chicago's Swedish Club, a private enclave on LaSalle Avenue where they called a poor immigrant Mr. Nelson, and in which he could kick back, and feel he'd really made it; and in a dingy paint shop on Devon Avenue, above which my father grew up and whose heavy and wooden cabinets held powdered red and white lead, and which reeked with the pungent and chemical odors of benzene and oily resins.

And of course there was the sequence of automobiles that ran from a Model T and through a series of Studebakers and Chryslers on up to his last one, a diesel-spewing hog of an Oldsmobile, which he washed every day with a chamois, and which against all advice and even pleading he drove to Florida at the age of ninety, and the loss of which he mourned deeply when they told him not too much later it was over, that the nearly blind should probably stay off the roads.

He'd always known where he was going, and was always in a hurry to get there, speeding up at yellow lights in every one of his many cars, while we as children cringed and laughed and grimaced at each other in the backseat; traveling with Karin to Japan and Hawaii and Florida, and crossing the straits on a ferry to Cuba, even, when that was still possible; and working, working until he was seventy-six years old, Saturdays, too, in that dingy paint shop, afraid to stop, not being able to stop, afraid maybe that if he did they'd come and take away his cars, and the smorgasbord at the Swedish Club, and his worn Oriental carpets and RCA color television, everything, in fact, for which he'd risked his life that day at that goddamn road.

Like tourists on a lark, the Americans wondered at and were at times enchanted by this Old World, and its seeming backwardness; to John Nelson and some of those with him—the Russian Abe Sachs, the Pole Zygmunt Misiewicz, the Sicilian Benjamin Baucaro—France instead surely must have brought back hard memories, flashbacks to pogroms and worn-out soil, to the wrinkled and careworn furrows in their own parents' faces, to the stifling of ambition in the day-to-day simple act of surviving, to a pestilent tenement in Lodz or an ancient and stingy and rocky plot in Smaaland, and to the doling out, perhaps, of a single pot of thin gruel to a gaggle of starving children.

John Nelson had worn—and would continue to wear—wooden clogs; he'd seen the same piles of shit in Sweden, lived with cows off the kitchen and seen as well the same worry lines etched into the faces of his mother Ingrid and his father Nils, and lived enough of that tough life to have gotten out while the getting was good, and so for him there would have been no patronizing wonder, no tourist's awe or interest in this drab and depressing place, this France.

I can imagine some of the things that went through John Nelson's mind as his forty-and-eight rolled across France that June, foremost being not the adventure, nor the cause, but a certain dread and apprehension that he might not live long enough or be able-bodied enough to go back to enjoying the new life he'd found, the hustle and bustle of simple American *promise*, and I have little doubt that all he wanted was to do his duty and live through whatever was coming and then get the hell out, out of this war, out of the A.E.F., and out of this France.

Marvin Stainton's problem that spring was the opposite: He was trying to get *in* to France, in to *it*, into the war, and even as John Nelson no doubt pondered his immediate future as he rolled toward the lines at Cantigny, the dull crump of the ongoing artillery duels growing ever louder and more ominous, Marvin Stainton worried that the thing would be done before he could make it Over There.

As the long months spent training black troops in the backwaters of Arkansas had dragged on—and as his own brother, Sam, had made the journey overseas with an airplane squadron—Marvin at every opportunity had sought a way to France, and had grown increasingly despondent about his chances.

On April 18, Marvin wrote to his mother, and seemed to be trying to convince himself as much as her that all would be well if he did go. "As for me going to France, I want to go very bad," he told Mary Stainton from his new post at Little Rock's Camp Pike. "Everyone that goes to France are not killed, some people say that if you are once in France you are gone. I think they are all wrong. Sam is over there and I will not be satisfied until I go."

Marvin added: "No I am not willing to stay behind while the others do their bit, the hardest and most dangerous part. Let me tell you dear mother that I would rather do my part over there, because it would be hard to get them after they are over here. It is just a fight between right and wrong."

Marvin also took pains to assure his mother he was leading a clean and Christian life—despite the revelation that he had—or *had* had—a girl-friend.

"I have a big bunch of pictures all over the walls," he wrote. "Mostly movie 'stars' but I have some pictures of George Washington cut out of the *Ladies Home Journal*. And I have a picture of Jesus over them all, next to the ceiling. It is one of the great artists Hoffmans paintings also out of *Ladies Home Journal*.

"I don't know whether I should tell you about my Memphis girl or not. I wrote and told her I did not love her and she seems to have taken it very hard. I had to because I felt myself getting into *deep water*.

"I really like her but I can't go too far and get myself engaged to her so I told her I did not love her any more. She is too young to tell whether she loves anyone or not."

Joseph Cannella, a fellow lieutenant and friend of Marvin's, would confirm Marvin's state of "mental torture" that spring. "Things looked mighty blue," Cannella would write Mary Stainton in December 1918. "We spent many hours 'chewing the rag' about going over—he would console me and I console him—but it didn't do much good.

"We both talked about giving up our commissions so we could go as privates, but somehow or other our plans about resigning never materialized."

Cannella would add: "I never will forget him when he was sitting on the cot, with his head between his hands and he said to me, 'Joe, I don't want anyone to think I want to be a hero, or want to kill other men or be a murderer, but this is the biggest thing that was ever pulled off and I want to have a hand in it and by Jove I am going to get in it.'"

Fortune, such as it was, finally arrived for Marvin's ambitions in the form of a May 22 lottery at the post, by which sixteen lucky officers would be selected to go to France. "As luck would have it, Marvin and myself lost out," Cannella wrote. But one of the lucky officers soon took sick; Marvin, "almost on his knees," begged Camp Pike's commanding officer to be put on the list of those going to France—and his wish was granted.

"I never will forget how happy he was and how I envied him," Cannella wrote. "He would say, 'Well Joe in a few months I will be coming back with wound stripes on my arm and make you feel cheap.'"

Even as the news of the great battle at Cantigny dominated the newspapers that June 3, Marvin sat down to write to Mary Stainton and inform her of his great luck—and of his new worries that the war would be over before he could get his piece of it.

"Names were drawn again and I was lucky this time and the order for my departure will soon be here," Marvin wrote. "I don't know that it amounts to much though as I think the war will end just as soon as General Foch makes his big attack.

"I know it must be hard for a mother to have her sons go on such a long trip. I don't think there is half the danger that a person would naturally think. Somebody has to go so I think that I might as well go as anybody else."

And to what was it that Marvin was in such a hurry to get?

It was a question which Company D's survivors may well have asked themselves, had they known of the young Mississippian's conniving and inveigling to reach them.

Veterans now, they had learned all too well the war's realities, had seen George Anslow die in a swarm of bullets, had seen the mortally wounded Roy Hockenberry paw himself frantically, seen Dust, Davis, Durham, Wilson, and the others disappear before their eyes during the play of the machine guns and the mind-numbing bombardments in the last days of May.

The company's thinned ranks and missing faces in the billets in the rear of Cantigny were testament enough to the dangers they had already faced in battle—and as well were an ominous portent of the deadly and costly work to be done before war's close.

Another portent was the smell. The decomposing bodies of the Moroccans and Germans killed in April and the unburied remains of the Germans and Americans who lost their lives in the last days of May conspired to fill the air with a thick, nauseating odor.

"When the wind is right," wrote Major Raymond Austin, "you can smell Cantigny two miles away."

Company C commander Captain Charles Senay remembered one particularly foul and body-choked ravine between his position and that of Company A. "There were scores of corpses of French colonials," he wrote. "These bodies had leaked their substance into the ground beneath them. They could be easily lifted with one hand, but the ground beneath them was outlined with maggots. When attempting to eat, we were harassed by fat blue bottle flies which clung so avidly to our lips that they had to be plucked away."

However, the remains of one partially buried Moroccan in Senay's section of trench provided endless amusement. "The rain exposed his face and we said 'Heoo!' whenever we passed," Senay wrote, adding: "Exposed hands of cadavers were matriculously shaken."

It was a terrible place toward which John Nelson and his fellow replacements rolled that early June, and at which Company D and the 1st Division settled into what one commander would call "vigorous trench warfare"—the antithesis of the hoped-for open warfare and the dreams of long-legged American doughboys loping across open fields and through the German trenches, shooting and bayoneting their way toward Germany, toward Berlin.

Instead, the Americans found themselves in a stalemate, as had the British and French long years before, facing off against an enemy just yards away, within easy range of the dreaded snipers, once again manning forward trenches rife with cooties and watching men be buried alive, and crouching, hugging the sides of the ditch, as thousands of shells crossed overhead from both sides on each day, and all night.

(The doughboys faced other, less dangerous missiles as well. "Of course there are the usual calls of nature on the battlefield," Senay noted. "The normal procedure is to place dirt on the face of one of the tiny trench shovels, have a morning's morning and hurl the results, sometimes unaimed, over your shoulder in the direction of a presently empty shell hole. This can be disastrous if the other shell hole is occupied.")

Battalions rotated into the lines for eight or nine days at a time, to eat bad, cold food, to rest by day and to sculpt their trenches by night, digging and excavating and widening and laying claim to this small portion of France; or to slither into No Man's Land by night, under a sky by turns black and protecting or lit by the Very lights as bright and incandescent as a pool hall, under which they would freeze for long minutes, hardly breathing, until the darkness returned and they could again crawl, hearts pounding, chests about to explode, closer and closer to the Boche lines, where alert machine gunners waited to give a deadly burst at the slightest noise, a cough, a hiccup, the last utterance of some unlucky doughboy.

Second Brigade commander General Beaumont Buck would remember that in those first days of June 1918 the 1st Division's men were "bombed from the air, swept by hurricanes of machine gun fire, pounded by tornadoes of mid-range and long-range artillery," all the while digging, stringing wire, and consolidating the hard-won position at Cantigny.

With darkness, Buck wrote, life changed. "The rolling kitchens came as close as possible and distributed hot coffee and hot meals, the wounded were evacuated, patrols came and went, bulletins and messages delivered, new trenches staked out for vigorous digging in the intervals between enemy flares which lit up the scene bright as day."

For Company D, such fun was put off for a week, as the men of the 28th Regiment were allowed to regroup and lick their wounds. In his memoirs, George Marshall remembered how the ordeal at Cantigny had "badly racked the nervous systems of both officers and men," and left them exhausted. Now Company D's survivors reveled in a week of refitting and relaxing after being trucked to safe positions away from the front.

"The sky was clear and warm sunlight bathed the fields, filled with poppies and other spring flowers, making the little villages appear havens of comfort," Marshall wrote. "By the hundreds men cast themselves on the grass or slept or regaled themselves with the peaceful beauty of their surroundings."

Even as Company D lolled in the back lines, some of its dead were being eulogized and memorialized back home. When word of the death of one of the fallen, Private Ranzie Adams, reached Paragould, Arkansas, several weeks after Cantigny, the local paper sent a reporter to interview his mother, Emma Mayo.

"My boy said just before he left me, 'Mother, don't worry. I will give the last drop of my blood for my country, willingly and gladly, before I would see those Huns overrun our land and deal with you and sister as they have with the women of Belgium and France,'" Emma Mayo was reported to have told the paper.

"It nearly breaks my heart to lose my boy. To have died so far from home, but I am glad to give him for his country. Glad that he had the strong heart, courage and honor to volunteer and go gladly."

In Janesville, Wisconsin, the death of Richard Ellis, who at the age of just twenty had become the first of the Janesville boys to die Over There, had a marked effect on his grief-stricken younger brother Lyle, who was just eighteen and ready to avenge his brother, though perhaps prudently not from a frontline trench.

Lyle Ellis instead made plans to join the navy. "There is nothing for me to do around Janesville anymore and I am going to Chicago to offer myself to the navy with the intention and hope that soon I will have a chance to get a few of the Huns that killed my brother," he told the local paper.

His family and much of the town's residents, meanwhile, filled the pews of Janesville's Methodist church on June 9 to hear patriotic consolations— "It is sweet and glorious to die for one's country," one very alive parson would report—and well-wishing from a small army of reverends attending Richard's memorial.

The next day, the *Janesville Daily Gazette* reported that the first speaker, a Reverend Ewing, "likened the chivalry of the ancient days to that of the present time. The best instinct which humanity cherishes is that which leads men to lay down their lives that others may live.

"Our boys have gone forth as protectors and not as aggressors on the old theory that the strong shall protect the weak, not that the weak be made to fight against the strong.

"Richard Ellis died protecting us. Someone had to be the first and, though, we may hope not, others will follow; but always at the head of the list written in gold letters will be the name of the boy whose memory the entire community honors today."

Another minister, F. F. Lewis, would also speak of the glorious crusade in which Richard Ellis had fallen: "I consider this the most wonderful age in the days of Jesus. With all due honor to the boys who fought to preserve the Union in the days of the Civil war, I say that the boys who are fighting to-day are sharing the greatest honor which can be conferred upon man. I am most thankful that I have been given the privilege of living in these stirring times."

The men in the trenches needed no such reminder of the "stirring times" in which they lived. They knew by now that death could arrive from above, behind, or blithely from anywhere in front of them, and that even a stay in the hospital could not guarantee a free pass, as Company D's Sergeant Howard Tenbroeck, wounded in the shelling that claimed the life of Ellis, complained in a letter to his mother in Middletown, New York: "The Hun has great sporting, joyful times sniping our stretcher bearers who are plainly marked with the Red Cross. Then, to further amuse himself, he shells our first aid stations and ambulances going to the rear.

"But his greatest pleasure seems to be in bombing hospitals for a couple of hours at a time, and for further amusement he flies low and rakes with gun fire any wooden buildings or tents that he thinks may contain patients. Tell them about it in Middletown and that I have been all through it. My idea of 100 percent [happiness] is a dead Hun."

Even in those back lines, tensions were high as the great German offensive begun on May 27 rolled on to the right of the 1st Division's lines in a great, gray, engulfing tide that seemed almost unstoppable. By early June, the vanguard of the massed Germans was just fifty miles from Paris, where some residents gave up hope and fled for the coast and points south, even as the marines of the 2nd Division were fighting furiously to check the swarm at Belleau Wood.

Meanwhile, the 1st Division's doughboys set to work improving and fortifying their still-imperiled lines in front of Cantigny—a position which, after the battle was over, Captain Stuart Wilder found to consist of "two trenches, one a front line trench along the line finally consolidated as the front line. It was about four feet deep, quite straight, and continuous. There was no wire." A four-foot-by-six-foot hole, "like a shallow well," served as his company's command post. "It was very secure as only a direct hit could harm it but the chalk spoil thrown out shows more clearly on an airplane photograph and it drew artillery fire of all calibers."

The movement of runners, too, brought heavy fire from the Germans. Wilder recalled one runner who on June 4 was sent forward through shot and shell to deliver what surely had to be a message of life-and-death importance: "He risked his life at every step. At last he reached the support trench and made his way over [to] the anxious men who sought to learn his mission, and gave the writer an envelope. The top of the P.C. hole was fringed with concerned faces as it was opened."

The message read, "You will report with the morning reports this date the names of all men in your company who are graduate chemists."

But, Wilder added, the men were emboldened with the arrival of night, especially when there was plunder to be had. On one such evening, he wrote, "Three men left the front line and beat through the wheat far to the front . . . looking, it afterward developed, for the body of a German officer reported by a patrol to have a great diamond on its finger."

The dangers of daylight required relief of the companies in the front lines to be performed at night, when darkness, shell holes, wire, and bricks and stones conspired with the constant shelling from the German lines to turn each changing of the guard into a nightmare.

"Everything dark and shell holes and ruins and wires that trip you up if you don't watch your step," Private Bert Tippman, of the 18th Regiment's Company G, wrote of one such relief. "After several hours we saw flares sent up and we marched on until—'whiz-bang'—and a shell burst at the road side.

"The buzz of the shrapnel is close and our guide says, 'Hello, baby.' Another one bursts near us just as we dive in a trench and here we stay during the night and the shells shake the ground all night. The next day we moved a block but the shells seemed to follow us to our new position."

On June 6, Company D performed such a relief, reentering the hard-won position that had cost it two dozen dead. Humbled by the Americans, the Germans were expected to have another go at regaining their old lines in the ruined town in an effort to relieve some of the pressure farther south, and intelligence reports led the 1st Division to expect another blow on its positions on June 9.

But when the assault came, the brunt of it fell to the south of the ground the 1st Division held in front of Cantigny, and after four days of heavy bombardment by the Germans, the immediate threat passed.

Life in the trenches settled down to a blasé existence of constant artillery pounding, keeping aware of ever-watchful Hun snipers, the ever-present threat of a raid, and mud, dirt, and the stench of death churning anew with every shell that stirred the soil.

Long days were also spent keeping heads down and out of sight of the the German airplanes carrying artillery spotters overhead, while shells rained randomly for hours at a time—and more precisely when the Germans thought they spotted a "chow party"—food carriers bringing to the front the men's one meal a day.

American faced German with just yards of pounded and shell-shocked earth between them. "We crowded right up to the German barbed wire entanglements, ready to give the alarm in case of an attack," Private John Johnston wrote.

"We were so close to the Germans that often at night we could hear them digging in their trenches, and frequently could hear them swearing. In the daytime when the Germans were using their machine guns you could see the wheat heads being clipped off prettily. The bullets sort of sang as they came through the air, with a little whistling 'ping, ping, ping.'

"The one-pound shells which were being used largely imitated the lonesome night howl of a hound dog. Sometimes it almost drove a man crazy—the sound was so continuous and doleful and unholy."

One of those "doleful and unholy" missiles found its mark on June 12 in the front line manned by Company C, collapsing a section of its trench and burying several men alive.

"We could hear them under the muddy dirt and dug frantically to release them with anything available: helmets, bayonets, bare hands, breaking finger nails and mauling our fingers, all to no avail," Senay remembered.

"They suffocated before we could reach them. One was a corporal Friday who had recently received a letter from a soldier named Tuesday."

The barrage also "mangled" the company's seventeen-year-old Private George Gassenberger, blowing off one of his legs "among other injuries," Senay wrote. "We bandaged where we could and applied a tourniquet on the dismembered leg. He fought us and cursed us for nearly an hour before he died. All this in shell fire and rain."

Two nights later, Company D's Private Maxwell Marshall, a nineteen-year-old from Piscataway, New Jersey, was killed by shellfire as he crouched in the trenches. Whether he fought and cursed as had young Gassenberger, no one said; the odds are, though, that he may well have suffocated before he could be freed from the sticky, chalky ground.

But compared to the carnage endured at the end of May, casualties among the men of Company D through June were light, despite the thousands of shells and the continuous machine-gun fire being traded back and forth between American and German lines throughout the company's stay.

Company D's men once again manned the forward trenches, where they would be the first sacrificed in the event of a renewed German assault, and where they were ordered to stand fast and hold the lines no matter the circumstances.

George Marshall wrote that the men in the far forward lines of surveillance "were explicitly forbidden to withdraw, even though it was apparent they must be overwhelmed. Brutal as this arrangement may now seem, it was essential if the main line of resistance was to be maintained."

While in the trenches, patrols frequently were sent out by both sides, small squads of men slithering from their holes at night to cut through barbed wire and move stealthily through the devastation of No Man's Land and toward the enemy's lines just yards away.

Sometimes the brass was looking for prisoners; other times the patrols were sent out to listen for the sounds of German activity, of digging or the pounding of stakes, anything that might indicate the inching over of their trenches in an attempt to envelope, or least creep closer, to the Americans.

Company A's Private Fred Gaw left the trenches at midnight one evening on such a patrol, crawling through a wheat field toward the German line. Feeling his way in the darkness, "I put my hand on the face of a dead Morocco soldier, and I can still feel the chills it gave me," he would write home to Waukesha, Wisconsin.

"Once when we stopped I was close to a shell hole and someone was in it. I kicked him once and he never moved, so I stuck my trench knife in his back, but he was already dead."

Creeping up on a machine-gun emplacement at the top of a rise, Gaw and his small patrol formed a skirmish line. Suddenly, a shot rang out, and one of the doughboys fell wounded.

"We could now see them and immediately opened fire," Gaw wrote. "We killed one and he rolled down hill. The other was wounded and he set off a red rocket."

Germans ran from every direction in the blackness as Gaw hid in the grass. "I could hear the wounded German groan and there were several voices," he wrote. "They were everywhere. I then started to crawl up closer but just then a German jumped out of the bushes beside me and tried to grab me, thinking I was wounded.

"I had only two cartridges left in my pistol but I let him have these in the head. I then rolled down the hill. I told the lieutenant what I had seen and he decided to go back, as they might call for a barrage and catch us in it."

The patrol, and its wounded man, made it back to the American lines.

Company D sent out another such patrol late on the night of June 11, with Lieutenant John Church leading eight men, plus a covering team carrying automatic weapons, from the shelter of the trenches on a mission to observe and listen close to the German lines.

"While he was out, 3 Boche approached front line," the 1st Battalion's commander, Major George Rozelle, would write of Church's foray. "One of our sentries said 'Halt' & the three Boche proceeded to go through the line. One of our men became suspicious and went after them."

Two of the Boche ran, while a third "threw up his hands & surrendered. The two Boche separated and disappeared behind our lines in the dark," Rozelle wrote.

It would turn out that there were *four* Germans loose in Company C's sector, and a wild midnight chase ensued.

Charles Senay would write that one of the infiltrating Germans "had lived in Chicago and deceived my outpost corporal with American slang" (in his own report at the time, Senay wrote that the German, when challenged, had told the American sentry to "Shut up").

One soon found himself trapped in a barbed-wire entanglement. "He was ordered to surrender but panicked and was shot," Senay would remember. Another was ambushed by an "irate" and deceived Corporal Michael B. Ellis and was shot "through the kidney." A third "found concealment," Senay wrote. "He was shot the next night attempting to return to his lines."

The fourth was discovered by Senay and surrendered. "As I marched him back he said, "Ich bin gewundert," Senay wrote. "I said, 'Who?' He said, 'In den fuss.' So we stopped. He had a wound in the heel. He was sent to regimental headquarters, talked freely, and received good treatment."

That was more than could be said for the men on both sides who manned the trenches that June at Cantigny, where night brought barrages and the threat of infiltration, and where daylight brought the threat of death by a sniper's well-aimed bullet.

Constant as well was threat of artillery fire, Private Wilbert Murphy noted. "One surely can have some narrow escapes from the big shells that sing over your head and occasionally drop uncomfortably close to your hole in the ground—for the trenches are nothing more than ditches with occasionally a shelter overhead for protection from the shrapnel," he would write. "These high explosive shells of Fritz's surely have me buffaloed and I like to keep down when the shells are coming."

On top of the danger, the food was lousy and cold and, like the old joke says, came in *such* small portions. Soldiers received one meal a day, "and nothing short of extreme hunger could have made that palatable," the 1st Division's history notes.

Cooties—lice—infested every man, adding to the torture, while "water for washing was unknown . . . and it was only during the rest in the back area that delousing could take place."

As well there was the noise—a cacophony of shell blasts and the chattering *pup-pup-pup* of machine-gun fire and the droning from squadrons of airplanes dropping here a bomb, and there a bomb, or diving now to strafe.

And it was into such a world, into such an inferno, and into Company D that John Nelson and fifty-four other unwashed Camp Grant replacements would be dropped that June, to take the places of those killed or torn apart at the end of May at this same ruined village, and to don their gas masks and watch the skies, watch for Death, and learn their way around these foul and muddy trenches and this fouler war, of which no end seemed possible, and of which as well survival seemed improbable.

10

"I Wish I Had Two Lives"

WILLIAM DWIGHT WARREN WOULD soon enough lead a platoon of
Company D men across that road, and up that hill beyond, and make it the
base of that next hill in the Argonne, but at the moment he was in his foul
and cramped dugout in the lines before Cantigny. Above him, dirt sifted
from the edges of a circular sheet of corrugated iron that, along with sandbags and a log, served as his roof; at his feet rats tap-danced across the
hard, wet floor; a strip of burlap hung by two nails, and which served as his
bunk, cramped the ten-by-ten hole further; and darkness surrounded him
in this lair, punctuated only by the flickering light of a tiny candle. Suffocating in the close and damp hole on the evening of June 30, 1918, he negotiated the twelve-foot ladder from his netherworld abode and found refuge
in a small, nearby wood hidden from the searching eyes of the Germans, and
in a letter described his situation to his sister, Anna.

"Yes, my darling sis, I am now High Monkey Monk of the 1st platoon
and hold sway over 51 enlisted men, who jump to do anything I tell them
without asking the why or wherefore, but simply because they have my orders," Warren wrote.

"At present I feel somewhat independent since except for another lieutenant who commands the 2nd platoon and lives with me here in a luxurious hole in the ground, I am all alone with my men and only have communication with the Company Commander by means of my runner, so I am sort of King as it were of 300 yds. or so of ground."

He added: "Although it's about 7 p.m. the day for me is just about equivalent to the middle of the morning back in the days when I was an ordinary citizen. I rise at 2 P.M. or 4 P.M. and usually go to sleep at 4 or 5 A.M. or perhaps an hour later. Altogether I am very comfortably situated and except for the exaggerated 4th of July activities that take place every so often, life might be unutterably dull."

Laconic, ironic, and detached, Bill Warren would find endless bemusement in the situation in which he found himself in 1918. The embodiment of a separate, and usually upper, class of young lieutenants in the A.E.F., young men who'd memorized their Voltaire and Rousseau and their Pliny, who went sightseeing to Gothic churches in their off-hours and could expound about the situation in the Balkans and the decrepit Hohenzollern dynasty, Warren was one of those who seems never to have quite got over the almost laughable irony that he, of all people, had found himself in the army now, and leading men into mortal combat.

"We were a rather carefree, happy-go-lucky group," Charles Senay would write of the 28th Regiment's young officers, "burdened with a new and awesome responsibility and actuated by a high spirit of patriotism and belief in the justice of our cause."

Thousands of such carefree and, like Senay, highly educated twenty-somethings had jumped to enlist in the spring of 1917, and by virtue of their full or partial college educations, and certainly in many cases their pedigrees, had been sent off to fill the first officers candidate schools.

Among the 28th Regiment's commissioned officers alone there were Paul Waples Derrickson, Washington and Lee University, 1915; the Cantigny casualty Richard A. Newhall, Harvard, 1917 (Ph.D., History); Robert O. Purdy Jr., University of South Carolina School of Law, 1914; William O. P. Morgan, Harvard, 1918; George Guest Haydock, Harvard, 1916; and George Buchanan Redwood, Harvard, 1910.

Bill Warren, though by all evidence as inspired by the cause as any of the above, had not been born with the proverbial silver spoon. He had aspired to attend Cornell University, and certainly had the grades to get in, but family finances were such that he could not afford the Ivy League school, and when war broke out he was finishing his sophomore year at the Cornell School of Agriculture.

The antithesis of Sorey Sorensen in his origins, and for that matter of the partially schooled John Nelson and many of the other rough and barely literate immigrants and backwoods American boys he would find himself commanding, Warren had been raised in Elmira, New York, in a home filled with the orations of his hard-luck father, Orson, and a domineering maternal grandmother, Mary K. Eastman Osborne, "a cultured woman, famous for her Shakespearean readings," one newspaper account would say, who held sway over the household in which Bill and his older brother, Roger, and younger sister, Anna, grew up.

Bill Warren's daughter, Dorothy Rinaldo, wrote in *An Imperfect Genealogy* that Mary Osborne "did the cooking, sat at the head of the table, gardened, and had quite a lot to say about the upbringing of children. Roger characterized her as 'domineering,' frequently quarreling with her daughter. Bill remembered being chased under the bed by his grandmother with a broom."

Roger, five years older than Bill, was a hellion—"not the good student his brother Bill was. Roger sometimes got in trouble with the police." The Warrens "didn't know how to deal with such a youth."

Orson Warren, born in 1860, seems to have had as little luck in achieving professional success as he had in controlling his oldest child. Orson would admit in an autobiographical sketch he apprehensively wrote in 1934: "The fact is, I have during my career lingered near the bottom rung. Then, too, my life has been so full of blunders it isn't pleasant to think of having them paraded."

After a childhood spent in North Java, New York, Orson Warren went on to attend college in Chicago, Michigan, and Pennsylvania. He met Fannie Osborne at Chautauqua, New York, in the summer of 1889; the following year they married, and settled into a pleasant life in Elmira, where Orson taught and served as principal at Public School No. 1.

A former student wrote of the school and Orson Warren's tenure there: "Old No. 1 was a great melting pot and Professor Warren had a goodly number of tough kids to handle, and he used a method that some of us called the 'Warren Twist.' He would place his strong right hand firmly on the skull of the miscreant and spin him around as you do a top. By the time the victim landed, he was cured of all misbehavior—for the day at least."

In April 1907 Orson Warren abruptly resigned under a cloud. Though he denied it, his resignation seems to have come about because he had been "censured by the father of one of his pupils for compelling his boy to work about the school as punishment for poor deportment or pranks played during school hours," the local newspaper reported.

Dorothy Rinaldo wrote that Bill's father after resigning "paced up and down in the attic, declaiming Shakespeare and other orations." The troubles with her husband and oldest child caused Bill's mother to turn to religion, although, Rinaldo writes, Fannie Warren "rejected conventional Presbyterian beliefs and embraced what was then known as 'New Thought,' which encompassed some of the ideas from Eastern religions. Anna was embarrassed when she brought friends home and her mother 'collared' them and began expounding her beliefs."

Times, it seems, were hard and chaotic in the Warren household in Elmira, New York, where at the time Bill was just eleven years old, and his teenage brother Roger continued upon a life of juvenile delinquency.

"Orson with no job and a wayward son might well account for their mother's preoccupation with religion, and their father's lack of 'understanding' of Roger," Dorothy Rinaldo noted. "Certainly, it would have made for tension in the family life."

Bill Warren negotiated the chaos by retreating into books, developing a calm and detached persona that would serve him well in the overseas battles to come, but in the end put him at odds with the absurd minutiae of army life.

The Elmira Free Academy 1914 yearbook said of him: "It is the mind that makes the body rich. During his stay in this dear place, he gained distinction in several ways. He bubbles over with sparkling wit and furnishes amusement for the rest of the class.

"No one ever goes to sleep when he is around. It is a mystery to us how Bill always makes such brilliant recitations, for we never see him study. We will miss his smiling countenance and his luminous monocle."

On May 8, 1917, Bill Warren, then just twenty years old, enlisted in the army, and so became a doughboy. He was sent to Fort Niagara for officers training and was commissioned as a second lieutenant exactly six months later. Shortly after Christmas he stopped in Elmira on his way to the port at Hoboken to say good-bye to his parents.

"He remembered that when he said good-bye to his mother, she said that she didn't think she would see him again," Dorothy Rinaldo wrote. "At that time, I believe, he thought she was overly anxious."

By January 29, 1918, Warren was off the coast of France, impatiently waiting to be let off the troopship *Mongolia*. On February 9, Fannie Warren died of pulmonary tuberculosis, news that would take more than two months to reach her youngest son, who continued to send his mother letters before the disturbing news caught up with him in mid-April.

"Poor Mother," he would write, "how I do wish I had done more things to please her and left undone those things that didn't please her. That always seems to be the way in this world.

"When it is too late, then we realize what we ought to have understood long before. I am so far away I can hardly realize now that Mother is really gone; it will always be to me, I suppose, as if I had just left her behind, gone on a journey and never returned to her."

Slowly, by degrees, Warren's steps that spring were leading him toward Company D. After several weeks in France, he was sent to Company H of the 26th Infantry Regiment, and when the 2nd Brigade of the 1st Division marched into the trenches at Seicheprey, Warren went with it; on March 24, Warren wrote home of his "cozy" but boring routine while out of the lines: "It hardly seems possible that I am here, for a year ago my wildest dreams never went so far as this. Everything seems peaceable here and war would be very vague and unreal but for the occasional dull boom of air H.E. exploding somewhere far enough away to keep us from being worried.

"One of the soldiers billeted here in this room just mentioned the fact that it is Sunday night which in fact surprised me, for one day is so much like another that I feel like Robinson Crusoe must have, and am almost tempted to cut notches on a stick to keep track of the days."

On April 12, Warren wrote from his billet on a farm: "Everything is peaceful and war seems far away for the farm work goes steadily on with the aid of several Boche prisoners who live an exceedingly soft life in my opinion. Altogether I shall be sorry to leave this place but judging from former experience we never stay long in one place."

Bill Warren had made that long slog to Picardy with the 1st Division, though his battalion had not been one of those to see action during those terrible days at the end of May, during which Max Buchanan had been killed, and Lieutenants Ross Gahring and Frank Cooper put out of the war with severe wounds. The division had been quick to pluck Warren and Lloyd Bronston from the 26th Regiment, to replace the fallen, and according to Company D's morning report for June 6, the two appeared at the company's headquarters "and joined this date."

Bronston, too, had shipped across in January, taking leave of Cecile and Jason just weeks after completing officers training at Fort Sheridan, where near the end of his schooling one of the fort's French instructors had written and passed around a letter to the camp's newly commissioned officers.

"For him who has faith, the command of a company under fire has a powerful attraction," Captain George Etienne Bertrand of the Sixth Alpine Chasseurs had written, adding: "One of my comrades said, 'War would have passionate interest without shells, bullets, mud or barbed wire.' He was right, but he could have added, at the risk of complimenting himself: 'It is that which makes it inspiring.'"

In other words, "It is good that war is so terrible or we should love it too much." Shells, mud, barbed wire, bullets, mayhem—Lloyd Bronson in a few months would write home to Cecile and express his frustration that the 1st Division "seems to be doing all the fighting while the others hold the lines."

But for a short while, the wilderness of the trenches seemed as inviting to Bronston as the French gentleman had said, and after his first ten-day stint in those wilds with a platoon of Company D, Bronston would write home to Cecile and impart a read-between-the-lines idea of the "inspiring" dangers he and his men had faced.

"Have been up in the front line," he wrote. "Didn't expect last time to ever get back but am here again. I wish I had 2 lives one of my own and could keep in reserve yours and Jason's. I could afford to risk it oftener. I don't like to trifle with yours and Jason's but I'm afraid I have over-stepped a little sometimes.

"I can certainly tell many fairy tales when I get home. I haven't any souvenirs yet as I didn't want to collect any but have had hold of one Boche a few minutes after he was snuffed off. They get through the lines sometimes then you have to hunt for them. If you get drop on them, they yell Komrad, Komrad put up their hands and beg. They claim Americans are a bluff but I notice they are scared to death of them."

He didn't—couldn't—tell Cecile of the specific dangers he faced; but after the war, Bronston would describe the Cantigny sector as "one of the worst we were ever in, the Germans shelling us almost every 15 minutes and at no time more than 1/2 hour intervening, during the day.

"We kept shovels and tools in small piles to dig out men when a shell would hit in the ashey and dusty soil and succeeded in un-earthing many a man from smothering after a shell had buried him alive."

On June 17, Company D and the 1st Battalion left such dangers behind, and were trucked to the village of Chepoix, several kilometers to the southeast of Cantigny. Private Wilbert Murphy would note, "We got replacements here, and needed them, too, for several of the familiar faces were gone and quite a few boys were in the hospital."

The company's morning report for June 18 says simply: "55 recruits assigned to Co. . . . and joined this date"—among that bunch the Private First Class John Nelson, the son of Nils Jonsson, the son of Jon Nilsson, sires and scions of peace and peasantry.

And I wonder now what he thought of the situation in which he found himself as he was sent packing to his billet with his Springfield rifle in hand, and that faint and ominous *pup-pup-pup* and that constant and dull thudding drifting toward Chepoix on the wind from the northeast, from Cantigny.

"We don't get anything green here except recruits," Sergeant Willard Storms would tell his mother while ruing his soldier's diet; and while the replacements being trucked up to the lines had to have had some idea of what they were in for, playing war in the faux trenches back home couldn't prepare anyone for this, the ruination and destruction, the burnt smell of cordite and the stinging hot tinge of the mustard gas, and the quickly gained and fearsome knowledge that death lurked random and hungry and always on alert in the trenches, where experience helped keep one alive, but where the element of luck couldn't be counted out.

As well, Company D's veterans must have been a sight to John Nelson and the other newcomers—filthy and grimy and mud-spattered and bearded and exhausted, stacking their rifles in the musty storefronts and the vacated, spare homes of the village and falling out on the floors, as the crisp, innocent, and well-washed lambs to the slaughter were assigned to platoons and began to find their way around.

It was a varied group that entered Company D in mid-June. Besides the Swedes, John Nelson and August Hedblom and Edward Svejcar, there was the Greek, George Chiodras, and the Sicilian Ben Baucaro, whose immigrant father could be found sweeping the streets of Chicago's downtown each morning.

There was also the Pole, Zygmunt Misiewicz, who had been working as a florist on Chicago's Milwaukee Avenue when duty called; and Abe Sachs, a Russian immigrant who had worked as a teamster on the Chicago's West Side, and whose mother had told him to "go with God's blessing" when his number had come up the previous fall.

There were country boys, too, from all over the States, among them Solon Paul Gunderson, a son of Norwegian emigrants to Mindoro, Wisconsin; and the Norwegian immigrant Thomas Eidsvik, who had followed an older brother, Johan, to the promise of the United States, and who had been working as a ranch hand under the big sky around Enid, Montana, when the draft found him.

Many of these recruits—just a few of the more than thirty thousand replacements the 1st Division alone would call on before war's end—had had little time to partake of the American dream before being gathered up and shipped back to the Old World from which they'd fled, and as a bunch they contrasted sharply with many of the company's original members, some of whom could trace their American pedigree to the turn of the previous century and beyond, and who had ancestors who'd fought on both sides in another great calamity—this one a domestic clash—just fifty years before.

But with the entry of the new recruits, the company became a true melting pot (maybe even more complete than the ones in all of those hackneyed Second World War movies), a mélange of foreign and regional accents, and a better reflection of the ethnic revolution the United States was undergoing as it entered the twentieth century, where in the first ten years alone almost 9 million immigrants arrived on American shores.

From this vast amalgam of different tongues, traditions, and experiences the A.E.F. drew heavily, enlisting half a million immigrants before the war ended.

By mid-June, Company D's ethnic makeup—the purebred Americans, the Swedes John Nelson and Otto Swanson, the Pole Zygmunt Misiewicz, the Argentinian Ralph Pol, Niccolo Bracco and Pasquale Carravetta from Italy, the Irish Bartley Larkin, the Pole Joseph Nichyporek, and the Norwegian Eidsvik—closely mirrored that of the fictional unit described by James Wharton in his book *Squad*: "Ole Anderson, a Swedish-American rancher from the Texas Panhandle. Stanley G. Allen, American, a high school youth from San Francisco. James Marzulak, Serb, a miner from Coal Valley, Pennsylvania. Harvey Whittaker, American, from Oklahoma City, Oklahoma. Emmanuel Waglith, Jewish proprietor of a shoe store in the Bronx, New York. Giuseppe Novelli, from 'Little Italy,' South Eight Street, Philadelphia. Michael O'Connors, itinerant Irish-American worker."

The mélange of races and languages proved exasperating to some officers who liked their army homebred and white bread. General Beaumont Buck, commander of the division's 2nd Brigade, wrote of an episode in October 1917 as he visited a gang of 1st Division soldiers constructing trenches, and to his consternation found few who could speak English.

Espying an Adonis with blue eyes, brown hair, and rosy cheeks, Buck thought, "Aha! At last I have found a real American! I will speak to him."

Buck wrote in his memoirs: "I said, 'Young man, what is the idea of having this hump of earth projecting out into the trench?'

"He looked up brightly, and without hesitation replied: 'Dot, Sir, ees to brodect dem mens in der trench from bullets goming from der flanks!'

"I said, 'Right you are,' and passed on."

Captain Stuart Wilder wrote that while many among the first batch of replacements sent to his company in the 16th Regiment in 1918 were foreign-born, they were willing and able soldiers.

"Thirty-six were German-, Austrian- or Turkish-born, and several could speak no English whatsoever," Wilder wrote. "There were many Poles and Russians and Jugo-Slavs of various sorts; a racial group of high quality were Cornishmen from the mines at Butte."

Wilder would write as well that he found "no difference between them and native Americans in courage or willingness or the conduct which we commonly consider to be inspired by patriotism.

"They were generally more amenable than the true American to discipline, particularly the Slavs, and were as enduring of physical hardship. They lacked in quickness of perception but much of this can be explained by the language difficulty."

In Company D, the entry of this immigrant class constituted a second generation of soldiers, all having been rousted from their pursuit of life, liberty, and happiness in the hope they could stop bullets as well as the native sons.

Warren took some of these men into the first platoon after he left the trenches, and surely some of them must have wondered at this teacher's son, this detached intellectual, who must have seemed educated beyond all reason to the grunts who could barely spell their own names.

But Warren took quickly to his new command, telling his father, without further explanation, that his transfer from the 26th Regiment "was much to my liking, for the men seem to be a much better type than I formerly had."

And he was patient and circumspect when describing his men: "My platoon is made up of all types of men, from ignorant men who can scarcely write, to intelligent men who can write very interesting letters. As one of my duties is the reading and censoring of all letters written by my platoon, I can thus get very good insight of their characters. Most of them are good men, anxious to do the right thing and brave in the face of danger."

One of these men may have been John Nelson; I'll never know. I do know it's improbable that he wrote any "interesting" letters back home to his parents Nils and Ingrid. I know he could write, but never did, not a birthday card or a letter to a grandchild at camp or even a grocery list.

But I can relate some of what he saw through the words of Bill Warren, who seemed unable to stop writing, at every stop and in every conceivable situation describing what he was seeing, and some of what was happening to him, in a letter penned on June 21 describing his billets in Chepoix: "This village is not torn up by big shells, it is practically deserted by civilians and I am occupying a house which belongs to an old lady living here all by herself at present. The front yard is what you and I would call the barn yard, as it is littered up like one with a manure pile, odds and ends of implements and the like.

"Between the house and the street is the barn in which resides a solitary cow that furnishes milk which I buy from the old lady for our officers' mess. I have a splendid bed to sleep in and even though it is shared by another lieut., it pleases me considerable, for the cold hard ground often serves a soldier for a bunk."

And there was this vignette from the evening of June 30, 1918, when, back in the front lines with Company D, he scribbled in that small copse next to his luxurious hole in the ground, and a small drama played out over his head: "As I was writing I heard some aeroplanes buzzing overhead and some machine guns popping away. I had just finished the sentence, when someone said one plane was coming down.

"I hustled to the edge of the wood and saw the plane come down in flames inside our lines, but didn't know whether it was a German or Allied machine. I sure hope it was the former."

Despite the ongoing nuisances of war, Warren was happy and content. "Really the whole aspect of this little place is delightful," Warren wrote to his sister on June 30. "The sun is about 2 hours up from the horizon and sheds just the right kind of a warm glow to give light to writing and heat for warmth.

"You see the world is topsy turvey as you may have decided by this time. We sleep in the day when all supposedly civilized people are awake and at night, we are wide awake and perform all our duties.

"Consequently I have become wonderfully well acquainted with all the stars of the universe, see the sun set at night and watch it rise in the morning."

Lloyd Bronston wrote home a few weeks later to tell of a hard-won battle trophy: "I am enclosing 2 pieces of a Boche helmet, a souvenir taken right up close to the Boche. We didn't figure on giving it back to the Dutch either until the last man was gone.

"Well I made some noise pounding that piece of helmet off the Boche's helmet just around where the hole is in it, I don't know whether he was killed by shrapnel or bullet. I didn't kill him anyway."

In his inimitable deadpan style, Bronston would also intimate some of the particular miseries being endured by the men in the front lines: "Well I've found out how to go without sleeping. We can't sleep much in the trenches but if I drink 3 or 4 cups of coffee (black) I don't need it.

"You know they almost discovered how to live without eating and I guess they would have it down pat only the subject happened to die just as they were completing the experiment. If he hadn't and people would take that course of mine about sleeping they could keep a lot of chow party's from getting shot up."

And Bronston, like many doughboys, had a few things to say as well about one particular misery of trench life: "O I forgot to tell you about the 'cooties.' Almost all the officers get them as well as the men and I had never had any until this last trip, had almost made up my mind that I was immune and I wouldn't have had but one except it happened to be a lady cootie.

"Well next morning the old lady presented me with her off springs and I had me a family. I went back to first aid station and got some antidermic but I got so nervous waiting around for the Boche to come over I had them all scratched off so gave it to my runners (not the cooties, the lysoseptic)."

Out of the lines, away from the shelling and the constant zipping of machine-gun bullets and the long and exhausting nights spent on post, some normalcy reigned.

Ball games, band concerts, and the ministries of the Young Men's Christian Association—whose work, and that of the Red Cross, was lauded by each and every doughboy who was ever in need of a cup of coffee, a cookie, or a pack of smokes—provided some connection to home, and some respite from the grinding trench warfare that Pershing had hoped to avoid, but in which his army had almost inevitably become entrapped.

While strict censorship prevented the description of a doughboy's whereabouts or his unit's actions, lest an unmailed letter fall into the hands of the Germans upon death or capture, the subalterns who spent evenings reading their men's mail allowed some mention of their back-line activities, the weather, and allusions to the action they had seen.

Also allowed was talk of what they would do when they got home. Charles Senay remembered censoring the letter of one soldier who had "a sweetheart who was always writing about scenery. His remark was, 'Sweetie, look at all the scenery you are able to. When I get home you are going to see nothing but the ceiling.'"

(The officers, though, censored their own mail in many instances with a light pen; Lieutenant Harry Martin's vivid account of the Battle of Cantigny brought him a reprimand the following September after it was discovered that his letter home "duly found its way into a weekly publication" in Martin's hometown of Emporia, Kansas. "In the future, Lieut. Martin's letters will be censored by his commanding officer," the 1st Division's General Order No. 59 declared.)

Sounding somewhat shell-shocked, Private Murphy wrote home that June to tell some of what he had experienced in the front lines, and to describe some of the blessed boredoms of backline life: "We're billeted now in a good looking French town and are getting a much needed rest," he wrote. "It seems good to get away from the sound of the guns. It gets on my nerves. Bombardments and barrages are nerve racking worlds of noise, clouds of smoke, and showers of rock and shrapnel.

"There is a Y.M.C.A. where we can buy cookies and sweets and get paper to write on, and then there is a Red Cross here. They give away hot chocolate and 'smokes' and treat us fine, in fact they are about the best quarters I've been in in France."

And on June 23, he sent these lines about a Sunday in the rear lines: "We had a ball game this afternoon. Our company beat the machine gun company. It was quite a game and a diversion from the ordinary routine of events.

"This morning there was a band concert. The music was good and I surely believe the man who said that music hath charms. I know it made me feel a whole lot better."

In the last days of June, Company D returned to the trenches, this time with its complement of replacements. The action was slight, and even the shelling decreased as the war's hot spots drifted to the south and west, where the Boche continued their march toward Paris even as the 1st Division held the line in Picardy.

Conditions in the trenches had not become any better since the company's last tour in mid-June. After inspecting the lines around Cantigny, 1st Division adjutant Major H. K. Loughry reported on July 2: "Clothing is fairly satisfactory; there is need, as reported, for a greater supply of breeches, shoes, underclothes and socks. Major Whitener was of the opinion that no evening hot meal should be served in Cantigny. There have been a considerable number of casualties among the carriers.

"The firing trenches are almost continuous but of insufficient depth. Latrines are being dug but sanitation is poor; men are deflacating [*sic*] in shell holes."

Loughry also discerned a troubling change in the character of the units, a change wrought by the slaughter in the same lines just one month before: "Physical condition of men is good but they are tired mentally and physically. Have 'trained off.' There are too many new men, received as replacements, that the men do not know each other and companies have ceased to be homogenous units."

Despite the continuing hardships, on July Fourth some levity prevailed in the form of a destructive fireworks display sent into the German lines. "We made things warm for Boche the 4th of July," Rollin Livick would write in one of his last letters. "They retaliated in the evening. Some place to celebrate the 4th in the front line."

On the same day, the last of the wounded from Cantigny passed on. Corporal Phillip Peterson, who had heroically advanced seventy-five yards in front of the company on the morning of May 28 and used an automatic weapon to help deter a German counterattack, died of his wounds after lingering for more than a month.

"I used to go in and see him every day and he seemed to be getting all right," said another of those wounded at Cantigny, Private Charles Lynn. "He died suddenly on the night of July 4th, 1918. He being one of the first men to die in this hospital he was given a military burial and a very beautiful ceremony."

On the night of July 7, the company withdrew again from the trenches. Billets were found in the village of Breteuil, where vacated homes and shops offered a haven from the cootie- and filth-infested front lines.

The company's men fell out, thankful for a respite from the action—

and hopeful of a long stretch in the rear lines in which to clean up, reorganize, refit, and train the newcomers to the dance.

Lloyd Bronston sat down on July 10 in his billet on the Rue de Voltaire to write a long, rambling letter home to Garnett, Kansas, in which he described his situation, alluding to his mother, Beulah, and brother, Manford, also serving with the A.E.F. in France: "Well I just got in and find my windows all camouflaged and my pistol oiled and holster shined and bunks made everything in fine shape. I had a whole lot of letters to censor and when I got through I took them to the orderly room and the Serg't. handed me some mail. It was U.S. army emblem paper envelopes from Beulah, came just in time to use as this is all paper I could find.

"I wrote Manford here in France but didn't tell him if he did not receive the letter to write and let me know. Had to write it on back of blank checks."

On the same evening, John Church sipped "a nice bottle of wine" and wrote to his cousin Charles Crispin in Brooklyn, and, as Bronston had, mentioned the plague of lice in the trenches: "I have managed to keep the cooties away fairly well but the last time in I sure got lousy but of course after getting over I got rid of them."

Though obviously wanting to say more, Church adhered to the censorship guidelines while alluding to the great victory at Cantigny. "One of the engagements I was in my regiment went over and cleaned up several Boche ones drove them back about 1 1/2 miles and held what they took, sure was a hot time for awhile. My platoon went over in the first wave. 7 counter attacks were [made] against us to their sorrow."

Rollin Livick was also busy writing home to Edgerton, Wisconsin. "It's not necessary to tell you the reason for my delay in writing. I have been at the front again," he wrote on July 10. "Things were the same as usual, possibly a little more quiet.

"We are now resting quietly in a fairly large town. Will probably be out of the trenches for a while. Have a large house to sleep in. The first since leaving home. It was used for a store before the town was evacuated."

And in his last surviving letter, penned to his brother Jim on July 11, Rollin wrote: "Have been at the front several times since writing you last. To make a good job of it we went over the top. Surely it is some experience. We are now stationed in a fair sized town. Our billet is a large store, which has been vacated. The town is in reach of the Ger. guns. It's the first house I've slept in for some time. It's by far the best billet we've had since we landed here.

"The weather is rather cool. The days are real long. Showers are frequent. I'm getting along dandy and feeling fine."

Within days, the company's hard-won reverie would be ended, and the men's hopes for a long rest denied, as the fluid events on the Western Front would pick them up and place them not back in the dank and treacherous trenches, but upon a vast, rolling, and sunlit plateau where the next, great event of the war was to take place.

The name of the place: Soissons.

11

Into the Wheat

AND HE'S INTO IT up to his neck now, the Old Man, lying here broken, bent, and paralyzed but awake on some cool, dark field in the Old World, with a hole on either side leaking blood, and the terrible and guilty confessions of some other sorry son of a bitch pouring into his ears, two almost lifeless soldiers come to lick the kaiser but instead they're pinned into the wheat damp with the midnight dew like throwaway doughboy rag dolls, with the faint flutter of Death tickling the back of his neck, but, luckily for him, there's just too much for Death to do this night, with so many bent and broken boys, and so little time.

And how many times would he return there, while staring into the television with an unread newspaper on his lap, return to that unmentionable night, to the sounds of sporadic artillery fire and the groans and screams of the others just beyond the Paris-Soissons Road, so many years to live with that, so many July nineteenths to bring back the strange sensation of drifting, maybe, drifting helpless like one of God's castaways.

And I wonder if he returned there years later, so many years later, when toward the end of his life he was dragged kicking and screaming from all that he'd known in Chicago to the tiny Wisconsin town to which my parents retired, and he found himself quickly adopted by the boys in the local Veterans of Foreign Wars chapter, who would stick him in a jeep in the holiday parades, and where he would sit, not waving, just a crease of a smile on his face, his Purple Heart pinned to his brown jacket, as he rolled down Highway 42, parting a small sea of fluttering red, white, and blue flags as if he were some Doughboy Moses come down from the Mount.

They advertised him as the last living First World War veteran in the county, and it may have been then that he felt he was for the first time in his life receiving the proper respect for what he'd done, for the bullet he'd taken, and for the night he'd spent in the wheat by the Paris-Soissons Road.

They'd even written him up in their newsletter, his one latent and small measure of fame, with a photograph of him in his brown suit and his VFW cap and his Purple Heart, the tough old doughboy at the age of ninety-eight looking wan and overexposed and very, very frail.

"On July 19th in a major battle outside of Swoosa, John was shot in the abdomen, and made his way to a field hospital where he found help and was evacuated for major surgery to an Army hospital in Paris. According to John, the hospital's chief surgeon said only a tough Swede could have survived his type of wound."

That they had mangled the name of the place didn't matter. They had cut to the heart of the story, of his story, of my story—*Soissons*.

Today the area southwest of Soissons in summer looks much as it did in 1918, with long rows of wheat ripening in the sun, narrow and ancient roads slicing across an impossibly flat tableland before twisting and winding through the deep ravines of Missy and Ploisy, and picturesque villages—Missy-aux-Bois and Ploisy, Chazelle, and Berzy-le-Sec—marking the edges of the plain like thumbtacks on a gold-and-green tapestry.

The area looks much the same, but the sounds are wholly different, the gentle rustle of the wind through the wheat obscuring the long-ago echoes of the big guns, the *pup-pup-pup* of the machine guns, and the screams, memories, and last words of the men who fell during what Wilbert Murphy in a long letter home would sum up as "Five Days I Will Never Forget."

It was here that so many of Company D's men would go "missing since recent operations," and be listed as such on that August roll, the living tangled up with the dead in the confusion wrought by a costly stop-and-go advance, of all-out charges and retreats and more charges, until the fields ran red with doughboy blood and the Germans grudgingly gave way and lit out for the east, leaving behind—so legend claims—many of their bravest chained to the Maxims hidden in the wheat.

And it was here that the Old Man would fall on the second day, just one of hundreds of boys who did so, many never to arise again, one of hundreds of Moroccans and Americans and Germans and Frenchmen, and just one of many from Company D itself who would fall over the course of those five days, each one a tiny turning point within a larger drama that, the historians would later write, became the "turning of the tide" of the Great War.

But none of them could have known that when, on July 7, 1918, Company D was relieved after an eight-day stint in Cantigny's trenches and fell out in the village of Breteuil. Lounging, cleaning up, writing letters home, eating decent chow—none expected any action for weeks.

In fact, rumors sweeping through the 1st Division went so far as to have its work in France done, and its next mission that of promoting Liberty Loans in the States, or putting down a rebellion in Ireland, or action in Italy, or intervening in the revolution then convulsing Russia.

Such wild and uninformed musings still held the day by July 13, when Company D moved with the 28th Regiment to Plailly for further rest and refitting. "The whole countryside was mantled in green and the people received the 'Men of Cantigny' with warm hospitality," the regimental history says. "Many of the men were strolling along the country roads; others were sleeping, and all were enjoying the quiet that prevailed. Everything seemed to indicate that there was to be a period of rest."

At 3:30 P.M. on July 15, the reverie was broken, and orders were handed down for the 1st Division to saddle up, once again, this time for a destination unknown. It's a soldier's lot to grumble, and certainly within the ranks of Company D there were mumbled protests at a quietude cut short. But as the division packed up and began trucking along the narrow French roads, the mood of the men changed when they realized they were headed not back to the trenches at Cantigny, but to new and open country.

Murphy later described the excitement that raced through the Americans as their forces gathered.

"Very short notice was given to get ready to move and it only took us twenty minutes to get our packs rolled and get into the trucks," he wrote. "We went by trucks to the Bois-du-Compeigne, and what a sight that line of trucks made on the road. Strung out for miles as far as one could see were trucks. It seemed as though there were an endless number of them, all filled with happy but expectant Doughboys. We imagined something was up."

What was up was a plan that had been in the works for weeks—a seizing of the initiative from the Germans, who had unveiled five separate offensives since March 21, but whose last was running out of steam. Between May 27 and June 5, the German's had rolled south to the Marne across a fifty-mile front extending from Noyon to Reims, creating a pocket more than thirty miles deep that had swallowed the ancient city of Soissons. From there a key road—the Soissons to Château-Thierry highway—and a railway kept the forty German divisions within the salient supplied with guns, ammunition, food, and replacement troops.

But the deep bulge—"Look at that balloon!" Frederick Palmer quoted Pershing as saying every time he viewed the situation map that June—whose southern limit lolled at the northern bank of the Marne was seen as an opportunity by Pershing and those on the French staff to whom reacting, and not taking the fight to the Germans, had grown tiresome.

A bold counterstroke was needed, and the place for it was right there on the situation map before them. So even as the German advance crested, and even as the German general Erich Ludendorff sensed final victory and made preparations for what he hoped would be one last, successful push on Paris, the Allies made plans for an offensive of their own that might pop that "balloon."

It was on the shoulder of the pocket that the offensive would be launched, its aim being to slice east across the salient just below Soissons and breach the German supply lines and force a retreat; if the assault could be made quickly enough, it might even encircle the Germans.

An all-out German push to cross the Marne and expand that bridgehead southward was expected, and even encouraged, by the Allies, who hoped that it would carry that many more men and that much more matériel into the bag—the "trap" Foch would call it—to be cut off by the Allied counteroffensive.

Artillery on the south side of the Marne was pulled back, as were front-line infantry positions. And when the German drive was launched in the early hours of July 15, the German artillery fired into empty trenches; when assault troops manned boats to cross the river, they were cut to shreds or cut off from their support by quick-arriving Allied troops—including those from three American divisions—that rushed to the front.

By the end of July 17, Ludendorff called off the offensive, and a crucial first element of the counterstroke had been gained: The Marne had been held. And by that time, thousands of Americans were on their way east, marching through the dark Retz Forest to jumping-off positions just a few miles southwest of Soissons, ready to seize the initiative from the Germans once and for all.

The 1st and 2nd Divisions, both veteran outfits now, were attached for the assault to the French Tenth Army to form, with the 1st Moroccan Division (including elements of the celebrated French Foreign Legion), the XX Corps, and would attack at the neck of the bag below Soissons, the 1st Division on the northern edge of the advance and the 2nd on the south, with the Moroccans in between.

The knife thrust at the northwest edge of the pocket, set days prior for a jump-off on July 18, would "aim for the jugular," Douglas Johnson wrote in his study *Soissons 1918*, while the Allied divisions still holding the line farther south, at the bulging southern limit, "would pummel the body."

The 28th Regiment, on the northernmost flank of the 1st Division, was assigned the toughest task, that of advancing through the deep ravines that split the countryside, which offered a host of defensive positions in gullies and caves and the stone buildings of small villages and large farmsteads.

On the 28th's left would be a colonial French division, the 153rd, and to its right would be the 26th Regiment, with the 16th Regiment to its right and the 18th Regiment advancing on the southern flank of the division's assault.

Timing was everything for the Allies, who planned to smash the German forces before they could fully consolidate the gains they had made. To that end, on the night of July 15 the 1st and 2nd Divisions were hastily assembled and began moving toward the front, bringing up men and artillery. Early on the morning of the sixteenth the 1st went into bivouac in the Compiègne Forest. Company D spent July 16 under cover of the woods to avoid being spotted by German aircraft and "doing our best to scrape up what 'chow' was available," Murphy wrote. "Some of us found a deserted garden with plenty of 'spuds' so we were fortunate in that way."

Meanwhile, the American buildup continued even as the German effort was ebbing. "All the time we were in the forest the main road was just jammed with traffic, troops, tanks, guns, trucks with ammunition and supplies," Murphy wrote.

"In the distance one could hear the steady rumble, like thunder, of the exploding shells and cannons. Somebody was getting h— at that time, you know Fritz was just being checked in his last drive."

While most of the division moved on July 17 to the area around Mortefontaine—eight miles west of the jump-off point—Company D and the rest of the 1st Battalion, 28th Infantry, were held in divisional reserve at Pierrefonds-les-Bains, about six miles to the west, and would have to travel that much farther to the front line.

At 9:00 P.M. on the seventeenth, the bulk of the 1st Division left Mortefontaine. As the huge assemblage of men, horses, and artillery wended its way east, with much of the infantry following trails pocked with shell holes, a violent rainstorm started. Major Clarence Huebner, commander of the 28th's 2nd Battalion, remembered: "The darkness became so intense that it was impossible for the men in ranks to see the men in front of them. The trail, which was bad at best from recent shelling, now became a quagmire of mud and it was necessary to close the units without distance and have the men hang onto the equipment of the man ahead. Great difficulty was experienced in keeping the column from being broken as the men were constantly slipping and falling in shell holes.

"As the column approached the front, the roads and trails were filled with hundreds of horses, cannon, motor trucks, tanks and artillery on the way to their positions. It was only by almost superhuman efforts on the part of the officers and the men that the battalion ever reached its destination."

Things were no better to the south, where the Janesville boys' former commander, Captain Edgar Caldwell, was leading his new command, Company A, 16th Regiment, on its slog to the battlefield.

"It was tough going," Caldwell would write, "climbing up the sides of steep ravines with the ground so slippery from the rain that you could scarcely keep your footing. The woods were full of shell holes, half filled with water, and a man would miss his footing and fall in one and half a dozen more would pile on top of him in the inky darkness. I fell in at least a dozen times and was mud from head to foot."

The assault was set to begin with a brief artillery bombardment of the German positions just prior to the 4:35 A.M. jump-off. Because of the traffic and difficulty moving forward through the rain and mud, many units struggled to be in place at the appointed hour. Complicating things as well was the fact that big changes had been made in the leadership of the 1st Division on the very cusp of battle, the foremost being that its commander, General Robert Lee Bullard, was promoted to corps commander and was replaced by the 1st's artillery commander, General Charles P. Summerall.

In addition the 28th's commander, Hanson Ely, was given a brigade command in the 2nd Division under James Harbord; taking Ely's place, just sixteen hours before the 28th was to jump off, was Colonel Conrad S. Babcock, a former cavalry officer with no combat experience, who over the next four days would struggle as mightily (and to the detriment of his army career) as had Ely at Cantigny to prevent the ruination of the regiment.

More pressing to the regiment's company commanders were other unknowns: There was a paucity of maps and an almost total ignorance of the ground over which the march to the battlefield was to be made as well as the terrain over which the attack was to roll.

French guides had been assigned to each company to lead them to their spots in the assault trenches, but even guides could become lost, as happened with the Frenchman leading Company H to the front. Harassed by artillery fire, the guide lost his sense of direction and began leading the unit back west. An officer with the 26th Regiment finally set things right, and Company H made it to the jump-off trenches with minutes to spare.

Once in the front lines, which stretched for 2,800 meters across the division front, soldiers fell out, some instantly nodding to sleep and others quietly pondering what lay ahead. Caldwell and his company arrived at 2:30 A.M. "Most of them took to their places and immediately fell fast asleep," he wrote.

Private First Class John Nelson, 1917.
(*Courtesy of the author*)

Private First Class John Nelson, seated third from right, Christmas
morning, 1917, Camp Grant. (*Courtesy of the author*)

John and Karin Nelson in 1991.
(*Courtesy of the author*)

Captain Soren C. Sorensen.
(*Courtesy of Margaret Brackett*)

Captain Charles T. Senay.
(*Courtesy of Timothy Senay*)

Lieutenant Marvin Everett Stainton.
(*Courtesy of Hubert M. Stainton Jr.*)

Private Rollin Livick.
(Courtesy of Linda Matzke)

Lieutenant Marvin Everett Stainton.
(Courtesy of Hubert M. Stainton Jr.)

Private Paul Davis (SEATED). *(Courtesy of Arnold Davis)*

Back Row, left to right: Mabel Davis, Paul Davis, Viola Davis, Beulah Davis. Front Row, left to right: Linn Davis, James Hyrum Davis, Eliza Davis with baby Ernest on her lap. (*Courtesy of Arnold Davis*)

Sergeant Willard Sidney Storms.
(*Courtesy of Diane Williamson*)

Lieutenant William Dwight Warren.
(*Courtesy of Dorothy Rinaldo*)

Company D's Lieutenant William Ross Gahring. (*Courtesy of Judy Balzer-Cash*)

Lieutenant George E. Butler.
(*Courtesy of Tom Butler*)

Sergeant James Whalen with his wife,
Gilla Mae. (*Courtesy of Michael Whalen*)

Major George Rozelle, left, commander of the 28th Regiment's 1st Battalion, with Company B's Lieutenant James Howland Donaldson on July 15, 1918—just three days before jumping off at Soissons. (*Courtesy of Rita Rozelle Schimpff*)

Lieutenant John Huston Church.
(*Courtesy of Ann Cooper*)

Corporal Tempton Corwin Hall.
(*Courtesy of Beverly Rush*)

Private Leigh Ellsworth Wilson.
(*Courtesy of Dorothy Geduldig*)

Huckleberry Shell, as a sergeant in 1919. (*Courtesy of the William Hammond Mathers Museum*)

Lieutenant Jason Lloyd Bronston. (*Courtesy of Jason Bronston*)

Thomas Dewey Slinker, as a sergeant in 1919. (*Courtesy of the William Hammond Mathers Museum*)

Officers of the 28th Regiment's 1st Battalion, April 24th, 1918. FRONT ROW, RIGHT TO LEFT: Co. D commander Soren C. Sorensen, Co. C commander Charles T. Senay, Co. D Lieutenant Max Buchanan, Co. B Lieutentant James H. Donaldson, 1st Battalion commander Maj. George F. Rozelle. (*U.S. National Archives*)

Company D, 28th Regiment at rest in the back lines near Seicheprey, March 10th, 1918. The company entered the trenches for the first time just a week later. (*U.S. National Archives*)

Bois de Cantigny   Montdidier – Cantigny road   Cantigny   1st U.S. Div Monument

Bois Carré   Bois Suisse

Cantigny, view from the southeast of the village, circa 1925. (*American Battle Monuments Commission*)

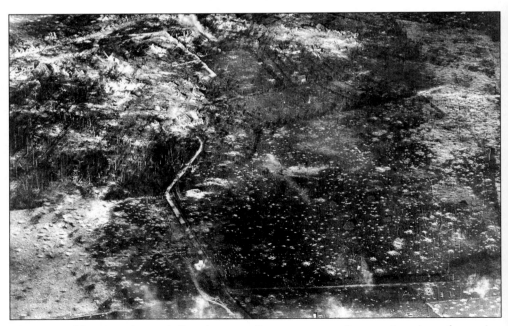

The ruins of Cantigny (upper left) and surrounding area as seen from an American observation plane, May 28th, 1918. (*U.S. National Archives*)

Troops from the 28th Infantry Regiment following the barrage in their assault on Cantigny, accompanied by French tanks. (*U.S. National Archives*)

The 28th Infantry Regiment goes over the top at Cantigny, May 28th, 1918. (*U.S. National Archives*)

Germans captured at Cantigny being escorted to the back lines by military police at Mesnil-St.-Fermin, May 28th, 1918. (*U.S. National Archives*)

The ruins of Cantigny in spring 1919. (*U.S. National Archives*)

American dead at Cantigny. (*U.S. National Archives*)

The village of Cantigny in 2008, looking east from the Bois Suisse, from which Company D jumped off on May 28, 1918. (*Courtesy of the author*)

Ploisy and Ploisy Ravine, looking east toward Berzy-le-Sec (out of sight to the right), circa 1925. (*American Battle Monuments Commission*)

French cavalry moving up to support the First Division advance south of Soissons, July 16, 1918. (*U.S. National Archives*)

Captured Germans carrying wounded 1st Division soldier near Soissons, July 19, 1918. (*U.S. National Archives*)

Advanced aid station of the 1st Division at Missy-aux-Bois, July 20, 1918. (*U.S. National Archives*)

Germans and machine guns captured by the 28th and 26th Infantry Regiments, near Lahayville, France, September 12, 1918. (*U.S. National Archives*)

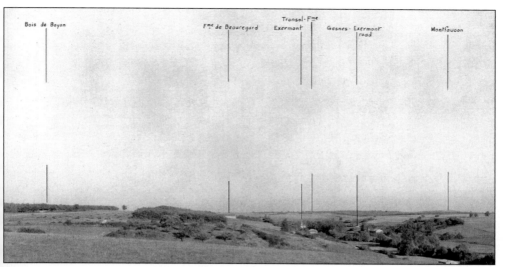

Bois de Bayon   Fᵐᵉ de Beauregard   Transol·Fᵐᵉ Exermont   Gesnes· Exermont road   Montfaucon

Scene of the fighting at Exermont and Beauregard Farm, viewed from the west, circa 1925. (*American Battle Monuments Commission*)

Captured German huts in the Nonsard Woods, September 12, 1918. (*U.S. National Archives*)

A machine-gun company of the U.S. 1st Division in action near Exermont, October 4, 1918. (*U.S. National Archives*)

Soldiers of the 18th Infantry Regiment dug in on Hill 240, October 11, 1918. (*U.S. National Archives*)

The village of Exermont. (*U.S. National Archives*)

Arietal Farm in 2008, center, looking north. Hill 263 rises above the Petit Bois in the background; the Bois de Moncy is on the right, while on the left the grassy slopes rise to the crest of Hill 272. (*Courtesy of the author*)

"The fact that in an hour or so they were to go over the top in one of the greatest attacks of the war did not make any apparent difference to them. They were just all in. I did not dare sit down or even stand still, for if I had I would have been dead asleep in a minute. I just kept moving up and down the line, talking to the men and trying to keep them cheerful."

Looking east, Caldwell surveyed a landscape of almost surreal beauty, the long wheat fields beginning to glow in the predawn light. "The storm had passed and the sun was just peeping above the Boche lines," he wrote. "Day broke rapidly and it bade fair to be a wonderful day. The birds were singing as if there were no such thing as war, and out in the big field of ripe wheat in front of us, which stretched away as far as one could see, the meadow larks were soaring and bursting their throats almost with their song of joy at being alive on such a glorious morning."

Taking his place in a shell hole to the company's rear, Caldwell surveyed his men. "It was great to study them as they stood thus ready, waiting for they knew not what the day might hold for them," he wrote.

"Each man's face was a study. The strained, eager, expectant look was wonderful to behold. One man rolled up his sleeves and soon they all had them up. Here was a man testing his bayonet to see that it was on securely; there one was working the bolt of his rifle. One or two men were reading letters, possibly the last they had had from sweetheart or mother."

In line with Company H of the 26th Regiment to the left of Caldwell, twenty-two-year-old Sergeant Gerald V. Stamm wryly remembered the sorry state of his platoon's "wet, shivering" men and, as was no doubt the case with the thousands of other doughboys that morning, certain feelings of dread.

"We seemed not soldiers but caricatures of soldiers," Stamm wrote. "I saw no sign of the fictional do-or-die spirit, not even of any desire to fight. I remember thinking it seemed unlikely that such muddy, sodden scarecrows had enough stuff left in them to break up a quilting party, and marking down the forthcoming assault in my mind as a complete washout.

"I felt less warlike than my companions looked, if that was possible. It suddenly dawned on me that I didn't even know the Kaiser, and that I had no personal grudge against any of his minions. And I wishfully hoped the Germans would feel the same way."

Twenty-year-old Corporal Emmett J. Donahue, of the 28th Regiment's Company G, recalled nervously checking and rechecking his watch as he waited for the signal to advance.

"We had just five minutes," he remembered. "I raised halfway upon my knees. I saw many boys kneeling in the sloppy mud, their heads raised to Heaven in fervent prayer, their gun lying by their side, ready to grasp at the spur of the moment, while others grasped a picture of their gray-haired mother, or perhaps a picture of their sweetheart, kissing it good-bye and replacing the string to which it was attached, and putting it around their neck, pressing the picture to their heart."

Suddenly breaking the early morning reverie, German rockets shot up all along the line. On the far left, German outposts had detected the advance of a battalion of the French 153rd Division and sent up flares—signals for the artillery to lay down a protective barrage. And at 4:29 A.M., six minutes before the attack was to commence, the Germans began pounding the doughboys' front with shells.

The barrage fell just twenty-five yards to the east of where Caldwell and his company crouched, "four platoons in the space usually occupied by one, shells falling all around," he wrote.

The shells crept nearer and nearer to his unit, killing several men, and finally trapping and almost burying Caldwell in a thick ooze of mud and slime. "I got myself out with the help of my two runners and, looking over to the right found that the regiment over there was getting out of the trenches and moving forward," Caldwell remembered. "I could do nothing then but get my outfit started.

"I jumped over the trench and gave the whistle signal for the two assaulting platoons that formed the first two waves to follow me. They came over the top magnificently, cheering like wild men. They never faltered at the Boche barrage, in spite of the fact that it knocked out quite a few of them, but moved right on through it."

At 4:35 A.M. the 1st Division's artillery, 108 pieces, launched its own barrage on the German line of surveillance. And with that barrage, the first waves of the 1st Division's men—some four thousand men—stepped into the wheat.

Hoping to catch the Germans in the open, the American barrage was set to roll forward rapidly, moving one hundred meters every three minutes before standing at designated objectives for from fifteen to forty-five minutes.

The German line of surveillance, a series of shell holes and shallow trenches, sat three hundred meters from the jump-off. One kilometer farther east, along the 28th Regiment's first objective for the day, the 6th German Division was organized on a line of resistance with light and heavy machine guns.

Farther beyond, German reserves had occupied Missy Ravine, a kilometer-wide gash in the Soissons plateau, and emplaced machine guns to cover "every approach with dense bands of enfilade machine gun fire," Huebner wrote.

The 28th Regiment jumped off with Companies G and H in the first wave, and Companies E and F in the second. The 3rd Battalion—Companies I, K, L, and M—was to follow the assault wave at a distance of five hundred yards. As the assault waves stepped out, American shells flew over their heads, and German shells continued to batter the eastern edges of the jump-off trenches.

"We were going merrily along walking in a skirmish line when one of the shorts from our barrage dropped within five feet of me," Corporal Nelson Thompson of Company H remembered. "It killed a man and wounded more but did nothing to me except to knock me out for a few minutes.

"When I had come to and gotten the dirt out of my hair and eyes and had joined the front wave they had already passed over the support wave and were bucking machine guns hidden in a wheat field."

"We were advancing rapidly, men falling about me like large drops of rain," Donahue would remember. "The boy next to me dropped, shrieking as he rolled over and over in the mud, for his right arm had been severed completely, and we had to drive on, and probably allow him to die on the field."

Another one of Corporal Donahue's squad members was soon hit, "and the top of his head was blown off, and I had to wipe his blood out of my eyes, which had been blown in by wind from the shot, so fast do they travel and with such velocity. I saw instantly that he was mortally wounded and I grabbed his rations off him and also his ammunition and pushed on, the shells falling about me."

One of those shells caught Captain Ray P. Harrison, commander of Company F, who just four days earlier had celebrated his twenty-seventh birthday. One of Harrison's noncoms remembered that Harrison had been wounded in the bombardment that greeted the 28th's advance and left the front to have his wound dressed.

Harrison quickly caught up with his company. "He had only been with them a few minutes when a shell burst about ten feet in advance of Ray," an account of his last moments would say. "Ray was struck in the chest by a piece of shell and fell at once. He had passed away when the men came up to him."

Another of Company F's lieutenants, twenty-four-year-old Paul Greenwood Cox, also succumbed quickly. Sergeant Elmer E. White remembered: "At first the Boche shells came rather thick and fast and I guess quite a few of the fellows were hit, but after about ten minutes, our artillery began to have its effect, and the Boche shells began to thin out a little.

"I saw one of the lieutenants get killed and I thought it was the lieutenant of my platoon. After that I guess I went mad and started out to raise hell by myself."

The loss of Harrison and Cox left White's unit disorganized, and precious minutes were lost as platoon leaders struggled to restore order. Even as this was being done, the 3rd Battalion stepped off in support, and within minutes 25 percent of its men were killed or wounded by the German barrage.

Corporal Ben Bernheisel of Company L remembered the din of battle drowning out all other sounds as his company stepped out. Commanders had to resort to arm signals, and as his unit headed east, "German shells came at us," Bernheisel recalled. "One came for a direct hit. We fell on our faces, all but one, he knelt. My head turned in his direction and I watched from under my helmet. Several yards to the left rear of his squad column, the shell burst. I batted my eyes. We all arose, all but one.

"The kneeling man never quivered. His rifle was at high port as he knelt.

His head was slightly ducked but no change. As we formed in the line again, I glanced back. What is he waiting for, thought I. Then I forgot him." (Bernheisel would find the soldier in the same position the next day—dead from a shell fragment that "had no doubt pierced his heart.")

Company I's Sam Ervin watched in horror as his platoon leader was torched in a freak incident. "It was sort of a horrible death," Ervin recalled. "He had a bunch of signal rockets in his knapsack on his back and some shell or something exploded behind him and ignited them and they spewed in every direction." Though just a private, Ervin assumed command of the platoon.

The first waves advanced steadily through the chest-high wheat, following the thin barrage of the artillery. Bullets from unseen machine guns clipped the stalks and took their toll on the doughboys; within minutes, the assault washed up on one of the many lanes the Boche had sculpted in the wheat parallel to the assault, open fields of fire that gave the German machine gunners a clear view of their enemy.

The Germans had spent the past few weeks digging pits seven to eight feet deep at the eastern edge of the lanes, from the bottoms of which they could quickly scoot up ladders to man their guns. "As soon as the barrage rolled past, the men could climb the ladder, poke their machine gun or automatic rifle up to the edge of the standing wheat and, well hidden, take up perfect positions to fire on the hundreds of steel hats that they could see advancing through the wheat," Babcock wrote.

The men under those steel hats, meanwhile, tried to locate their tormenters, hidden in the sea of wheat, painstakingly outflanking the nests as machine-gun bullets cut scything patterns. "This took lots of time, was deadly work," Babcock added.

Hundreds of doughboys fell while racing over these lanes to flank and carry the emplacements; the survivors moved on. Two hundred meters short of the German line of resistance in the 28th Regiment's sector, the men now encountered fierce rifle and machine-gun fire from a strongpoint at the Raperie—a large, rectangular farm building surrounded by a stone wall—and were pinned to the ground.

Huebner called up the 2nd Battalion's scout platoon, made up of thirty-five of the best shots and bravest men, who maneuvered on the German flank, while a platoon from Company H made a full-frontal charge, capturing five heavy machine guns and one hundred Germans.

The Americans continued to roll forward as the captured Boche were sent west. Emmett Donahue recalled that these Germans "passed us as going to the rear of our lines, as is the rule for captured prisoners, where the intelligence unit takes care of them. I know there was a large number who passed me with their hands up yelling, 'kamerad.'

"We never bother them unless they start something, as we save our ammunition for when we reach the trenches, for here they do not always give up easily."

Babcock remembered encountering one very happy German soldier after leaving his command post to follow up the advance at 5:00 A.M. "One wounded American soldier was being carried on a litter by four prisoners. One of them, a nice looking little Bosch who didn't look a day over eighteen, smiled and chanted in the gayest manner, 'La guerre est finie,' repeating it over and over, at the same time imitating the 'passage steps' of a dressage or trained horse."

The captured Germans, Babcock would add, "did not mind holding their hands up. I saw many of them running to our rear with their arms held as high as possible, they made me think of a young bird trying to fly."

Even as the doughboys labored through the bloody work in the wheat, dozens of airplanes battled above them, German, French, and American fliers pirouetting and looping and rolling in a colorful and macabre dance that at times enthralled the ground troops.

"The aeroplanes, too, were busy scouting in the air," Donahue recalled, "finding ranges for the artillery in the rear of our lines." He watched as a German plane "appeared on the scene and a battle above us was started, we had no time, however, to watch the outcome for we were engaged ourselves in routing the enemy from the positions they held.

"All I know is that a number of German planes soon arrived and likewise American. I remember that one German plane fell to the ground on the left of us about 100 yards, and we heard or seen no more of the rest."

Pressing on, the doughboys ran into the German line of resistance. As Donahue approached, a well-hidden machine-gun opened up, raking the advancing Americans. Donahue located the nest and, creeping up in the wheat, "soon cleaned them out by tossing a hand grenade into the bush."

Passing over the shallow frontline trench, in which German and American bodies lay sprawled in a tangle of khaki and green, Donahue continued on to the Germans' reserve trench, in which lurked "several reprobates, and showing fight. We leaped in upon them. One was making for me with his bayonet fixed as he had no chance to fire at me, for he was out of ammunition, I learned later. As he drew near me, I leaped upon him plunging my bayonet into him just above his heart.

"I heard the poor devil give a groan and I could distinctly feel the impulse or sudden jar as the bayonet pierced him. He shrank and I placed my foot against him and thereby extracted my bayonet, and lifelessly he fell to the ground."

So this was good work, a good morning's work indeed, just two hours in and the Germans on the run, the doughboys slogging on, their tin hats bobbing just above the wheat as if they were turtles skimming across some golden, wavy pond, young American men like Emmett Donahue dishing it out to Heinie, dishing it out but getting back almost as good as they gave, the orange sun ascending on the morning of July 18, 1918, over ground pocked with the prone and unmoving khaki forms of hundreds of doughboys and long dark lines of Germans snaking west, their four long years of war over, *La guerre est finie*.

As they had at Cantigny just six weeks earlier, the 28th's men had shocked and steamrolled an unsuspecting foe, given him the bayonet and the grenade and rifle and routed him from his hiding places, but it was early yet, early in the day and certainly early in the battle, and as at Cantigny, the trials of these "operations south of Soissons" would stretch on for days, too many days for the lucky few survivors to count, or want to remember, though none would ever be able to forget them.

12

"Kamerad!"

As such life-and-death dramas raged across the plain, Company D was still struggling to the front. Having started its march some six miles farther to the west at Pierrefonds-les-Bains, and with but one map and no guide, Huebner wrote that the 28th's 1st Battalion was "forced to make its long march over roads that were congested with almost every kind of military transportation and equipment."

The battalion was still several kilometers from the front when the crescendo of the Germans' preemptive bombardment—and the subsequent cannonade heralding the 1st Division's attack—echoed across the countryside. "All was quiet and every one was tired out," Wilbert Murphy wrote. "All of a sudden there was a snap as if something broke and every gun in the valley—there must have been a thousand of them—broke the stillness with a tremendous roar. It seemed like one continuous roar of thunder. It was a terrific drum fire and it served it's purpose to surprise the Jerries."

The men stumbled across fields toward the sound of the guns, lost, "exhausted from the fatigue of the long march forward and . . . badly in need of rest," Huebner wrote. Finally, "the Brigade Adjutant found the battalion and ordered its Commander to move his command forward in the regimental zone of action."

A small record of the company's presence that morning survives in a few lines in the Second Brigade's records:

5:00 a.m. Lt. Braunston reports with 1 platoon of D Co. 28th Inf. Claims Major Roxell ordered him to go towards artillery firing. No further orders. (Brigade commander is of the opinion that this officer was scared.)

5:30 a.m. Lt. Sorenson D Co. 28th with his company outside of Brigade P. C. Absolutely lost. Had no maps.

5:30 a.m. Adjutant reported whole 1st Bn. 28th lost in woods La Fosse Trure. They did not know what to do or where to go. I ordered them forward at once.

(Lloyd Bronston would put the lie to 2nd Brigade commander general Beaumont Buck's opinion of his spine, winning a Silver Star for bravery before the five days of Soissons had passed.)

Once he had his bearings, Soren Sorensen led his men to the shallow jump-off trenches from which the 28th Regiment's second and third battalions had moved out an hour before. "We rushed past the artillery and into position on the crest of a hill from which we were to jump off," Murphy wrote. "Bayonets were fixed, rifles loaded—ready to fire when we should run across the Jerries in our advance."

As had their predecessors, Company D's men surveyed the fields before them and wondered what the day might bring—and how they might hold up in the certain trials to come. Murphy settled in next to his twenty-year-old squad leader, Corporal Clarence A. Butts, from Rocky River, Ohio.

"We each rolled a cigarette and started to smoke—it helped our nerves, in fact I am sure it helped mine, for though I was rather weak in the knees I tried to brace up and be as brave as he was," Murphy recalled.

"We had all forgotten about being tired, even though we hiked all night. The excitement was great though none of the fellows near seemed the least bit nervous. 'Porky' Flynn, of Chicago, was about the most cheerful of the crowd and he had been even more tired, I believe, than myself on that night hike."

Sorensen strode the line, his simple presence steeling the men. "Just as we were smoking the Captain came along and gave orders to get ready to go over," Murphy remembered. "He was an exceptionally fearless man and that gave us all confidence. Soon the order came to go over and over we went. Just as we went over the man at the telephone back of me said, that over half of the German batteries had been knocked out by our artillery fire."

Advancing east, Murphy could see the lumbering French tanks crawling across the plain in the distance, one exploding into pieces from a direct hit. After an hour the company halted in a "battered up" German trench and watched in amazement as a swarm of Germans headed its way.

"Flynn touched me on the shoulder once and said, 'See that bunch of Jerry's coming,'" Murphy wrote. "I looked and imagine my surprise at seeing nearly a battalion of them coming without their helmets or rifles.

"They had surrendered to the men out ahead of us and were now on their way to the rear. That made us happy because we felt that there would be less fighting to do the next day."

"We advanced rapidly, under shellfire, over the scarred fields," Captain Charles Senay later wrote of Company C. "We soon passed the first casualties, both German and American. There were a few disabled tanks, several burning."

Farther east, the bloodied 2nd and 3rd Battalions continued their advance. They came across a fortified German position at St. Amand Farm, in the French 153rd Division's sector, where stone buildings concealed heavy 77 mm artillery, machine guns, and trench mortars that inflicted devastating enfilade fire on the left flank of the advancing troops. With the assistance of the French, a squad from Company G attacked the farm and captured it— and one hundred of the foe—in hand-to-hand fighting.

With such diversions and small attacks all across the front, the battle turned into a chaotic tapestry, a blending and weaving of small groups of soldiers—often from different units, or, in the case of the Moroccans, different divisions—operating together to eliminate machine-gun nests as the assaulting forces became tangled on the plain's wide expanse.

Side by side, doughboys and the dark and feared Senegalese, Algerian, and Moroccan warriors from the famed French Foreign Legion—"they'd go over the top with rib-stickers in their mouths, looking like pirates," one veteran recalled—moved ever east, while captured Germans inexorably moved west.

"Part of the time I was scrapping along side of Yanks and part of the time of Moroccans," Elmer White wrote. "I only remember seeing a few of my company so I don't know how they fared."

As did many a doughboy that morning, White soon became a victim of a machine gun. "A bunch of us had rushed a blind trench in a wheat field and had run the few remaining Boche from it. Those that got away alive beat it back to another blind trench in the wheat along the side of a ravine where they had a bunch of artillery.

"We ploughed into them and had just gotten them on the run beating it out of the trenches, when a concealed machine gun over on our left front along the ravine opened up and mowed a bunch of us down. They got me in the right leg above the knee and as I fell one hit my cartridge belt and nipped me in the left side. However, the cartridges in my belt glanced the bullet so it gave me just a scratch."

White took refuge in a shell hole, and encountered two wounded doughboys. "One was shot through the arm and the other through the shoulder. Both were bleeding fierce and I helped them get tied up the best we could. I guess the machine gun had beat it for I didn't hear it anymore and the fellows kept right on going."

A little farther south in the 16th Regiment's support line, Bert Tippman's company advanced past "guns, helmets, blankets and everything" that had been dropped by the frantic and "scared" Germans.

Those captured by the doughboys, he wrote, had "faces as white as chalk as they come running with their hands up and yelling, 'Kamerad!' The sun shines on their yellow helmets as they run and they look like a bunch of bulls coming instead of human beings. The fight is all gone from them this day and they can't run fast enough to our rear."

After capturing a German artillery position, the doughboys turned the tables on the Germans—only to become targets themselves. "The shells burst around us all over and as our pals fall we keep on going as far as we can," Tippman wrote. "A bullet clips the straps on an ammunition bag of my partner and he throws the bag away, keeping the ammunition but never stopping a second. Pretty soon our gunner goes down with a bullet in his side, but jumps up again and walks away leaving his carrier [to] handle the gun. If he goes down, I take the gun next."

As hundreds of wounded began the long crawl back to aid stations—
"Believe me, of all the journeys I have ever made, that was one," White
would recall—the assault battalions of all four of the 1st's regiments approached Missy Ravine, a once-pastoral refuge of fields and woods now
bristling with more than thirty German artillery emplacements and numerous and well-sited machine guns.

German artillery also ranged on the slope's eastern edge, and several
small villages—Breuil, Saconin-et-Breuil, and Le Mont d'Arly—provided
cover for German riflemen. All three villages had been assigned to the 153rd
Regiment's sector, but the French "had been unable to to enter the ravine
at all," Huebner wrote.

Unable to continue the advance unless the intense fire on his left was
extinguished, Huebner ordered Companies G and H to descend into the
ravine and attack north toward the villages. They managed to advance just
one hundred yards, so Huebner then ordered his two support companies, E
and F, to resume the attack. These units advanced three hundred yards
before heavy losses stopped them. Meanwhile, five of the tanks supporting
the 28th's advance were brought up, only to be quickly destroyed at the
ravine's western edge by German artillery.

Hearing the intense firing, Captain Willis Tack, commander of the 3rd
Battalion, rushed up to meet with Huebner. Both concurred that Tack's
men should press through the ravine. Two of the battalion's companies
carried the attack across the ravine toward Breuil, while another assaulted,
and took, Le Mont d'Arly, before slicing south of Saconin-et-Breuil and
gaining the ravine's eastern edge. The French 153rd Division, meanwhile,
pushed east and overran the German defenses in Saconin-et-Breuil.

"There was but one way to pass and that was to wade the swamp," the
28th's regimental history says. "This, the doughboys did, sometimes sinking to their waists in mud and water. On one occasion a high German officer buried himself in the mud and water until his head and arms were
exposed and continued firing on the slowly advancing doughboys until he
was killed and trampled into the mud by the infuriated soldiers."

"The fighting was very severe and the enemy defended his positions to
the last," Huebner recalled. "In fact, very few, if any, prisoners were taken

by the troops of the 28th Infantry in this advance. Our men waded in mud and water, in many places up to their hips, and continued to advance in spite of heavy casualties.

"Many glorious feats of valor were performed during this attack and the entire success of this advance was due to the efforts of individual soldiers who continued to advance regardless of the casualties."

Sergeant Gerald Stamm, on the right with the 26th Infantry, recalled wading through a "morass, waist-deep in spots," on the ravine's bottom.

"A hurricane of rifle and machine-gun fire churned the oozy water underfoot, and spattered us with slime. Shells too swooped down, the bursts flinging up huge geysers of black ooze.

"The swamp was full of concealed machine-gun nests, and the opposite bank seemed alive with them too. All of them kept on chattering. Several 77's coughed away steadily, nor were they silenced until their gunners were shot or bayoneted at their posts.

"The stifling swamp was a bloody, ruthless place of fighting business. Few prisoners were taken in it."

Among the "glorious feats of valor" near Missy Ravine that morning was one performed by Lieutenant Samuel I. Parker of the 28th's Company K. When the 153rd Division was unable to advance in the face of withering German fire coming from machine-gun nests in a quarry northeast of the village of Breuil, Parker gathered his platoon and about forty poilus and attacked the quarry, capturing forty men and six machine guns.

Parker received help in his feat from his University of North Carolina classmate, Sam Ervin, who with five men from Company I rushed and took a machine-gun position that was sweeping the quarry with fire during Parker's advance.

Two of Ervin's men died in the assault; Ervin was hit by a shell fragment. "Right before I got to the gun pit I felt a blow like a sledge hammer on my left thigh," he recalled years later. "It just knocked me down flat. I had an automatic clip bag slung over my shoulder with several clips or cartridges and whatever hit me just cut through the clip bag and cut through the cartridges like it was a sharp instrument."

Parker, who years later would win the Congressional Medal of Honor for his bravery that day, encountered Ervin at the captured gun pit. "I saw Sam Ervin standing down there and he was leaning on his rifle and he was bent over," Parker recalled. "Blood was all over him. I told him he should go to the rear. He said, 'No, I want to stay with you. I'll help you organize for a counterattack.'"

Ervin stayed long enough to help consolidate the position, then hobbled painfully—as he had at Cantigny—to the rear.

The eastern slope of the ravine was carried by 10:30 A.M., and the 28th's attack continued, always eastward, spilling out of the ravine until heavy fire stopped it three hundred yards east of Breuil. Huebner and Tack paused to reorganize. Counting heads, both were astounded at the sorry state of their battalions, which had hit the wheat on the run just four hours earlier with close to one thousand men each.

Huebner's battalion was reorganized into "five small rifle platoons and one machine gun platoon, all commanded by sergeants. All the officers, excepting the Battalion Commander, had been killed," he wrote.

Tack's 3rd Battalion was in similar shape; together, the two assaulting battalions had lost 90 percent of their men. Tack would say in a message to Babcock: "We are held up at this point and can not advance as the total strength of the 2 Bns is about 200 men. The French on our left are held up. The 26th on our rt has not as yet come up to our present line. Dont believe we are strong enough to repulse a determined counter attack as M.G.s are practically out of ammunition. Request reinforcements at once."

Still, the day's last objective remained: higher ground just east of the poplar-lined Paris-Soissons Road, which sliced across the golden plain on a northeasterly course. German snipers hidden in the trees fired at anyone brave enough to lift his head over the ravine's rim, and the broad fields on either side of the road gave the Hun a clear field of fire.

Babcock arrived at the eastern edge of Missy Ravine at about 11:30 A.M. to find the battalions "halted and consolidating." Huebner and Tack told him "that the men were exhausted and after the fighting in the ravine west of them, the assault died out," Babcock would report.

Babcock also discovered that part of his regiment, including Samuel Parker's platoon from Company K, had drifted north and into the zone allotted to the French 153rd Division in order to cover a gap on its left.

Babcock located the commander of the unit and requested that he move his men to the right; a battalion of the French infantry shifted over, allowing Parker and his men to return south to the American lines.

(Babcock would remember vividly his encounter with one of the 153rd's colonials, a "tall, swarthy fellow," who, recognizing Babcock as an American, asked: "How many battles have you been in?" When Babcock replied that the day's action was his first, "He tapped his Croix de Guerre ribbon, and, in a patronizing tone, enumerated the battles he had seen," Babcock wrote.)

Tack's decimated 3rd Battalion then took over the front line, while the equally battered 2nd Battalion moved back to the eastern edge of Missy Ravine. The 1st Battalion's Company C was brought up to the ravine's western edge at about 11:00 A.M. to act as a blocking force, "doing considerable mopping up en route," Senay wrote.

A renewed attack was set for 5:30 P.M., but because of the men's dismal shape, and the horrendous casualties they'd suffered, the day's fight was done for the 28th and 26th Regiments, having petered out several hundred meters short of their final objective.

While the fighting for the ravine raged, elements of the 3rd Battalion mopped up caves passed over in the initial advance, from which Germans could be seen popping out to fire at the backs of the Americans.

"We saw our First Sergeant run to a cave opening," Ben Bernheisel recalled. "He carefully took his grenades from his pocket, and setting them off, he threw them into the mouth of the cave. After the thud of the concussion, German soldiers with hands raised emerged to the opening. A Frenchman opened a large pocket knife. He slashed at their belts and suspenders. Thus handicapped, they moved to the rear as directed.

"They were hastened with well-placed kicks."

Germans were seen emerging from a larger cave near Le Mont d'Arly, and the 3rd Battalion's reserve unit, Company M, was sent forward to subdue them. The Germans raced back into the recesses of the cave, leaving machine gunners to guard the entrance.

The company laid siege, and the Germans held out until 4:00 P.M., when under a white flag the "entire force, consisting of twenty officers, including a Commandant, and between three and four hundred men" sullenly walked out, Huebner wrote. Inside, the men found "a great number of machine guns and trench mortars," he added.

According to Babcock, the total haul from the caves was 604 enlisted men and officers. Babcock reported the delight with which the grimy and mud- and blood-spattered doughboys patted down and searched the imperious German officers for weapons.

"The German major was a Prussian, I was told he was a relative of the German Crown Prince," Babcock wrote. "It was amusing to see those haughty officers when one of our husky, sweaty, dirty soldiers frisked them for arms. We even took their dirks or daggers, although they claimed they were only for mess purposes. I do not suppose many of those Prussians had ever before had an ordinary man lay hands on him, unless it was to help with his coat or pull on his trousers."

Senay couldn't resist the temptation to investigate the cave. With his runner and first sergeant, he probed its recesses and found a storehouse holding bread, canned horsemeat, cases of mineral water—"We proceeded to eat and drink, but the horsemeat was strong and I threw it up," he remembered—and thirty more Germans, hidden in a dark storeroom.

Beyond was a larger room, the floor crowded with German wounded. "When they saw armed Americans coming in, they screamed and tried to crawl away in cringing terror," he wrote. "We promptly got out of there."

Though the 28th arguably had the toughest assignment of the day, the fighting was fierce and costly all along the line. The 16th Regiment's Edgar Caldwell remembered his unit's push to, and through, the village of Missy-aux-Bois that morning.

"We pushed on, cleaning out the Boche trenches as we went along," Caldwell wrote. "We were taking a great many prisoners and the slightly wounded men were taking them to the rear in groups of twenty to fifty.

"The Boche would not stand up and fight like a man to the finish, but many of them jumped out of their trenches and ran toward us, shouting 'Kamerad!' Our losses had been heavy and our men were in no humor for this kind of thing. They killed lots of them."

Caldwell took a bullet in the left shoulder as the unit closed on Missy-aux-Bois. The impact sent him sprawling, but, he wrote, "I did not notice any bleeding and got up and caught up with my company again."

Overcoming stiff resistance from German machine gunners, the village was taken after two hours of hard fighting. Caldwell paused to take a head count and, like many company commanders in the 1st Division that day, was astonished by the sorry state of his unit. "When we started to consolidate, I found I had men with me from three different regiments and half a dozen different companies. They had become lost in the confusion and joined in with us. Of my original company, 226 men, I could find only seventeen and not an officer or noncom left."

With Missy Ravine taken, the assault ebbed all along the 1st Division's front as it confronted a wall of German machine-gun bullets and shells.

Wrote Bert Tippman of the 16th's Company G: "We are safe now and dig in so we can keep the boche back. While we dig the shrapnel is flying around us and a chunk lights near my leg just missing me, but a miss here is as good as a mile.

"While they are digging the machine guns of the boche open up and a ditch digger hasn't got anything on us who never followed this trade. Our gunner ahead of me gets a bullet through the side but we keep to the original position and hold them, firing until our rifles get hot. Then the boche turns on the gas and high explosive with shrapnel but can't drive us off. I see more of my pals down with shot or shrapnel but we only get mad."

Sent forward during a short lull in the firing, Tippman's part in the great battle soon came to an end. "Got one in the leg at last and had to give up running and lay down in a shallow trench barely deep enough to cover me and the bullets still coming. I was safe until night. When I think of the bullets that were coming my way, and only one hit me, I'm glad to be alive."

Such harrowing experiences would have to wait for the men of Company D. Hanging back of the advancing front waves, the company suffered just a few casualties from shells that overshot Missy Ravine and from harassing fire and bombs sent the company's way by some of the numerous German aircraft buzzing and droning and strafing overhead.

Wilbert Murphy would remember at one point counting sixty-five airplanes in the sky overhead as Company D advanced. "They weren't all French or American either—several were British and not a few were German."

In the late afternoon the company paused along a lane running parallel to and about one kilometer west of Missy Ravine. Though more than two kilometers from where the 2nd and 3rd battalions were hanging on just east of the ravine, even here they were well within the Germans' reach.

"The whiz-bangs were coming over fast and you didn't have to listen very hard to hear the 88's and 77's whine thru the air and light a short distance from you," Murphy wrote. "Some of the explosives nearly took my breath away, the concussion was so great."

Ordered to dig in, Company D's men pitched furiously into the earth with whatever implements they could find. "It didn't take very long to dig a rather deep hole either," Murphy wrote. "The shells were landing pretty close and a hole was some protection from flying shrapnel. We improved our trench and prepared for a counter attack, which we felt sure would come for the Germans were well prepared here."

Company D's Private John Cibulka added: "It was every man for himself. All we had to dig in with were the covers of our mess tins—little things—and our bayonets. First you made a little hole to stick your head in, and then dug hard for a place to shelter your body. Every bullet that went by your head made you dig a little faster."

"The shellfire was continuous but not particularly deadly," Charles Senay remembered; still, he added, dangers abounded even on the western edge of Missy Ravine, where late in the afternoon he watched with Lieutenant Robert Rayburn as a German shell sent one of his men sprawling. "I remarked to Rayburn that we'd probably lost that one," Senay wrote.

But soon the "disheveled and bleeding soldier dashed toward us holding his shattered rifle." Sobbing, the soldier showed Senay his broken weapon and said: "Captain, see what the Germans just did to my rifle."

Added Senay: "It must have made him real angry, for the next day he was potting Germans like jack rabbits in the wheat fields where they checker boarded with their machine guns."

Towards dusk, Senay was ordered to bring Company C back from the edge of Missy Ravine to the 1st Battalion's position "for a meal and consolidation with the other companies." Noting the abundance of "magnesium flares and bombing planes" filling the air, he ordered a retirement by platoons across the plain.

"The German bombers were circling overhead dropping strings of contact fuse, 8 inch artillery shells with whistling vanes on them," Senay recalled. "A bomb hit the head of the second platoon, wounding Lieutenant McKenzie and his platoon sergeant so severely that neither could help the other. The men near them were dead.

"Each told the other that he was bleeding to death and nothing could be done. A French first aid team came along in time and they were brought to a French hospital."

While the 28th's 1st Battalion ate a meager meal provided by its rolling kitchen, other men, hungry and thirsty after the all-night march and the hard fighting under a July sun, walked the rear, rifling through the packs of American and German dead, looking for sustenance.

"Hunger got the best of us," the 26th Regiment's Gerald Stamm would write. "All afternoon small groups wandered up and down the valley, searching discarded enemy packs for food. I went into a deserted village on our left, Saconin-et-Brieul, if the signs spoke correctly, and found some wine. This, plus some salvaged crumbly sausage and some dark hardtack that I found on a dead German, helped my hunger."

Private Albert Hoppe of Company D remembered risking life and limb, as did many, to retrieve water for himself and his parched squad amid the shelling that day. "An officer asked where I was going and advised me not to go down a certain road because it was under fire and they're getting everyone that tries it," Hoppe said. "I thought it wouldn't be any worse to die by shell than thirst so I kept on going until I saw a shell land right between a team of horses and the water cart they were hauling."

Told by another soldier of a well in a village nearer the German line, Hoppe headed toward it. "About every six minutes shells would wreck another wall in the little village I went to," he said. "But I got the water and got back safely, though I never expected to."

On the far right of the division, Private Frank Last of the 18th Regiment's Company G loaded himself with more than a dozen of his comrades' canteens and went looking for water, with the admonition of his captain, F. W. Huntington, ringing in his ears: "Look out for poisoned water."

Along the way, he ran across the ruins of a farm building turned to use as an aid station, where wounded Americans lay side by side with wounded Boche. "A shell had landed not long before and got several of them. It was an awful sight," he wrote. "I soon reached a spring. There were a number of 'kammerads' there and I took my pistol in my hand. I pointed my pistol at a bunch of Germans near the spring and said, 'Drink.'

"They drank from the spring. Without asking any questions I waited a while and then began to load my canteens."

By nightfall, thousands of doughboys—at least three thousand in the 1st Division alone, according to one army source—had been killed or wounded. The 1st had brought with it just six hundred litters "and the usual number of blankets," according to *The Medical Department of the United States Army in the World War.* "In five or six hours the supply was exhausted."

A medical-supply officer raced to Paris and several other cities and scrounged three thousand more litters and blankets, but, as the battle raged on, "even these proved insufficient, for as evacuation from the field hospitals was retarded and they were overcrowded they were obliged to use litters as beds."

On the field, doughboys resorted to using their blouses or ponchos to carry off wounded comrades, with their rifles for holders. More often, the wounded were better off taking refuge in shell holes and waiting for night than making a slow, upright hobble to the rear, as the sweeping, indiscriminate firing of the German machine guns was deadly.

Many of the wounded on both sides were simply left to slowly die in the wheat, unable to crawl rearward or find shelter as the battle raged over and around them.

Major Raymond Austin remembered that by the close of the first day's battle, "Just back of us in a large wheatfield there were many dead and wounded of both sides. One Boche, shot in the back, lay there all day calling 'Kamerad' whenever anyone came near."

"There are many pitiful sights on a battlefield," wrote Senay, who saw his share while trailing the 28th's advance to Missy Ravine that day. "The dead are at peace. They feel no pain. Not so the wounded."

He added: "There are many ways of being wounded. Among the worst is being shot through the spine. It is heartrending to pass some poor chap, friend or foe, dragging himself painfully by his arms and begging oncoming troops to give him the *coup de grace.*

"Then there are the soldiers who have abdominal wounds. On occasion a shell splinter would rip a man's stomach open and he would be staggering around trying to hold his writhing insides in their natural cavity. They might fall out and he'd scoop them up, dirt and all, and thrust them back.

"Combat elements," Senay added, "cannot stop to care for their wounded, except to give them hasty first aid or a few drops of water. Troops from the rear are charged with salvaging the human wreckage."

Despite the day's savagery, there were some small acts of doughboy kindness, such as that displayed by Sergeant Jay Teeple of the 16th Regiment. A newspaper account of Teeple's part in the battle on July 18 says that he and his scout platoon "came upon two nests (eight men) of German machine gunners and he ordered the enemy to throw up their hands.

"Seven did, but the man in charge refused and it was necessary for Teeple to shoot. The bullet entered the stomach of the German and he fell to the ground, while the other seven were disarmed and sent back of the lines."

Leaving the wounded German behind, Teeple and his squad moved on. Later in the day, he "began to think of the poor fellow he had shot" and went back to find him. He dressed the German's wounds and shared some bread and coffee with him.

"The German was so touched that he took from his finger a large gold signet ring and gave it to Jay with his compliments, saying the ring stood for good luck. What became of the German he does not know, but said the chances were against him."

Although set amid a landscape wrought with tragedy and carnage, scenes of beauty still managed to stir the soul, such as that witnessed toward dusk by the 18th Regiment's Captain F. W. Huntington on the edge of the 1st Division's boundary with the Moroccans.

"About 6:00 PM French Cavalry was seen approaching from the west along the Coeuvres-et-Valsery road," Huntington wrote. "It continued to pass the bivouac area for about two hours. It presented an enthralling and never to be forgotten sight to those who saw it. From whence this cavalry came, or where it went, no one ever knew, for we never saw it again."

In fact, the French *cuirassiers* had spent much of July 18 creating a massive logjam in the rear of the American army, impeding the ability of men, artillery, and supplies to follow up the day's breakout. In the afternoon, Austin would remember, the French put "large bodies" of cavalry on reconnaissance—"and the Boche went after them pretty hard."

Senay also witnessed one such charge across the plain toward a gap in the German line late in the day on July 18. As the mounted French advanced, "they were enfiladed by intense machine gun fire. The mass of troops disintegrated in minutes. Dead and wounded horses and men marked their trail. The survivors dashed back off the field. There were riderless horses, horses with double mounts, horses with running men grasping their stirrups or their tails. Complete disaster for an outmoded weapon of war."

Robert Lee Bullard would write simply of the brave French horsemen: "I was perfectly sure they would do no good, and they did none."

The insane Old World dash into mechanized warfare was one of the last of its kind in history, as the machine gun added cavalry to its list of victims. For once, the 1st Division's men who watched could thank their stars they were in the infantry; they were happy to lie low after the bloody day's work on the Soissons plain.

As darkness fell, they licked their wounds and counted their dead, as long lines of wounded doughboys and German prisoners continued to amble west. The night of July 18–July 19 was "fairly quiet," affording the men some rest, Huebner wrote.

They would need it.

13

The Paris-Soissons Road

While the exhausted doughboys tried to sleep, the Germans set to business, bringing up another division—the 34th—and positioning it to the right of the 28th, in front of the village of Ploisy, which lay a little more than a mile across open wheat fields to the east-southeast. German snipers and machine gunners raced forward, some to the Paris-Soissons Road and others to locations in the wheat where they could cover the most ground.

The German line of resistance lay a full half mile across the wheat, midway between Missy Ravine and Ploisy. A former French strongpoint 600 meters north of the 28th and east of the Paris-Soissons Road in the 153rd's sector had also been turned to good use by the Germans, who threw down wire and placed a battalion of riflemen and numerous machine guns within. This position—known later as the "Vauxbuin position" for the village just behind it—covered 1,200 meters of front, and in the hours to come would lay many a doughboy—including John Nelson—to the ground.

The Germans had learned much about establishing fields of fire over four years of war, and had come to regard light and heavy machine guns—and not the rifle—as its weapons of choice. A 1st Division report written after Soissons noted, "Every attempt is made to secure the greatest possible field of fire, and especially is direct fire sought after." The guns, the report noted, were placed in "checkerboard formation"—staggered in groups of up to six guns, each one sited on a limited front, "the more easily to control a very large volume of fire" against advancing infantry.

It was against this opposition that a renewed 1st Division push opened at 4:00 A.M. on July 19. The remains of the 3rd Battalion carried forward the 28th's attack on the left and the 2nd Battalion of the 26th Regiment pushed ahead on the right in an attempt to close ranks with the left of the 1st Brigade, whose lines had advanced a full kilometer farther east the day before. But as the attack spilled into the wheat and toward the Paris-Soissons Road, little ground could be gained in the face of the Germans' withering machine-gun fire.

Sergeant Gerald Stamm remembered being rousted "in the graying dawn" of July 19 and ordered to renew the advance. "We formed section columns in the semi-darkness and moved out into the dew-laden grain," he wrote. "There was an ominous quietness, but before we had gone one hundred yards it was shattered by a wailing that swooped out of the fog and materialized in a wall of spouting flame and dirt that paralleled the forward waves.

"Waspish fragments sang past us and acrid fumes made us cough. Magically, big black gaps appeared in the wheat. Soon the staccato of scores of machine guns built up in the din. It was plain that Fritz was in an ugly mood, and that there would be hell to pay."

The 28th would also pay that day—and in dividends. Quickly, the firestorm left 3rd Battalion commander Willis Tack severely wounded, and Company M, which had accepted the surrender of several hundred cave-bound Germans the day before, lost its way during the advance into the fog and veered too far to the left, becoming trapped by enfilading fire from the Vauxbuin position.

"The enemy had evidently prepared for such a movement as not a shot was fired at the company until the Paris-Soissons Road was reached," Clarence Huebner wrote. As the company approached the road, "a withering enfilade fire from the enemy strong point on the left was opened on it. This fire was so intense that the entire company, with the exception of four or five men, was annihilated."

Among Company M's dead was Lieutenant Robert O. Purdy Jr., a twenty-seven-year-old graduate of the University of South Carolina School of Law. Though he had been wounded on July 18 and urged to seek aid by Captain John Manning, Purdy insisted on staying with his men. "Fearlessly leading his platoon" that morning, Purdy "was struck by a machine gun bullet in his heart and instantly killed," an account of his death says. He was later buried on the spot.

Sensing an opening in the ashes of Company M, the Germans began preparing a counterattack. But a message, relayed through the 26th Regiment, quickly brought up a battalion of the 7th Field Artillery, which raced to the front, placed its guns hub to hub, and so disrupted the forming enemy that the counterattack was abandoned. In the meantime, a few men from the 28th's 3rd Battalion managed to make it to the Paris-Soissons Road before flinging themselves against the bank on its western edge and going to cover. "The Germans machine gunned us severely," Ben Bernheisel recalled. "A lad on my right threw his gun in the air and clutched at his knee. He rolled over and over."

Racing for his life toward the hard-packed, tree-lined road, Bernheisel witnessed from the corner of his eye an incongruous scene. "From the hedge alongside the road ahead, a rabbit jumped," he wrote. "A soldier near me shot at it. Force of habit, I judged. He laughed. He did not hit the rabbit."

Finally, "We made the road," he added. "Men were trying to cross and some succeeded. Some fell in the road. As hard as I could run, I made for the far side. Down behind a tree. A fox hole at hand. In I went."

Headquarters Company's Captain Francis M. Van Natter—the same who, as captain of Company L, had pleaded for mercy as night fell on the first day at Cantigny—also sought refuge in the ditch that lined the eastern side of the road, only to find himself in the middle of a squad of Moroccans, who refused to believe he was an American.

Lieutenant Herman Dacus, of Company I, would recall that the Moroccans were feared even by other Allied troops, and left an easily recognizable and deadly mark across the Soissons plain that July. "I went down one German trench where half a dozen or more had been killed, all with the bayonet—a sure mark of the Moroccans," Dacus recalled.

That morning, Dacus and his platoon were held up on the western edge of the Paris-Soissons Road, with no idea where the rest of their company was located. Raising his head to scout across the road, Dacus heard a familiar voice call to him. It was Van Natter.

"I heard, 'Hey, Dacus! Come on over! Have a fine, deep trench over here!'" Dacus wrote years later. "I recognized Van and dashed over. There he was, with a dozen or so French Moroccan troops. The Moroccans thought he was a German officer, and wanted to shoot him. He found one who understood French and convinced him he was an American captain, even if he had no horse, which French officers of his rank had."

Still seeking an opening, Huebner brought up his 2nd Battalion—120 men were all that remained—and, moving through murderous machine-gun and rifle fire, "30 to 40" of the battalion's men were likewise able to find cover on the road's western edge while a few slipped across.

But as the sun burned off the morning fog, the 2nd and 3rd Battalions' survivors remained checked by the intense German fire and clung to their precarious positions in the wheat as Babcock struggled to close a kilometer-wide gap between the regiment's left and the right of the French 153rd.

At 11:15 A.M. the French attempted a "minor operation" to close the gap, but, Babcock reported, "This operation was not highly successful as machine gun nests still operated very effectively from on our left flank causing continued and heavy casualties."

Because of this, Babcock ordered the left of the 28th "refused"—bent back to cover the flank—and asked for artillery fire to be placed on the Vauxbuin position, and as well for the 153rd "or some force be sent up to clear the areas to our left." But nothing happened, according to Babcock.

With the 28th's 2nd and 3rd Battalions virtually used up, the division had little choice but to release the 1st Battalion, three companies of which remained in reserve one kilometer west of Missy Ravine. (Company C had once again been brought forward at 3:00 A.M. on July 19 and placed "in depth behind the Paris-Soissons Road just north of the 28th Infantry," Charles Senay recalled.)

It was time for fresh blood, fresh meat, fresh legs to continue the fight, and as snipers and machine gunners pinned down the hungry and thirsty survivors of its brother battalions, the 1st Battalion's men climbed from their improvised holes and struck for Missy Ravine.

"About noon orders came to advance," Wilbert Murphy wrote. "Packs were adjusted and over we went. It was necessary to expose ourselves very much in crossing the crest of the ridge—consequently as soon as Jerry saw us coming he opened up; and we had very little barrage of our own ahead of us.

"Double timing over the crest and down into the valley we went. Gas was in the valley so we couldn't stop. A few adjusted gas masks on the run. Most of us didn't. We gained the next slope O.K. and without a single casualty. Then we spread ourselves out in a wheatfield to await the signal for a further advance."

German machine gunners probed for new targets among the battalion's men, one bullet nearly ending Murphy's great adventure. "Jerry must have seen us enter the wheat field for his machine guns kept up a constant put-put-put, and we could see the dust rise where the bullets hit around us," Murphy wrote. "I had a queer feeling once when I felt something slap against my pack. When I got a chance to look I saw that a machine gun bullet just grazed my helmet and hit the pack going through the mess kit and finally stopping in the handle of the small shovel I carried. I felt pretty lucky."

"It became a rough afternoon with mounting casualties from shell and bullet fire," Senay would write. But it wasn't until 3:15 P.M., according to Babcock, that the division sent word that a renewal of the attack would "probably" be ordered for 4:00 P.M.

Reaching 1st Division headquarters by phone to discuss the order, Babcock had the misfortune of having 1st Division commander Charles Summerall himself pick up—and their subsequent talk would result several weeks later in the relief of Babcock from command of the 28th.

Babcock told Summerall that it was impossible for the 28th to launch its attack from the area ordered by the division, as that position was in fact held by the Germans. Summerall told the colonel to attack and that "troops would come up on my left."

Babcock, still bitter a quarter of a century later, added of Summerall (who had once replied to a question about his men's capabilities: "Sir, when the First Division has only two men left they will be echeloned in depth and attacking toward Berlin"): "Later, he informed me that this message indicated to him I was prone to see obstacles; that he did not want officers in his Division to make reports concerning obstacles in their sector. That he knew all about the difficulties, didn't wish to be told about them. That he was prepared to sacrifice the entire division if he thought it best to carry out his orders (I can well believe that) and that all he wanted was for us all to simply go forward regardless of conditions."

Summerall would almost get his wish this day at the Paris-Soissons Road.

With the understanding that the French 153rd intended to move forward in the late afternoon, the division's order called for the 28th to attack with the aim of linking the French and American forces and clearing the German positions on the left, and as well to push two kilometers across the wheat to Ploisy Ravine, and then another kilometer beyond to the strategic village of Berzy-le-Sec, which had originally been an objective of the French but which was turned over to the 1st on the morning of the nineteenth.

The order from 1st Division headquarters to Colonel Babcock reads: "General Summerall directs you to send a battalion to close the gap between the left of the 28th Infty and the 153d Div. The gap is said to be about 1 kilometer wide. Gen. Summerall directs that you see that the 28th Inf advances immediately and establish close liaison with the 153d Div. if that Division advances."

And it is upon such words that worlds turn, nightmares spawned, indelible memories etched, and lives obliterated.

I'll never know what thoughts raced through the mind of twenty-six-year-old John Nelson, who lay there in the wheat that afternoon as the hot sun was just beginning its descent and shrapnel burst in every direction, and a staccato *pup-pup-pup* from the machine guns split the air, and while every shadow pointed east, over there, that way, over bunches of dead doughboys and through wheat fields pocked by machine guns and well-hidden German riflemen.

Physically, he was at that moment as close as he had been for seven years to the bucolic and ancient pleasures and deprivations of the family farmstead of Kangsleboda, but considering his lot there at the Paris-Soissons Road, he was at the same time as far away as he would ever be.

We are not soldiers, except for him, our genes bespeaking that long line of flip-flopping and peaceable stay-at-home Nils Jonssons and Jon Nilssons, centuries of wooden clogs and a few coins and a skinny cow in the pasture and a family Bible on the table, not grand tales of heroism and sacrifice on the slopes of Bunker Hill, Missionary Ridge, or Mount Suribachi.

But he was surrounded at that moment by other such accidental soldiers, all in the same boat, and as he had not a philosophizing bone in his body, I can only guess that John Nelson's thoughts at that perilous moment were similar to those that had occupied Emmett Donahue as he waited for Company G to jump off into the wheat the morning before.

"It is next to impossible to describe the anguish and mental suffering and agony that a man passes through while waiting for the time," Donahue recalled. "As each man is equipped with a time piece, he watches those tiny hands creep around the shining face hoping against hope that it will never reach there, and then again wishing it would come sooner, in order to get it over with."

But it seems reasonable as well that thoughts of the coming and unknown trials that lay beyond that road, and the question of whether he would even find a way to stand and move his feet toward it, tickled the mind of John Nelson, and the minds of every other as yet untested soldier who lay with his head pressed into the wheat on that terrible afternoon.

It was a question that all men have faced in all wars, a question that can't be answered until the dust has settled and the dead are being carried off the field. And it was certainly a question that faced all of the men at Soissons through those four days, including Gerald Stamm, who, after facing his own initiation into battle at Soissons, was able to write matter-of-factly: "I had answered one question that probably haunts every thinking man on the eve of his first battle—'Will I be afraid?' I was afraid—definitely and terribly afraid, but that fear decreased with action. I went forward and did my share of the fighting. It was not a hero's share and I won no medals, but it was a share of which I had no need to be ashamed."

Captain Edward S. Johnston, who led Company E of the 28th Regiment at Cantigny and Soissons, would later write that the double traits of bravery and cowardice could be found in the enlisted men of his unit—and in all soldiers, for that matter: "Most of them went into Battle because they were soldiers, because it was ordered, because it was fitting, because it was expected. They were themselves in doubt as to what they would do to the Battle, and what it would do to them.

"They did not know, themselves, whether they were brave or cowardly—and never did find out. When almost all are heroes, and nearly every one is frightened, how is a fellow to know?"

So it was that the Old Man no doubt found himself plumbing his own well of courage, as was every other man of the 28th's 1st Battalion as they lay in the wheat, waiting for the order to go over.

Less than half a mile away, and at the crest of the gently sloping rise before them, the lollipop-shaped poplars picketing the Paris-Soissons Road stood silhouetted against the azure July sky, across which airplanes flitted and swooped and dived, oblivious to the ongoing drama below.

Bullets and artillery shells rained among the prone ranks of the 1st Battalion's men, as each one pressed to the ground and prayed, or simply went numb and mindless, refusing to even consider the pending, perhaps penultimate—and perhaps final—experience that awaited them at that road.

"These were tense moments," Charles Butler, a twenty-six-year-old lieutenant on the 1st Battalion's staff, recalled. "The troops of the battalion lay on the ground in thick lines, waiting for the zero hour. Boche gas and high explosive shells were raking the roadway and taking their deadly toll. Bullets from the distant, high-angled fire of the Boche machine guns peppered the ground like rain. These lagging moments before the zero hour tried men's souls. Some prayed. Mormons read their pocket Bibles. Others collapsed from exhaustion and fear."

Battalion commander George Rozelle met with Babcock just south of Breuil, and remembered being told by Babcock that the 1st Battalion was to attack at 4:30 P.M., the assault straddling a country lane running from Breuil to the first objective of the Farm du Mont de Courmelles, on the northern edge of Ploisy Ravine.

Once at the edge of the deep ravine, the battalion was to wait for twenty minutes while artillery shelled the ravine, after which "the battalion would continue its advance with Berzy le Sec as its second objective," Rozelle wrote.

But at the appointed hour of attack, the American artillery failed to appear. Babcock instructed Rozelle to postpone the attack "until he gave the order to do so," and then left the scene to take a phone call at his command post.

At 5:30 P.M., Babcock sent a message ordering the 1st Battalion forward, although the promised artillery support had still not arrived. According to Rozelle, he and Company B commander Captain Clarence Oliver moved forward one hundred yards "to get a view of the terrain over which the battalion was to advance."

Company commanders, meanwhile, relayed orders to their junior officers. While there was later confusion as to the exact objective of the assault, "I remember quite distinctly that my company commander, Lieut. Sorensen, gave me my final objective on the map as Berzy-le-Sec," Bill Warren would write.

Organized into square formation, with Companies B and D in the lead, from left to right, and Companies A and C in support, the battalion's men rushed forward on Rozelle's signal, a lusty cry from a thousand parched throats merging into one as they charged across the wheat and ascended the rolling incline that crested at the Paris-Soissons Road.

And John Nelson was one of them that day, at that moment, perhaps emitting a primal howl as he raced toward the rest of his life, as he raced to judgment day at that road, racing because he was a soldier and this was what soldiers do, this was what soldiers did, all the while certain he would die, he would tell my sister many, many years later, because "boys were dying all around me."

And when it was all over he would leave us with just the following brief summary of his hair-raising and grand adventure, as he crossed that road and headed toward the abyss, the tide of a world war turning on his very footsteps, the tide of his own life nearly ebbing and leaving the Old Man, and us, high and dry in the middle of a sea of wheat:

"My outfit started advancing on July 18 and moved forward several miles in the first two days. About six o'clock on the 19th I was struck by machine gun fire from our flank, was knocked unconscious and did not come to until about midnight. Was picked up by stretcher bearers in the morning and taken to a first-aid station."

And I can see him now, his bayonet glistening in the fading late-afternoon sunshine, racing through that golden grass alongside Wilbert

Murphy and Willard Storms and Rollin Livick and the rest, racing ever closer to that road, then up its west bank and across the hard-packed dirt bed strewn with dead and dying doughboy flotsam, and then down again, and a pause, perhaps, just a moment to catch his breath.

And then it's up again, and dashing across another open field, lungs on fire and legs turning to lead, until the moment when some of that miserable spray from the Vauxbuin position catches him, so perfect now and so expected that *of course* the bullet entered from the left, and then he's falling, going blank and dark into a dreamless sleep—and as the battle rages on, ever eastward, he'll be there in its wake, safe and bleeding and oblivious; and so we will leave him there, to what in some ways would be his good and unconscious fortune, and pick up the story of Company D's rolling assault across the plain toward the village of Ploisy.

By all accounts, it was a bloodbath. After crossing the Paris-Soissons Road, the 1st Battalion quickly began to suffer the full effect of the enfilading fire from the numerous machine guns just to the north at the Vauxbuin position—especially Companies A and B, on the left of the assault, who were ordered by Rozelle to veer slightly north and envelope the Breuil-Courmelles Farm Road.

"The enemy machine gun fire was terrific, particularly from the left flank, where there was a powerful strong point," Charles Senay would write. "The casualties were heavy," Clarence Huebner added, "but the battalion continued to advance."

Charles Butler would recall: "The German artillery and machine-gun fire doubled until it seemed that the advancing waves would be entirely swept away. Timed shells exploded overhead, raining red hot shrapnel down on the dashing doughboys. Men fell like grain before a reaper, but the avenging line never faltered. Some fell, some died, but the charge went ever forward."

The 1st Division's history says that the 1st Battalion "passed through the rest of the regiment with a dash that defied all opposition. It swept over the most severe resistance at every step and clung to the heels of its barrage. Casualties were heavy and when the objective was reached only eight officers were left to command the front line."

"This time the machine gun bullets were hell," Wilbert Murphy would write. "Some of our best friends dropped, but it only made us more determined to stick it out and get our revenge.

"We went a couple hundred yards and hit the Paris-Soissons road and then an open plain which was fairly level. The road was covered with dead Huns and not a few Americans. They had had hard fighting. Still we went on and with a cheer, a shout of defiance to the Huns, we swept across that highway and into the open field beyond."

Exposed to the raking fire from the Vauxbuin position on its left and to machine-gun and rifle fire coming from the German positions to their front, the 1st Battalion's doughboys fell in bunches as they raced for Ploisy Ravine. Losses approached 80 percent as the battalion's men spread across the naked plain, taking machine-gun nests in mad, brave rushes.

The former berry picker Tempton C. Hall was among the casualties, falling with seven bullets in one leg after charging a machine-gun nest. Dragged from the wheat by the Germans, the corporal was carried to Berzy-le-Sec, where German medics would care for his wound over the next two days.

Scores of other Company D men would also fall that day as they raced east through choking dust and the dangling bits of chaff kicked up by the machine guns—among them Sergeant Thomas Ayer, Privates James Carney, Henry Fanning, Denis J. Cullity, Joseph E. Person, William J. Dawson, the Janesville boy Walter Meyer, and the Camp Grant replacements George Chiodras and Pasquale Carravetta.

Private Sam Terman, another Camp Grant replacement, was shot in the abdomen; like the Old Man, "he was evacuated to the hospital," Private Edward Backley remembered. Unlike John Nelson, "he died of the wound," Backley added.

Another Camp Grant replacement, the former Chicago teamster Abe Sachs, would find refuge in a shell hole after catching a bullet in the face. "When I got near their first line the Huns leaped out, threw down their guns, and ran like greyhounds," Sachs said later. "I heard one boy near me say, 'You couldn't catch that outfit with a motorcycle.'

"Their machine gunners are what hurt us. If it had not been for them, I guess that first bunch of Huns would be in Berlin by this time, if their legs held out."

The experience of Company B's Private Paul Vogel—another of the

Janesville boys—was eerily similar to that of John Nelson. Crossing that open plain with Company B, Vogel took a machine-gun bullet near his left eye; another broke his leg.

"After I 'came through,' I saw my corporal laying in front of me," he would write. "He was wounded in the right leg, but was able to handle himself. I said to the corporal, 'Let's dig a little hole with our bayonets. It will help to protect us from machine gun fire.' I had not any more spoke to him than I got hit in the left shoulder."

Vogel added: "A fellow came along just then and he asked if there was anything he could do for us. I told him that he could dress my wounds to keep me from losing too much blood, so he dressed my wounds and also dug a hole for me so I wouldn't get hit again.

"I laid there all night and finally about six o'clock in the morning an ambulance came along and rushed me to the hospital." Vogel, like John Nelson and so many others, would spend much of the rest of the war in Red Cross Hospital No. 1 in Paris.

German artillery, held back until the 1st Battalion had advanced about five hundred yards, was added to the misery of the machine guns. One shell caught Company D's Private Joseph Zerwes and sent him sprawling; he would lose his right leg—and his shell-shocked mind—and spend the rest of his life in veterans-care facilities.

"The fire of the enemy's artillery was not felt until after the firing line had crossed the Paris-Soissons highway," Rozelle would remember. "Some of the fire from the enemy artillery seemed to be direct or low angle fire coming from one or two forward guns stationed in the immediate vicinity of Berzy le Sec."

As the doughboys raced for life and limb across the plain, the French 153rd finally advanced on the 1st Battalion's northern flank, and by 5:45 P.M. carried the problematic Vauxbuin position, allowing the battalion's survivors to make a run for Courmelles Farm and the edge of the Ploisy Ravine, where at the bottom the fortified village of Ploisy awaited them.

"We had broken their defense and they were in retreat," Wilbert Murphy would write. "Our line of skirmishers across that plain was beautiful—yes marvelous. Nothing but Jerry 'G.I.' cans bothered us now and he was throwing a bunch of them over. (By G.I. cans, I mean H.E. shells.)"

The battalion split as it moved across the plain, the survivors of Companies A and B halting just northwest of Courmelles Farm, along a road that ran from the farm to the village of Courmelles, one kilometer to the northeast.

Companies D and C, meanwhile, veered south toward Ploisy to cover a gap between the right of the 28th Regiment and the left of the 26th. The battalion's survivors waited in vain for the promised artillery support at the edge of the ravine for twenty minutes before Rozelle ordered his men forward again.

"We crossed the plain and went down a hillside into a valley and captured the town of Ploisy—but we could not stop even though we were nearly exhausted," Murphy remembered.

"My throat and mouth were just parched dry, my legs ached, and my head swam from the concussion of exploding shells—but I couldn't quit. I kept up with my Corporal and we passed through the town and up the next hill."

Companies C and D entered the ravine and enveloped Ploisy, the former attacking from the north and Company D along the ravine's southern edge. All told, Senay would write, the two companies captured seventy-five men and several machine guns in the village.

Senay remembered that as he made his way through Ploisy, he picked up a loaded rifle that had been thrown down by a doughboy after its stock had been shot away. "Suddenly I heard, 'Kamerad,'" Senay wrote. "Slightly to my right was a German soldier, but he wasn't looking at me. Following the direction of his gaze, I saw a GI coming toward him." The German soldier "dropped his hand and shot the American with a concealed pistol. The boy fell like a sack. I'd immediately covered the German. He turned and saw the menacing rifle muzzle.

"His hand shot into the air and he pleaded for mercy, calling on God, his mother and his family. I let him feel the full terror of death and then shot him beneath his armpit."

As this drama played out, soldiers from Company D found and liberated some American prisoners from caves that pocked the southern slope of the ravine. Companies A and B—whose commander, Clarence Oliver, was "killed shortly after reaching the 1st objective while observing the ground to his left front," Rozelle wrote—assaulted the German garrison at Courmelles Farm.

"After a series of attacks and counter-attacks by opposing handfuls of men, in which quarter was neither asked nor given, the farm finally remained in the hands of the 28th Infantry," Senay wrote.

Huebner wrote of the fighting there: "One officer and about one platoon of Company B attacked and captured this farm, only in turn to be counter attacked by the enemy. The enemy counter attack was so powerful that the few men of Company B that had just captured the farm were all overwhelmed and all died fighting gallantly. Other men of Company B made a second attack on the farm and succeeded in recapturing it."

After a pause, Companies C and D continued on toward their final objective—Berzy-le-Sec, which sat strategically on the edge of the plateau, and from which the Germans could guard the valley of the Crise River.

"Organization had temporarily disappeared because of the heavy casualties," Senay wrote. "The remnants of the battalion were here organized by Lieutenant Sorenson and myself."

Senay cautiously led the mixed contingent of companies up the steep southern embankment of Ploisy Ravine. "Before I reached the top, I placed my helmet on my bayonet and lifted it slowly over the rim," he wrote. "There was no fire."

Turning east, the one hundred soldiers followed Senay and Sorensen up a sheltering rise, moving parallel to woods lining the ravine's edge. Reaching the crest, the doughboys found themselves at the western edge of the wide and exposed plain before Berzy and soon ran into "a massed force of Germans counter attacking from the direction of Berzy-le-Sec," Senay wrote.

"The enemy advanced shoulder to shoulder protected only by slight small arms fire and an ineffectual screen of potato masher grenades, thrown well beyond range, apparently for moral effect."

Senay added: "It was duck soup. The Germans were too distant to reach us with their grenades and we simply mowed them down by rifle fire. Entire groups would fall at one time. I was nearly incoherent with battle frenzy and was ahead of my firing line. One of my men pulled me behind the line."

The Germans quickly retreated. Wilbert Murphy remembered seeing a "wonderful sight" of several hundred Boche racing for the safety of Berzy-le-Sec.

"Going down the road ahead of us, at a distance of about 300 yards was nearly a company of Jerries in full retreat. They didn't even stop to yell 'kamerad' or take their guns or anything. They just beat it. We let loose on them with our rifles and saw quite a number of them drop."

The Germans in Berzy soon began sweeping the plateau with dense machine-gun fire, forcing the doughboys to retreat west 1,200 yards to where the plain descends toward Ploisy, leaving numerous dead and dying doughboys and Germans behind.

"Bodies were everywhere," Senay remembered. "One lieutenant was dead on his knees. He had been hit in the head and a grayish mass of blood and brains dribbled down his shoulders."

With no support on either flank, the isolated doughboys were certain a counterattack was imminent. Darkness, and a lack of aggressiveness on the Germans' part, forestalled an attack.

"The machine gun fire got so intense and deadly that we had to stop and seek shelter behind the crest of the hill," Murphy wrote. "Our company was there alone—the outfits on our flanks had not gone as fast as we did. It was nearly dark—getting near the close of the second day of fighting."

Lieutenant Charles Butler found shelter at the edge of Ploisy Ravine, while other men remained strung out on the reverse slope directly west of Berzy. "Within half an hour the entire front wave was back on the reverse side of the rocky, wooded slope, where the men put up their shelter halves and dug in as best as they could," he wrote. "Thus they were partly protected from flying bits of shrapnel and from the rain which had begun to fall.

"At intervals all night long the Boche artillery threw gas and high explosive shells into the valley of Ploisy below, but little damage was suffered by the men on the hillside except for disturbance of their sleep."

As the battles at Courmelles Farm and in Ploisy Ravine raged, Huebner, following the 1st Battalion with the pitiful remnants of the 2nd and 3rd Battalions, spread his few men thinly across high ground halfway between Missy Ravine and Ploisy. As this small force moved across the field

Captain Van Natter fell. He had left Lieutenant Dacus earlier that after-noon at the Paris-Soissons Road, setting out with two runners from Dacus's company. "An hour or so later he returned, after losing the two men to sniper fire, and confirmed that we were to go over at 5 p.m.," Dacus re-called. "We did, about two squads, a Capt. and a 2nd Lt. In about ten min-utes, Van was hit—it looked to me like it was in the throat. I did not expect to see him again."

(Dacus and Van Natter, wounded not in the throat but in his cheek, would indeed meet again the following October, "in a smoke-filled café in Nice" while on leave; once again, Van Natter would greet the startled lieu-tenant with the words, "Hey, Dacus!")

Huebner, pausing with his small command on that bit of high ground before Ploisy Ravine, was wounded when a piece of shrapnel drilled through his helmet and caught him above the right eye.

Lieutenant Samuel Parker, who had been injured in the foot during Company K's heroic assault at the quarry near Breuil the previous day, fol-lowed the advance on his hands and knees. He remembered hearing the words "The major is hit"; turning, he saw Huebner on his back, his face covered with blood.

Parker wrote later that his first thought was "that a machine gun bullet has shattered his brain." But Huebner opened eyes, telling Parker only: "Take my maps and carry on."

With that, Huebner's eyes closed and, so Parker thought, he died. But that evening Huebner "stumbled" into the 28th Regiment's headquarters at Le Mont d'Arly. Second Brigade commander Buck remembered: "His steel helmet was broken in front, his face and shirt were bloody. Upon see-ing me he said, 'Well, General, they got me at last!' I examined the wound. He smiled and said, 'It doesn't amount to much,' but I could see he was dizzy while he was talking to me."

Buck credited the tin hat with saving Huebner's life; Parker was aston-ished to encounter the battalion commander back on the job just a few weeks after leaving him for dead.

Meanwhile, Rozelle, the 1st Battalion's commander, was nowhere to be found, having been so far out in front of the assault that he and four run-ners wound up on "the final objective"—Berzy—and found themselves "in danger of being killed by machine gun fire from the front and rear or of being captured."

Before escaping and making contact with a platoon from Company A at Courmelles Farm late that night, Rozelle tore up his communications codes and buried the papers in some brush "in order to prevent them from falling into the hands of the enemy in case that we were killed or captured."

Rozelle—who had been reported killed—and several staff members and runners meandered through Ploisy Ravine, lost, until 2:00 A.M.

Rozelle would in 1926 explain his actions after the battalion had paused before Ploisy Ravine: "It was at this point that the Batt. Comdr. made the serious mistake of trying to play the heroic role by actually 'leading his men' instead of driving them."

At daybreak, he sheepishly reported to Conrad Babcock. Rozelle would spend years living down his misadventure, but on the morning of July 20 Babcock had his own issues to deal with, including an immediate and bitter regret that he had remained behind at his post Le Mont d'Arly when the 1st Battalion jumped off: "Although our Divisional training neither required nor advised brigade and regimental commanders to accompany front line battalions in action, I am certain that when Ploisy was captured I should have been there. Perhaps, I might have had sufficient energy to push on the weary men of the 1st Battalion and taken Berzy that night."

The man who would twice defy orders in an effort to limit casualties during the 28th Regiment's ordeal at Soissons would add: "A little of our Civil War medicine is what we lacked in the Great War."

In fact, the battalion was spent, its assault taking three hours to wrest one and one half miles of ground from the Germans. There was little the weary men could do but consolidate a new front line, which that evening ran from Courmelles Farm on the northern edge of Ploisy Ravine to the high ground west of Berzy-le-Sec in the south.

As much as the battalion had suffered, Huebner wrote, the Germans had suffered even more. "The losses of the enemy were appalling. At least one battery of 77's had been captured and many prisoners were taken. The enemy dead were piled everywhere."

Charles Yuill, who commanded Company B of the 3rd Machine-Gun Battalion, recalled the chaotic scene as stragglers, survivors, and even

Moroccans washed up at Ploisy Ravine. "An Algerian liaison platoon reported to the company command post. The machine-gun company commander drank the platoon sergeant's wine and then directed him to report to the American troops in the valley to the left.

"A captain of the 28th Infantry arrived alone and showed evidence of, and talked about, his narrow escapes until told to organize the 28th Infantry and move forward on the slope."

By the end of the second day's fighting, the men were thirsty and ravenously hungry, many of them having had little to eat or drink since jumping off the previous morning. Extra effort was made to bring food and water forward to Ploisy across the shell-raked plain—and German artillery again took its toll on the rolling kitchens as they were moved forward. Six were destroyed, and "many casualties were inflicted among the men and animals of the train," Huebner would write later from secondhand information. "It was only with great difficulty that the food was brought forward but it was a case of where the gain was worth the sacrifice."

But the good old Y.M.C.A. would once more go where even the army feared to tread and provide succor for the troops. Charles Yuill remembered the amazing sight of a truck pulling into Ploisy Ravine at dusk "with chocolate and cookies. The truck was unloaded and left"—unharmed.

And John Nelson would sleep through all of this, to awaken in the drizzling midnight with no idea at first of where he was, or of what had hit him, or whether he might live or die, as day two closed on these operations south of Soissons.

14

"Shooting, Yelling, Swearing"

ARTILLERY AND MACHINE-GUN FIRE punctuated the night of July 19–July 20, as the exhausted doughboys fitfully tried to get a few winks beneath their shelter halves. Rain fell, too, cooling the night and making sleep more attainable, but the knowledge of what tomorrow might bring certainly haunted the survivors as they attempted to drift off.

As dawn broke, German artillery and machine guns began to pour flanking fire into the doughboys' positions from the eastern edge of the Crise Valley, and as well from the north, where the French, once again, hadn't been able to keep up with the 28th Regiment. The fire rose in intensity with the sun, the Boche showing "that he was nervous and that he expected the attack to be resumed," Lieutenant Charles Butler wrote.

"His artillery and machine gunners kept up a steady fire, while his observation planes hummed overhead. The American field pieces returned the fire with vigor but failed to silence the Huns. Under these conditions, it was extremely difficult to reorganize the waves resuming the attack."

Charles Senay remembered that shortly after daybreak "a two seater German observation plane floated up the little valley below us, looking for artillery. The observer saw us and leaned over the side of the fuselage and emptied his Luger at us.

"I was so astonished that I stood with open mouth gazing at him while my own 45 lay snugly in its holster at my side." (Senay was evacuated from the battlefield shortly thereafter, a wound he suffered to his right hand the day before having turned swollen and black overnight.)

A field memo sent by the 3rd Battalion's Captain Howard E. Hawkinson painted the doughboys' situation that morning:

"1st, 2nd, & 3rd Bns 28th Inf occupy crest of hill to east of Ploisy. We have touch with 26th on right. A post of ours on west slope of Ploisy ravine has touch with French on left. The enemy is sweeping us with machine gun fire from left rear. His present line crosses ravine to north of Ploisy and bends around down through Berzy-le-Sec."

Berzy-le-Sec remained the ultimate prize, and in the early afternoon of July 20 Conrad Babcock—who had finally made it to Ploisy late the previous night—received orders from the 1st Division to make another attack on the village with the remainder of the 28th Regiment, which at 2:00 P.M. was to once more simply form and attack across that open plain, following a small barrage.

Once again, Babcock objected to the order, and in a phone call to 2nd Brigade commander Buck asked for heavier artillery support for the advance: "I notified the Brigade Commander that, in my opinion, a heavy barrage especially in the vicinity of the enemies machine guns across the valley north of us and also east of Berzy-le-Sec should be put down, that the ground over which the troops were to pass was practically flat and under heavy shell fire and cross machine gun fire, and that we probably would sustain more heavy losses if we attacked in the open at 2.00 p.m."

The plan for the attack, he bitterly noted, "was not altered."

Babcock recalled the state of his regiment that early afternoon—and his fears that the attack over the open ground toward Berzy would amount to little more than murder: "Having just come from the front line; knowing how small in numbers and how weary the men were and what great losses had already occurred, I felt it my duty as the regimental commander to make an effort to save some of their lives and get my gallant soldiers some real artillery support."

By the afternoon of July 20, the 28th Regiment was nearly used up, its twelve companies consisting of just ten officers and fewer than four hundred enlisted men. The remainder of the 3,247 men that jumped off on July 18 were either "dead, wounded, or shirking—hiding—in the wheat or in the stone houses at Breuil, Missy, or Ploisy," Babcock remembered.

"To attack Berzy-le-Sec over a flat plain 1200 yards wide under clear observation by the enemy, with their guns sweeping it from three sides, was sure to cause further heavy casualties unless we were given strong artillery support."

Babcock hastened to meet with George Rozelle, back on the job after his previous night's misadventure. Rozelle, who according to Babcock "appeared mentally well below par" because of exhaustion, told him that he had already arranged for Soren Sorensen to lead the 1st Batallion in an attack on Berzy.

While reading the order, Babcock noted that it was suggested that the battalion use "the infiltration method of attacking," and Babcock— obviously as distressed as Hanson Ely had been with the division's willingness to use up the 28th Infantry—seized on what seemed an "out" for Sorensen's doomed enterprise.

Babcock ordered Rozelle to send "three or four small groups" of about sixteen men each toward Berzy under the protection of the barrage—and "attempt to filter these groups into Berzy-le-Sec by passing through the trees bordering Ploisy ravine and to enter Berzy-le-Sec from the north then try to bring over more groups until he had passed his entire battalion over."

But the village's defenses were extreme and impregnable, especially to an attack in broad daylight. Its stone houses had been "converted into veritable forts and every avenue of approach was swept with dense bands of machine gun fire," Clarence Huebner wrote. A battery of 77s guarded the approach.

At 2:00 P.M., Sorensen made his move on Berzy with his small groups, moving from tree to tree and stone to stone under a hail of gunfire. Meanwhile, a battalion of the 26th Regiment followed the barrage and attacked directly east over the ravine bluff south of town "accompanied by the devastating fire of the enemy's artillery," the 1st Division's history says. "Men struck by the enemy's fire either disappeared or ran aimlessly about and toppled over."

The 26th's attack quickly faltered: "The attack had met the resistance of a strong position occupied in great force by the enemy. It could not be taken at this time by our worn soldiers, and, after this advance, they could go no farther. The thin lines lay down in shell holes, while long files of wounded hobbled painfully back."

Sorensen's group ran into similarly intense fire as it attempted to close on the town from the northwest, and Sorensen was forced to give up the novel attempt at taking the village.

"The attempt was made by Sorenson, a courageous, energetic officer; and he and his groups reached the outskirts of Berzy; but heavy enemy machine gun fire made it impossible, in Sorenson's opinion, to enter the village until after dark," Babcock recalled. (Two of Company D's men—the regular Sergeant John Licklider and the Camp Grant replacement Private Edward Backley—would earn Distinguished Service Crosses for their roles in reducing several German machine-gun nests during the attack.)

Sorensen was told to try again at 11:00 P.M.—but Company D would be spared potential disaster just minutes before jumping off, when it was discovered that the 1st Division's artillery planned to bombard Berzy at 4:45 the next morning, at which point elements of the company might be the only living things there.

Babcock would recall his "frantic state of mind, my effort to think and act clearly" after receiving notice of the planned bombardment—"A notice that showed there was absolutely no coordination between the Division and its attacking elements. Instead of saving some of the lives of my men, my plan, had it gone through, might have caused further heavy loss."

"Routing out" Rozelle, Babcock ordered the attack abandoned, and Sorensen and Company D were ordered to fall back to Ploisy. The 28th Regiment's men dug in for another long night. Hunger and thirst overtook them, and led some to leave the safety of their holes to forage for water and food.

"Still nothing to eat and no water," Wilbert Murphy would write. "When it got dark on the evening of the third day I and a couple other fellows went after water. We succeeded in finding some after a couple hours looking for it and ducking shells. Got back to our company O.K. and found that a little chow had arrived. It surely tasted good even though there was but little of it."

There was hope among the men that night that they would be relieved (to the south, the 2nd Division had been relieved on the evening of the nineteenth after suffering losses equal to or fewer than those of the 1st). But of course, there was one more thing for the men of 1st Battalion to do.

Once again, they were ordered to assault Berzy.

And, once again, the attempt would be made in broad daylight.

Rozelle remembered receiving the order to attack at 1:30 A.M. on the morning of July 21 and casting about for reinforcements. Before daybreak, he managed to scrounge up one squad from the 3rd Battalion, and another thirty men from the 2nd Battalion.

Buck, who according to legend was ordered by General Summerall to take the village or face cashiering, arrived at Ploisy on the night of July 20–July 21 and met with the exhausted, battered survivors of the 28th Infantry, strung out in their pitiful foxholes before the village, to explain the mission almost individually.

"So exhausted were the men that it was often necessary to take hold of them and shake them to get their attention," Buck would remember. "By flash light, beneath a shelter-half," Buck explained the order for the 8:30 A.M. assault, and "gave each petty commander a copy of the sketch map to guide him in the formation and attack and told them I expected them to be with them at jump-off."

Buck added: "This handful of brave men never once questioned the order to go forward against the strongly fortified village which, the afternoon before, repulsed the attack of ten times the present numbers! And I felt as I looked at them that I would run through a dozen barrages to keep my promise to be with them at the jump-off."

There was nothing fancy about the plan. The 28th's 1st Battalion—by that morning consisting of fewer than three hundred men—was simply to form for the attack right under the noses of the Germans.

Following a rolling barrage, the doughboys would have to cross one kilometer of flat, exposed ground in full view of the Germans, who were being reinforced by their 46th Division even as Buck was giving the orders for the assault to his skeleton command.

(Just how much artillery support the doughboys actually received remains in question. Major Raymond Austin of the 6th Field Artillery, supporting the 1st Brigade to the south, would write that the 6th "shifted our fire out of our own sector to help them with a rolling barrage." Babcock and Rozelle would complain that the artillery support came too late, and was too feeble, to provide any real help.)

Continuing to scrounge for help for the assault on Berzy, Rozelle by 8:00 A.M. collected another handful of men from the 2nd and 3rd Battalions; as well, some scattered survivors from the 16th, 18th, and 26th Regiments were thrown into the second waves. In all, about four hundred men were available to form lines for the attack.

Sorensen was to lead Company D in the first wave, but just three minutes before jump-off, as he was going over the plan of attack one last time with Buck, a shell exploded five yards away from him. A fragment hit him in his left hip, "and he had to be carried away to a safer place at the edge of the ravine," Buck recalled.

The front waves were then placed under the command of two junior officers. Lieutenant James Howland Donaldson, twenty-six, would lead Company B on the left. The studious, calm, and bemused Lieutenant Bill Warren, just twenty-two years old and one year removed from that oration-filled home back in Elmira, New York, would lead Company D on the right. Two support lines, spaced two hundred meters apart, were to follow the lead wave, the men spaced five paces apart.

A fire for destruction was to be laid on the village beginning at 5:30 A.M., but, Babcock remembered, "it was a beautiful morning and not a shot was being fired by either side."

The promised rolling barrage that was to harken the 8:30 A.M. attack was late in arriving, Babcock remembering that just prior to jump-off, "Not a projectile was heard passing over head. At 8:40 a.m., a few friendly shells were heard passing on their journey to the enemy, but it was a misnomer to call such artillery support a barrage."

After waiting in vain for the promised artillery support, Rozelle "received permission from Gen. Buck in person at 8:40 a.m. to advance without it," Rozelle remembered.

The 1st Battalion's survivors—"only a thin line of skirmishers," Buck would write—pulled themselves from their holes and formed on the reverse slope where the plain before Berzy-le-Sec descends west toward the Paris-Soissons Road a mile away.

Marching steadily east up that slope, the doughboys soon found themselves facing the wide plateau that lapped up to the western edge of the village. Already, spent machine-gun bullets plopped at their feet, and a battery of German 77s coughed away, the shells ploughing new furrows into the wheat. The first wave paused for a moment, the men perhaps reconsidering the odds.

Seeing them stop, Buck rushed forward "to see what was the matter," he wrote. "Before I could reach them they resumed the advance." Looking back, Buck found the second wave lagging far behind.

"I rushed back to the jump-off line and started them forward," he recalled. "They were, apparently, perfectly willing but nobody had given them any command to move out!"

They moved on his order, as Buck "hastily gathered up every man left, mostly machine gunners, and directed them on the run to the brow of the slope, where they took posts."

From his position below the plain, Babcock could not see the assault— but he could hear it. "Immediately, the crash of bursting shells and swish of small arm bullets made their presence known all along the line," he wrote.

"The advance was taken up immediately," Rozelle would write. Pivoting on the "left element of the left company" at the edge of Ploisy Ravine, the first wave took to the level plain.

"The ground over which the battalion was to advance was already under fire from enemy artillery," Rozelle wrote. "Our own rolling barrage had failed to drop," he added, while the enemy artillery was "increasing in intensity as the battalion approached Berzy le Sec."

The thin lines moved steadily forward into a wall of machine-gun and rifle fire from well-protected emplacements in Berzy-le-Sec, where the red steeple of the village's ancient church marked their destination, its sharp triangular apex looming larger with every step the doughboys took.

Point-blank artillery fire from a battery of 77s felled the men in khaki heaps as they neared the village, and yet Company D and the 1st Battalion moved on, ever east, behind Warren and Donaldson, the doughboys bending forward as if bucking a strong gale as they crossed the open field.

Rozelle watched in horror as a shell landed amid a group from a machine-gun company, "evidently making casualties of the entire crew as no one member of that crew was seen to move after the smoke cleared." And still the others went on, their anger and bloodlust increasing as their friends fell to the right and left.

Raymond Austin would remember that the doughboys advanced "with all the calmness and unconsciousness of danger of a drill ground. Shells striking among them, men falling dead and wounded, seemed not to affect in the slightest the ones who were left. Not a man ran forward, not one lagged behind—it was just a normal steady walk forward."

A swath of dead, dying, and wounded soon marked their path. "We hadn't gone three hundred yards when over a hundred of the fellows were laying on the ground wounded or killed," Wilbert Murphy would remember. But, he added, "The second wave rushed up and filled the gaps in the first wave."

Despite a sickening feeling that his number was up, Sergeant Willard Storms dutifully formed for the assault and led his platoon toward Berzy. "I think every man in the company had the 'hunch,' I know I had it," Storms would recall. "Then the zero hour, the time appointed for attack arrived and we went 'over.' It was a scene that I will never be able to forget."

Leading his first-wave platoon of fifty men against "hundreds of machine guns as well as artillery fire," Storms recalled that the withering storm of projectiles "stopped lots of us, but couldn't break the line."

Storms fell with a bullet in his abdomen halfway across the field, as his men continued on. "I went about six hundred yards before they got me but I was the last non-com to fall of that platoon," he wrote. "They showed the world the marksmanship of the U.S. Doughboys, sniping the gunners as they went, blowing them up with hand grenades, but holding their line, always.

"When I last saw them they were still advancing, shooting, yelling, swearing, every man intent on getting more than one before getting hit.

The support, or the second wave, dwindled down to nothing, but always advancing."

It took a full ten minutes under heavy fire before the surviving dough-boys, their blood up, swarmed the battered town in a final, frenzied rush, clubbing, bayoneting, and shooting the Boche at their posts, even as more of their comrades fell riddled with bullets at the village edge.

Sensing no quarter would be given, the surviving Germans hied through the narrow, steep streets of the village, heading for the safety of German positions across the Crise River below.

"That day we took only a few prisoners," Wilbert Murphy wrote. "Not that we didn't have a chance to—but we were so 'Damn' mad at the Hun beasts that we killed most of them."

Bill Warren led Company D's survivors—"only about seventy out of two hundred and fifty men," Murphy would write—through Berzy-le-Sec in pursuit of the fleeing Germans, stopping at a tow path on the western bank of the Crise.

"Our front extended to the left to where the French were supposed to be but were not," recalled James Donaldson, who led Company B's survivors in pursuit of the Germans. "The Germans had us cornered by enfilade fire from the left through this space, as well as by direct frontal fire. Lt. Warren of D Co. also reached his objective, on my right. We two were actually at the extreme line of advance, which we held."

Warren would remember doing more than just holding. Pushing Company D across the shallow Crise, he led an advance of almost two hundred yards through the sodden, swampy ground of the Crise Valley while enduring withering machine-gun fire from a German strongpoint behind the Soissons–Château-Thierry railway embankment.

"A few of us pushed on beyond Berzy-le-Sec to a railroad track," is all Warren would write, "but fell back to join the rest of the Battalion that were formed along the crest of the hill, just north of Berzy."

In fact, things weren't as casual as Warren noted, for Company D found itself in danger of becoming cut off. A subsequent citation for bravery awarded to Sergeant Ernest E. Carlson gives an account of his platoon's near annihilation: "His platoon passed thru a second machine gun barrage in attempting the flanking of several machine guns across the valley. When it was discovered that the line had not advanced beyond Berzy-le-Sec, he nobly aided his platoon commander in extricating the men in the command from their perilous position."

Warren and his men joined the 28th's other survivors—just 280 men—as they spread themselves on Berzy's northeastern edge and dug in amid intense artillery fire from across the Crise. All expected a German reprisal, Beaumont Buck wrote. Hostile artillery fire searched out "every ravine, every cross road, every P.C., town, woods, trail, trench and possible shelter. I became impressed with the idea that it meant an impending counter attack and so advised the Division."

But the counterattack never came. In fact, the Germans had already begun a retreat, orders to pull back from the Marne having been issued even as the first battalion was attacking across the plain and toward Ploisy two days before.

With Berzy and the heights above the Crise beyond taken, and Buzancy farther to the southeast in the hands of the 1st Brigade, disaster had come to the German military machine. The significance of the bloody and costly assaults over those four days at Soissons was lost on no one, and went far beyond the loss of the 3,500 German soldiers and sixty-eight guns the 1st Division captured.

The neck of the bag hanging ominously toward the Marne had been tightened and was in danger of being closed entirely. The entire German pocket was in dire peril, and the Boche were forced to retreat.

From that point onward, the German army would gain not one foot more of French soil, and instead would begin a slow deflation of its lines, ever east toward the German border.

In his postwar book *Out of My Life*, the former German field marshal Paul von Hindenburg noted how those five never-to-be-forgotten days at Soissons had crushed the ambitions of the five great offensives undertaken in the spring: "From the purely military point of view it was of the greatest and most fateful importance that we had lost the initiative to the enemy. How many hopes, cherished during the last few months, had probably collapsed at one blow! How many calculations had been scattered to the winds!"

The German chancellor, Georg von Hertling, would write of the surprise counteroffensive below Soissons: "We expected grave events in Paris for the end of July. That was on the 15th. On the 18th even the most optimistic among us understood that all was lost. The history of the world was played out in three days."

By 9:30 A.M., the taking of Berzy-le-Sec was already turning to legend. Beaumont Buck would return home a hero, and dine out for the rest of his life on the stirring story of how he led the first wave of the attack, the subject of such idealized versions of his actions as that penned by Joseph Mills Hanson for *The Home Sector* in 1920: "As the second hand of his watch marked 30 minutes past 8 and the barrage fell, General Buck stretched his long legs out in front of the first wave, advised his men in no mincing words to follow him and get the _____ boches this time, and led off the streaming rush across the open.

"They followed—who could not with such a leader? On and on they went toward the hot muzzles that flamed through the cracks of split walls and behind fallen masses of masonry, on past those muzzles, yelling, cursing, striking down with swinging blows the desperately resisting Germans behind."

Laurence Stallings got into the act, too, writing in *The Doughboys* that Buck led the charge "like a platoon leader in front-line sweeps . . . Buck, waving his tin hat, took the village on the 2nd Brigade's second try."

In fact, Buck never claimed to have led the attack, never claimed to have oh-so-bravely urged his men on with long and artful sweeps of his tin hat. (At the same time, he does not seem to have ever gone too far out of his way to correct the image.) After urging the second line on, Buck had, in fact, remained behind. Babcock would remember encountering him near Ploisy as the attack progressed: "Just as Rozelle and the last wave of his little force climbed out of Ploisy ravine . . . I found him with one or two of his staff officers and Sorenson . . . seated in an enlarged shell-hole on the plateau east of the ravine," Babcock wrote.

Hell, at least Buck was *there*. Babcock would assert years later that General Summerall—whom Babcock would never forgive for relieving him from command of the 28th Regiment despite the taking of Berzy—had some flunky write up a nice bit of balderdash that put Summerall, and not Buck, at Ploisy on the eve of the desperate dash for Berzy.

Summerall's DSC citation claims that the general: "Visited, with great gallantry, the extreme front lines of his division and personally made a reconnaissance of the position in the face of heavy hostile machine gun and artillery fire, exhorting his men to renew the attack on Berzy-le-Sec, promising them powerful artillery support, and so encouraging them by his presence and example that they declared their readiness to take the town for him."

"The only time I saw General Summerall near the front was on the night of the 19th in the Missy-aux-Bois ravine," Babcock would remember bitterly. "Ploisy had just been captured. If he exhorted any of the 1st Battalion that evening, after their strenuous and fierce 3000 yards advance, I was never told of it."

The men who'd actually done the deed, meanwhile, were left to marvel at what they'd done, and what they'd seen. They would have no Tennyson to extol their awe-inspring feat, but they did have the *Collier's* correspondent James Hopper, who stumbled across a group of exhausted, wounded Americans at an aid station on the morning of July 21.

There Hopper found an atmosphere of "tranquil gravity" among that bunch of battle-weary doughboys: "The fighting that morning had been hard and long; these boys had seen many of their comrades die, and they bore themselves with a quiet dignity which was not quite sadness, but rather a deep realization of the sad beauty of what they had seen. I shall always remember the tone of the first whom I asked if the fighting had been hard. 'Yes, sir,' he said, 'it was hard. It was hard but the boys sure did stick to it! The boys sure did stick to it!'"

Thirteen of Company D's noncoms would be cited for sticking to it that day—among them Willard Storms and Clarence Butts. Each of the thirteen, the identical citations read, "after three days of most intense and prolonged fighting, showed his exceptional bravery, courage and endurance by leading his men thru heavy and terrific machine gun and shell fire in the attack on Berzy-le-Sec."

Warren and Bronston would also be cited for their actions at Berzy. Bill Warren's citation reads: "The other officers of his company having been casualties, he took command during this operation, giving an example of calmness, decision and courage at all times. Owing to his leadership, he and his company captured and held their final objectives before Berzy-le-Sec, although at all times exposed to heavy bombardment and intense machine gun fire."

Lloyd Bronston, characterized as "scared" by Buck in the early morning chaos before the jump-off on July 18, wound up having the last laugh. His citation reads in part: "During this operation he showed exceptional courage and devotion to duty. Disregarding personal safety, he willingly exposed himself whenever necessary and in this way inspired confidence in his own men and determination to hold on at whatever cost."

Soren Sorensen, too, would have another citation to go with the DSC he'd won at Cantigny. Sorensen, the citation notes, was wounded prior to the attack on Berzy "but refused to leave his post at the jumping off point until the progress of the attack and his own inability to advance with the men necessitated his removal to the rear.

"During the attacks made July 19th–July 21st, and in the organization and preparation for the attack on Berzy le Sec Lieut. Sorenson set an inspiring example to all around him by his coolness, intrepid courage and conspicuous gallantry. To his cool leadership is greatly due the success of the operation."

Those who had paid the supreme price, meanwhile, lay splayed and bleeding on that level plain before Berzy. While some of Company D's survivors spent the afternoon watching for a German counterattack, others returned to that field to see to the dead and wounded, finding many familiar faces among the forms that littered the ground.

Here lay Private George Dwight Cook of Ellenville, New York, whose law studies in the office of H. Westlake Coons had been interrupted by the draft the previous September. "A large shell hit at his feet and blew him into the air killing him instantly," Private John Settle would remember of the twenty-three-year-old's death.

There lay Private Dewitt Arbunoth Facundas of Denham Springs, Louisiana, his body found at the edge of the village—"shot from the stomach up to the neck, all full of holes," Private Edward Berry would say.

Supply Sergeant William Dengler, from Reading, Pennsylvania, was thrown into the assault as every available soldier was scraped up; his body, seemingly unscathed, was located on the field before Berzy, and it was decided he must have died "from shock—not a mark on his body, but he did have a weak heart," Corporal William Wright would relate.

The bodies of the Minnesotan Frank Sager and the Norwegian immigrant Thomas Eidsvik lay among the dead, as did those of the Pennsylvanians Alton C. Cole and Theodore Manitu and the Missourian Olen Fletcher.

Corporal Joseph Nichyporek became one of the eternally missing in the confusion of the morning. "He was last seen as he was sent a message," remembered Private Arthur Beauvais.

The former Chicago florist and Polish immigrant Zygmunt Misiewicz also was felled in that mad dash for Berzy. "He was hit by a machine-gun bullet while advancing, the bullet passing through his head," Private Edward Backley remembered.

Twenty-one-year-old Private Otto Beard, of Leakesville, Mississippi, had survived Cantigny, but to their dismay his comrades found his body among the corpses littering the field. Another Otto—Otto B. Swanson, a Swedish immigrant to Chicago who had trained with John Nelson at Camp Grant—was found dead in the village and was buried in a mass grave in a farmyard.

Private Merrit Booth Durham of Blue Mountain, Mississippi, made it into and through the town before being killed. His body was found east of the village, and was buried on the spot.

Private Willie B. Day, of Mariba, Kentucky, died because of a tragic miscommunication. The company's medic, Sergeant Fred Gunn, would relate after the war: "They found Day dead in the village. Nearby was a dead German. They had been dead abt 5 hours. Day was a Battalion runner and was probably on his way with a message from Hq. to Company D, whom he thought were in the village. The Company had not then taken the village. The Germans were holding it when Day arrived."

Of those fifty-five greenhorns who had reported for duty with John Nelson at Chepoix on June 18, a dozen were killed in this, their first battle, while another twelve who had trained at Fort Benjamin Harrison and Camp MacArthur—veterans of Cantigny all—had also perished (one bright spot was the discovery and liberation of Corporal Tempton C. Hall, who had been made prisoner in Berzy, where the Germans tended his mangled leg.)

All told, in the five days which Wilbert Murphy would never forget until his 1982 death, twenty-six of Company D's men would be killed outright or die of their wounds, and as many as one hundred would be wounded to some degree—many severely.

(According to Company D's morning reports, the unit went into action on July 18 slightly understrength, with 4 officers and 233 enlisted men, including 179 privates. After taking Berzy-le-Sec, acting company commander Bill Warren noted there were "4 Sgts 18 cpls. 102 Pvts missing in action"—a total of 124 men, or 52 percent of the company.)

Among those wounded on the twenty-first were Willard Storms, who took a machine-gun bullet in the right abdomen, and Murphy's squad leader, Clarence Butts, who would be left severely disabled and die before his thirty-second birthday. Chicagoan Daniel "Porky" Flynn, at Murphy's side throughout the first day's advance, also suffered a severe wound from machine-gun fire.

They found the Swedish immigrant and reluctant soldier, Private August Hedblom, prone and clinging to his weapon, a gaping hole below his nose exposing teeth that hung by a thread. "The bullet went up under his nose, and came out on his left cheek," Hedblom's nephew Emil Eliason would tell me. There was a small struggle as his comrades tried to wrestle his Springfield from the Swede's hands—"He was afraid that he'd be charged for it if he left it lying there," Eliason said. "And so they had a little trouble getting it away from him."

On the afternoon of July 22, reconnaissance parties from several French and British regiments arrived at Berzy. Beaumont Buck would later write that a Scotch officer expressed amazement at the work done by the 1st Division, exclaiming: "No, you do not mean 4 attacks in 4 days! That is a whole year's work!"

That night a Scots brigade and the French 69th Division relieved the 1st's troops, and the 28th Regiment's pitiful survivors tramped out to the Paris-Soissons Road over a battlefield thick with German and American dead and burned caissons and blasted and useless artillery pieces, to receive their first hot meal in five days.

Corporal Nelson Thompson of Company H remembered that as the 28th's men trudged back west, the Scots arrived with full fanfare: "We were relieved from this sector by some kilties and on our way out we passed some of them going up. Their pipers were piping away and were playing their outfit right into the trenches. There's something thrilling in their music. I never thought a bagpipe sounded very martial before but it certainly did put the fight into the men there."

The Scots weren't there just to relieve and hold. They had been charged with resuming the attack across the Crise Valley, and on to the heights beyond. Babcock remembered the powerful sight of the doomed Scots moving up: "Under a cloudless sky, the country bathed in full moon light, I watched the platoons of the Scots as they marched briskly forward out of the Ploisy ravine on the road to Berzy-le-Sec the evening of the 22nd of July.

"Led by an upstanding young officer, each platoon—many of them pitifully small in numbers—passed in perfect formation, a sergeant and two litter bearers bringing up the rear.

"Three or four hours later we heard the thunder of the guns heralding their attack; their losses were severe and I fear many of the casualties were beyond the need of a litter or bearer."

After assembling and hungrily chowing down at the rolling kitchens that lined the Paris-Soissons Road, Company D's survivors climbed into trucks and began their trek to a rest area. "We moved back to Plailly, a pretty little town, where we remained for a week," Wilbert Murphy remembered. "There we got new clothes and equipment for we were a sorry looking bunch, dirty, torn clothes and most of us minus a great deal of our equipment."

Victory at Soissons came at an incredible cost to the 1st Division, which had put some 12,000 infantrymen into action and suffered casualties of about 60 percent—1,714 men killed in action or died of wounds, and another 5,492 wounded.

The 28th Regiment, which had lost one-third of its men at Cantigny, suffered even worse casualties at Soissons, this time losing more than half of its men. The regiment's history notes: "The casualty list of the 28th Infantry for this action was greater than that for any other action in which it has ever been engaged. It was almost unbelievable that a Regiment could maintain its unity and fight on after losing so many men as this

Regiment had lost in the battle near Soissons—a total of 56 officers and 1760 men."

Among those left to an unknown fate was Private First Class John Nelson.

Sometime on the morning of July 20, as the company's men had huddled in their shallow foxholes before Berzy amid a rain of shells and shrapnel, two Algerian stretcher-bearers had set out to gather wounded from that field stretching from the Paris-Soissons Road to Ploisy.

A *Chicago Tribune* reporter described the battlefield over which they passed as "a vast plateau covered with waving wheat, marked by new dusty roads, helmets, guns, battered equipment, heaps of dead Germans and scattered American dead, with rifle butts standing up above the wheat where bayonets had been thrust in the ground to mark where others of our heroes lie—such is the battle ground over which the Americans advanced southwest of Soissons."

The Algerians had found the Old Man where he had fallen, one of them roughly kicking his prone form in an effective, if less than textbook, test to see if he was alive. When the Old Man had responded with an agonized groan, the pair roughly lifted him onto the stretcher and carried his nearly lifeless body back to an aid station at Missy-aux-Bois.

From there, he was trucked all the way back to where all this had begun, Pierrefonds-les-Bains, where surgeons at Field Hospital No. 12 were working furiously, their blood-soaked tables filling first the lobby of a hotel and then taking over "all the neighboring buildings and streets," as one source would say, the 1st Division's wounded overwhelming the town during those four days.

John Nelson's war—and his army career—ended there. Sent on to a Red Cross hospital in Paris and thence on a medical odyssey across the United States, it would be almost nine months before he was whole enough to return to Camp Grant to receive his honorable discharge.

He would speak little of his war, but his memories of those days—and of July 19, 1918, in particular—never dimmed. And the images that floated back during fitful nights of sleep, or on those July anniversaries of battlefield salvation he kept with his wife for seventy-five years, may have been similar to those so eloquently conjured by Edward M. Coffman in *The War to End All Wars* in 1968: "All that remains of the exhilaration, the exhaustion, the fear—the complex emotions which Soissons provoked—are the memories of men now grown old. For those who were not there, there are only the words. A rabbit jumping from a hedge in front of an assault line; the flies on the corpses; twigs and leaves falling gently, cut by a hail of machine gun bullets; French mounted cuirassiers drawing sabers and charging machine guns with the inevitable result; the incessant din; lines of sullen prisoners moving to the rear; the wounded, thirsty and in pain, lying in the sun—Soissons."

15

"Most of the Old Crew
Have Been Killed"

EVEN AS JOHN NELSON lay busted up in the wheat, even as Company D was ruining itself there at the gates of Berzy, its future commander was on the move, Marvin Everett Stainton having flown the coop from that backwater post in Arkansas and entrained for the docks at Hoboken and a berth on a transport that now sailed east across the Atlantic toward Brest, with a bellyful of doughboys whooping and hollering and puking their guts out as their own grand adventures took wing.

And I can't help but think that as Marvin Stainton walked the deck of that ship and breathed in the cool, salty, Atlantic air, every lungful served to give him a growing sense of "fateful purpose," as Willa Cather had in her novel *One of Ours* described the feelings of her own tragic hero, Claude Wheeler, as he stared out to sea from a troopship in 1918 and reflected: "Something was released that had been struggling for a long while, he told himself. He had been due in France since the first battle of the Marne; he had followed false leads and lost precious time . . . but he was on the right road at last, and nothing could stop him . . . The feeling of purpose, of fateful purpose, was strong in his breast."

Marvin Stainton had nearly escaped his own fate, and his own tragedy;

but perhaps the real tragedy would have been that Marvin never lived it out, never found a purpose, never felt the excitement that came to him now as he steamed toward a war, worrying not so much what might happen to him but that it might all be over before he could reach it and find his rightful role and place in this crusade, this gathering of hosts, this struggle, so they had all said, between what was simply right and what was simply wrong.

As had Claude Wheeler—modeled after Cather's cousin, Lieutenant G. P. Cather, who died on May 28, 1918, while serving with the 26th Regiment at Cantigny—Marvin now found his "right road," which in the third week of July 1918 led to the village of Gierves, from which he wrote home on July 28 to tell his mother of the cheering reception he and his cadre of doughboys had received, first in England during a short stop, and then again while on their journey from Brest: "They sure gave us a welcome coming on over. They cheered and threw flowers in the road before us and the women ran out and pinned them on the soldiers coats. The people ran out and cheered us all along coming over and of course the Americans returned with an Indian yell."

Marvin Stainton sailed toward a war where the news was, for once, mostly good for the Allies. The Germans stacked deep in the Marne pocket were slowly evacuating, the American troops of the 3rd, 4th, 26th, and 32nd Divisions on their heels. More than one million Americans had landed in France, and another 300,000, Marvin included, would land in French or British ports just in July.

Just weeks later, at Amiens, the Germans would face another "Black Day" at the hands of the British army, such as they had experienced at Berzy-le-Sec on July 21; the tide of the war had certainly turned, though not so much that Marvin would play no part, as he had so desperately worried as he wheedled and cajoled and pleaded his way out of Camp Pike in early June.

Marvin would have his war, and find his fateful purpose, but for a few weeks in late July and early August he was something of a free man, and he took in the sights and sounds of France as would a man deprived too long of food and drink, and for those few weeks his letters home carried the tone more of a foreign-exchange student on a summer's lark, an all-expenses-paid European vacation, than a commissioned officer facing imminent action.

To his delight, Marvin found his brother, Sergeant Sam Stainton, serving with an airplane squadron just miles away, and for a few weeks they roamed the countryside and villages together: "Only yesterday I went down to see him, and we walked over to another small town named Pruneirs, which is near Sams barracks. We came by the river and saw some Chinamen fishing. They had a long net they were throwing into the river. They were catching perch, almost the same kind we catch in the creeks back there. Of course it made us want to go fishing."

But Marvin's thoughts always returned to the war, and to the Cause, and his admiration for those fighting men whose ordeal at Soissons had turned the tide: "Tell them that our fellows went over the top with there hats off, and there sleeves rolled up and when the order was given to halt, they would not halt but charged straight ahead and won the battle you have read about. It is the American way that is going to push the Germans back across the Rhine."

What Marvin left unsaid—whether through greenhorn ignorance or through disinclination to trouble a mother's heart—was that "the American way" was going to involve gallons of red American blood.

Despite new innovations—including tanks, which had at least terrified the German defenders at Soissons and Cantigny, but were still slow-moving, prone to mechanical problems, and easy prey to artillery—the machine gun continued to rule, taking an astounding toll at Soissons, finding American targets as easily as it had found French and British in the slaughters of the previous three years.

By the first week of August, the price of victory at Soissons was becoming much clearer for Company D and the 28th Regiment, as the fates of many of those "missing since recent operations" were being determined.

A memo from the 2nd Brigade adjutant, Captain W. H. Woolworth, spelled out in black and white just what had occurred in the treacherous ravines and the bloody wheat at Soissons, and what would be needed if the 28th was to continue: 2 majors, 10 captains, 31 lieutenants, 106 sergeants, 245 corporals—and "1503 Privates and Privates First Class."

Soissons had been costly from top to bottom of the regiment, with two captains killed and nine wounded. In one of two reports he wrote after the battle, Colonel Conrad S. Babcock listed eight lieutenants dead, fifteen wounded, and another twenty-three missing. Among the wounded were Soren C. Sorensen and John H. Church.

They found Church on the field before Berzy, soaked in his own blood— "I must have lost a gallon," he would write—after taking a bullet to his upper chest. Taken to a field hospital, where because of the blood his clothes had to be cut from him, and then to Base Hospital No. 202 in Orleans, Church just six days later was well enough to write to his cousin Charles Crispin to say that he was "shot a week ago by a sniper, I think, while leading the company.

"Was hit at the junction of the throat and chest, the bullet piercing the upper part of my left lung and coming out under the shoulder blade, but don't worry, I'll get well again sometime soon."

On July 30, Church in another letter elaborated on his condition, and prognosis: "Just now I can't speak above a whisper, but don't think my vocal cords are permanently affected. On the surface my wound is healing nicely, but it is the inside of which I must be careful, as the healing of the lung will, of course, be slow, and I'll probably be unfit for active duty for several months. However, it will heal all right eventually, of that I am assured; have quit spilling blood now and cough less."

Some of his ward mates were worse off than he: "There is a young lieutenant from South Carolina in the next bed to me, who has lost his hand, and in the next a Scotch officer who had his chin blown off. Some awful wounds I have seen, especially on the battle field."

(Church would also enclose a postcard taken from the body of a dead German machine gunner at Soissons. Addressed to "Musketeer Sumkotter," of the First Battalion of the 24th Infantry Regiment, it began: "Dear Brother, as I have heard nothing from you since Nov. 17th I thought I would write you a few lines. I hope everything is well . . .")

Across France, Company D's wounded lay in straits similar to that in which John Church found himself, some of them dying, others hoping, like Church, to get patched up quickly enough to go "over" and rejoin the company, and continue the momentum begun at Cantigny and in the bloody fields around Soissons.

Sergeant Willard Storms was one of these, writing home from Red

Cross Hospital No. 1 in Paris to say he was "getting along wonderfully, for the kind of wound I had."

Anticipating his return to Company D, Storms rued the thought of having to train yet another group of green recruits (he would, in fact, spend the rest of the war in various hospitals): "When I go back it will be practically a new Co. and no doubt they will need lots of work but if they are the kind of men my last platoon was I don't mind it. They were the kind of men one enjoys going over with. The kind of men who die with a smile on their face or looking toward the front."

Private Abe Sachs was another. On July 19 a bullet had hit him in the face and exited through his neck, and like John Nelson he had endured a long night on the battlefield before being rescued.

Chicago Tribune correspondent C. N. Wheeler found the former teamster in the hospital, and reported that Sachs's comrades "say he displayed wonderful bravery and fought like a tiger until bowled over. When he regained his bearings he crawled into a shell hole and lay there from 6 in the evening until 9 the next morning, when he was picked up and carried back."

Sachs told the reporter, "I didn't mind it much, except I lost a lot of blood, I guess, and I was weak. At that I am luckier than some boys, who didn't have water. I saved my canteen, and that kept me going in the shell hole."

Asked about his future plans, Sachs "tried to smile, but the sore and stiffened muscles of his face cut it short," Wheeler wrote. Finally, Sachs replied: "Going back with the boys, I guess. All the boys want to go back and see it through."

There would be no going back for many—among that number Rollin Livick, who lay in Red Cross Hospital No. 1, or so it was said, perhaps sharing space and breathing the same Parisian air as John Nelson and Willard Storms and some of the others who'd raced across that road that day.

In the months to come Rollin Livick's family would hear rumors to the effect that he was having his lower jaw rebuilt, but that information would come secondhand and long after the whistles had blown and the folks had whooped and hollered at the news of the breakthrough on July 18—and months after a piece of disturbing news had rocked the sleepy town.

Six weeks after the offensive, the local papers had begun to carry the

familiar names of boys from Edgerton and surrounding Rock County under such headings as Killed in Action, Wounded Degree Undetermined,
Missing in Action, the maddening Previously Reported Severely Wounded
Now Reported Killed in Action, and of course Severely Wounded—and it
was under that heading that the name Rollin Livick could be found on the
morning of September 3, 1918, in any one of a number of papers, including
The Sheboygan Press, Chicago Tribune, and *Milwaukee Journal*.

Rollin's place on that dreaded roll shocked Edgerton out of its "compla-
cency," the Edgerton native and author Sterling North would write many
years later of the summer when he was twelve years old, a time when "personal tragedy came to one home after another," and "we seemed much
nearer to the trenches and the shell-shattered wheat fields of France, red
with poppies and blood."

As the grim lists of dead and maimed grew longer and longer, parents
in North's fictional "Brailsford Junction"—Edgerton—had prohibited
their sons from playing "the war games we had been playing each Saturday
on Earl's Hill," North remembered.

"It seemed a shame, after all our work constructing dugouts and opposing trench systems; for we had thoroughly enjoyed our desperate battles."

But the children of Edgerton were given new tasks, he wrote: "There
was a flurry of patriotism among the children of the town, the girls knit-
ting khaki wristlets by the score, and the boys competing to see who could
collect the most peach pits, used in making charcoal for gas masks. Another lively contest was the scramble for tin foil. Up and down the streets
and alleys went the tin-foil hunters, each child for himself."

News of Rollin's severe wounding had been received a full week before
his name appeared in the casualty rolls, in the form of a telegram that arrived at Hain, Livick & Arthur on the afternoon of August 24.

The news could have been better, but it obviously could have been worse.
With no official word that the diminutive go-getter was dead, at least there
was hope; he was wounded, yes, and severely; but then again there was the
comforting thought that he was probably getting good care in a hospital,
giving Robert and Emily Livick some hope on which to cling.

Optimism ruled in the Livick family, with Rollin's uncle, Frank Livick,
that same afternoon writing in a letter to Rollin: "Your father got a

telegram about two hours ago stating that you was severely wounded July 20th. We are all hoping and praying that it is not serious. I also hope that you got a few huns before you got knocked out. Write as soon as you can and as often. By the way, how the tide of war has turned."

Ten days later, Rollin's name surfaced in the casualty lists; five weeks after that, Frank Livick's letter to Rollin was returned, with a notation on the envelope, "Wounded." In France, Company D carried him on August 1 as "Missing since recent operations"; by September 1 Rollie was carried as "Wd in Hosp."

And still no word came to the Livicks from the nicest boy in Edgerton, Wisconsin, he who had hardly hesitated to volunteer for duty Over There, and whose last letters home from the back lines at Cantigny assured all that he was "getting along dandy and feeling fine," displaying no sign of that brooding angst with which he'd marched to war, no dark flicker of the doubt that had led him to worry over a possible disfigurement, and which had also led him to tear that ticket stub in two back at Waco and hand one half to his cousin, should help be needed in identifying his body.

Rollin's letters home from France were instead filled with cheery and long-obtuse half responses to questions posed by family members in their letters to him. "Some joke on dad going to Madison for the car," he wrote on July 10. "No wonder you called him 'Dr. Yak.'"

In a reference to a newspaper account of Jimmy Hopper's coup at Cantigny, Rollin wrote: "Did you notice the piece which told of a scribe taking fifteen prisoners. That['s] straight dope."

To a query regarding the fate of Private Richard Ellis, Rollin wrote simply, "Ellis was in the same co. and reg. as myself."

A few more snippets:

"Tell Frank I've done all that Empy told his pal to do—also that 'Lieut.' had returned from hospital and I delivered his message. Lieut. just gave a little grunt when I told him.

"Tell Roy the picture of Gert. and I was recd.

"How did the dam at Stebbensville effect the river this spring? Did it flood much?"

By October, Rollin Livick disappeared from Company D's rolls, as would John Nelson and many others put out of the war at Soissons; by then a distraught Robert Livick had already written the War Department seeking more information about Rollin, and been rebuffed by Adjutant General Austin A. Parker, whose reply offered no news, just the suggestion that Robert Livick write to the commanding officer of Company D, which at that moment was on the move, heading toward yet another battle, one of its platoons now commanded by another earnest small-town boy, another hero in the making who remained enthralled with the country, and with the cause, and who was at that moment anticipating his first taste of real action, which had been so long, too long, in coming.

"You may be sure I am going to do my part when the time comes," Marvin Stainton wrote to his mother that September. "Because the better each man fights the quicker the end. And I am sure no one wants the war to end worse than I.

"It doesn't take a fellow long to change after he comes over here. Yet every one I have seen that has been wounded has the same determination to go back. There are no cowards over here."

Marvin was one of them now, his quest to get into the show made possible by the wounding of Church and the transfer of Lloyd Bronston, who made it through Soissons unscathed and with that Silver Star on his lapel and who, before the dust had even settled at Berzy-le-Sec, was reassigned to Company G, 2nd Battalion, allowing Marvin, the fresh-faced tenderfoot, to take his place at the head of a platoon.

Marvin received his orders to join Company D in mid-August, and wrote to his brother Sam on August 13 to rue having missed a planned outing, explaining that duty had called. He was at that moment, he told his brother, "on my way to the front. Have stored my baggage, that which I could not take with me at my old billet. If you have time to I wish you would drop by and get your raincoat. I could not take it to the front line and you might find it useful."

Having spent a few days at Plailly after Soissons, the company had moved by train to a French camp near Toul called Camp L. "The few days spent here were given over to rest and, needless to say, they were days of enjoyment for the men," the 28th Regiment's history says. "The most popular pastime was swimming in the Moselle River, which was but a short distance from the camp."

By the time Marvin caught up with Company D, it was back in the trenches in the quiet Jonc Fontaine sector for an eight-day stint, a good venue for replacements such as Marvin to get their feet wet, the 28th's history notes, as there was "very light patrol activity and practically no artillery fire . . . this front seemed more like a rest area than a battle line."

Still, there was *some* action. "I joined the division just in time to get a taste of trench warfare," Marvin told his brother. "We had some fighting, some men being killed in patrols. D company was in the trenches one day & we had an out-post of two men in no-mans-land. Twenty Germans tried to take it but they got the most of them and the others ran."

Marvin added, ominously: "We have to reorganize the out-fit again, new men and officers as most of the old crew have been killed. The Division I am in is known as the Shock division. So you may guess we are going to have a nice time of it. Our orders thru-out the division are (Never Surrender) (Never Retreat) so I guess we will fight to the finish."

During August, recruits—many of whom had been inducted as recently as May—were folded into Company D, the aim being to make it "the same old fighting machine that started out July 18," as Wilbert Murphy put it.

As after Cantigny there would be little time for these unwashed lambs to become acquainted with the few old hands who had survived so far, some of whom went out of their way to impress—or perhaps scare—the new men.

One such veteran who was certain to make a mark on the company's greenhorns was Private James "Slim" Jones, of Fairmont, West Virginia, whose peculiar battlefield habits were brought to the attention of the International News Service's Bert Ford: "Jones is lean and reckless and has a musical drawl and his comrades say there is no braver man than he. At the request of his fellow soldiers Jones showed me his famous belt labelled 'Gott Mitt Us,' studded with brass buttons, each button representing a German, killed or captured."

Slim Jones told Ford: "Every button represents a German I have killed or captured with my own hands. Of course, there is only twenty buttons on it now, but I got three more in my pocket that I've had no time to hitch on it. And, believe me, no button goes on this belt unless I'm sure I've got my man."

Jones, Ford wrote, "puzzled over the questions of scalping his German victims Indian fashion," but compromised on the buttons: "I had sort of an Indian idea, but you know you couldn't tote so many scalps, so I decided to put buttons on instead. I heard so many fellows talking about Fritzies they had got that I just naturally decided to keep count.

"There was a few that I could not get near to so I just had to shoot them. In most cases, though, I have used this little trusty jack knife (his bayonet) because our gang always goes forward to meet them."

Such stories took a toll on the impressionable and green recruits filling the 28th Regiment's 1st Battalion as it geared up for yet another push. Its new commander, Charles Senay, noted: "The morale of the new men was none too high. The old timers regaled them with ghastly tales of Soissons and other places, and consequences were none too desirable. There were a number of self inflicted wounds and at least one suicide in the fortnight prior to the operation."

But veterans such as Jones were becoming a rarity. The 28th Regiment's ranks instead were being filled with recruits who had been rushed through training camps and hurried to France to stave off the German offensives that had put Paris in peril. Their lack of training was apparent, Senay noted. "Few of these men had any conception of the military scheme of things and they were particularly deficient in knowledge of the handling of weapons."

And it wasn't just the grunts who needed work. The 1st Battalion of the 28th Regiment had a desperate shortage of veteran officers after the five bloody days at Soissons. Senay commented: "The battalion had only two lieutenants to each rifle company. The solitary captain of the battalion was in command. Of the total of ten combat officers only six had been in action. Four were very recent arrivals from training camps in the United States"—among them Marvin Stainton.

Ready or not—and according to Senay the new men and officers were definitely *not*—plans were being drawn for another huge offensive. And once again, Company D would find itself "in the thick of it," as Marvin Stainton later told it.

In the second week of September, Company D packed up and moved toward the 1st Division's old haunts near Seicheprey. Wilbert Murphy remembered: "Immense preparations were going on, trucks were coming up getting ready to take their part in the fray. Big naval guns were set up, 75s, the most wonderful guns were being set up in the gun pits. The weather was rotten for such preparations but nevertheless they went forward at a considerable pace."

The company's objective this time was the St. Mihiel salient, which poked into the Allied lines like a great Gallic nose and encompassed 150 square miles. The salient had been created in 1914 when Bavarian troops attacked French positions and drove a wedge into the stabilizing Western Front in a stab at isolating and reducing the fortress of Verdun.

The scene of great fighting in early 1915—the French alone lost forty thousand men in back-and-forth battles while trying to take it—the salient had gone quiet after April of that year. Since then the Germans had fortified the area with an array of artillery positions among the steep hills of the Meuse heights on the west and strung trenches and fixed machine-gun posts across its width on the Woëvre Plain.

Since their arrival in France in June 1917 the Americans had regarded the salient as a natural locale for an all-American effort, and preliminary plans for its reduction had been produced by September of that year. The crisis of the spring German offensive had left the operation against the salient an afterthought, but after the great success at Soissons, the Allied high command met and divvied the responsibilities for continuing the pressure on the German army. The job of reducing the St. Mihiel salient was restored to Pershing, who would employ his newly created First Army in the operation.

On August 10, Pershing's staff dusted off its plan for an assault on the salient, and began to design a new strategy that aimed to push through the salient's base, then swerve east to invest Metz—from which east-west railways were able to supply the German army on the Western Front—and then push on to the Briey iron fields, the largest in Europe.

But on August 30, Foch presented Pershing with a new proposal: He wanted the Americans, with some French support, to make a limited attack against the salient's southern face only—"and that immediately after the attack the Americans participate in two operations further to the west, with a number of their divisions going under French command," wrote Charles Senay.

Pershing wanted nothing so much as to keep his doughboys under American command. After much recrimination and wrangling, he compromised: The Americans would perform a limited attack on the St. Mihiel salient beginning September 12, then turn their attention and their army to the northwest, and two weeks later launch a massive offensive against the daunting and heavily defended area between the Meuse River on the east and the Argonne Forest on the west.

The burden of planning these two large-scale assaults fell to George C. Marshall, the former operations officer of the 1st Division, who was now performing the same mission for the entire A.E.F. With the aim of the attack on the salient now limited to the reduction of the salient itself, he revised his plans to include one French division to attack at the apex, and six American divisions to converge on its western and southern sides.

The 1st Division would again have what seemed to be the toughest task, that of piercing the center of the salient along a one-and-a-half-mile front, which was ominously dominated on the west by Mont Sec, bristling with German artillery.

After jumping off, the 1st Division would bypass the hill on the east, move quickly north to the village of Nonsard, then push northwest to the village of Vigneulles to connect with elements of the eastward-advancing 26th Division and slice the salient in half.

Senay wrote that the 1st's task, at least on paper, seemed daunting. There were several lines of trenches and thickets of wire, and the Madine River formed "a difficult obstacle with steep banks and of considerable depth. It was reported to be strongly held and supported by numerous batteries."

At the Rupt de Madt—"a creek reported as unfordable, and with steep banks"—the Germans had well-established machine-gun positions. Adding to the difficulty, Senay wrote, "both the Rupt de Madt and the Madine were reported to be filled with wire."

The Germans had roughly 25,000 men to defend the salient, but, Senay wrote, its divisions were "generally low in numbers and not rated high in morale. This had become a rest and reorganization sector."

In fact, the Germans had long before recognized that they did not have the manpower to resist a determined push on the salient's southern face, and orders had been given to begin a withdrawal to the Michel Line on September 12—even as the Americans would be jumping off against them.

Expecting stiff opposition, extra and intense training was ordered for the 1st Division's green recruits. "The new men were instructed in rifle marksmanship by having them shoot, under individual supervision, at empty tomato cans inverted on stakes, driven in the ground at a distance of about fifty yards from the soldier," Senay wrote. "About two hours a day were devoted to tactical formations. During this training period the entire division rehearsed its part in the drive, going through a gigantic maneuver over steep and wooded terrain, as a unit."

On September 6 the 1st Division moved to the Faux Bois de Naugisard, five kilometers from the jump-off line. "There was a steady drizzling of rain and circulation in the woods kneaded earth and water into a sodden, gripping mass," Senay wrote.

On September 11, orders for the attack were received by the 28th Regiment. The 2nd Battalion would lead the assault, with the 1st Battalion in support, B and D Companies in the lead.

"One evening just at darkness we moved out of the woods and after a few hours hike in rain and on muddy roads arrived at a quarry where we were to 'jump off' in the morning," Wilbert Murphy recalled. "About midnight our preparation fire started and from then until daylight the sky was bright with the flash of our guns and the air was full of the noise of the exploding shells."

German shells "punctuated the march into position," Senay wrote, and the regiment's replacements came under fire for the first time. "Fortunately the shells sank well into the spongy ground before exploding," Senay wrote. "As it was, several men were wounded and one company threatened to stampede, being held in line only by the strenuous exertions of a few good NCOs."

At 1:00 A.M., the American artillery—some three thousand pieces—poured shell after shell—the first of what would be more than a million in all—onto the German front lines. In the 1st Division's zone alone, 168 guns opened up and continued for four hours. "The bright flashes from the muzzles of so many big guns seemed to turn night to day," Senay wrote.

"Every known battery position was drenched with gas by at least two heavy guns or howitzers. The waiting infantrymen were rendered jubilant by the spectacular drama and all along the line the men burst into cheers and songs like children on a holiday. Cries of 'let's go' clarioned from eager throats and these words became the battle cry of the First Division."

As the hours-long bombardment continued, the night grew frigid, and bonfires were built to ward off the cold. "Steaming buckets of coffee were sent up and down the line," Senay wrote, "saving many men for the morning's effort. Around one fire were gathered the battalion headquarters and some company officers whiling away the hours before the attack, perchance the last few hours on earth, in song and story. Favorite among the songs, but sung in rollicking vein, was 'Just Before the Battle, Mother.' "

One of the singers was Frank Arthur Howe, a twenty-two-year-old lieutenant new to Company A. The product of boarding school and Philadelphia's Girard College, Howe was "utterly despondent, asserting he was going to be killed in the battle," Senay recalled. "We used every means to change his thought, but all to no avail."

At 5:00 A.M. the infantry stepped off, "appearing as a line miles long moving slowly forward," Major Raymond Austin remembered, "followed at intervals by succeeding waves, the latter waves being broken up into small squads instead of being continuous long lines, as the telephone squads running wires, engineers, stretcher bearers, etc. advanced."

Austin added: "It was a great sight, that broad expanse of country dotted everywhere with men and tanks, bursting shells, rockets rising and bursting into white, red, green stars, Mont Sec looming up dark and forbidding and showing here and there on its sides white puffs of smoke which told where our big 8 inch guns were dropping their shells—all in the gray light of early morning under the broken storm clouds against which the fast, low-flying airplanes were sharply silhouetted."

Watching all of this in awe as well was Marvin Stainton, held out of the grand spectacle for a few moments as the 28th Regiment's 2nd Battalion stepped off into the dawn. Soon enough, Marvin's war was on.

"At 5 a.m. the command was given by platoon leaders 'all set and then forward,'" Marvin wrote to his brother. "It was still dark and a good many of my men fell in shell holes as we were going over no mans land.

"The barrage of our guns was terrific and blew holes in the ground 15 feet deep and 15 ft. across. It was raining and the mud spattered for hundreds of yards. At a distance the explosion of our shells looked like an explosion of a mine or an earth-quake as we could feel the shock."

Before long, the Germans responded. "The Germans harassed slightly with thinly scattered shell fire and some machine gun fire but this was not serious enough to affect the advance of our troops," Senay recalled.

Still, a few were lost—among them Lieutenant Frank Howe, who had had such a foreboding of his own death, and who, Senay would write, "was killed before he had gone a hundred yards."

Marvin would write of his first taste of battle: "The German shells soon started over and bursting all around us but we came thru O.K. only three of my men being hit. We passed the German barb wire O.K. and as our tanks came forward and advanced.

"It was a great sight, the long string of tanks just behind and barrage and the advancing waves of our troops just behind. They were stretched out as far as one could see to the left and right down the valley."

Soon, though, "the German machine guns began to play," Marvin recalled. "My platoon had to lie flat on our stomachs on a ridge for 15 minutes. The bullets from a machine gun were right over our heads. We weren't bothered by him but a short time. We had to 'mop up' the dugouts as we passed."

The feared German wire in most cases proved to be no trouble, it having rusted and weakened over the past three years; as well, the 1st and 2nd Battalions were hardly stopped at the Rupt de Madt, which had been dammed at its source by American engineers and proved to be only waist deep.

The 1st Division met strong resistance only at one point, a strip of woods called the Bois de Rate. Here a hail of machine-gun bullets poured forth at the advancing doughboys and caused a few casualties.

Clarence Huebner, recovered from the wound he'd received at Ploisy and once again commanding the 2nd Battalion, wrote later that "every arm" at his disposal, including Stokes mortars and a 37 mm piece, quickly smothered the wood with fire. The 3rd Battalion of the 26th Regiment, advancing to the right of the 28th, joined the fray, sending its scout platoon—and its complement of Native Americans—forward and through the trenches leading to the wood.

"I suddenly saw my big Indian 'Bear Ghost' walking along the parados of the enemy position playing a most wonderful tune, closely followed by about thirty of the flanking party," Captain Walter McClure of the 26th remembered. "Individual Germans began climbing out of their trenches and coming in our direction with their hands reaching for heaven."

The German contingent of eighty-five men was quickly rounded up. "One prisoner, who spoke English, said it was certain death for any one to raise their head to fire therefore they quit as soon as they could make us understand," Huebner wrote.

Among the prisoners taken by the 26th's 3rd Battalion were four officers, one wearing "a beautiful pair of boots that I was very envious of," McClure would write, "but they were too small."

Another prisoner asked to speak to McClure and told him in confidence that "he was a French spy and it was imperative that he be taken to a French officer at once." Amazingly, the prisoner's story checked out. The German officers were sent on to battalion headquarters—"minus their field glasses and Iron Crosses," McClure added.

By previous arrangement, at 11:00 A.M. the 28th's 1st Battalion took up the assault and soon approached the Madine River, beyond which sat the hilltop town of Nonsard, its first-day objective and an expected German hot spot. The battalion was now faced with moving two kilometers over "absolutely open" ground, Senay wrote. "Company commanders were nervous and needed encouragement before crossing this potential death trap."

Scouts raced ahead, fording the Madine and appearing in silhouette on the road above it, and a few tanks came up, further reassuring the doughboys, who now boldly marched toward Nonsard, losing just two men from friendly artillery. "The infantry was advancing faster than our artillery knew," Senay wrote.

With its left flank covered, the 1st Battalion climbed the hillside just south of the village. Suddenly, Senay wrote, "vicious" machine-gun fire spewed from the town's church tower: "Bullets whipped through the mass of troops and lashed dust sprays over a considerable area. But only for an instant. Nearly coincident with this German fire the entire flank burst into flame and a shower of missiles rained upon the stone face of the tower."

Patrols were sent in under the cover of fire. An "ambitious tank" came up and began "one pounder marksmanship against the tower window," Senay recalled. "Fritz quit cold and the patrols brought in five forlorn prisoners, one of whom was retained as an industrious and efficient orderly for the headquarters mess."

The feeble resistance at Nonsard over, the doughboys searched the town and found a storeroom filled with Turkish cigarettes and another filled with German blankets. News of the troves brought soldier stragglers from far and wide to pillage and loot, and guards had to be posted.

More alarming was a report that eight thousand Germans were forming somewhere in the front of the battalion for a counterattack. The expected attack never materialized, and it was later learned that the mass of Germans seen from the air by an Allied pilot was a group of the enemy who had surrendered to the Americans.

Marvin Stainton would write that despite the odd pillagers in Nonsard, the doughboys were welcomed warmly by the residents after their German occupiers of four years had been chased out or killed.

"I have never seen anything that was quite so touching to see as the old women and men and children run out kissing the dough boys and crying and shaking their hands and calling us 'brave Americans,'" Marvin wrote.

"Then the women of the town killed their chickens and rabbits and everyone had a celebration. We tried to pay them something, but they would not take a cent.

"When we insisted that they take something for their trouble and expense, they stated that the Boches came four years ago and took everything they wanted without asking for it, and what they had now the Americans should have free of charge."

Marvin added: "I have yet to see a happier bunch of old women and children, some of them being wounded by the shells. The scenes there in that village that day alone made me glad that I was in the war, and made me feel pardonable pride in the country whose soldiers could win the love and respect of these people."

While a liberated Nonsard celebrated, the horizon to the north soon became black with smoke from fires set by the retreating Germans. But hours were lost as the men waited for orders to resume the advance.

When the 28th Regiment's adjutant, William Livesay, arrived in the town, "he was asked why we couldn't go ahead while there was no resistance and we had the advantage of good light in which to pierce the dense woods ahead," Senay wrote. "He responded that the regiment wished to push on but higher headquarters were not yet ready."

With darkness falling, the 1st Battalion was ordered to move out from Nonsard to the Nonsard Woods, about two miles north of the village. Senay sent Company C ahead to cut the railway to Vigneulles while the rest of the 1st Battalion's men hunkered down in the dark woods like spiders, snaring anything that crossed into their web.

At one point a German major and four lieutenants wandered into the battalion's lair just off the road to Vigneulles, and were captured. Four guides on bicycles likewise were "dismounted by a pole placed across the road and captured," Senay wrote.

It was during that long night that one of the more momentous moments in Company D's history occurred, when at about 10:00 P.M. a patrol intercepted a wagon train of supplies, killed an officer and two enlisted men, and captured thirteen prisoners. Another feast—the second of that long day—was had with the plundered German goods.

"I want to say the Germans are not starving like we have been led to believe—at least this wagon train did not indicate that," Marvin wrote. "Every one of the wagons were loaded with hams, bacons, apples, sugar, bread, and a case of German beer. We had been living on hard tack and 'monkey meat' for nearly three days, and right then and there we proceeded to have a feast which will linger long in my memory."

Their German prisoners, meanwhile, "appear to be glad that they are prisoners, with the exception of the officers. They all held their hands up from the advancing lines until they reached the rear, and I suppose they would have been holding them up yet had they not been told to take them down. Some of the men were smiling, especially the more intelligent looking.

"The simple-minded and ignorant were frightened. I found one who could speak English. He said that they had been told that the Americans would not take prisoners, therefore they were not to surrender. They all said they were tired of the war."

At 3:15 A.M. on September 13, the 1st Battalion once more advanced, and took a position southeast of Vigneulles at the western edge of the Bois de Vigneulles. At 6:20 A.M. the battalion's scout platoon reached Hatton-ville and took five prisoners—and "barely missed capturing a staff automobile, firing into it as it scurried out of town," Senay wrote.

At 7:15 A.M., the scout platoon hooked up with advancing scouts from the 26th Division coming from the east at Hattonchatel, and the St. Mihiel salient was cut in two.

That afternoon, advancing elements of a French division and the American 42nd Division "pinched out" the 1st, and it was withdrawn to the Bois de Nonsard and Bois de Vigneulles. The division could count among its trophies 6 German officers, 1,190 enlisted men, thirty pieces of artillery, and fifty machine guns.

Its casualties, especially in light of those horrendous days at Cantigny and Soissons, had been exceedingly light: Only 3 officers and 90 enlisted men had been killed, and 10 officers and 431 men wounded.

Within the 1st Battalion, only 3 men were killed and just 27 were wounded during the thirty-two-hour drive; Company D had just 1 man killed—Private Herman C. Fritz, a replacement from Benton, Pennsylvania—and 3 men wounded in the drive.

One of the wounded was a former billiard-room manager named Orrin "Spider" Smith of Savanna, Illinois. "I had a little hard luck," Spider would write his sister. "Old Fritz had my number but not the right range. I am in a Red Cross hospital and getting along fine.

"I will be out soon and I sure will give them hell again, so don't worry about me. When I left the battlefield the Germans were on the run and we dough boys were on their trail."

In fact, the doughboys were not hot on the Germans' trail. Pershing's contract with Foch called for a limited offensive against the salient, and that is what Pershing had given him. Many have since faulted Foch for his shortsightedness in insisting on limiting the operation, arguing that had the Americans pressed on to Metz as originally planned, the war might have come to a quicker, and less costly, end.

Senay would complain that during the crucial day of September 12, "Front line battalions were held back until the Germans were free from peril, even though their leaders pleaded for orders to advance. The delay of more than six hours permitted a badly beaten enemy to extricate himself from an apparently hopeless position and to occupy, without serious opposition, a partially prepared rear line."

An opportunity to take Metz had been lost. "Lacking in troops, under sufficient pressure, the Germans were ready to evacuate the city voluntarily and place their main defense behind the Rhine," Senay would write, and even Pershing agreed: "Without a doubt an immediate continuation of the advance would have carried us well beyond the Hindenburg line and probably into Metz."

German commander Erich Ludendorff later wrote that a golden opportunity had been botched. "I venture the opinion that it would have been possible for the Americans to win a much greater and more decisive victory if their initial successes had been exploited with more decisiveness and firmness of intention."

Those greater ambitions meant little to the men of Company D, who were left to enjoy their great and nearly bloodless victory in woodland huts in which the Germans had hoped to while away the coming winter. The officers grabbed the more luxurious bungalows originally intended for German officers, and it was from his bunk in one of these that Marvin summed up his first battle experience in a letter to his brother: "The good old U.S. airplanes pass over every hour of the day where we are camped in the beautiful woods. Also a real American railroad runs by our camp. The old trains and the American engineer certainly looks good to us.

"I have an excellent pair of field glasses that I 'captured' and lots of other things, spoils of war, that I am going to try and bring home with me for souvenirs."

Exulting in finally having played a small role in one of history's great dramas, Marvin couldn't help but feel the war would soon enough come to an end: "Things look mighty good for us now. The Germans are on the run everywhere and we are all beginning to think the war will soon be over—maybe not in a few weeks but in a few months anyway.

"When we attack the Germans they run and we have a hard time catching them. It looks like they are scared of us. Of course, we have a hard fight some times, when we get hold of a bunch that wants to fight, but they are very few, it seems to me."

Marvin added that he had found out "what it is like to fight for a great cause like ours. The little scene in the village that day was a striking example of what the Allies hope to accomplish for the entire world—freedom for all mankind."

The reduction of the St. Mihiel salient had seemed like a walk in the park: Resistance was light, the soldiers had been welcomed as heroes by the French, there were few Germans to be seen, and the ones they had encountered had seemed all too happy to surrender.

Marvin, who for so long had craved action, was already thinking and talking of making it home alive, as were no doubt many others among the company's men now lounging in the former quarters of their enemy in the Bois de Nonsard, especially the dwindling few who'd made it through Cantigny and Soissons.

But within weeks, such idle and wishful reveries would be run to ground in another patch of woods, from which the Germans had no intention of withdrawing. This time, the affair would be no cakewalk, but bloody, desperate work that would make grizzled veterans out of every man in the company—at least, that is, those lucky or willful enough to survive.

16

Montrefagne

A_ND IT'S INTO THE_ fog now, into the darkness, this time with a better idea, perhaps, of what awaits, and then racing anxiously across black earth drenched with rain and sodden with mustard gas, their objective revealed only momentarily in the brilliance of exploding shells, the shrapnel showering from above to rip some of them limb from limb, and the steady and deadly *pup-pup-pup* sparking from the machine guns; and it was amid such horrors and toward the unknown that they raced again, heading north in the dawn toward that hill, that last hill, which awaited Company D with indifference, except for the welcoming salvos of Boche artillery and machine-gun fire sent forth from its crest.

And Marvin Stainton was one of them that day, as Company D jumped off in support of the 28th Regiment's 3rd Battalion, but he would find quickly that this would be no cakewalk, no St. Mihiel, but an inching forward against a determined German foe that contested every yard of ground, every ravine, every stand of shell-shocked and bark-stripped trees on this early morning of October 4, 1918, the Hun having already broken and scattered one American division sent in to take that hill.

And for the next seven mornings Company D's men would find themselves in those murderous woods, trying to simply survive in a nightmare world of seesaw advances and retreats, of lying low for days on end and ducking and squatting helplessly as death ranged at them from above, from the 77s and machine guns and *Minenwerfer* aligned on the range of hills that hovered over pieces of ground the French had named the Petit Bois and the Bois de Moncy and the Bois de Boyon, which surrounded the once-bucolic Beauregard and La Neuville-le-Comte and Arietal Farms.

The end had seemed so near, so close, the light at the end of the tunnel beaming bright, so it seemed, in the eyes of all those prisoners, its coda in the songs Company D's men sang during those easy few days in the Nonsard Woods, while the German front crumbled from Cambrai in the north to those abandoned barracks where the boys lounged, where the days were filled more with wine and song than the whine of German shells and machine-gun bullets, where they gorged on plundered Heinie sausage, and where for a little while life was good, where it almost made sense to think that they might make it back home alive.

Slowly, and as if answering some siren call, or some nagging urge to resolve unfinished business, some of those wounded at Cantigny and even Soissons had drifted back to their units for the last "push," the last go, among them John Church.

Having spent six weeks lying in a hospital bed staring at the ceiling following Soissons, Church did some pushing of his own, and managed to get discharged from the hospital at Orleans on September 2 and sent on to Blois, a dreaded destination for some officers designated for cashiering, but just a crossroads for those who, like Church, had been knocked out for a while and were awaiting reassignment.

Church wrote to his cousin on September 2 to say he had been classified as "B2"—"which means that I will be in the Service of Supplies for at least two months until I can come up for another examination. I am back for light duty and will very likely be made an instructor until I can get in 'A' class."

He added: "There is nothing whatever the matter with me except the fact that my wound was of a serious character and the disability board was afraid that I would not be able to stand hard work and hardships [found] at the front. I am feeling bad as I hoped to get back to my regiment as I have very good friends there."

The restless Church finally managed to convince the medical board at Blois that he was ready for action. "Yesterday went to the medical board and persuaded [it] to change my classification to an 'A' class," he wrote on September 15. "So am starting back towards the front tomorrow. Sure will be glad to get back as am tired of hanging around in the SOS. I feel OK again and really believe I am."

Bill Warren, too, caught up with Company D in those barracks at Nonsard. Sent to officers training school on August 20, Warren had missed the company's almost bloodless walk across the marshes and woods at St. Mihiel, but he'd heard all about it as soon as he rejoined the company.

In a letter to his father, Warren took note of the ease with which the company had cleared its portion of the salient: "According to all the information that I've gathered since arriving, this last affair was like a big maneuver for us, as the resistance offered by the Huns was so slight. I'm sorry I wasn't there, for it must have been much more fun than the one I was in."

The postbattle digs were better as well, Warren wrote: "There were long rows of barracks, arbors, bowling alleys, recreation houses, cement dugouts. Pianos in many of the houses, canteens and in fact everything was fixed up as if the Boche intended to reside there indefinitely.

"The men have told me tales of capturing a whole train load of supplies, many German cigarettes, food, etc. And yet the German newspapers talk of an intended withdrawal and speak of drawing back their troops without being hindered by the enemy! Astonishing amount of humbug isn't it."

By the time Church and Warren reported to the company, talk of yet another offensive was rife. Marvin Stainton wrote to his brother Sam on September 21 and obliquely mentioned the likelihood of another "push" by the 1st Division: "We will have another push 'tout suite' and will try and keep them going. We are in open warfare all the time now. Keep your eyes on the news because I am going to be in it, (not the news) but the next push."

Even as Marvin wrote, the furies were gathering sixty miles to the northwest, where the second part of Pershing's pact with Ferdinand Foch would soon come into play, and where an American army that had in most cases tripped ever so easily over the light defenses on the Woëvre Plain would come nearly to ruin on the pitted, forested, blighted slopes of a pile of hills that ran from the Meuse River on the east to the Argonne Forest on the west.

It was in the Meuse-Argonne that John Pershing would realize his dream of employing an all-American army in a single, determined offensive, so to better showcase the unique abilities and rugged individualism of the doughboy. But it was also here that Pershing would watch as some divisions cracked under the strain and seemed to dissolve, and where rain, mud, blood, and suffering would run together and produce several legends, including the sad story of the 77th Division's "Lost Battalion," and as well the enduring tale of the hero Alvin York, of the 82nd Division.

Both of those war stories would play out a few miles to the west of where Company D and the 1st Division were now headed, over a countryside blighted by war, through villages flattened to paste, and toward a dark and pitted forest where even at that moment the 35th Division was splintering into little more than small groups of shell-shocked and exhausted survivors frantically seeking safety, as if being pursued onto open ground by a wounded animal which was lashing out desperately and wildly in its own last throes.

The greenhorn 35th was unblooded and untried, a National Guard division whose recruits came mainly from Kansas and Missouri, among them the artillery captain and future president Harry S. Truman. In the grand scheme designed by George C. Marshall, it had played just a reserve role at St. Mihiel, and when that affair was over it had quickly been put on the march toward the Argonne, where it joined eight other American divisions in the last great American effort of the war in an offensive that kicked off early on the morning of September 26, 1918.

Attacking almost due north, these nine divisions had been expected to advance ten kilometers on the first day over some of the roughest terrain France could offer—and toward an enemy strongly entrenched amid ravines and on hilltops and that was, quite literally, fighting with its back to the wall, knowing that if the heights between the Argonne and the Meuse were taken, and the gates to the rolling country toward Sedan opened, his left flank would become unhinged, and his lines of supply cut.

Frederick Palmer wrote in *Collier's*: "No sector in the old German lines was considered more redoubtable than the Meuse-Argonne sector. It was as essential to the integrity of the German front, from Flanders to Switzerland, as the hills of Verdun to the French; for it protected the Germans' lines of communication to all their armies in Belgium and northern France."

The 35th had been assigned the area on the east bank of the Aire River, and was the eastern prong of the three divisions—from left to right the 77th, the 28th, and the 35th—that made up First Army's I Corps, under the command of Hunter Liggett. George Cameron would lead the Army's three-division V Corps in the center, consisting of, from left to right, the 91st, 37th, and 79th Divisions. On the far right of the sixteen-mile front, Robert Lee Bullard took command of the III Corps—from left to right, the 4th, 80th, and 33rd Divisions.

The terrain facing each division was beyond formidable, the Germans' defensive line embodying "all the experience of four years of stationary warfare," Frederick Palmer wrote. "The Hindenburg Line was not stronger than the Meuse-Argonne, while, once the Hindenburg Line was broken, the country beyond was much more favorable for rapid advance in open warfare than back of the Meuse-Argonne line, where the commanding hills, many wooded or with wooded slopes, rose in a kind of whaleback to a depth of some ten miles."

At 5:30 A.M. on September 26, and after a two-hour barrage, all nine divisions jumped off, and progress initially was good.

On the east bank of the Aire, the 35th Division made quick gains in the opening days of the drive, taking the villages of Varennes and Cheppy, and moving ahead six miles over heavily defended ground. By September 30, the division had taken six thousand casualties, and was in disarray after briefly taking and then being kicked out of the village of Exermont, behind which lay the key German defenses strung along the Romagne Heights.

Its most forward elements, disorganized and dispirited, were counterattacked by the Germans, and engaged in what amounted to a running fight from Exermont Ravine and over several kilometers of countryside, leaving behind their dead and dying in order to reach the dubious safety of an amorphous new line south of a commanding bluff known as Montrebeau Wood, near which the 1st Division would take up the attack.

But the dismal state of the 35th, while extreme, was not unique. All along the front, the nine divisions had bogged down and stalled after making quick gains; and the first phase of the grand offensive between the Meuse and the Argonne ended when Pershing suspended operations on September 29. Round one had been something of a draw.

Pershing and the First Army knew now just how bitter, bloody, and costly would be the work to come and laid plans to bring in several veteran divisions—the 1st, of course, as well as the 3rd and the 32nd—to smash through those daunting defenses on the heights of the Romagne.

The 1st Division had already been on the move, by foot and by truck, it having originally been attached to the III Corps for a possible and future offensive to the east of the Meuse. "We crept toward the battlefield by muddy stages," Charles Senay, still in command of the 28th's 1st Battalion, would write. "It rained incessantly and we bivouacked in slimy mud. Needless to say we were usually marching."

On September 29, the division was transferred to I Corps, and moved by trucks from Nixeville, near Verdun, to the vicinity of Neuville. The trucks were operated by Annamese soldiers, Senay remembered. "There were two drivers on a seat and one drove while the other slept, as the trucks were driven continuously for several days. Each truck was loaded with from thirty to forty men with their equipment."

That night, the 2nd Brigade bivouacked in woods northwest of Aubreville, some ten miles directly south of the battle line, where from his billets that evening Bill Warren wrote to his father to describe the exhausting movement: "Since I wrote you last, we have moved about considerable, partly hiking and partly moving by trucks. On some of the hikes, I have been so tired that during the ten minute halts every hour, I have lain down on hard rocks and thought they were the softest bed in the world.

"At present we are rather comfortably located. I had a bunk with a straw tick last night, and slept under a roof. I hated to get up this morning."

On September 30, the foot-weary infantry moved out again, this time on a sixteen-kilometer forced march to plug the gap left when the 35th Division imploded. The miseries of that march, all would agree, rivaled that of July 17–18, when the division had raced through a blinding rainstorm to its jump-off position below Soissons.

"The march," wrote Captain Lyman S. Frasier of the 26th Regiment, "was one never to be forgotten. It was raining, as usual. The night was very dark. The roads were very muddy and congested in places. Shell holes rendered them almost impassable at some points.

"However, the infantry made its way through. Dead men, dead horses, and dead mules lined the roads, and one stumbled over dead men when he left the roads. It immediately became apparent that the 1st Division had not come to a 'rest sector.'"

Private Alvord Kemp, of Company F, 18th Regiment, remembered as well the urgency of that march, as tough, old-line noncoms continually prodded their men to keep up: "Up ahead one would give the order to 'hurry up you birds' and along the line the platoon sergeants would give their orders to keep closed up and not get lost, while back in the rear some poor little sawed off soldier would be getting a bawling out from a sawed off corporal because he couldn't keep up."

Despite the "cussing and discussing," as Kemp put it, the 1st Division's men were in high spirits. After the heavy losses at Soissons, seven thousand replacements had been woven into the division, and, the 26th Regiment's Captain Barnwell Legge would write, "The psychological effect of a rapid and successful advance of 13 kilometers in less than 48 hours, with practically no losses" at St. Mihiel "had an astounding effect on these men," many of whom were under the assumption that they had "proven their worth on the field of battle and the Germans were not so good after all."

The reality, Charles Senay would write, was much different. "We never again were the coherent irresistible tireless soldiers who turned the tide of the war at Soissons. Our dead and hopelessly wounded were irreplaceable."

In the black of night on September 30, the division began its relief of the beleaguered 35th Division, finding utter confusion at what were presumed to be its new lines. "No definite line existed on the right of the 35th Division," Lyman Frasier recalled. "No one could be found who knew where the enemy was except that he was in a northerly direction.

"The most definite information secured by the 26th Infantry was given by a young first lieutenant who was wearing no overcoat, blouse, helmet, or gas mask. He rushed up to the commander of the advanced guard of the regiment from out of the darkness and demanded a [sniper] rifle, saying that he had located a German general in a tree and desired to shoot him out."

With the 16th Regiment on the left at the eastern edge of the Aire Valley, followed west to east by the 18th, 28th, and 26th Regiments, the 1st Division took up positions early in the morning of October 1 along the Charpentry to Eclisfontaine Road.

Charles Senay led Company D and the 1st Battalion to its place on a reverse slope from which the men could hear the pleas of the 35th Division's wounded. "Just beyond the troops to my front lay the dreaded Exermont Ravine filled with wire and mines," he wrote. "In it lay dozens of dead and wounded.

"There was an endless crescendo of groans and outcries for help. It was impossible to reach the sufferers in the ravine due to constant shellfire and also enfilade fire." Most, Senay added, would die long before the 1st's men could reach them.

When dawn broke, the leading battalions "could get some idea of the task before them when the order to attack finally came," Legge would later write. "It was not difficult to see the problems which had confronted the 35th."

On the left, the dense Argonne Forest rose three hundred feet above the valley of the Aire, and German artillery positions on the west bank were well situated to pound the valley below, as well as positions to the far east and west, with devastating fire; for that reason, Pershing considered the front facing the 1st Division "of vital importance to the continuation of the general advance" of his army.

Facing the 1st to the north in the first light of morning on October 1 were "row and row of buttress like hills with wooded crests and glacis like slopes with small fringes of brush and woods," Legge wrote. "The most imposing of these were the Montrefagne (Hill 240), the barriers of Hill 263 and 269 and a great forbidding ridge Hill 272 which seemed to defy all progress."

These Romagne heights comprised a southern "switch" of the imposing Kriemhilde Stellung—the main German defensive position known as the Hindenburg Line. Here, as all along the line, the Germans had made good use of the terrain, employing endless bands of barbed wire, concrete machine-gun emplacements, deep redoubts and trenches, and well-sited artillery positions. Each and every approach was subject to enfilading fire from machine guns and artillery.

The village of Exermont sat in a deep, east-west ravine at the head of what amounted to a canyon, with the steep and wooded slopes of Hill 240 a mile or so to its northwest, and the massive Hill 272 running almost directly north from that hill to terminate at the daunting Hill 263. Just to the east of Hill 263, the slopes of Hill 269 edged back south to a series of ridges that terminated at Hill 212, directly east and about one mile from the Montrefagne.

And if you had survived this far, if you were Private Leroy Bright or Sergeant Ernest E. Carlson or the returned-from-hospital Private Abe Sachs or Lieutenant John Church, this was the apogee of your Great Adventure, no golden poppy-laden fields before Cantigny or dew-laden wheat at Soissons but nasty, nightmarish hills festooned with Hun artillery and machine-gun emplacements, manned by a foe who had already rebuffed earlier attempts at dislodgement and was ready for a real fight to the death, sending unending canisters of gas and high explosive your way with zeal, with deadly intent, although the consensus was that the thing was over, the war virtually won, if only the Boche would give up and save himself so the world could move on.

But the Hun wasn't quite ready to throw in the towel, and quickly made that clear to the 1st Division's men. During the day on October 1, the guns on these hills opened up, forcing the 1st's men to go underground as the Boche "pounded the area with high explosive and drenched the ravines and woods with gas, and machine guns and snipers harassed constantly whenever movement was observed," Legge would write.

Mustard gas, he added, so impregnated the ground "that when the Sun came out after the habitual morning fog, severe burns developed on many men and the casualty list increased hourly."

One of the casualties was Charles Senay, who, after suffering a slight wound in one of the "downpours of shells," was sent to a hospital at Clermont-Ferrand. Taking his place at the head of the 1st Battalion was Soren Sorensen, finally recovered from the wound he had suffered at Berzy-le-Sec on July 21.

In the early hours of October 2, the commanders of the frontline battalions were assembled and given orders to send out strong patrols in an effort to locate the Germans' positions. "No objective is designated for this patrol," the 28th's commander, Colonel George Barnhardt, who had replaced Conrad Babcock on August 5, wrote in his order, "but it will be vigorously pushed forward until such obstacles are encountered that cannot be overcome. If no serious resistance is encountered the army may order an advance of our lines."

Jumping off at dawn, Company K's Lieutenant Samuel Parker and his fifty-man patrol made it almost to the eastern edge of Montrebeau Wood before encountering such "obstacles." Parker recalled: "The patrol suffered very heavy casualties and was unable to advance across the field in front of the woods which was occupied by the enemy. The patrol dug-in along [a] hedge . . . and held this position until it was picked up in the general advance of our lines."

The results were the same across the 1st Division, as patrol after patrol encountered strong German resistance and was punished for its curiosity. Still, Legge would write, the patrols had accomplished their missions. The enemy's dispositions had been located, and "information was now available to lay the barrage for the initial attack."

That attack was delayed for two more days as the division waited for its artillery to come up. Each day as it waited, five hundred of the 1st Division's men were made casualties by the German artillery, gas, machine guns, and, in some instances, Hun aircraft.

Alvord Kemp remembered hearing "the zoom of a Fokker coming our way" on one afternoon, "and so we dove for our holes like so many rabbits. Soon Fritz came sweeping down the valley, not over fifty feet above the ground."

To his dismay, Kemp watched as one of his company's men leapt out and started firing at the startled German aviator, who in return let loose his machine guns. "Nobody got hit but the fellow who jumped out and started shooting, and he got it through his arm," Kemp wrote. "Well, he got out of it easy, we all agreed. By jumping out of his hole he had given away our position, so that toot sweet or tooter, we would be getting a whole flock of G.I. cans, rolling kitchens and everything."

On the morning of October 3, two of Company D's privates were killed. Having left the dubious safety of the hole they shared, the recent replacements, Wisconsinites Frank Marquardt and Edgar Linder, were lying outside of it "when a German shell came over and hit between them killing both men instantly," Private John Settle remembered.

On the same day, the division's battalion commanders were brought together and handed their orders for the assault, to begin at 5:35 A.M. on October 4.

Two battalions of the 16th Regiment would push north along the eastern edge of the Aire to the town of Fléville, several kilometers away, while battalions from the 18th, 28th, and 26th Regiments would attack from left to right in line—the beginning of what would be an eight-day, superhuman effort to drive a wedge through the German defenses before and on top of the Romagne Heights.

The 18th was to connect with the right of the 16th Regiment and push over the eminence holding Montrebeau Wood and through the ravine sheltering Exermont, both of which had been taken, and lost, by the 35th Division less than a week before.

The 28th Regiment, on the right of the 18th, was to push across Exermont Ravine, through Beauregard Farm, which sat just northeast of Exermont, and up and over Hill 240 in conjunction with the 18th Regiment, and then assault Hill 272; the 26th was to advance on the right of the 28th, clearing La Neuville-le-Comte Farm and Hill 212, and push on through the Bois de Moncy to the northern edge of Hill 269 on its right.

Two companies of tanks were to accompany the lead battalions; divisions on the right and left would move in line with the 1st, the 16th Regiment's push on Fléville supported on the left by the 28th Division in the Argonne Forest, and the 26th's advance supported on its right by the 32nd Division.

Once again, ambitions for the first day's assault were almost ludicrous, the optimistic A.E.F.'s brain trust betting that the 1st Division could in one day advance several kilometers through the stiff German defenses and take the heavily defended heights before it and establish a new line running from Fléville on the left through the Côte de Maldah and Bois de Romagne on the right. Once astride those heights, it was all downhill over open country to the fortified Hindenburg Line.

In the 28th Regiment, the 3rd Battalion readied itself to lead the assault, with Company D and the 1st Battalion in close support. Third Battalion commander Captain Howard E. Hawkinson, who had made it unscathed through Cantigny and Soissons, was given final orders, and some personal mail, shortly after midnight as he waited to jump off. After placing his assault companies on the jump-off line, Hawkinson "sank back into the hole to wait—and think," a newspaper account of that morning would later say.

At 5:25 A.M. the 1st Division's massed artillery fired a barrage that fell two hundred yards in front of the division's jump-off line; it stood there for five minutes and then rolled forward one hundred yards. Signal rockets were seen above the German positions, and then came the inevitable German counterbarrage of artillery and machine-gun fire. "Into this hell of death and destruction the gallant infantry dashed with a courage and steadiness that could not have been surpassed," the 1st Division's history says.

At the jump-off line, Lieutenant Herman Dacus led the men of Company L to a gap in a line of barbed wire. There he encountered Lieutenant Maury Maverick of Company I. "We shook hands, wished each other good luck, and went over," Dacus would write. (They would not meet again until 1939.)

Maverick remembered there being "no bugles, no flags, no drums, and as far as we knew no heroes" as he stepped into the maelstrom at 5:35 A.M. that day. "The great noise was like great stillness, everything seemed blotted out. We hardly knew where the Germans were. We were simply in a big black spot with streaks of screaming red and yellow, with roaring giants in the sky tearing and whirling and roaring."

Hawkinson—"a very demon for luck," Maverick would remember—and an entourage of thirty aides, runners, and signalmen led the way; within minutes, "the enemy machine gun and shrapnel barrage had reduced their number to six," Hawkinson's hometown paper in Syracuse, New York, would report.

Moving blind, the party emerged from a small wood and into a clearing covered with dense fog. In the early-morning light, Hawkinson saw a group of about thirty men across the way. "Thinking they were men from one of his own companies who had lost their bearings, Hawkinson led the way toward them," the paper reported. "Not until within a very few yards of them did he discover them to be enemy troops. The surprise was mutual."

Hawkinson did the only thing he could do: "Captain Hawkinson drew his automatic and rushed straight at the bewildered group, shouting and shooting into their midst, while the other five quickly followed his lead. The Hun, taken off his guard . . . quickly surrendered."

Two of the Germans, though, raced off for a nearby wood, with Hawkinson—carrying an empty .45 and guessing that the two were headed for a waiting machine gun hidden among the trees—and Lieutenant Victor E. Garrett in pursuit.

The Germans made it to their gun first and put it to quick use, and Hawkinson's luck soon ran out. *The Syracuse Herald* would later report that Hawkinson "slipped into a shell hole and fell, just in a position to receive, point blank, at twenty yards, most of the contents of the gunner's magazine." Garrett, it added, was within a few yards of the Germans, "when they swung their weapon and got him too. The piece then jammed and the gunners made their escape."

Such dramas were playing out all along the front as the sun rose and some of the mist and fog lifted. "In a few minutes there was hand-to-hand fighting all along the line," the 1st Division's history says. "Bayonets and grenades supplemented bullets, and the line swept on."

Advancing after a pause, Maverick was hit by shrapnel from a shell that exploded overhead. "It tore out a piece of my shoulder blade and collar bone and knocked me down," he wrote. Quickly getting the attention of a medic, Maverick found that his four runners had been killed by the same blast—"the two in the middle had been cut down to a pile of horrid red guts and blood and meat, while the two men on the outside had been cut up somewhat less badly, but no less fatally."

With Maverick's company commander, Frank Felbel, already dead as well, Maverick remarked "there was no one to take my place." He continued on for an hour, before the loss of blood forced him to the rear; Dacus, who had been with the company before being transferred to Company L a few days before, took over what was left of I, his old outfit.

One Company I private, Carl Mitchell, was wounded in the hip during the assault and fell prisoner. "They did not want to carry me, so I lay in that woods all day, and about dark a German Red Cross man fixed my hip up for me and told me to go back of their lines." With no one guarding him, "I went back a little ways and hid myself under a bush until morning." He would make it back to his own lines the next day.

Leaving wounded men such as Mitchell in its wake, the attack spilled onto open ground south of Exermont, without the support of the tanks, which, as at Soissons, had quickly succumbed to the German artillery.

"Anti tank guns on Hill 240 prevented a single tank from reaching the assault waves," Legge wrote. Only five would make it to Exermont Ravine; just one would remain to actually enter the town. Casualties among the crews were 84 percent.

From Montrebeau Wood on the west to the open ground south of Exermont on the east, the 1st Division's men found themselves fighting over ground carpeted with dead from the 35th Division.

Alvord Kemp remembered that as his unit advanced from Montrebeau Wood, "There in an uneven row across the field, and close enough together so a man could walk on dead men and hardly have to touch the ground, lay American soldiers.

"When the men of the First Division saw that awful sight, they swore that they would win back this ground and drive the Germans back or there would be another line of silent men there, too."

On the left of the 28th Regiment, the 18th advanced with two battalions to Exermont Ravine. After taking the deserted village, the 2nd and 3rd Battalions of the 18th began ascending the open slope toward Hill 240, about a kilometer to the north, advancing "every foot of the way . . . in the face of a withering fire with no cover from which they could reply," the 1st Division's history says.

Reaching the top of the hill, the remnants of the battalions were shredded by heavy artillery fire coming from the emplacements on the Aire and were forced to retreat to the hill's southern base and dig in for the night.

On the extreme left of the division, the 16th Regiment took horrendous casualties while fighting its way into Fléville, but it would be the only regiment in the division to achieve its objective for the day. As arranged, the 2nd and 3rd Battalions evacuated the town soon after, figuring, rightly, that the Germans would pound it with artillery once the Americans took it.

On the extreme right, the 26th Regiment advanced and immediately took fire on both flanks and as well to its center, a battery of 77s at the La Neuville-le-Comte farm firing point-blank at the Americans from a distance of just eight hundred yards.

"The combat liaisons group which was to protect the right flank was annihilated by machine gun fire at the 'jump off,'" Legge wrote.

Company D and the rest of the 28th's 1st Battalion, meanwhile, jumped off from the Charpentry-Eclisfontaine Road in support of the 3rd Battalion. They made good progress until they reached the open crest of Hill 185, about half a kilometer south of Exermont, and were pinned by heavy fire. Working their way forward in rushes, the battalion's doughboys eventually reached Exermont Ravine that afternoon.

Joining with elements of the 26th Regiment, the 1st Battalion helped subdue the crews manning the 77s at La Neuville-le-Comte Farm and, sweeping west through the ravine, captured Beauregard Farm in vicious, hand-to-hand fighting, putting out of action another German 77 that had destroyed several of the American tanks.

Two of Company D's privates did the deed, Berte Kinkade and George Gardner making "an encircling movement amid heavy fire" from numerous machine guns and capturing the gun's crew. "They cleaned out the enemy dugouts in the vicinity and returned with forty prisoners, including an officer," their subsequent DSCs say.

At the end of the day's fighting, the division's line ran west to east from just south of Fléville to the southern base of Hill 240 and then to Beauregard and La Neuville-le-Comte Farms. There the 26th Regiment was forced to refuse its flank "to prevent infiltration from the Bois de Morine on the right, which was still strongly held by the enemy," Legge wrote.

Spent, both sides settled in to lick their wounds and ready for another day's fight to come. Artillery dueled across the evening sky; Lieutenant

Charles Butler, now with Company C, dug a "funk hole" and spent the evening watching "the enemy's heavy shells level the aged stone walls of now deserted Exermont."

(Butler would also recall an encounter that day with two immigrant stretcher-bearers from Company D. Asked to carry a wounded Company C sergeant to the aid station, one of them demurred, saying in broken English, "He no from our company. Dot's our orders. We only take wounded from Company D." After Butler pulled out his .45 and threatened to shoot them, they quickly loaded the sergeant onto the stretcher and carried him off.)

"We tried to dig in but we were so tired and hungry and the ground was just like the rest of that Argonne mud, seemed like it was a mixture of putty and glue," Alvord Kemp remembered. "So after trying to dig a little we gave it up, but we couldn't sleep because all around us were wounded men."

As the night wore on, Kemp added, "Now and then a high explosive would come screaming and hissing a message of death. All together it was terrible, and the only thing I could compare that night with would be *Dante's Inferno.*"

The attack was resumed on October 5, this time with the grand ambition of taking Hill 240, and as well the northern reaches of the strongly fortified Hill 272, from which artillery and machine-gun fire had taken a heavy toll on October 4.

The 18th Regiment was to storm the western side of Hill 240, the 28th the eastern side and the rolling plateau to its right; after a pause of two hours at the hill's northern base, these two regiments were to continue on northward and assault and take Hill 272, while the 26th Regiment was to push north and take Hill 212 and, farther on, the western limits of the Bois de Moncy at the base of Hill 269.

In a key innovation, control of supporting artillery was passed to regimental commanders in an eventually successful effort at making the preparation fire and barrages more effective.

At 6:15 A.M., the American artillery opened on the ground facing the 18th, 28th, and 26th Regiments. Company D and the 28th's 1st Battalion jumped off at 6:30 A.M., the men leaving the relative safety of their holes to follow a rolling barrage through the valley leading slowly upward through the eastern edge of the Bois de Boyon and toward the eastern slopes of Hill 240.

"The enemy had constructed strong shelter trenches and dugouts north of Beauregard Farm as well as along both crests of the valley," the division's history says. "With the falling of the barrage . . . the 1st Battalion, fresh and impatient, sprang forward and closed upon the line of bursting steel. Men fell fast, but on swept the successive waves. More than fifty bodies of their brave number were afterward counted in front of a single group of shelter trenches."

Ascending an open slope with the 18th Regiment on its left, the 1st Battalion swept away the German line at the foot of the Montrefagne. "Rifles were used at close quarters and the bayonet came into its own," the division's history says. "The position was won by extermination."

As his own unit advanced upward onto the hill, "we received a galling crossfire from both flanks," Kemp wrote. "We kept on and finally reached the summit."

Sliding down the northern side, the men found shelter in shell holes and foxholes and prepared for an immediate counterattack, but, Kemp wrote, "Our fears were needless as either they did not have the heart to storm us or else they were so disorganized that they were not in shape to."

Wrote Company C's Charles Butler: "From all directions, the sharp rat-a-tat, rat-a-tat, tat-tat of the Boche machine guns seemed to be coming. An occasional Yankee went down, but the lines pressed forward. German whiz-bangs burst in their midst, as the boys closed with the Boche first line of resistance."

And Marvin Stainton was one of them there, on that day, enduring or reveling in or perhaps even relishing his first taste of hand-to-hand combat, of pulling himself up the steep slope of the Montrefagne with his left hand and firing away with his right, with a mad look in his deep-set eyes, jaw set, his time finally come, his "fateful purpose" arrived.

George Butler would remember that Marvin stuck to it that October 5 on Hill 240, and was "in the thickest of that fighting and did splendid work overcoming 4 enemy machine guns while going through very heavy shell fire."

Others matched Marvin's aplomb, one, Corporal David B. Stewart Jr., an old hand from Massachusetts who'd trained with the company at Fort Benjamin Harrison, winning a DSC for his conspicuous actions on Hill 240. Held up by fire, Stewart, his DSC says, "called for a German-speaking comrade, and advanced thru woods for about one hundred fifty yards in front of his Company, capturing two machine guns and twelve prisoners who delayed the advance."

The hill took its toll: After making it unscathed through Soissons and St. Mihiel, Wilbert Murphy finally met his match there, catching a machine-gun bullet in the left knee as he fought his way up its steep slope. Three days later, he wrote: "We were surely making it hot for Fritz this last time, let me tell you. The morning we started it was still dark and there was a heavy fog so that one couldn't easily see the fellows near him. Just the second we started, our barrage opened up on them and all you could hear was the crash of our shells exploding."

As Company D spread itself in the thick forest and advanced in twos and threes, taking machine guns or being blown to pieces by the whiz-bangs that pierced the woods, many men fell unseen, and their deaths would not be noted until an accounting was made when the company was relieved on October 12.

Among those killed on Hill 240 was Private Raymond A. Horton, twenty-four, the only child of a farmer in Greene, New York, who was "hit by a machine gun bullet" that "passed through his stomach" while fighting that morning, Murphy recalled. "He was carried back to the aid station where he died from the wound."

Another, Private John Young of Seaman, Ohio, was killed "by concussion from a large German shell," Sergeant Anthony Vedral would recall. Young was buried where he fell, his grave marked by a stick, his helmet, and his identification tag, just one of a burgeoning picket line of sticks and upended rifles following the 28th's advance up that hill.

Many others from Company D would die in those woods over the next week, many recent replacements who had no doubt marveled at the ease of war while traipsing the Woëvre Plain, and as they relaxed in the luxury of those abandoned quarters in the Nonsard Woods.

With the taking of the Montrefagne, the 2nd Battalion of the 28th Regiment passed through the 1st Battalion and, according to plan, attempted to take Hill 272, but was repulsed.

"As the battalion advanced beyond the cover of Hill 240 a hurricane of fire met the lines," one officer would relate. "Enfilade and frontal fire wiped out entire platoons. In a period of a few minutes after the jump-off the battalion lost over fifty percent casualties and retired to the cover of the woods, unable to bring in their dead and wounded."

The 26th Regiment, meanwhile, after a mad dash across open ground captured Arietal Farm in the center of the valley.

"Veritable sheets of steel from the machine guns on the hill across the valley and from the Farm d'Arietal swept knee-high over the ground, mowing down the advancing ranks and killing them after they fell," the 26th's Lyman Frasier wrote. "Hand-to-hand fighting raged for a short time in le Petit Bois and at the Farm d'Arietal. Artillerymen were bayoneted at their guns. Machine gunners fell on the piles of their empty shells."

The men quickly found themselves being pounded by German artillery and taking withering fire from as many as fifty machine-gun emplacements above them on Hill 272. The regiment's 3rd Battalion attempted to storm the offending hill several times, and placed men on its lower reaches and on Hill 263 as well, but the intense fire broke up the assaults.

Friendly fire also took a huge toll, one company alone losing forty men dead and wounded. The survivors fell back to the edge of Arietal Farm and dug in for the night.

The second day's fighting came to a close with the 1st Division's lines having budged, at terrific cost, just over a kilometer in the vicinity of Hill 240, and about one and a half kilometers to where the 26th Regiment occupied Arietal Farm and the western edge of the Bois de Moncy.

In one key and fortuitous move—"one of those remarkable incidents that place a premium on daring and resourcefulness during war," the division's history would note—a patrol from the 26th Regiment's 1st Battalion ascended and occupied a knoll on the western slope of Hill 269 on the regiment's far right flank, putting the Americans behind the German lines.

The presence of this bunch of doughboys in the German rear "confused his circulation so greatly that prisoners were constantly captured while trying to pass through the Bois de Moncy," the division's history says.

Over the next few days, detachments of the 26th Regiment, the 32nd Division, and, finally, the 1st Battalion of the 1st Engineers would occupy and hold this key ground despite attacks and counterattacks by an enemy chagrined at having given up such prime real estate so easily.

On the evening of October 5, Germans and Americans settled in for the night with little having been decided, and with the Americans' original objective of the Bois de Romagne and Côte de Maldah still far, far out of reach.

Giving up the dream, for now, of a lightning advance to the top of those offending hills, the doughboys instead dug in; in some places just a few dozen yards separated friend and foe, including the funk holes occupied by Company F of the 18th, which spent the night in the woods at the northern base of Hill 240 "within ten or twelve rods of the Jerrys' front lines," Kemp wrote, adding: "They had a row of machine guns set up there, just a little way from the edge of the woods. Believe me that was some night. I shudder now to think of the awful suspense of waiting, knowing that if any of our men should cough or sneeze that we would be slaughtered like sheep.

"We could hear the Jerrys talking and now and then we could see the flicker of a match as one would light a pipe. I knew that we were going to hell and back again if we stood the pressure."

After two days of hard fighting, the woods and hillsides were filled with dead and wounded. Lyman Frasier's battalion lost 9 officers and 240 men killed and another 7 officers and 350 men wounded just on October 5, well over half the battalion's strength. The 26th's severely wounded—120 men— were collected in an aid station near Arietal Farm, unable to be evacuated because of the constant and intense shelling.

"Over eighty men died at this aid station," Frasier wrote, "some of them living as long as three days after being brought in. The sight and experience will never be forgotten by those who were present."

Such experiences were common along the 1st's front line. From the safety of his funk hole above Exermont, Charles Butler could plainly see the day's toll in the broken bodies of the wounded gathered at an aid station: "The sight below was a tragic witness to the cost of the ground gained during the day's battle: row upon row of broken, tossing, bleeding bodies. Miles back of the line, ambulances were waiting to receive the wounded riflemen and to rush them still farther back to the base hospitals. Many died of mortal wounds long before their turns came."

Many more who dug in alongside Butler that evening would die before their time, but for now the 28th Regiment caught its breath, the men using heat tabs to warm a cup of coffee and wash down their tinned monkey meat and goldfish, awaiting the last push against that hill—"that appalling hill," as Charles Butler would write—that loomed like death itself in the fading sunlight.

17

Hill 263

HE HAD WANTED THIS, he had asked for this; hell, Marvin Everett Stainton had *begged* for it, and by October 9, 1918, Marvin was well on with his war, awaking from a cold and fitful sleep and stumbling through the gloom of a heavy fog to a large shell hole, where a small group of Company D's noncoms and officers sat waiting—all "joking and of good humor . . . waiting for zero hour to go over after them," Sergeant Lynn Barnes would remember—to begin one more day of war, one more day of hunting Germans in yet another place they called Death Valley, all the while ducking and dodging the blind barrages and fusillades that whooshed from the artillery emplacements on Hills 272 and 263, amid the wails of the unseen wounded and the chugging *pup-pup-pup* of the machine guns, all of these sounds merging into a resounding echo of violence that careered across the valley floor like the waters of a flash flood.

A long way from Cantigny, a long way from Soissons, Company D's men awoke that October 9 to follow a new leader, a kid who just a few months before kept a picture of Jesus on his wall but who had now become one of them, muddy and wasted and gritty and mean; and if Marvin Stainton was not the actual source, he was certainly a kindred spirit to a "kid lieutenant" the correspondent Frederick Palmer had found in those woods below those hills, and who had told Palmer:

"This is a mean, nasty war, but it is the only war we have had or most of us ever want, and we will have to put up with it and fight the boche in the meanest, nastiest way possible, if that is the way to lick the mean, nasty boche.

"This," Palmer added, "was certainly not a sophomoric view of war, and it was characteristic of an officer of the 1st Division."

And it was as a company commander that Marvin took his place that morning, what with Soren Sorensen—who had taken over the 1st Battalion from Charles Senay—out of the war once more with yet another wound, suffered October 4, and Company D's commander George Butler, the next most senior officer in the depleted battalion, taking Sorensen's place, and naming the company's second in command, John Church, as his adjutant.

And it was at 8:52 A.M. that Lieutenant Marvin Stainton led Company D's men from their places near Arietal Farm toward Death Valley, stringing out into the woods to fight singly and in small groups, any meaningful contact between units lost amid the brambles and stands of trees and slicing ravines fortified with German bunkers and machine-gun nests; and it was at 8:52 A.M. that Marvin Stainton marched off to war, again, toward that hill and whatever destiny might await him there among those dripping trees, and in that thick fog that clung to the ground like suffocating down.

For three days following the taking of Montrefagne, the company had clung to its position just a few hundred yards to the northeast in the vicinity of a natural spring called St. Germaine, digging in at any handy spot that offered protection from the artillery and constant machine-gun fire coming from the northwest, north, and northeast.

Patrols were sent out in an effort to keep contact with the enemy and probe for weaknesses on Hill 272 and Hill 263, creeping through barbed-wire entanglements that choked the Petit Bois, each man constantly on alert for the burst of an unseen Maxim from the front or rear, or the whine of an incoming round that would shatter the very treetops and send shards of hot metal and wood in one hundred different, and dangerous, directions.

Hill 272 had remained a menace, its guns continuing their bombardment of the 28th and 26th Regiments' lines below, and on October 6 the

3rd Battalion of the 26th was given permission to assault the German positions.

"Enemy activity on Hill 272," Captain Lyman Frasier would write, "indicated that he was feverishly strengthening his positions there. The 3rd battalion commander felt that if he had to take the hill he better take it now."

The battalion set out, its aim to send two companies across Death Valley—southwest of Hill 263 and east of Hill 272—and roll up the German left flank. The 28th Regiment's 2nd Battalion, in the front lines north of Hill 240, would contribute suppressing fire "until the attacking troops should appear on the hill," Frasier wrote.

The 7th Field Artillery as well was to lay strong fire on Hill 272 until friendly soldiers could be seen on its crest. A strong patrol also would cover the assault's right flank from a position south of Hill 263. At 2:00 P.M., the 26th went over the top, and "all went well for a time," Frasier wrote. Amid clouds of smoke and dust, the assaulting companies reached the German positions on Hill 272 "and drove him from his position on that part of the defense."

However, at 3:00 P.M. the situation changed. A German counterattack from the vicinity of Hill 269—Frasier estimated its strength as being that of a full regiment—quickly drove in the company protecting the right flank. Seeing Germans in their rear, half the troops on Hill 272 broke and ran as well, about forty of them subsequently being stopped and steadied with the help of several old-line noncoms.

Two machine gunners supporting the 26th's advance on Hill 272 went to work on the Germans, who brought up another company to clear the Petit Bois on the 26th's right flank. Frasier, hustling to the area to arrest the retreat of his assaulting and supporting forces, gathered up forty men and quickly ordered a counterattack.

"They outnumbered us three to one," Frasier wrote. "We had no support. We had no line of retreat. We had to attack them. This was done, the men firing from the shoulder and advancing very rapidly.

"The interval between the men was wide and produced the desired effect of deception and surprise upon the Germans. They fled in some confusion straight into the fire of the two machine guns. The casualties in the enemy ranks were very heavy."

The artillery went to work on this force as well, shelling the woods and causing eight hundred casualties among the Germans. The counterattack had been broken, but it had achieved one of its aims; the 26th's assault on Hill 272 was called off.

The 3rd Battalion had also suffered enormous casualties: "The strength of the battalion that night was three officers and one hundred and eighty-two men," Frasier wrote.

The lines would remain as they had been, the 16th Regiment holding its own but unable to advance on Fléville; the 18th Regiment in the woods north of Montrefagne, taking fire from Hill 176 to the northwest and the slopes of Hill 272 to its north; the 28th Regiment dug in to the northeast of Hill 240, and the 26th Regiment at Arietal Farm, its right flank refused to guard against German infiltration from the Bois de Moncy in front of Hill 269.

Conditions were horrendous, as the 1st's men huddled in their shallow funk holes under a barrage of shot, shell, and gas. Private James "Slim" Jones remembered: "I ain't got much religion, neighbor, but as I was laying in the shell holes with the machine guns and cannon balls roaring around, I've often said well, sir, here I am alone with God, and I sure put my trust in him."

Neither food nor water could be brought up through the maelstrom, and decaying corpses littered the ground, as burial parties had been suspended as far back of the lines as Montrebeau Wood.

"There was no such thing as breakfast to be had, no water to drink, nothing to do but crouch there in our hole and wait," the 18th's Private Alvord Kemp would write. And as they waited, the deluge of German shot and shell was so intense it in some instances ignited the blasted woods on the hills surrounding them, adding a thick veil of choking and acrid smoke to the miseries that bedeviled them.

"Frequently, the Montrefagne looked like a veritable volcano," the 1st Division's history says. "For hours at a time the smoke from bursting shells in the Exermont ravine, and in the depressions north of it, resembled forest fires. By night, the crackle of machine guns, the bursting of shell and the flare of signal rockets were confusing and awe-inspiring."

"For two days and two nights," Charles Butler would remember, the men of the 28th's 1st Battalion "in thin lines lay dug in along the Romagne

Road. Boche airplanes purred overheard constantly, as they tried to search out the hiding places of the Yankee infantry, and to detect the artillery emplacements of the Yankee field pieces.

"Whenever a Hun observation plane swooped low over the lines the order would be passed along the entire position: 'Keep down, don't move, and keep under cover!'"

Alvord Kemp would learn the hard way what ingesting mustard gas could do to a man's insides. On October 6, his company was elated when a chow party finally made it through with beans and coffee and bread. "Well, we ate and were sick, the whole of us," he wrote.

Unknown to the men, the carrying party had been shelled with gas, ditched their food cans, "and then when it was over they came back and got the chow and brought it up." The mustard gas had permeated the food and drink. That night, Kemp wrote, the men were too sick to sleep. "If the Jerrys had known it they could have gobbled us up like ginger bread men, but they didn't," he wrote.

As the heavy guns on the west bank of the Aire continued to take their toll, and as the 1st Divison's doughboys burrowed farther and farther into the ground, Pershing and his staff found themselves casting about for a means not only to resume the 1st's advance, but also to solve the vexing and well-publicized plight of the so-called Lost Battalion of the 77th Division. Its situation several kilometers to the southwest of where the 1st Division's men hunkered in their holes was dire, and becoming worse by the hour.

The Lost Battalion was not actually a single battalion, but an amalgam of troops from three different regiments under the command of Major Charles Whittlesey, who had jumped off with his 1st Battalion of the 308th Regiment on September 26 on the far left of the Argonne drive, and found himself cut off for seventy-two hours in the dense forest before the first phase of the drive was suspended.

Pushing ahead again on October 1, Whittlesey and his command made good progress despite taking heavy casualties. On the evening of October 2, the men stopped on the southern side of a road running northwest from Binarville to Fléville. A battalion of the 307th Regiment tried to reach him from the west to help exploit his gains, but only one company made it through the dark woods.

On the morning of October 3, Whittlesey found that he and his 553 men had been cut off during the night. Over the next five days, as its food and medical supplies ran out, this "lost" command would endure attacks by German infantry wielding hand grenades and flamethrowers, high-angled mortars that devastated their ranks, and a misguided bombardment from their own artillery.

Whittlesey's plight preoccupied Pershing's staff even as it sought a way to overcome the standoff in the 1st Division's theater. Finally, a proposed solution to the situations facing both the 1st Division and Whittlesey's Lost Battalion was offered by I Corps commander General Hunter Liggett.

Liggett proposed sending a brigade from the untested 82nd Division across the Aire below the tiny village of Chatel-Chéhéry, still out of reach of the 28th Division. This force would then pivot to the north and attack a series of hills—180, 223, 244, from which German artillery had pounded the 1st Division—and threaten the rear of the Boche holding up the advance of the 28th Division on the west bank of the Aire. If successful, the 82nd's assault would also force the Germans encircling Whittlesey to pull back.

Over the objections of some on Pershing's staff who felt the move was too risky, the 164th Brigade was moved up along the traffic-choked roads that supplied the 28th and 1st Divisions.

At dawn on October 7, understrength elements of the 327th and 328th Regiments crossed the Aire, their right "in the air" and exposed to the German artillery to the north, and quickly seized Hill 180. The 28th Division at the same time advanced, and together with the 327th Regiment managed to take Chatel-Chéhéry and move to the heights beyond.

Though they were held up before a strong German position at the town of Cornay, the move outflanked the German force that had encircled Whittlesey and his men. The Boche began to withdraw. On October 7, help reached the pitiful survivors of the Lost Battalion, and on October 8 Whittlesey and 193 men walked out of their formerly forlorn position. Another 144 wounded had to be carried.

It was also on October 8 that Private Alvin C. York of the 328th Regiment's 2nd Battalion would perform what is beyond doubt the most legendary of doughboy deeds, killing around 28 Germans and capturing thirty-five machine guns and 132 prisoners near Hill 223—just a few miles to the west of where the 1st Division continued to hold its positions, vainly probing for openings among the German positions in those hills above Exermont.

As Whittlesey was being rescued, and Alvin York was capturing what seemed to be "the whole German army," Lyman Frasier was being ordered to make another push against Hill 272. Frasier led his battalion over the top at 5:00 A.M., leaving a gap between the 28th Regiment and the attacking battalion of the 26th, but, Frasier would write, "It was felt that the 28th Infantry could take care of this in addition to its own sector."

Frasier's force soon ran into machine-gun positions on the hill's lower slopes, each protected by fifteen riflemen. "These were gradually reduced but at the expense of time and at the expense of men," he wrote. But just as Frasier's men reached the eastern crest of Hill 272, Germans were seen approaching on their right flank—as they had two days before.

Another force of Boche was seen advancing toward them from the northwest; Frasier decided the best course was to retreat, reasoning, "If the enemy should succeed in eliminating us from the fight it would be an easy matter to roll up the flank of the 28th Infantry and possibly the entire division." Frasier's force "retreated by leaps and bounds, keeping our right flank constantly refused."

For the rest of that bleak day, the 1st's artillery poured high explosives onto Hill 272, the Germans responding in kind with heavy concentrations of gas. To Frasier, the heavy American fire indicated "that some new move" as yet unknown to him was to be made.

In the evening, Frasier and the 1st Division's other battalion and regimental commanders were indeed apprised of a new plan, set to begin the next morning: The 16th Regiment's 1st Battalion, held in reserve until now, would be inserted into the 28th Regiment's lines north of Hill 240 and attack northwest at dawn with the aim of capturing Hill 272.

Frasier was told he would be relieved from his position at Arietal Farm by Company D and the 28th's 1st Battalion, and slide to his right and into the western edge of the Bois de Moncy. On Frasier's right, the 1st Battalion of the 1st Engineers, which late on October 7 relieved a detachment of the 32nd Division atop Hill 269 and on the next day attacked and gained the crest, was to pivot west and clear the Bois de Moncy, while the 361st

Regiment of the 91st Division—now attached to the 1st—would guard the engineers' right flank.

On the left, the remaining battalions of the 16th and 18th Regiments would attack north, to keep pressure on the German right flank. The 28th and 26th Regiments were to shift their direction of assault slightly, turning from their positions facing northwest to follow Death Valley's north-northeasterly course toward Hill 263, with the right of the 26th also sweeping the lower reaches of Hill 269.

Company D and the 1st Battalion would lead the 28th's assault toward Hill 263 on the morning of October 9, with the 3rd Battalion in support; each move would be made in stages, with the division's artillery leading each individual battalion's advance with a rolling barrage, shifting ranges and directions on a prearranged schedule.

The objective, as always, remained the crests of those hills that had continued to rain death on the doughboys over the previous nine days, as well as the heights of the Côte de Maldah and the dark woods of the Bois de Romagne, which dribbled out into open country north of the Romagne Heights and pointed the way to Germany itself.

By midnight, the 28th's 1st Battalion had relieved the 26th Regiment at Arietal Farm. Shortly thereafter, Lieutenant Charles Butler, of Company C was rousted from his foxhole and told to report to the regiment's command post. There, he was instructed to guide John Church and two runners to the battalion's front line to ensure its two forward companies were in liaison with each other—no mean feat in the shell-hole-pocked, wire-tangled woods of the Petit Bois.

Moving through "the familiar smell of poisonous gases, while the dank air was laden with the odor of high explosives," Butler crossed paths with many of the 1st Division's wounded, some of whom had lain in their positions of agony for four days.

"As the fevered brains of the wounded perceived the approach of the detail, they would try to rise and would call out water, water!" Butler remembered. "Many fell again to the ground, perhaps to arise no more. These wailing cries of the wounded continued to pierce the night. The distressing sounds wrung the hearts of the detail."

Locating the series of funk holes that marked the battalion's position,

Church and another lieutenant groped their way to the line of resistance on the left, while Butler established liaison with the front line on the right. After several hours, Butler and Church managed to find each other and returned to the regimental command post, where Church, still weak from his severe wounding at Soissons, "fell into a wire bunk, exhausted," Butler wrote.

Heavy fog greeted the early risers the next morning. "Never was there a denser fog than that which ushered in the morning of October 9th," the 1st Division's history would recall. But the dank clouds had a silver lining, it added: "Fog is the best protection that could be provided for assaulting machine gun nests."

At 8:30 A.M., using the advantage of the thick mist, the division began its last great push of the war, as the 16th Regiment's 1st Battalion moved to relieve the 28th's 2nd Battalion near St. Germaine spring.

As the battalion approached the hill, the 28th's men passed through it, coming "out of the fog in front and running to the rear as fast as possible," Capt. Leonard Boyd would remember.

Fearing the fleeing men would sow "the seed of panic" in his own battalion, one of Boyd's company commanders stopped one of the retreating soldiers and asked what unit he belonged to. After hearing he was with the 2nd Battalion of the 28th, word was passed to the 16th Regiment's men to "let the men of the 28th Infantry go through," Boyd wrote, adding that the knowledge that the fleeing force was not part of his regiment's 1st Battalion "restored the steadiness of the men."

As Boyd's men ascended Hill 272 behind a rolling barrage, infiltrating and eliminating machine-gun nests, Company D and the 28th's 1st Battalion prepared to move out, their destination Hill 263 at the north end of the valley.

And when Company D moved out, it was behind Marvin Everett Stainton, twenty-three-years old, the kid who'd pined for this for more than a year, and who'd chafed under the stifling boredom of Fort Logan Roots and Camp Pike, withering under the ignominy of those domestic backwaters while the history of the world hung at a precipice and others were doing their part, *his* part.

It was the biggest day of Marvin's life, and the best day, the culmination of all that he had wanted as he had stewed in the Arkansas heat through most of 1917 and the first half of 1918; and one can picture him laughing the loudest as Company D's noncoms and officers sat around that shell hole at Arietal Farm on the morning of October 9, 1918, "all of good cheer," as Lynn Barnes would write, even as mustard gas–tinged fog wrapped around their ankles, as machine-gun fire raked the air overhead, as the deep crescendos from exploding 77s and the screams of *Minenwerfer* seeking their targets further collapsed the woods of the Petit Bois, and as hell itself seemed to erupt with the 16th Regiment's storming of Hill 272 just to the west.

They moved out at 8:52 A.M.—"Lieut. Stainton and Sargt. Vedral of this Co in charge of the first line and first wave of the second platoon, and I with the second line of the first wave," Lynn Barnes would write.

Moving north through the battered valley and splintered woods of the Petit Bois, the company's platoons had not gone far before they were separated. German bunkers were cleaned out the old-fashioned way. "My pal and I went past a German dugout, and my pal said, 'there is someone down in that dugout," Private John Durbrow of the 28th Regiment would recall.

"He hollered in German for them to come out, but nobody answered, so I threw a hand grenade down and pretty soon a German came out with his hands up and limping and hollering 'kamerad.'

"We then threw another bomb down into the dugout, and after it went out we told the German to go down and bring out all the killed and wounded. He brought up two dead and two wounded German soldiers. One of them was suffering pretty bad, so I finished him with his rifle."

Company D advanced the same way. About 11:30 A.M., "The Huns drop a nice box barrage just back of our first waves and as the [terrain] of our advance was wooded hills, we got more or less separated," Sergeant Vedral would write. "When partly reorganized [the] Co. proceeded on towards our last objective, Hill 263. Lt. Stainton being at that time being cut off by enemy barrage, proceeded a little later with 7 men in reconnoitering patrol on our left."

Slim Jones would recall one "dirty pocket" which in particular consumed hours as Marvin and his men worked to pin down and encircle machine-gun emplacements, and then, with grenades and automatic rifles, force either the deaths or surrenders of the German machine gunners and infantrymen that lurked inside.

"A German machine gunner was giving our outfit trouble," Jones remembered. "Stainton asked how many of us would follow him. Seven of our guys stepped out. Well, sir, we went into that Dutch bunch with all pistols blazing and we got 132 prisoners and captured nine machine guns, got a colonel, a captain and a lieutenant in an officer's dug out."

Marvin, Jones added, had become a leader "that the men sure would [go] to hell for if he gave the order. Nothing but a kid, too, always ahead of his men, yelling out to encourage them and giving them a good example."

Barnes agreed. "In this valley through the Lieuts. good leader ship we captured 7 machine guns and 64 prisoners. Among their killed I cannot say only I got 8. For us we lost none there."

Marvin's mood was right, his fateful purpose intact, a well of heretofore unknown abilities located deep inside himself, and one can't help but imagine that it was in the midst of that mean, nasty work being done there in those woods against the mean, nasty Boche that Marvin for the first time truly found himself, finally attained that ephemeral right of passage between youth and manhood, bridged the life-changing divide between dreams and reality, and set himself upon a new course, a new life, and toward a foreseeable and agreeable future.

Even as Marvin and his mates finished their work that afternoon, others were gaining dark new insights into their mortality, among them Lieutenant Bill Warren, who was very nearly killed by a round that barely missed his carotid artery.

"A machine gun bullet started at my chin, passed along the right side of my neck and came out above my right shoulder," Warren would tell his father in an October 15 letter. "In its path it miraculously avoided all vessels of importance. My wound will probably leave a slight scar on my neck, which will be an emblem of my part in the war."

He was happy enough to let the war run its course in his absence. "It gives me a chance to rest up a bit and perhaps the war will be over before I have a chance to get back into the fighting again."

As Marvin and his squad continued clearing Death Valley, elements of the 28th Regiment's 1st and 3rd Battalions began ascending Hill 263. "The steep, heavily wooded slope of Hill 263 presented many difficulties, and the men were often compelled to pull themselves up by clinging to the brush and small trees," the 1st Division's history says.

"The hostile defense consisted of dispersed machine guns which were taken by groups of men who flanked them under the cover of the brush and the deep ravines along the slope."

Halfway to the crest, Company C's Lieutenant Otus Lippincott's platoon was stymied by German machine-gun fire that caused severe casualties. "A runner sent to the platoon on my right reported he was unable to locate this unit, or that from any other outfit," he recalled. "A runner to D Company on my left reported that company badly shot-up, with no officers left in the Company and that they had been ordered to fall back and dig in."

Company D had indeed taken severe casualties on the hill, among them Private Solon Paul Gunderson, the Camp Grant replacement from Mindoro, Wisconsin. "He was in my squad at the time and was killed about four paces from where I was," his best pal, Private Martin Mikkelson, also of Mindoro, would write home. "He was not the only one who went 'west' up there, I'm sorry to say."

Private Steve Bolis, a Greek immigrant to Warren, Ohio, also fell on the approach to the hill. "He was killed by several machine gun bullets, he died instantly," Private Herbert Maltman remembered. "We had just about reached our objective when he was hit."

The Irishman and private Michael Walshe's American odyssey ended in the same manner, and nearly in the same place. Private Noble Jackson— who had enlisted the previous May 28, even as Company D was holding on at Cantigny, and whose body would eventually travel back to the U.S. on a transport named after the famous village—and privates Stephen Curran, Stanley Latuk, Ross Walker, Cecil Johnson, Frank Gura, and Otto Brunst would also find that hill to be a permanent impasse on that day.

While part of Company D dug in alongside Lippincott's platoon in the center of the hill—"From about noon of October 9th, until about 8 a.m. October 10th, we were completely cut off from the units in our rear and had no contact with troops on either flank," Lippincott would write— others found a way up Hill 263, among them Marvin Stainton.

Delayed by the work in Death Valley, Marvin and his small squad emerged at the base of the hill in the late afternoon, by which time the hill's northern reaches had been reached by elements of the 1st and 3rd Battalions.

"Then it was just about 5 min walk to Hill 263 and our objective," Barnes remembered. "We made it all right but the bullets sure were coming our way."

Under fire, Marvin and his squad wearily climbed Hill 263's south escarpment to near its crest, where Vedral found him. "At about 6 o'clock that afternoon (just at dusk) Lt. Stainton arrived to our position and started to dig in, as we were under heavy artillery fire," Vedral would later tell Sam Stainton.

"Your Brother preserved his good nature and humor in spite of all the hardships. And he preserved it to the very last for when he found me on Hill 263 he was full of joy when he related to me how himself with only seven men captured some 63 prisoners and 7 machine guns."

Marvin picked up a shovel and began digging a hole for the night. But as he dug in, there suddenly was a low whistle, and then a dull crump, as a shell coming from the German positions north of Hill 263 cleared the rise and dropped in the middle of the company.

Rising from the brambles and underbrush and shaking mud from their uniforms, the men checked for casualties, and found Marvin lying on his face, strangely unmarked—but ominously still.

Next to Marvin lay his runner, a small-town Illinoisan private named Frank Kelly. A few feet away lay the body of Private Fred Lauersdorf, of Gillette, Wisconsin.

Barnes would remember: "The Lieut. was not there over 15 minutes till this catastrophe came to him. It was either shrapnel or Trench Mortar that sent the missive on account we were all digging in on the opposite side from the Germans. He was further down the hill than I was and with the same shell killed his runner, Kelly by name, one other man and wounded 4 others."

Vedral would add: "Before he was able to remove some 5 shovels full of dirt, a shell exploded 5 paces in rear and below him. He was thrown on his face, slightly laying on his right side. There was only one small wound visible, one under his right shoulder. He was killed more by concussion.

When the news of his death reached the men in rear, they produced a sad effect."

It had taken one quick second to snuff out one of the brightest lights in the company—and perhaps the entire A.E.F.—and it may well be that as the company's men gathered around his body to mourn and bemoan his passing, they could see the worst of the war's waste and sacrifice there before them on that forlorn hill.

But while it could be said that Kelly and Lauersdorf had been in the wrong place at the wrong time, it was hard to argue that that was true for Marvin. His efforts of the past year and a half had all pointed toward his being there, on that hill, in the middle of one of the largest and most costly drives of a war whose intentions he believed in so.

And in the end, it may well be that he was born to be on Hill 263 on the evening of October 9, 1918, that he had been born to die there at the hand of that single shell, its explosion the culmination of the day on which he had truly found himself, become himself, toward the end of a war in which his restless spirit had finally found a cause on which to spend its energy.

His brother, Edwin, would say as much in Marvin's obituary for the *Laurel Daily Leader.* "He did not enlist from any desire for excitement or adventure—it was purely a question of patriotism and right with him. He died a glorious death, such as a true soldier craves, in the cause of righteousness and humanity—the cause that Jesus Christ himself died for—on the eve of victory."

Edwin added: "He told us when he was at home last that he was ready to die and that if it were his portion to make the great sacrifice all was well and good. He said that somebody had to die and he might as well be one of them.

"The only thing he seemed to fear was that the war might be over before he could get into the fight. His heart was in the war."

John Church had the sad duty of burying Marvin. "I personally saw to the burial and marked the grave which is on the highest point of Hill 263 he so materially aided in capturing and holding," he told Mary Stainton.

Kelly and Lauersdorf were laid to rest near Marvin, who "was buried 15 ft.-20 ft. from where he fell, further up the hill & slightly to the right," Barnes remembered.

Others besides Marvin, Kelly, and Lauersdorf would die that day. As at Cantigny, and Soissons, the company had suffered enormously in the Argonne. As in each of those battles, 10 percent of the company—twenty-two men—would be killed, and records list another 108 who were debilitated by wounds, from gas, and even, in a few cases, "shell shock."

But no death seemed to touch the men as much as that of the fresh-faced lieutenant from Mississippi, the eager beaver whose boyish enthusiasm for his great adventure seemed to have lifted the spirits of the entire company.

And the saddest part of all, George Butler would write, was that the worst of the company's work was done, its war almost finished, at the very moment Marvin Stainton was being buried on the scrubby, shell-pocked heights of Hill 263.

George Butler would tell Edwin Stainton: "Lieut. Stainton had taken all of the objectives assigned to him and had I think won as hard a fight as any American has ever fought, against odds and the saddest thing to we officers and men who knew him for the man and officer that he was, was the fact that his work was completed, and all fighting that Regiment was to do was finished when a stray shell killed him and several of his men."

"I knew Lieut. Stainton for about three weeks but in this short time formed quite a warm friendship with him as he had a warm coat and I a warm blanket, we shared them and slept in the same hole," John Church told Marvin's mother in an October 24 letter. "Believe me, madam, friendships are formed in a short while or never when men share a common danger continuously. In action, he never thought of his own safety, but always the success of the engagement was paramount and I assure you that his courage was always of the highest and the soldierly qualities displayed by him of the finest type."

Slim Jones would add his two cents in a letter to Sam Stainton: "I was with Lieut. Stainton from daybreak on the 9th day of October until 4 p.m. in the afternoon, and I can say that I have not met any man that was braver or had any more nerve than your brother, and you can take one man's word to another.

"I am proud, and so are the rest of the men, that I had the pleasure of having a man like Lieut. Stainton to lead me in the face of death. For he was always cheerful and had us in good spirits all day long. He would keep saying, 'Boys, that hill is where we want to go,' and you can take it from me, we went.

"That day will always be indelibly impressed upon my mind, for I think that we, meaning Lieut. Stainton and what few of the men that were left, did our bit for the freedom of the world."

Marvin Stainton died on the ninth day of October 1918—the ninth day of the company's perilous stay in the Argonne. And as George Butler had written, perhaps the biggest shame of all in his demise was the timing: With Hill 263 taken, the company's most deadly work was done for the war, its suffering nearly over.

Along the entire front that day, the 1st Division had finally achieved its objectives. On the left, the 16th Regiment once again occupied Fléville, establishing a new line just north of the town.

The 18th Regiment found it hard going on the left of Hill 240, its 2nd Battalion taking heavy casualties, but its 1st Battalion was able to join the 1st Battalion of the 16th—which in just several hours had accomplished its mission of finally taking Hill 272—and with it briefly take and hold the Côte de Maldah, before German fire forced a retreat to Hill 272's crest.

Hills 263 and 269 remained in the doughboys' hands on the morning of October 10, though the going was tough once out of the cover of the Bois de Romagne. That morning another advance was ordered, this to fully clear the woods of Germans and the way to open country before the entrenched Kriemhilde Stellung, which ran just south of the villages of Landres et St. Georges and St. Georges.

Patrols from the 28th's 1st Battalion pushed the 1st Division's boundary to the northern edge of the woods, and on October 11, the 28th's 2nd Battalion, which had already suffered terrible casualties while trying to take Hill 272 on October 5, had the unfortunate duty of pushing into the open country, to test the defenses of the Kriemhilde line. But the effort was futile.

"The attacking line would emerge from the woods only to be mowed down before any man had advanced fifty yards," Lyman Frasier wrote.

"Three attempts were made but these heroic efforts came to naught and the battalion commander decided to attempt no further attack."

That commander, Clarence Huebner, wrote simply: "At 8:00 A.M. on Oct. 11th, 1918 combat patrols were sent forward . . . but were held up by heavy machine gun fire and were compelled to fall back into original position."

That evening, troops from the 42nd Division began relieving the 1st Division, whose survivors numbly tried to grasp the fact that their eleven-day ordeal was over.

"We stood and watched them go by and it seemed that we were awakening from a horrible nightmare and that a century had passed since we went to sleep," Alvord Kemp wrote. "We sat and pondered whether we who had come through the ordeal were any better off than those who had made the supreme sacrifice."

Once again, the 1st Division's casualties were staggering, its losses in the Argonne amounting to 35 officers and 816 men killed, and another 7,703 men wounded, gassed, missing, or captured.

As usual, the 28th Regiment suffered hugely. Leaving a party of one hundred men behind to search the woods and hills for dead and wounded, the 28th would ultimately find that 8 officers and 211 men had been killed, and 1,434 wounded or gassed.

There remained twenty-four soldiers "for whom no account could be given," the regiment's history says. "Left behind were those who had died, going forward with the light of battle in their eyes and those who, after being wounded, had dragged themselves to shell holes or into clumps of bushes and there felt their strength grow less and less with agonizing slowness and pain until they, too, lay cold upon the battlefield."

Cold, tired, hungry, and shocked by what they'd experienced in the deep gloom of those October days, the 28th Regiment left it to the 42nd Division to continue the advance; and in a vicious, costly fight led by brigade commander Douglas MacArthur, the 42nd in mid-October took the heights of the Côte de Chatillon, finally breaking through the Kriemhilde Stellung.

By then the dazed survivors in the 28th Regiment could only marvel that they hadn't been killed. "There was but little moving around, most of the men preferring to make use of this chance to rest," the regiment's history says. "There was a dazed sort of expression on their faces and a quiet, almost awed tone in their voices as they sought for and spoke of missing comrades. To them, it seemed little short of a miracle that they had not met a similar fate."

George Butler, sick with the flu and suffering as well from exhaustion, characterized his stay in the Argonne as "12 days of hell if there ever was such a thing, for when you win a hard fight like that it means a heavy loss to yourself as well as to the enemy, and I lost some of my best friends there."

Given seven days' leave to recuperate, Butler headed on a train to Nice; there, he caught "a fever," and wound up in a hospital bed in Paris for several weeks.

As Company D headed to bivouacs in a patch of woods near the village of Parois, south of the Argonne, Bill Warren was also recuperating from the bullet that had slit his neck and very nearly ended his life. By October 16, when he wrote to his sister Anna, he was able to joke about his near demise: "I am sitting up in bed in a ward of Base Hospital No. 67, so you can judge from that that I am feeling pretty good. Having no way of getting shaved, I have been shaveless for over a week, and you can imagine how much like a gorilla I look. I'm thinking of borrowing the nurses' curling irons and curling the whiskers."

An exhausted Lloyd Bronston also had seen hard fighting in the Argonne with Company G of the 28th. In a letter written to Cecile on October 19 he could only hint at what he'd gone through: "Roughing it don't hurt me. I layed in water 3 days where you got your head shot off if you stuck it up 18 inches. I didn't have my clothes off for 18 days or my shoes off for 10 days. But after all is over it is some fine old war when you come out victorious in the end.

"The Germans didn't win this time, they died."

"Whenever there was a fight the 1st division was always in it," George Butler would write his mother, and despite its losses since entering the trenches in the Sommerviller sector exactly one year before—5,448 officers and men killed, some 16,500 wounded and gassed, and another 275 captured or missing—the 1st would be called on again.

On October 28, the men were rousted once more, and the 28th Regiment began marching toward Eclisfontaine, near where it had jumped off on October 4. Company D's last, anticlimactic push of the war had begun.

By November 1, the Western Front was crumbling. The American First Army had finally broken through the Kriemhilde Stellung, and on that day launched a seven-division drive towards Buzancy, Vaux, Stenay, and—the ultimate prize—Sedan, taken from the French by the Prussians in 1870.

The French, meanwhile, had taken Laon and continued to advance toward Germany; the British, too, had broken through and taken the ports of Ostend and Zeebrugge in Belgium and the French city of Lille.

Turkey on just the previous day had surrendered, Austria-Hungary was on the verge of leaving the war, and German sailors had refused orders to engage the British fleet. On October 30, the kaiser declared himself licked, and abdicated and fled to Holland.

Following the new advance, Company D and the 28th Regiment marched hard and fast from November 1 to November 5, when the 1st Division received orders to relieve the 80th Division and attack toward Mouzon, ten kilometers southeast of Sedan, the next day.

On the afternoon of November 6, as the 28th Regiment waited in reserve near Beaumont-en-Argonne, new orders came to the 1st Division; Pershing had issued what one author would call a "blue-sky order," letting it be known that he wanted American boys to be the first to enter Sedan.

A ridiculous race ensued, the 1st dangerously crossing the front of the 42nd Division below Sedan. Doughboys of the 1st wound up famously and briefly "capturing" the 42nd's Douglas MacArthur, mistaken in his ersatz military accoutrements for a German officer.

At the end of the race, the 28th settled into a support role just south of the village of Chéhéry. German machine-gun fire came from the heights just east of the village, and the 3rd Battalion was ordered to attack, with the 1st Battalion in support.

Thus began the last "push" of the war for the 28th Regiment.

With no artillery support, the 28th's 3rd Battalion went over the top on the morning of November 7. "In the face of incessant machine gun fire from the slopes and top of these hills, the men of the 28th pushed on, forward and upward, and at 8:30 a.m., had established their lines on the ridge south of Sedan," the regiment's history said. After being subjected to machine-gun fire and trench-mortar fire all day, they were relieved that evening by a French unit.

The 28th Regiment's war, for all intents and purposes, was over, but not before Company D suffered its last combat losses there at the gates of Sedan.

Private Claude Girdley, from New Albany, Indiana, died with its spires in view. Corporal John Farrelly was killed "by a 77 mm shell, while digging in, the shell making a direct hit in the hole in which he was digging," Private George Tarantino recalled.

Private Alva Sheridan Odle, the twenty-three-year-old son of a Civil War veteran from Franklin County, Illinois, had written a brother from within the United States just the previous August 23 to say his army training was done and his unit was on the move: "Hello brother I am on my way but don't know where. I am well and having a grand time."

But Alva's great adventure ended on November 7 when he was hit by fragments of a high-explosive shell, and he became the eighty-fourth—and last—doughboy in Company D to die in combat or from wounds received in combat.

"His last words were, 'Oh, I'm wounded,'" Sergeant James Whalen remembered. "He died shortly after."

The 28th Regiment, after suffering 217 further casualties in its few hours in front of Sedan on November 7, was pulled out of the lines the next day, and was on the march at 11:00 A.M. on November 11, 1918, when the armistice ending hostilities went into effect.

"An officer announced the fact to the companies as they marched by," wrote the 28th Regiment's intelligence officer, William Livesay. "The announcement caused no demonstration in the ranks, only here and there weak cries of hurrah."

"We stood around and cheered a little bit," Ralph Loucks, a private with Company A of the 28th Regiment and one of the few Janesville boys to make it through to the end, recalled. "We saw some columns of Germans advancing with fieldpacks on their backs. They marched right through our company. No one said, 'Hi Heinie. Look at the guys who whipped you.' No one wisecracked. We figured, 'What if it had been us?' "

After spending most of the previous year under fire, the stillness that day "was awesome," Private Frank Groves of Company H would recall. "You could feel it—almost smell and taste it. There was no singing, no shouting, no laughter. We just stood around and looked and listened.

"The officers then gave us permisson to build fires to dry ourselves and our clothes. We made coffee. My buddy and I sat up and quietly drank and talked in our pup tent until 2 a.m."

The sheer cost in lives made for a bittersweet victory, George Butler would note. Still recuperating from the flu and the effects of those twelve long days in the Argonne, Butler was in Paris on November 11, but the faces of the Company D men sacrificed over the past months haunted him even as he moved amid the joyous crowds.

The next day he wrote his mother and told her: "While I was happy that it was over I could not help thinking of my many friends of last winter who have been 'bumped off.' For this reason I could not cut loose like the whole of Paris did. Even yet today the streets are jammed with people who are half mad with joy, and still parading with all the allied flags."

The war was over, but it would be long months before the men of Company D returned home, and longer still before a full accounting of the price of their war was tallied. From Cantigny to Sedan, the company's dead lay in graves shallow and graves unknown—among the latter the brave young lieutenant who had found redemption and purpose only in his last hours of life amid the forests of the Argonne.

18

"In the Interest of Humanity"

I AM AT THAT road, that village, that hill. If I close my eyes I can see them racing, some of them; falling, some of them; continuing on, some of them; on to Ploisy, its deep recesses lurking below the plain and screened behind a curtain of forest-green foliage; on to Cantigny, perched on high ground and floating beneath a blue and cloudless sky; on to the steep slopes of Hill 263, its heights unseen and unknowable behind a miasma of choking and dripping brush.

I have come to see something of what they saw, what *he* saw in that last moment, that image I'd carried with me for forty-odd years, the culmination of my search. So much seems familiar—whether from the maps I've pored over or the accounts I've read or from my own dreams, I can't be sure—but all seems oddly in place: the poplars lining the Paris-Soissons Highway and marking the horizon like a string of bristly pinwheels; the slopes at Cantigny, that village long since rebuilt, falling away to a mosaic of golden and green fields; bushy Hill 263 silent and lording over a rainy Death Valley like an imperious and indifferent sentinel.

I see the wide and rolling field on which John Nelson fell, just past the

Paris-Soissons Highway, which on a gray and drizzly September day in 2008 is choked with trucks and Renaults and Citroëns moving blithely and impossibly fast on a track once paved with the bodies of doughboys.

I trudge that last kilometer of wheat from Ploisy Ravine to the level ground at Berzy-le-Sec, to be greeted not with a plaque marking the place where Willard Storms and Zygmunt Misiewicz and the others had fallen, but a memorial to the village's own boys gone missing during four long years of war.

I stand at the spot straddling the Framicourt Road where Company D's men dug in east of Cantigny, from which I see the dark blobs of forest that hid the German artillery; on a rainy and miserable day I climb Hill 240, its thick woods still pocked with shell holes, and in the deep, moist silence I try to conjure the guns, the explosions of the *Minenwerfer*, the chattering of the Maxims, the misery of those days.

It was the drama of war, all of the unknowns of *his* story, which drew me to their names, and to these places; but there are deeper dramas, more permanent images, which will stay with me long after I put Company D, and its war, back on that shelf.

They're the images I hadn't expected to find, the ones hidden behind those names, images I might have seen in the Old Man's eyes had I looked close enough, and not of war but of peace—of Company D scattered into pieces, its next of kin seeking in the absence of a body or a dead boy some solace, some meaning to take from a war already on its way to obscurity, its outcome ambiguous, but its suffering, for many, for John Nelson, just beginning.

Anna Wilson is in one of these images, sitting in the ink-smeared office of the local newspaper in March 1919, pouring out her heart amid the clutter of cold type and the chugging of the presses, the editor dutifully taking notes; he will run the results in the next day's edition of the *Janesville Argus*, the headline "What Became of Leigh Wilson," the story detailing Anna Wilson's search for Leigh, for the boy lost at Cantigny just the previous spring, the sixteen-year-old boy she perhaps begged not to go; within its margins the story will relate the supposed fate of Company D, from the horse's mouth of a surviving member returned to Fort Snelling. "From him she learned that Company D had been almost literally wiped off the map, only six men surviving the terrible assault in battle. If Leigh were alive, he would be one of the five others.

"The war department must have a record of Company D and if that company has been submerged in the maelstrom of battle and entirely lost, it ought to have that record, and upon that basis it ought to relieve the anguish of a mother's heart by giving out the facts."

Robert Livick is another. He is writing again—the War Department, the medical department, the headquarters of the 28th Regiment, the surgeon general, the chairman of the U.S. Senate's War Committee; and finally Soren Sorensen, looking for answers, looking for his boy, Rollin Livick, from and of whom word has not been received for seven long months; but none can help, not even Sorensen, who will tell Robert Livick in early 1919: "I really cannot explain why you have not heard from Rollin if he is alive, and from the Surgeon General's report the wound was not a serious one. My honest opinion is he has probably recovered from his wound and has been returned to duty with some other organization and very likely gone into action again, you will get this all from the records office."

George Butler is another. He is at his desk in Rupprecht, Germany, answering yet another inquiry from yet another someone searching for a boy, searching for a soldier lost at that village or at that road or on that hill—*Leigh Wilson, Rollin Livick, Michael Duron, Edward F. Meyers, George Dust, Thomas Eidsvick, Paul Davis* . . . and George Butler is trying to find just the right words, the right tone, settling finally on the following in answering a Dr. Sam Pool of Leakesville, Mississippi, who has inquired on behalf of Private Otto Beard's family as to his whereabouts. "I cannot say how the error was made in carrying him as missing for he was always carried on the records of this company as killed in action, as some of the men of the company saw him after he was killed.

"As his commanding officer I knew him intimately all the winter of 1917 and spring of 1918 and in the battle of Cantigny and I am proud to say he was a good soldier, always willing and ready to do whatever was asked of him, and I know of no higher service a man could render the world than a good U.S. soldier who gave his all to the cause.

"My sincere sympathies go out to the parents, but for consolation they may be proud of his great adventure, in the interest of humanity."

And the strongest image of all is of Sam Stainton, who is climbing that last hill on a beautiful spring day in mid-May 1919, looking for answers, looking for a brother, looking for Marvin Everett Stainton, who, unseen, is going to dust right under Sam's feet.

Using maps drawn by Sergeant Anthony Vedral and Lieutenant John Church, Sam digs and pokes the thick clay of Hill 263, half mad with grief and loss, vainly searching for the body so as to bring his brother home to Laurel, Mississippi, and a proper burial in the family plot. But that hill won't release Marvin, despite the best efforts of Sam, who will tell Mary Stainton: "My trip is over Mamma and again I will have to admit defeat for I could not find Marvin's grave. I followed out all the instructions that was received from Sgt. Vedral and the other and searched again as I did before every inch of the hill and surrounding territory but not a trace could I find of it.

"I did every thing that was in my power to do Mamma and I don't know what I would go thru to know his body is not lost to us forever."

That hill, that image of Sam, would not release me, either, try as I might over the years to look away, to move on, and leave Marvin Stainton and all of the rest of them on that shelf. It was an image that seemed to embody everything about Company D's story: the sacrifice, the waste, the suffering, the courage; the reality that each of its dead was mourned by someone, somewhere; and the cold fact that so many of them died, so many of them simply disappeared, so many were left broken, all in the interest of "humanity" or whatever less-lofty ideals and interests and accidents of fate had put them at that road, and that village, and that hill.

I'd set out to gather some sense of what John Nelson had endured in that wheat, and I found some of that; but I discovered Marvin Stainton and Rollin Livick and Soren Sorensen and the rest as well. And I should have known that, as with John Nelson, the story of Company D did not end with the silencing of the guns on November 11, 1918.

I should have known that the effects of their great and now almost-forgotten war would continue to be felt for months and years, comprising and consuming entire lifetimes, the fallout wafting west across the Atlantic as if it were the fine ash from some far-off Vesuvius, and arriving aboard every returning hospital ship and troop transport to settle into the thousands of homes from which a doughboy had set out on his Great Adventure, only to disappear or be killed or wounded.

For the thousands of doughboys arriving home in early 1919 the war was over, their guerre *finie*, but not so for Company D and the 1st Division. Less than a week following the armistice, the division saddled up once more to head east toward Germany, leaving behind its dead, disappeared, and wounded, among the latter Bill Warren, still recuperating from the bullet that had nearly severed his carotid artery.

The war would leave him permanently scarred, despite several operations and even, as he would write in 1919, "x ray treatment" at Walter Reed General Hospital. But, writing to his grandmother from his bed at Base Hospital No. 67 on December 7, 1918, Warren expressed more concern about his immediate future in the army than he did about his looks.

"My wound is practically healed, though it is still open and must be dressed every day," he wrote. "I'm wondering whether on my recovery I will be sent back to the outfit or will be sent home. It's hard telling.

"My regiment at present is marching toward the Rhine. Transportation must be hard to get, for there are several hundred officers here, completely well, only waiting to receive orders to go."

In early January, 1919 Warren's orders arrived—and he was elated to find himself heading not for Germany, but for the U.S. "At last I'm started somewhere and that place is home," he told his father. "I have my orders for embarkation and am waiting for a ship. Now that I have started I am impatient to arrive. Believe me it will be a happy day when I walk down the gang plank to the other side."

Willard Storms, as well, was on his way home, his five-month tour of various base hospitals over. In late January, 1919 Storms landed in New York.

"It sure seemed like I was destined to stay in the land of the Frogs," he wrote his mother. As his ship, the *Maui*, passed the Statue of Liberty, he told "The Old Lady" to "take a good look at me for she would have to do an 'about-face' to look me in the face again."

Company D, meanwhile, left for Germany on November 17, its new mission to help enforce the terms of the armistice. And when it moved out, it carried on its rolls just thirty of those 185 men who'd sallied from Fort Benjamin Harrison in the fall of 1917, just nine of those fifty-five Camp Grant replacements who'd turned up with John Nelson at Chepoix, and just four of the thirty-six Janesville boys who'd left Edgar Caldwell in tears the previous March.

On December 1, these few who'd carried the ball much of the way crossed into Germany. "Many of the people expressed surprise at the orderly conduct of the Americans and said that they had been told to expect harsh treatment," the 28th's history says.

On December 13, the regiment reached Coblenz, and scattered to different towns and villages. Lloyd Bronston, still with Company G, found himself in Heiligenroth, Germany, quartered in the home of a local family that had for a time lived in Wisconsin. He wrote to Cecile: "I have a fine place to stay with an old German lady, her son 35 years old, calls himself a boy. Was in Dutch army 4 years and sorry of it. They lived in America for 15 years and the son wanted to stay but the old man wanted to come back to Germany.

"They are sure sorry they came back. He said if he had stayed in Wisc. he would have been in the American army. But a Dutchman is a Dutchman and after they are licked they whine like pups."

(Having not seen his toddler son for a year, Bronston would add: "How is Jason? Tell him he had better practice up with his dumb bells because I'm going to have a fight with him when I get home.")

For those troops stuck in Germany, homesickness ran rampant as the weeks passed and many marked their first anniversaries in Europe; the arrival of Christmas was especially hard. Wilbert Murphy no doubt expressed the sentiments of all doughboys when he wrote to his family to say: "Early this morning I woke up and by glancing out the window saw that it was to be a white Christmas. Snow, beautiful white snow was everywhere. The air this morning was crisp and fresh and really seemed like Christmas morning. But something seemed lacking and I guess it was because I was far from home in a strange land."

Within the bridgehead, battalions took turns manning positions on the border of the neutral zone. "With the daily routine of drill, maneuvre, practice march or fatigue the weeks and months passed slowly," the 28th's history says, "but with few exceptions every officer and man performed his tasks with a thoroughness and zeal which was characteristic of this Regiment."

John Church was put in command of Company B, headquartered with Company D in Rupprecht. "In addition I am also provost court which is our main military court for trying and punishing misdeeds of civilians in this district which my co. occupies," he told his cousin. "I can close up any store or café or anything I decree necessary for the good of the military service. Let's hope the 'Boche' behave as I am not looking for more work."

While the enlisted men drilled and stood guard at their border outposts, the officers at least had the solace of the officers club—"a luxury casino in Coblentz," Captain Charles Senay remembered. "We wassailed there Saturday nights and some officers became rather drunk. It was not unusual to see well known company and battalion commanders in full uniform splashing through the fountain of the casino in ardent pursuit of frantic goldfish."

Amid such hilarity, there continued to be deaths, as the flu epidemic sweeping Germany reached out to the doughboys as well and took the lives of several Company D men who had fought through four great campaigns only to fall to an invisible virus. Charles D. Estes of Heber Springs, Arkansas, was one of these, dying on March 10, 1919, as the occupation of Germany dragged on.

By then, the men of Company D, especially the few survivors who had left the States in June 1917 or on the following Halloween, lusted for home. Sergeant Anthony Vedral described his feelings, and the scene in Coblenz in a letter to Sam Stainton as spring bloomed on the Rhine: "There is one question that hangs on everyones lips, 'when do we go home'? and there is no one to give us satisfactory answer. Our Division was the first American Division to arrive in France. But we are still doing our watchful waiting on the Rhine. How long yet? There are rumors that, if all is well, Gen. Pershing will go back to the good old Gods country, and this Regt. will go with him. Sounds good and let us hope it will come true."

As he wrote, Germany vacillated over the draconian peace terms.

"The Germans have another week to register their kicks: if that is all they are looking for, kicks, well I think we could easily oblige them and finish the job," Vedral wrote. "And we could make a good job out of it, too."

Vedral's stout service in the army and his actions on the previous October 9 had earned him a DSC, just as it had brought Marvin a posthumous award. Vedral brought up Marvin's legacy as he described how John Pershing had personally pinned it on his chest.

"I received mine from Gen. Pershing himself in later part of March," Vedral wrote. "It is unnecessary for me to say, that the day when gen. Pershing pinned the D.S.C. on my breast was the proudest day of my live. I wish Lt. Stainton was there, I would like to see him wear it."

Still, he would tell Sam: "I know if you had two ways to choose from, one of seeing your Brother alive and hiding somewhere in safety, the other one seeing him perform his duty as he so nobly did, I know you would choose the later."

Sam Stainton had no expectations of finding his brother alive; Vedral, Barnes, and John Church had told him all about Marvin's last day, and his death, on Hill 263 the previous fall. But Sam was intent on finding Marvin's body, and in mid-May—as his own aero squadron was readying to return to the United States—he motored to Verdun, and thence across the bomb-battered roads of the Argonne to Romagne, from which he launched an effort to find his brother and bring his body home.

"I think I shall be able to go out to Romagne this afternoon and tomorrow I will begin the search for Marvin's grave," he wrote his mother from Verdun on May 10. "I have learned that they have removed a great many of the bodies to the cemetery there. Anyway I know that if they have not already moved the grave from hill 263 I will at least be near both places."

Four days later, a dejected Sam Stainton wrote his mother to tell her his search for Marvin had been in vain—although he was able to turn up *a* body very near to where Vedral and Church had placed Marvin's on their crude maps: "Just one thing in connection with the search that makes me think that I had the correct location and that is I found what I thought to be a grave altho there was no mark of any kind and all traces of any one being buried there had long ago disappeared. I took a shovel and dug down and discovered that it was a grave and contained the body of an American soldier."

Sam returned to Romagne to report his find to the local headquarters of the Graves Registration Service, charged with consolidating thousands of battlefield graves into permanent American cemeteries—the largest of which is located at Romagne—and, when the option became available, shipping the remains back home.

Through the last half of 1918, nineteen companies of the service followed the advance of the Americans across France, its burial details performing the often grisly work of collecting and burying the American dead—many of which had lain on the battlefields for days in the heat or rain or mud or lay in shallow graves marked only by an upright rifle or crude cross—in temporary cemeteries.

Identification tags were collected, and the exact coordinates of the burials often noted; at war's end, the job began of disinterring and collecting the bodies of the more than 110,000 dead—53,000 killed in action or died from wounds, and another 63,000 dead from disease, accidents, or other causes—for placement in permanent cemeteries.

The service also had the often-exasperating and frustrating duty of identifying remains, which in many instances involved disinterment and, in extreme cases, comparing the deceased's dental records. More frustrating still was the process of finding a soldier's battlefield grave, which in many cases was hastily dug, poorly marked, and then left to the elements and the whims of German artillery as the dead soldiers' comrades moved on.

Under the aegis of the Quartermaster Corps, a small army of searchers was kept busy well into the 1920s, as investigations were launched at the request of parents seeking some idea of when and where their boys had been killed and buried.

An avalanche of resulting correspondence sits in the National Archives—including that from Rev. J. J. Morley, a 1st Division chaplain who buried many of Company D's men in the rain and mud of the Argonne on November 3, 1918. Responding in 1926 to a request for information on the whereabouts of the body of the company's Private Thomas Kukla, he wrote: "As far as I can remember, Thomas Kukla was buried near Noble Jackson. Next to him was a soldier unidentified. One soldier was found in a shell hole [on] the side of the road and was buried there in a sitting posture.

Another soldier was found stripped to the waist with a couple of body wounds, and buried with a blanket over him."

The Milwaukeean Thomas Kukla remains one of more than three thousand American dead still missing from the Great War, his name inscribed on the wall of the missing in the cemetery at Romagne. Were it not for the efforts of Sam Stainton on that May day in 1919, the name of another Company D soldier might be inscribed on the same wall.

Returning to Hill 263 on that day with three graves searchers, the quartet disinterred the body Sam had discovered, only to find it was that of Private Frank Kelly, a Camp Grant replacement who had been unlucky enough to have been Marvin's runner that day. They would find in Kelly's pockets a pass from Camp Grant, "a purse, a little French money," and "a plain gold ring," Sam wrote.

"Lieut. Church tells us that Pvt. Kelly was the only other soldier buried near Marvin but if Marvin is buried there I don't know how we can ever find the grave unless perhaps by digging up this whole side of the Hill which I couldn't do not having any more time."

Frank Kelly, of Shabbona, Illinois, had reported for duty alongside John Nelson and the rest of those Camp Grant replacements the previous June 18, and made it through Soissons and St. Mihiel unscathed, only to die at Marvin's side in that single shell blast on October 9.

His family had learned of the twenty-six-year-old's death on November 23, 1918, but as the months passed, no further information had been received regarding where or how he died, or where his grave was located. In February 1919 one of his sisters, Nelly Evensen, had written the Graves Registration Service to learn what she could.

"We rec'd a telegram saying he was killed in action and never have been able to learn how he was killed if he was shot or gassed you know we are very anxious to know any particulars about him," Nelly wrote.

"He wore my mothers wedding ring (a plain band) and two wrist watches and a sign. ring but I don't expect there is any chance at all of getting jewelry back. We would like to have them for keep sake and especially my mothers ring for she is dead to."

And in an exquisite irony, or perhaps just coincidence, it would be

Sam Stainton who, mad with grief and stabbing his shovel all over that potter's field on Hill 263, would become responsible for the discovery and return of that treasured wedding ring worn to the altar in 1882 by the late Margaret Kelly, who when she passed on November 18, 1901, had left her husband James with "a family of small children to raise alone which was no easy task for him," according to James Kelly's 1934 obituary.

Some months later, long after Sam's own departure for Mississippi, a small item ran in the *Shabbona Express* announcing the return of Frank J. Kelly's slightly tarnished personal effects from his heretofore lonely and isolated grave in the Argonne.

"Frank's pocketbook containing a quantity of French money, a part of what was returned, showed that the book had been buried, the leather being hard and crisp and the bills inside partly ruined and dilapidated, from the moisture and dampness of the ground.

"His mother's wedding ring was another one of his personal effects returned and that one will be prized highly by the folks here."

A live Frank Kelly would have been more highly prized, but at least the Kellys, who decided to leave Frank Over There in the permanent American cemetery at Romagne, had the solace of a body, and some idea of what had become of him, a closure that would ultimately be denied to many of the families of 3,350 doughboys—among those the parents of the nicest boy in Edgerton, Wisconsin.

Robert and Emily Livick continued to seek information as to Rollin's fate amid the hazy fallout of the war, but months of effort resulted only in the word that at some point during those desperate five days at Soissons, he'd been hit by a bullet in the lower jaw, and that several company members had seen him heading to the back lines for treatment.

On November 25, 1918, the *Janesville Daily Gazette* reported that Corporal Kenneth Lutz, one of the old Company M hands, had encountered another former Janesville boy in France who passed on the information that "Rollie had been gassed and was in a French hospital."

The Livicks, meanwhile, turned to a local doctor, Willard McCheaney, who, doctor to doctor, wrote to the U.S. surgeon general seeking to cut through the red tape and discover Rollie's whereabouts.

But the reply from Albert G. Love, head of the army's medical corps, was not helpful, either: "There is no medical record on file in this office in the case other than that of the diagnosis tag, which you already have. Consequently we feel sure that private Livick's wounds were of so slight a nature to require no hospital treatment or that he is still in a hospital, in which case we would receive no report until after the case was completed."

In the meantime, a query sent by Robert Livick wound up in the hands of Lieutenant Merton L. Aldridge of the 28th's headquarters company. Aldridge tried to put a bright spin on Rollin's situation, telling Livick that many Americans were sent to French hospitals, "owing to there location nearer that sector, and owing to the fact that our hospitals were pretty well filled.

"Mr. Livick," Aldridge wrote, "I wouldn't give up hope. My advice is for you to write to captain S.C. Sorensen, Co. D 28th Infantry. He was commanding your son's Co. at the time of the battle, and would probably be able to give you pretty definite information. In fact, he should be able to tell you exactly what became of him."

But Sorensen was no help. Increasingly desperate, Livick turned to F. H. Thompson of the Marine Corps, who attempted to pull strings with Senator G. E. Chamberlain, the chair of the Senate War Committee. Thompson wrote Chamberlain to say: "No one in his company seems to have seen him at any time after he was given first aid. Several of them saw him on the way to first aid, and there has been a rumor, which we have been unable to verify, to the effect that Rollie was placed in a hospital where they were building up a lower jaw.

"If he has died, it would seem that there should be some record of it, and if he is alive certainly some one must know where he is. It is a case in which it seems to me that some one ought to make a decided effort to get reliable news to the parents."

Anna Wilson, too, wrote letters, all to no avail, in her own frantic effort to discern the fate of her boy Leigh. And it was out of desperation that she turned to the *Janesville Argus* in early March 1919, which, and for whatever reason, put out its own A.P.B. on Leigh in its March 5 edition and described Anna's search: "During the months that have elapsed, Mrs. Wilson has communicated time and again with the war department, but with no results. No information ever came from the department which would indicate the location of the boy or what became of him.

"In desperation she appealed to others to write. Letters were sent to his captain and the colonel of the regiment. Six of those letters were returned marked, 'wounded in battle.'"

Nor could that unnamed Company D veteran at Fort Snelling help Anna. "From descriptions the soldier remembered him, but could tell nothing of what finally became of him," the paper reported, adding of the dearth of information on Leigh: "Mothers of the boys are entitled to better consideration than this. They are entitled to know what becomes of their boys. The right is sacred and should be so regarded. It is a travesty of justice that such a condition should exist. There is something wrong, radically wrong, somewhere or such a thing would not and could not occur."

Just weeks later, Anna Wilson finally received a response to one of her many letters. Either Sorensen or Lieutenant Asa B. Sutherland, who briefly took command of Company D in Germany, responded, and the somewhat chastened editor of the *Argus* bent over backward in an effort to retract his earlier, and impassioned, vitriol against a seemingly uncaring government.

The follow-up story appeared in the *Argus* on April 23, 1919, under the headline, "Fate of Soldier Seems Settled": "The mother informs us that she is in receipt of a letter from his captain, stating that the boy has been missing since the 28th of last May and that no trace of his whereabouts has been discovered since that time.

"The captain further intimates that in all probability he was among the number who were lost in the great battle in which the company was engaged at that time, only six of whom are known to have survived the terrible ordeal. It was one of the most sanguinary battles of the war."

The story concluded: "Mrs. Wilson tells us that there is still a lingering hope, but that it is very slight. She has philosophically accepted the conclusions reached as to the fate of her son whose life is sacrificed for his country. It is the supreme sacrifice laid upon the altar of freedom."

But Anna had not "philosophically accepted the conclusions." Just weeks later she would again write the government, her letter to the central records office of the A.E.F indicating a mind unhinged by grief: "I have lost my son Private Leigh E Wilson. If you can tell me of his whereabouts and conditions please as I have both waited and worried a long time. I think he would write me if he could, I think he is held as a Prisoner in Germany as has'nt he lost his mind and he cannot tell who he is. All these things come to me so many times a day . . ."

Still biding its time on the Rhine, the 28th Regiment was called out that June, as Germany seemed to balk at signing the peace terms that followed the armistice. "Very careful plans were laid and perfected for the immediate resumption of aggressive hostilities in the event that Germany refused to sign and the Armistice ceased to exist," the 28th's history says.

On June 17, the 1st Division was ordered to assemble on the perimeter of the bridgehead for a possible move toward Berlin, but at 5:00 P.M. on June 23, the final peace terms were accepted by the Germans—"much to the regret of the entire Regiment," the 28th's history says.

The 1st Battalion of the 28th, with Charles Senay in command, was ordered to pull back. By then, he noted, a winter and spring of relative ease had taken its toll on the troops. "When the columns formed, we looked like Sherman's bummers," Senay would remember.

"There were a variety of pets including ducks, geese and rabbits. Some men had bundles on sticks or tied to their rifle barrels. As we marched down the road, one drunken sergeant staggered in the rear, gradually losing distance and, all the while, yelling 'Company Halt!' Fortunately there were no inspectors."

Their work long done, by September Company D's men had returned to the United States, ready for discharge or, for those staying in— lieutenants John Church and George Butler among them—reassignment in the army.

But one soldier was not with them.

Once out of the hospital after being wounded in the Argonne, Soren Sorensen had been assigned as an infantry instructor with the I Corps School under former 1st Battalion commander George Rozelle.

Sent on to be an instructor at the III Corps School in Germany—one of several schools created to help the doughboys further their educations and, it was hoped, keep an army full of idle and restless minds occupied—Sorensen on February 8, 1919, asked to be transferred to the III Corps's military police, saying he considered himself "especially qualified for this duty, as having served about seven years as Prison Overseer U.S. Military Prison."

His request was accepted, with Major Spencer Merrell writing that Sorensen's services "have been excellent, but owing to his numerous wounds he is not physically capable of doing strenuous outdoor work in inclement weather."

While Sorensen's wife would write that Sorensen hoped at some point to return to the 28th Regiment, and perhaps even Company D, fate intervened; on June 2, 1919, Sorensen died after wrecking his motorcycle while out on an early-morning ride within the bridgehead, whether on official police duty or no, it was never said.

Reports in his burial file blame his death on massive internal hemorrhaging brought on by the accident, details of which were duly noted in *The Amaroc News*, which chronicled the occupation forces in Germany from 1919 to 1923: "Capt. Sorensen had left Neuwied about seven o'clock Sunday morning going toward Honningen and in turning a sharp curve in the road ran into a telephone pole with the side car of the machine, wrecking the vehicle and injuring the officer so severely that he died several hours later at the hospital.

"There were no eye witnesses to the accident and when he was picked up he was unconscious. The injuries were internal principally, only a few minor contusions."

An H. J. Klinge would eulogize Sorensen as "a friend and a man toward all who ever knew him and few men in the A.E.F. covered themselves with more glory and more honor than did our Sorey. His grave is upon a hilltop overlooking the valley of the Rhine, and the memory of his loyalty should be the motto of America."

Though there is no mention of foul play in any official account of Sorensen's death, family legend holds that he was killed in an ambush, plotted by friend or foe, no one can say. James Underhill, a descendant of Sorensen's widow, would tell me that the widow of one of Laura Evelyn's brothers had one evening pulled him aside in the 1970s to tell him all about the family's deep and dark secrets—including that pertaining to the lonesome death of Sorey Sorensen.

"They ambushed him," Underhill told me. "They called him out at night, and strung a wire across the road, and when he went by on his motorcycle, he ran into it and was decapitated. Whoever recovered the body wrote to his widow and explained in the letter what had happened."

Foul play or no, it was a strangely ignominious end for the thrice-wounded commander whom Wilbert Murphy had characterized as "exceptionally fearless," and who'd risen the hard way from buck private to mess sergeant to captain, and earned a DSC as well as a Croix de Guerre before war's end.

Hoping he'd return whole, Sorensen's widow was instead left to grapple with a common postwar issue: whether to leave the body of her beloved husband in Europe, or have it brought to the States.

The federal government, after some debate, decided to leave the decision to the soldiers' families, while offering to pay for the return of any doughboy's remains, though John Pershing had come down squarely on the side of leaving the bodies in France.

On September 5, 1919, Laura Evelyn wrote the adjutant general's office and revealed her own tortured feelings, saying she had "talked with several men who have returned from overseas, and each one has expressed the wish to have been left over there 'with the rest of them' if he had been killed or passed with disease.

"This matter has caused me a great deal of agonized thought," she confessed, "but as my thought clears there seems a great comfort in thinking of my dear one as over there still 'with the rest of them' with whom he endured the hardships and sacrifice.

"I had asked this on the card already returned, but if it is not too late will change this and ask that his body be withdrawn from Germany and laid to rest in France with the others. So we complete our sacrifice."

Arrangements were made for an overseas burial, but by the following November, and for unknown reasons, Laura Evelyn had decided his body should be interred at Arlington National Cemetery. And on July 30, 1920, Sorensen was laid to rest there with military honors, his widow in attendance.

But there was one more thing for Laura Evelyn to do: persuade the government to spring for something grander than the simple wooden marker under which he was laid. In 1923 the government approved her designs for a small monument to the dead hero, and today the commander of Company D lies at Arlington under a stone bearing his name and that quotation from Revelations.

Others lost in France took longer to return, as the job went on of sorting out which among the 116,000 American dead would remain in cemeteries overseas and which would be shipped home.

In the end, about 70 percent of American families sought the return of their soldier boys' remains; about thirty of Company D's ninety-odd dead likewise were left in the permanent American cemeteries in France, or had their names inscribed on the Walls of the Missing. The others were shipped home through the early 1920s and laid to rest in family and church plots.

Marvin Stainton would be one of these, but not before becoming the subject of a bizarre newspaper story. The article, which ran in the *Washington (D.C.) Herald* on March 25, 1921, claimed that Mabel Lowery—with whom he had so nobly broken up before leaving for France as he felt himself getting into "deep water," or so he told his mother—had mysteriously received a note from Marvin: "A few nights ago a messenger boy rode up to her home, left a note and rode away. Lieut. Stainton's name was signed to the note. It said, simply, that he had arrived in Memphis, learned that she had moved from her previous address and would call on her the next morning. She has heard nothing further since."

Mabel told the correspondent: "The handwriting was his. I compared it with some of his letters. It was identical, signature and all."

The paper would note: "Sometimes Miss Lowery believes her sweetheart is in Memphis, and again she is afraid she has been the victim of a cruel hoax."

It was cruel; it was also, indeed, a hoax. Marvin had not risen from his shallow grave on Hill 263. In fact, he would lie there for another three years, until April 19, 1924. On that day, Marvin's remains were located in the shallow grave into which he'd been lowered by John Church and his grieving company mates.

It's unclear how his body was found, but it's likely that erosion did the job, completing the work that had so frustrated Sam Stainton five years before. A grimly descriptive Graves Registration report notes that Marvin's body was located in an "isolated, unmarked 'made' grave on top of southern point of Cote 263" and was "buried 18 inches deep in blouse of good quality issue material, OD Red Cross sweater, whip cord breeches and issue/shoes about 7D. Overseas cap on head with 2nd lieut.'s bar attached. Head and body wrapped in an oilskin blanket lined, trench coat with leather buttons. Flesh of body entirely decomposed—skeleton disarticulated."

The report also noted that Marvin had two broken ribs where a fragment of the shell that smashed into Hill 263 on October 9, 1918, had pierced his body and, unknown to Vedral and the others there that day, probably entered his heart and killed him instantly.

Mary Stainton asked for Marvin's return. And on July 23, 1924—six years to the day since he had written home to tell of the cheering crowds that had greeted him and his shipmates on arrival Over There—Marvin returned by train to Laurel, Mississippi.

In a story that shared the front page with the guilty pleas of "thrill" killers Nathan Leopold and Richard Loeb, and under the banner headline "Body of War Hero Long Lost in France Is Home to Rest at Last," the *Laurel Daily Leader* reported: "World War veterans who met the train formed a guard of honor and escorted the body to the fallen hero's boyhood home, where his brave-hearted mother, Mrs. L. Stainton, and his brothers and sisters received him with tear-dimmed eyes. Business throughout the city was suspended for the funeral that his home people might pay fitting tribute to this fallen hero of the war."

Even as memories of the war faded quickly from the national consciousness, the Livicks continued their futile quest to learn what had become of Rollin. Through the twenties they continued to prod the government, seeking some information as to the fate of a son who had seemed to disappear into thin air.

But no one, it seemed, could help them, and at times Robert Livick's exasperation exploded into written rage, as when the Graves Registration Service asked for Rollin's dental charts. On July 23, 1923, Robert Livick answered: "Just how do you expect to locate the dead by the record of their teeth? When they were reinterred did they make a record of the work they had on their teeth or will they dig them up again? Are the unknown buried by them selves or are they mixed in with the others? How many unknown are there who have been found and how many are entirely missing?"

The Livicks would descend at times into hallucinations similar to those endured by Anna Wilson, the worst being that Rollin had survived with amnesia and might be wandering Europe.

Once, Rollin's younger brother Jim thought he saw Rollin passing the other way on a Wisconsin train, another passing hallucination. Or was it? Could Rollin have in fact been in Red Cross Hospital No. 1 in Paris, where John Nelson and so many others had been patched up following Soissons, and survived with some new identity?

The possibilities are endless, but the probable answer is that Rollin died somewhere between Berzy-le-Sec and Paris, or perhaps even in Paris, and for whatever reasons—a lack of identification, a mix-up—he was placed in an unmarked grave.

Whatever happened, from the time of his last letter penned on July 11, 1918, through eternity there would be no more heard from the small-town hero who'd joined the colors in a pique of patriotism.

Robert Livick died in 1955, never knowing Rollin's fate. "His father once told me that every time the mail came he expected to receive some news about Rollie but he never did," Rollin's cousin, Frank Devine, wrote years later.

The family took some solace in the thought that perhaps it was Rollin's remains that were interred in the Tomb of the Unknowns at Arlington in 1921. "There is a long shot possibility . . . and that is good enough for me," Devine wrote.

As late as 1926, Willard Storms was still trying to help locate the bodies of the many Company D men still missing at Cantigny, as the relatives of Edward Meyers, Leigh Wilson, and the many missing Ds—Rufus Durham, Walter Dawe, George Dust, Michael Duron, Paul Davis, Hartman Dawson—continued to press the government for answers.

Paul Davis's mother, Louisa, wrote the Graves Registration Service and the Adjutant General on May 14, 1920, from McCammon, Idaho, to say: "O I wish you could tell me where he was for he was as good a boy as left home and it has been two long years since he left home and I havent heard yet where his body was buried. Can you advise what is Best and whether they can find our Boy and oblige a mothers aking heart."

Six years later, Storms—by then living in Rupert, Idaho—said in a reply to a request for information from Alma Dust, sister of the missing Private George Dust:

"As I remember them, Dust was buried where he fell or very near the spot. I believe Cpl Anslow was buried near the same spot, but somehow it runs in my mind that Duron was blown to bits by a large shell while still in the Cantigny woods.

"I was on that sector about July 1-9th and the men of my platoon pointed to the graves of several of our Buddies, among them Dust's and Davis."

It was also in 1926 that a former Company D private, Fay Robbins, wrote from Ellenboro, North Carolina to offer Anna Wilson his help in finding the body of her son Leigh, but there was a catch: "I know him and I helped to bury him to the right of where the Co.s headquarters were in an old chateau in the center of town about 300 yards to the right, as well as I remember. I could come nearer finding him if I was there. If you will pay my expenses there and back and pay me for my time I am making $3 a day."

Ignoring Robbins's offer, Anna Wilson instead sailed to France on the government's dime as a Gold Star Mother in 1931. Family lore says she made the trip in part so she could look for her beloved son, but if that's true, she got no farther than locating his name on the 1st Division monument at Cantigny.

Anna wrote to the War Department upon her return to Minnesota to say: "I had never been on a voyage before this and to think of all we saw in France and Paris and the beautiful cematry but a sad place to look at so large and then to know I only saw a few of them."

The loss of Leigh, and the eternal uncertainty as to his fate, haunted Anna. "The great grief of her life was the loss of her son Leigh in World War I," a family history written in the 1950s concedes.

Anna's granddaughter, Dorothy Geduldig, told me that when talk turned to her uncle Leigh when she was a child, "All I remember is a great deal of bitterness. My mother Myrtle, Leigh's sister, hated war, and she was very bitter about the fact that he was just taken as a young recruit, and given very little training—this was my understanding of it—and just sent over and killed almost immediately. That's the picture I got."

In the end, Anna did find a grave for Leigh, if for no other reason than to offer her grieving heart some comfort. A stone with his name and the words "Lost in Battle in France, May 28 Co. D. 28 Inf First Division" was erected in the Janesville Cemetery. When she died in 1948, Anna Wilson was laid to rest next to the cenotaph, its emptiness an echo still of the cost of that simple "straightening of the lines" thirty years before.

In 1933, searchers found the last of the company's remains. In September of that year, the body of the Camp Grant replacement Otto B. Swanson, who, like John Nelson, had left Sweden for a new life in Chicago, was found in a shell hole in the center of Berzy-le-Sec, where he had been hastily buried with three other American soldiers.

"Only one shoe, other foot and shoe missing," the report of the discovery says, perhaps giving some idea of the violence with which Otto met his end.

Otto's father in Sweden, Sven Akesson, was duly notified, and one has to wonder what he was able to make of it all—of the war, and of the boy who'd left home to make a new life in America, and of the country that had taken him in only to send him back to the Old World to die in that obscure village.

Another who'd been severely wounded on that July 19, Private Joseph Zerwes, was to return in body, but not in spirit, whatever hopes he'd had for his future lost in the explosion that took a leg, and most of his mind, at the age of twenty-four.

When Waukesha County, Wisconsin compiled the service records of its veterans, the compiler wrote on the back of Joseph's card: "Lost a leg in battle and cannot talk. Now in Iowa hospital." By 1920, he was in a psychiatric hospital for veterans in Dansville, New York, his diagnosis "dementia Praecox, hebephrenic type"—schizophrenia.

"Could not adjust, manifested homicidal and suicidal tendencies and was sent to Wisconsin Memorial Hospital," his medical history says. "At this hospital he developed grandiose and persecutory delusions, auditory hallucinations and ideas of reference."

In 1937, Joseph was sent on to a Veterans Administration hospital in Mendota, Wisconsin. There "he adjusted fairly well," one record says, adding: "Behaviorally, however, the patient had become well institutionalized and was apathetic, listless and indifferent."

Beyond his right leg, which had been amputated midthigh, the record holds other reminders of what happened to Joseph Zerwes during the 1st Battalion's attack across the Paris-Soissons Road on July 19: "Fracture, right mandible, old"; "Scar of shrapnel fragment wound, left thigh, and mandible."

In 1947, Joseph was relocated to a VA hospital where he "worked arduously . . . weaving rugs, and was granted open ward privileges." Joseph's niece, Sheila Rank, told me that on visits to Joseph Zerwes during her childhood, "He was very quiet. I guess 'subdued' is the word.

"I can remember my Mom and Dad always saying to me, 'Don't ask Uncle Joe about his leg.' So I'm sure it was a very touchy thing with him. He was just shattered by the experience.

"I remember one time my Mom and Dad were trying to talk him into coming and living with us, and he didn't want any part of it. I remember him saying, 'This is where all my friends are!' I remember Uncle Joe as being a sad person. He was remorseful—is that the word? I guess you'd say he had empty eyes . . ."

In 1958, at age sixty-three, Joseph Zerwes arose one night to get a glass of water, and tumbled down some stairs, suffering facial fractures and lacerations. He died two months later.

Tempton Corwin Hall also returned, but the wound he'd suffered when seven machine-gun bullets ripped his leg open that July 19 at the Paris-Soissons Road never healed.

In Anderson, Missouri, Tempton Hall did some farming, married and had some children, and liked to sip a little while sitting on his porch. But as the years passed, the pain from those seven bullets he'd taken at Soissons grew worse, and despite one or two operations a year, the wound remained an open sore because of a chronic bone infection.

"He was too disabled to work," his son, Wray Hall, told me. "He was 100 percent disabled on account of his leg. His leg never did heal. That part of his leg wasn't as big around as his wrist—just skin and bones. He had osteomyelitis, whatever that is, in that leg. And it would swell up and bust open. See, they didn't have the treatments then like they do nowadays.

"He was in his late 40s when he passed away in the spring of '41. He was in various veterans' hospitals a month or two every year. And then the last few years he was in so much pain he got to be a morphine addict. He just kept going downhill."

Another of those wounded severely at Soissons, Willard Storms, also died young.

Willard would marry his Willa May Estus, have three children, and after a stint homesteading near Rupert, Idaho, move to Riverside, California, in the late 1920s. But on December 11, 1934, Willard passed away at age of forty-seven "from the effects of his war service injuries," the local paper reported.

As to whether those "effects" came in the May 15 blast at Cantigny or that machine-gun bullet at Soissons, the newspaper was mute; his grand-daughter, Diane Williamson, told me that Willard may ultimately have died from complications from that "little touch" of gas he had suffered at Seicheprey sixteen years before.

There were happier returns: Wilbert Murphy went back to school upon his return to Brodhead, married his high school sweetheart, became a math teacher, and even wrote a textbook. But his February 1982 obituary sadly omitted the fact of his many letters from the front that had run in the same newspaper six and half decades before and kept the folks in Brodhead apprised of the doings Over There.

Bill Warren became a chemist and a professor as well, earning five university degrees and spending much of his adult life teaching at East Central State Teachers College in Ada, Oklahoma. He seems to have been as successful at putting the war behind him as he had been negotiating that chaotic childhood home in Elmira, N.Y.: Teaching chemistry at Western College in Oxford, Ohio, when the American Battle Monuments Commission in 1928 sought his input for its account of the movements of the 1st Division at Soissons, Warren replied that "the map and summary which you have enclosed brought back to my mind quite vividly those hot July days of 1918." Warren subsequently asked for a map and the completed summary—"to recall to mind an occasion so foreign to my present life."

His daughter, Dorothy Rinaldo, remembers Warren talking of the war on just one instance, when, in 1939, the family gathered around the radio to follow the German invasion of Poland. She wrote: "Daddy hovered over the radio, listening to news of the German invasion. It was probably then that lying in bed, I heard him telling Grandpa about his own wartime experiences. He said that when a German came toward them with his hands up, his sergeant shot him.

"When he was wounded, he said it felt as if someone had punched him in the jaw. The nights before battle, the chaplains prayed, making him feel not better, but worse."

Warren died of a heart attack in 1959, at the age of sixty-three. His daughter wrote in *An Imperfect Genealogy:* "I wish he had lived longer, to see how our lives have turned out. I wish at this writing that we could discuss what he thinks about this messy world and of the current state of politics—though I think I can guess."

Warren's old bunkie, Lloyd Bronston, returned to Garnett, Kansas, on June 3, 1919, after being picked up at the train station in Topeka by Cecile and Jason, by then a husky three-year-old. "Lloyd grabbed his little son as soon as he stepped from the train, and wouldn't let him go till they got home," the Garnett paper reported.

Bronston earned and lost a few small real estate fortunes following the war, and he and Cecile would also produce three siblings for Jason. Jason, like his father, joined the military—the marines—and was stationed overseas. Unlike Lloyd, Jason did not outlive his war, dying at the age of twenty-seven in a Japanese prison camp in the Philippines.

Lloyd died at age sixty-three on February 12, 1949, and today he, Jason, and Cecile lie in hilltop graves at the Garnett Cemetery, the love that flowed between them just a distant whisper in the wind on that lonesome knoll.

The company's first hero, Lieutenant William Ross Gahring, who won the DSC and a fistful of other decorations for his actions at Cantigny, went into the oil business in Shawnee, Oklahoma, with his best friend, George Bradfield, also a veteran.

Bradfield's son, George Jr., told me that for decades, the two old soldiers held court in their downtown office, good-naturedly belittling each other's military careers: "He and my dad liked to put on dog-and-pony shows in their office. My dad had been an enlisted man in the 35th Division, and Ross was an officer. Ross would say about my dad, 'Well that old fart over there, if he'd of done anything in the war he'd have got a pension like me, but of course he didn't do anything!'

"Then my dad would say, 'If you were so damn much of a hero, stand up and turn around and take down your pants and show them where you got shot. And then explain which direction you were headed when that happened!'

"If I told you how many times I heard that you wouldn't believe it . . ."

19

"To the End of Your Days"

HE IS HOBBLING THROUGH the gates of Camp Grant, having completed a medical odyssey that began with triage there at Missy-aux-Bois and ended at Washington State's Fort Lewis; stiffly, he's limping to the station, $60 in thank-you money from the government in his pocket, and now boarding a train for Chicago, to rent a small room on Briar Place and while away the first weeks of April 1919 playing his violin at its window, those two holes on either side of his abdomen just barely healed, the pain that will plague him for the next seventy-four years already a throbbing and constant reminder of those machine guns at the Paris-Soissons Road, and that long night in the wheat, and that great day, that great and terrible day, when he was grabbed back from the abyss by those great and exotic Algerians, to live again, to dream again, to pick up the pieces of his immigrant life and go on.

I'm sure John Nelson would have liked a parade down State Street, some acknowledgment, some gratitude, for having taken his bullet, and for having toughed it out during that long night in the wheat; instead, even as the 1st Division's survivors embarked from France, even as they *did* parade through the streets of New York and Washington, the Old Man quietly returned to work, only to quickly discover that his war, and his wound, would not let go so easily.

Within weeks of returning to his job as a painter, he filed a claim with the War-Risk Insurance Bureau, saying that because of his wound he was "not able to do a day's work as beforehand, and nothing without suffering. Have not been able to work every day.

"I walk with a pronounced limp; cannot run; cannot walk more than 2 or 3 blocks on account of soreness in leg on exertion; limited motion of leg, probably due to weakness and wasting away."

On May 25, 1919, a caseworker was sent to investigate John Nelson's complaint, catching up with him on the job.

"He was decorating a flat and he has the appearance of being a person physically fit to perform his line of work," the investigator wrote. "No doubt this impairment to the right leg is a handicap to him and it is a question as to whether or not the claimant will be able to do what is called rough work, such as outside work, climbing and standing on ladders any great distance above the ground."

Six months later, John Nelson's ability to work steadily was still in question. On November 25, 1919, his doctor reported: "Present complaint: Limited motion of rt. Leg, due to m.g. bullet injure. Back hurts after working a short time.

"Physical examination: Head and neck show no changes. The spine shows a scoliosis lateral rt. and a compensatory bulge of chest cavity on left side. The curvature dates from GSW going in just above pelvic brim on left side and exit just above brim on other side with history of spinal trauma and intestinal perforation. Rt. limb shows atrophy of femoral muscles. Loss of patellar reflex. Sensitive limb, with slight limp. Muscular atrophy.

"Diagnosis: Curvature of spinal traumatic.

"Prognosis: Guarded."

In the twenties, controversy emerged over the source of John Nelson's scoliosis, and whether it had been caused by the bullet—"I was shot thru my abdomen by machine gun and my right leg is weak, my back is bent," he told one doctor—or because of a childhood disease. But there was little the doctors could do despite his repeated visits, one doctor writing with some exasperation after examining him in April 1924: "This claimant was examined in January 1923 and in September 1923. He complained substantially as he does today. He says that with the exception of his back and leg his general health is good. There are no psychotic manifestations and no marked psycho-neurotic features."

He was given a 47 percent disability rating, ultimately reduced to 20 percent in 1933, which entitled him to somewhere around twenty dollars a month for his "residual gun-shot wound, right thigh injury to Group XVI and antero-cruro nerve."

And that, it seems, was that.

It would not be until John Nelson was gone, and I obtained his postwar medical records, that I—we—realized the toll his war had taken on him, and realized as well how that bullet he'd taken at the Paris-Soissons Road had plagued him through his long life.

And it wasn't until after he was gone that I understood that the lingering pain from that wound was no doubt the source of his sometimes gruff, even cranky, demeanor, an emotional state enhanced, perhaps, by an unspoken feeling that what he'd endured at the Paris-Soissons Road was underappreciated by us, and by a world that would come to regard the American part in the Great War as little more than a quaint crusade, an anomaly, a conflict that held, one historian would write, "no obvious meaning" in America's history.

Even the division in which John Nelson served ignored his small part. In January 1920 the 1st Divison issued its General Order No. 1, citing 14,228 of its soldiers for their "meritorious service," a list headed by Company D's medic, Fred L. Gunn, and which also included the names of almost two hundred others from Company D, among them Rollin Livick, Soren Sorsensen, Bill Warren, Willard Storms—even the reluctant warrior and Swedish immigrant August Hedblom.

But the Old Man's name was nowhere to be found, though certainly he'd done as much, or as little, as many of those on that long list.

He'd jumped when they told him, and stormed that road when they said to, and taken his bullet, and nearly died in that wheat. And no, as the 26th Regiment's Gerald Stamm had written of his own service, "It was not a hero's share." Still, Stamm had added, "It was a share of which I had no need to be ashamed."

In the end, it may well be that the true hero's share for John Nelson was in simply surviving, in enduring that night in the wheat and then, for so many years, finding some way to live a good life, a very long life, despite the almost debilitating physical pain that bullet had bought him—and whatever nightmares that long July night had left him.

And in the end, it was probably best that he was no poet, and no philosopher, just a poor farmer's son born at Kangsleboda, just an immigrant, just a hardheaded Swede who'd experienced some of the worst life—and war—had to offer and had come through, perhaps not whole, but intact enough to persevere.

He'd seen the alternative, and he would leave any sense of disillusionment with his Great War to others. He instead would feel for the rest of his life a quiet, unshakable pride—pride for having put his life on the line for his adopted country, for having found the courage to cross that road, for having paid with blood for his immigrant dream, and for having served in the company of men who believed in their cause, and who had performed glorious deeds there at that village, and at that road, and at that last hill, men who died "with a smile on their face, or looking toward the front," as Willard Storms wrote.

John Nelson had almost become one of these smiling dead, only by the slimmest of margins enduring to receive a second chance, and to revel once a year in the elation at having made it across that road, and through that night in the wheat, and of having made it home whole enough to pick up his immigrant's life—which he did, in 1925 opening a paint shop on Chicago's Devon Avenue with his childhood friend Joe Sholin, who'd been a conscientious objector and missed out on John Nelson's Great Adventure, a difference of opinion over duty that seems not to have harmed their friendship.

And for the next six decades he moved within the close-knit Scandinavian immigrant circles of Chicago's North Side, the fellow Swedish immigrant and former Karin Lindberg, the daughter of a tailor, by his side, she who would tell a newspaper on the occasion of their seventieth wedding anniversary in 1991: "We met at a party and a few days later I saw him walking on the street where I lived. I went up to him and asked him what he was doing there and he said he lived there—just a short distance from my home. Our first date was a movie show and my mother couldn't have been happier. She thought John was a wonderful catch—a good, strong Swedish boy with a steady job."

The nice Swedish boy and his Swedish princess had children, a girl named June and a boy named Howard, who upon enlisting in the army in 1943 was promised a new car by John Nelson if he made it back alive; assigned to the Army Air Force, Howard never even left the United States, and collected on the promise.

John and Karin lived blessedly boring lives, residing for many years above that paint store on Devon Avenue, and then in a modest house in a Chicago suburb. Karin did needlepoint and raised the kids; the Old Man read Colonel Robert McCormick's *Tribune* and watched men walk on the moon. She baked; he railed against Angela Davis and "Yane Fonda" and whatever else you had. She did the housework; he tripped through their home askew even seventy years after Soissons, his wound always there.

They took every July nineteenth to consider the alternatives, the unspeakable might-have-beens, the things about which he would not speak in any case.

They grew very, very old, and moved into the retirement home. And it was there that I left him for the last time, in July 1993—almost seventy-five years to the day since Soren Sorsensen had blown his whistle, and John Nelson and the men of Company D had raced off to the rest of their lives, which lay somewhere there beyond the Paris-Soissons Road, and which consisted at that moment of just seconds, or minutes, or a few days, or, for the very lucky, months or even years.

He would keep that day's horrors to himself—as would most others, as I learned when I stumbled across an account of that day written by a marine with the 2nd Division, which was plowing through the same wheat just a few kilometers south of Company D.

That marine, Russell Garrison, wrote to an uncle shortly after the war to say: "The worst we were ever hit at one time was at Soissons, July 19th, when we faced the enemy across an open wheat field. We advanced, showing no especial bravery, but just doing the thing that has won the war.

"On we went, losing a man here, another there, then two or three here, and so on. When we made our stand, I was the only one left of my squad.

Having a man walking by your side one second, and lying lifeless the next, is an experience hard to understand or explain.

"Well, if you have gone through in reading this what I have gone through in writing it, you have seen the turning point of a great war and undergone feelings that will follow you to the end of your days. Don't expect any more battle descriptions in letters, and maybe no verbal ones. I am trying to forget it as much as possible."

It wasn't until 1999, when I discovered that Company D roll from August 1918, that it occurred to me that there was so much more to John Nelson's story than he had let on.

And now that I know some of that story, and can put to it some of the faces and names of the men who disappeared from his side in the wheat at Soissons, or who were buried in the mud at Cantigny and in the underbrush of the Argonne, I can see that it was more than just the wound from a machine-gun bullet that plagued him for the rest of his days, and I think I understand why he clung so tenaciously to life until Death, finally, won its exhausting battle with him.

I'll never know exactly what thoughts occupied John Nelson on that last July nineteenth of his, as the old doughboy idled in the dim lobby of the retirement home, or sat alone in his small room, marking time and awaiting the inevitable. But I can guess that thoughts of the company he kept during that summer of 1918 drifted back, as he perhaps for the last time allowed himself to remember the things that happened in the trenches at Cantigny, or in the wheat at Soissons; I can guess that he was thinking of these things, but of course I'll never know.

I do know that when I think of him now, it's not as I left him for the last time—all alone and distracted, nearly blind, so frail and shrunken and old and wrapped in his heavy blue wool sweater despite the summer heat. When I think of him now, he's in the wheat by the road that runs between Paris and Soissons, twixt heaven and hell, about to step across beside Rollin Livick and Willard Storms and Soren Sorensen and the rest, with no idea of what will remain of himself, or of Company D, once he reaches the other side.

NOTES

Primary Sources by Individual

Abbreviations Used in the Notes

ABM RG 117, Entry 31—Records of the American Battle Monuments Commission, Correspondence with Former (First) Division Officers, U.S. National Archives, College Park, Maryland.

MWW Monographs of World War series, Donovan Research Library, Fort Benning, Georgia.

ROQC Records of the Office of the Quartermaster General, Cemeterial Division, 1915–1939. U.S. National Archives, College Park, Maryland. Record Group 92. Cited as ROQC.

WWR United States. Army Division, 1st. World War Records, Basic Maps and Overlays / First Division, A.E.F., vol. 1. Washington, D.C. 23 vols.

Adams, Ranzie. Emma Mayo's interview ran in the *Paragould (Ark.) Weekly Soliphone*, June 27, 1918.

Aldridge, Merton L. Aldridge's letter to Robert Livick is in the Rollin Livick Papers (see Livick, below).

Angell, Jerome. Angell's exhortations ran in the *Kalamazoo (Mich.) Gazette* (undated clip provided by the Kalamazoo Public Library. Biographical information from the *Hastings (Mich.) Banner*, July 11, 1918. Account of Angell's death from his burial file, Record Group 92, Entry 1942, ROQC.

Anslow, George. Account of Anslow's death, ROQC.

Austin, Raymond B. Austin's wartime letters from the *World War I Veterans Survey Collection*, U. S. Army Military History Institute, Carlisle, Pennsylvania.

Babcock, Conrad Stanton. Much of Babcock's account of the Battle of Soissons found in the Conrad Stanton Babcock Papers, pp. 505–52, Hoover Institution on War, Revolution and Peace, Stanford University. Used with permission of Babcock's granddaughter, Barbara Babcock. Also, two after-action reports written by Babcock—"Report on Operations South of Soissons, July 1918" and "Report of Offensive July 18–July 22 1918"—can be found in WWR 13: *Operations Reports 28th Infantry*.

Babson, Roger. Babson's casualty statistics from Myron E. Adams and Fred Girton, *The History and Achievements of the Fort Sheridan Officers' Training Camps*.

Barnes, Lynn. Barnes's account of Marvin Stainton's actions and death found in the Marvin Stainton Papers (see Stainton, below).

Baucaro, Ben. Information on Private Ben Baucaro from author interview with Baucaro's son, Robert Baucaro.

Beard, Otto. Letter from George Butler to Sam Pool, January 28, 1919, graciously provided to the author by Beard family historian Robert Beard. Also, Otto Beard, ROQC.

Beck, Frank L. Account of Beck's death, ROQC.

Bernheisel, Ben H. Bernheisel's account of Soissons comes from his unpublished memoir "Foot Soldiers," Robert R. McCormick Research Center, Museum of the First Division, Wheaton, Ill. Used with Permission.

Bertrand, Georges Etienne. His letter on the attractions of war comes from Myron E. Adams and Fred Girton, *The History and Achievements of the Fort Sheridan Officers' Training Camps*.

Boyd, Leonard. The source of information is Boyd's postwar monograph *The Operations of the 1st Battalion, 16th Infantry in the Second Phase of the Meuse-Argonne*, MWW.

Bronston, Jason Lloyd. Letters graciously provided to the author by Lloyd Bronston's grandson, Jason Bronston. Used with permission. Material about Bronston's assignment overseas was found in the *Garnett (Kan.) Review*, January 24, 1918; an account of his return home ran on June 5, 1919. Bronston's account of the conditions at Cantigny comes from Box 184, ABM. Bronston "scared" at Soissons from WWR 15: *Field Messages All Units.*

Brunst, Otto. Information on Brunst, ROQC.

Buchanan, Max C. Buchanan's letter on the verge of heading overseas ran in the *Brockton (Mass.) Daily Enterprise,* November 10, 1917. His account of training with a Canadian regiment found in the same paper, January 12, 1918. Also Max C. Buchanan, ROQC.

Buck, Beaumont. Buck's description of the Cantigny sector from the *San Antonio (Tex.) Sunday Light,* February 22, 1931. His discussion of immigrant soldiers, and his account of the attack on Berzy-le-Sec, from his *Memories of Peace and War.* Buck's fears of a counterattack at Berzy-le-Sec from WWR 13: *Operations Reports Second Brigade.*

Bullard, Robert Lee. Getting the First Division ready and opinion of French cavalry from Bullard, *Personalities and Reminiscences of the World War* (see separate entry in Bibliography section).

Butler, Charles E. See entry in the Bibliography section of the notes.

Butler, George E. Biographical information regarding Butler comes from author interview with Butler's son, the late George E. Butler Jr., and grandson, Tom Butler. Letters cited ran in the *Arkansas City (Kan.) Daily News*: the account of Butler's arrival overseas, December 22, 1917; his letter about the Battle of Cantigny, June 27, 1918; letter on the armistice, December 2, 1918; his November 28, 1918, letter on December 20. Butler letters to Sam Stainton found in the Marvin Stainton Papers. Butler's postwar paper *The Battle of Cantigny* found in MWW.

Caldwell, Edgar N. Caldwell's account of Soissons ran in the *Janesville (Wisc.) Daily Gazette,* September 7, 1918; earlier letters and interviews come from the *Daily Gazette* as well: his plea for volunteers, April 10, 1917; his sadness at the breakup of Company M, June 12 and August 23, 1918; his descriptions of the front lines, July 13, 1918.

Campbell, Stuart. Campbell's account of the Battle of Cantigny taken from "Report of Company E, 18th Infantry, July 5, 1918," in WWR 13: *Operations Reports 18th Infantry Regiment.*

Carns, Whitelaw Reid. Information on Carns comes from author interview with Norma Carns, Carns's daughter-in-law.

Church, John Huston. Church's letters regarding Cantigny, his attempts to be classified as fit for duty, and from the Coblenz Bridgehead found in *The Charles*

Crispin Scrapbook of John H. Church During World War I, 1918–1919. Long Island Division, Queens Borough Public Library, Jamaica, New York. Used with permission of Ann Cooper, Church's granddaughter. Letters dated July 27 and July 30, 1918, from the August 21, 1918, *Flushing (N.Y.) Daily Times.* Also WWR 15: *Field Messages 28th Infantry Regiment.* Church's letters about Marvin Stainton found in the Marvin Stainton Papers. Also *The National Cyclopedia of American Biography*, vol. 44.

Cibulka, John. Cibulka's account of the Battle of Soissons ran in the *La Crosse (Wisc.) Tribune and Leader-Press,* January 12, 1919.

Cook, George Dwight. George D. Cook, ROQC. Biographical material from *Ellenville (N.Y.)* Journal, Sept. 12, 1918.

Cox, Paul Greenwood. Biographical material from Adams and Girton, *The History and Achievements of the Fort Sheridan Officers' Training Camps.*

Dacus, Herman S. Dacus's 1984 reminiscences about the battles of Cantigny, Soissons, and the Meuse-Argonne come from letters to Ed Burke, executive director of the Society of the First Division, copies of which were provided to the author by Colonel Stephen L. Bowman, author of *A Century of Valor.* Used with permission of Dacus's niece, Marianne Moriarty. Further Dacus material comes from *The World War 1 Veterans Survey Collection*, U.S. Army Military History Institute, Carlisle, Pennsylvania.

Davis, William Paul. Davis's nephew, Arnold Davis, graciously provided the author the following: *Life Sketch of William Paul Davis as Remembered by His Brother, Ernest J. Davis; Story of James Hyrum Davis; Life Story of Eliza Ellen Marston Davis.* Used with permission. Also, *McCammon (Ida.) News*, May 31 and June 28, 1918; and Paul Davis, ROQC.

Dawe, Walter. Walter Dawe, ROQC.

Day, Willie. Information on Day's death, ROQC.

Donahue, Emmet J. Donahue's account of Soissons found in the *Fort Wayne (Ind.) Journal-Gazette*, February 16, 1919.

Donaldson, James Howland. Donaldson's account of the Battle of Soissons found in Box 185, ABM.

Dorr, Julian. Dorr's account of the Battle of Cantigny ran in the *Janesville (Wisc.) Daily Gazette*, June 11, 1918. Account of Dorr's ride in an ambulance from Dorr, *A Soldier's Mother in France.*

Dunkle, Elmer. Account of Dunkle's death, ROQC.

Durbrow, John. Durbrow's account of his actions in the Argonne ran in the *Fort Wayne (Ind.) News and Sentinel*, February 8, 1919.

Durham, Merrit Booth. Information on Durham's death comes from ROQC.

Durham, Rufus. Accounts of Durham's death come from ROQC.

Dust, George. Account of Dust's death and his sister's letter about him from Dust, ROQC.

Eidsvik, Thomas. Account of burial of Eidsvik, ROQC, and author correspondence with Eidsvik's grandnephew, Hans Peter Neergard.

Ellis, Richard. Account of Ellis's memorial service and Lyle Ellis joining the navy from the *Janesville (Wisc.) Daily Gazette*, June 10, 1918. Also Richard Ellis, ROQC.

Ely, Hanson. Hanson's messages from the Battle of Cantigny from WWR vol. 13 and 15; his comments on tactics at Cantigny from WWR 13: *Operations Reports 28th Infantry Regiment*. Ely's new appreciation of the battle from the *San Antanio (Tex.) Light*, May 29, 1938.

Ervin, Sam. Ervin's doughboy experiences from Paul R. Clancy, *Just a Country Lawyer*. Ervin's demotion to private from RG 120, Entry 1241, Boxes 138 and 140, *Organizational Records, First Division*, U.S. National Archives, College Park, Md.

Evarts, Jeremiah. His account of life in the lines at Cantigny from his *Cantigny: A Corner of the War*.

Farrelly, John. Information on Farrelly's death, ROQC.

Fishette, William. Account of Fishette's death, ROQC.

Frasier, Lyman S. *Operations of the Third Battalion, 26th Infantry, First Division, in the Second and Third Phases of the Meuse-Argonne Offensive*, MWW.

Gahring, William Ross. Gahring's account of his service comes from an undated newspaper article headlined "Shawnee's Man of Medals" in the *Tulsa (Okla.) Tribune*, provided by family friend George Bradfield Jr.; also, author interview with George Bradfield Jr. Biographical information on Ross Gahring from author interview with his son, George Gahring.

Gallagher, Neal. Account of Gallagher's death, ROQC.

Garrison, Russell. Garrison's account of Soissons from the *Garnett (Kan.) Evening Review and Journal Plain-Dealer*, December 26, 1918.

Gaw, Fred. Gaw's account of a night patrol from "Waukesha Boy in No Man's Land," *Waukesha (Wisc.) Freeman*, August 29, 1918.

Gehrke, Leo. Gehrke's comment on the advance at Cantigny from the *Janesville (Wisc.) Daily Gazette*, January 21, 1919.

Girdley, Clyde. Information on Girdley from ROQC.

Golladay, James de Armand. Golladay's letter to his pastor ran in the *Kokomo (Ind.) Tribune*, March 28, 1918.

Groves, Frank. Groves's account of the armistice from *The World War I Veterans Survey Collection*, U.S. Army Military History Institute, Carlisle, Pennsylvania.

Gunderson, Solon Paul. Martin Mikkelson's account of Gunderson's death ran in the *La Crosse (Wisc.) Tribune and Leader-Press*, April 20, 1919. Also Solon Paul Gunderson, ROQC.

Hall, Tempton Corwin. T.C. Hall's son, Wray, provided the author with the information on Hall.

Harbord, James. Pershing's insistence on an independent American army from Harbord, *The American Army in France, 1917–1919*.

Harrison, Ray P. The account of Harrison's death at Soissons appeared in the *Columbia City (Ind.) Post*, November 2, 1918; provided to the author by the Whitley County Historical Museum, Columbia City, Indiana.

Hawkinson, Howard E. Hawkinson's death is recounted in the *Syracuse (N.Y.) Herald*, June 1, 1919. Maury Maverick's characterization of Hawkinson as a "demon for luck" appeared in the *San Antonio (Tex.) Light*, October 6, 1927.

Haydock, George Guest. William O. P. Morgan's account of Haydock's death found in the Christina Morgan Papers, 1881–1930, at the Schlesinger Library, Radcliffe Institute, Harvard University. Anonymous account from M. A. DeWolfe Howe, *Memoirs of the Harvard Dead in the War Against Germany*, vol. 3, p. 142.

Hedblom, August. Author interview with Hedblom's nephew, Emil Eliason.

Hockenberry, Roy. Account of Hockenberry's death, ROQC.

Hoppe, Albert. Hoppe's description of the Battle of Soissons is taken from the *Waukesha (Wisc.) Freeman*, October 2, 1919.

Hopper, James. Account of destruction at front lines appeared in "At the American Front," *Collier's*, May 18, 1918; the account of First Division moving toward the front lines from "The Gypsy Division Goes In," *Collier's*, August 3, 1918; the account of the assault on Cantigny and of Hopper's having "captured" a group of Germans in "Our First Victory, Part II—Over the Top and Beyond," *Collier's*, September 7, 1918; the description of German prisoners in "Our First Victory,

Part III—After the Battle," *Collier's*, October 12, 1918; account of aid station at Soissons in "The Lucky Boy," *Collier's*, November 23, 1918.

Horton, Raymond A. Account of Horton's death, ROQC.

Howe, Frank Arthur. Biographical information from Myron E. Adams and Fred Girton, *The History and Achievements of the Fort Sheridan Officers' Training Camps*. Howe's foreboding and death from Charles T. Senay, "From Shavetail to Captain."

Huebner, Clarence Ralph. Much of Huebner's account of the Battle of Soissons comes from his postwar monograph *The Operations of the 28th Infantry in the Aisne-Marne Offensive, July 17–23, 1918*, MWW. Also Huebner's after-action report, "The Twenty-Eighth Infantry in the Aisne-Marne Offensive, July 18–21, 1918," WWR 13: *Operations Reports 28th Regiment*, which also holds Huebner's messages during the Battle of Cantigny and 2nd Battalion reports on the St. Mihiel and Argonne offensives. Huebner's wounding at Soissons is described in *The Bridgehead Sentinel*, Spring 1973, and Beaumont Buck, *Memories of Peace and War*.

Huntington, F. W. *Operations of Co. G, 18th Infantry, 1st Division, in the Aisne-Marne Offensive, July 18–23, 1918*. MWW.

Jackson, Noble. Information on Jackson's death and transport to the United States, ROQC.

Jimmerson, Angus Leslie. Biographical information on Dock Jimmerson comes from Virginia Knapp, *Remembering Rusk County*, provided to the author by the Rusk County Library, Henderson, Texas.

Johnston, Edward S. Johnston's postwar monograph *The Day Before Cantigny: Personal Experiences of a Company Commander*, MWW. Also, "The Day Before Cantigny" in Johnston, *Americans vs. Germans*.

Johnston, John. Johnston's recap of his doughboy adventures found in the *La Crosse (Wisc.) Tribune and Leader-Press*, March 2, 1919.

Joholski, Edward. Joholski's post-Cantigny letter ran in the *Janesville (Wisc.) Daily Gazette*, July 2, 1918.

Jones, James A. Letters from Jones to Sam Stainton and Bert Ford's story on Jones found in the Marvin Stainton Papers, carried in an undated edition of the *Laurel (Miss.) Daily Leader*. Shorter version of the same article appeared in the *Oakland (Calif.) Tribune*, October 27, 1918.

Kelly, Frank J. Notice of Kelly's death from *Shabbona (Ill.) Express*, November 27, 1918; return of effects from undated edition of the *Express*, courtesy of the Shabbona-Lee-Rollo Historical Museum; deaths of James and Margaret Kelly from the *Express*, November, 1934; also Frank Kelly, ROQC.

Kemp, Alvord. Kemp's account of the Battle of the Meuse-Argonne ran in two parts in the *Wellsboro (Pa.) Agitator*, April 19 and April 26, 1933.

Klinge, H. J. Klinge's eulogy of Soren Sorensen from the *Grand Island (Neb.) Daily Independent*, June 23, 1919.

Koubsky, Rudolph. WWR 13: *Operations Reports 28th Infantry Regiment.*

Lansing, Robert. His speech on the dangers of a German victory from Myron E. Adams and Fred Girton, *The History and Achievements of the Fort Sheridan Officers' Training Camps.*

Last, Frank. Last's writings come from his unpublished memoir, "Frank Last Diary," used with permission of Last's nephew, Rick Riehl.

Lauersdorf, Fred. Information from Fred Lauersdorf, ROQC.

Legge, Barnwell. Barnwell's postwar monograph *The First Division in the Meuse Argonne, September 26-October 12, 1918*, MWW.

Licklider, John D. Account of the burial of bodies at Cantigny from letter found in Paul Davis, ROQC. Account of actions at Cantigny from undated article in the *Martinsburg (W.Va.) Journal*, provided by the Berkeley County, W.Va., Historical Society. Account of his actions at Soissons from his obituary in the *Martinsburg Journal*, May 26, 1959.

Lippincott, Otus. Lippincott's account of the movements of Companies C and D in the Argonne found in Box 188, ABM.

Livesay, William G. *The Operations of the 28th U.S. Infantry, First Division, from Nov. 5th to Nov. 11th, 1918*, MWW.

Livick, Rollin. Letters and other source material regarding Rollin Livick are contained in the Rollin Livick Papers, graciously provided to the author by Linda Matzke, Rollin Livick's grandniece. Also, Rollin Livick, ROQC.

Loucks, Ralph. Loucks's account of the Battle of Cantigny ran in the *Fort Wayne (Ind.) Journal-Gazette*, August 11, 1918. His account of the armistice from the *Janesville (Wisc.) Daily Gazette*, August 14, 1985.

Lowery, H. K. Lowery's description of the trenches at Cantigny from WWR 12, pt. 2: *Operations Reports, First Division.*

Maine, Charles. Maine's account of Company M's Atlantic crossing ran in the *Janesville (Wisc.) Daily Gazette*, April 24, 1918.

Marshall, George C. Accounts of the effects of explosives and accounts from Cantigny and after the battle come from his *Memoirs of My Services in the World War, 1917–1919.*

Martin, Harry H. The *Emporia (Kan.) Weekly Gazette* ran Martin's account of the Battle of Cantigny on July 4, 1918; the resulting reprimand is found in RG 120, Entry 1241, Box 223, *Organization Records, First Division, General Orders 1918–1921*, U.S. National Archives, College Park, Maryland. Martin's account of the *Mount Vernon*'s voyage to France appeared in the *Emporia (Kan.) Weekly Gazette*, December 13, 1917.

McClure, Walter R. *Operations of Company M 26th Infantry (1st Division) in the St. Mihiel Offensive, September 13–September 16, 1918*, MWW.

Mitchell, Carl. Mitchell's account of his ordeal in the Argonne ran in the *Indianapolis Star*, November 11, 1918.

Murphy, Wilbert. Murphy's account of the Battle of Soissons was taken from two letters he wrote after the war—one published by the *Brodhead (Wisc.) Independent-Register*, March 26, 1919, and the other by the *Brodhead News*, March 6, 1919. Numerous other letters from Murphy come from both papers between May 1917 and April 1919.

Nelson, John. Information regarding John Nelson was provided to the author by the Department of Veterans Affairs. Additional information came from the *Door County (Wisc.) Advocate*, November 23, 1991; and June 1990 newsletter from the Liberty Grove (Wisc.) Veterans of Foreign Wars Post 8337. Found sleeping on guard duty from RG 391, Entry 2133, Box 3773, *Records of Regular Mobile Army Units, Company L, 344th Infantry*, U.S. National Archives, College Park, Maryland. Ancestral information compiled from church records in Sweden and translated by Karin Nelson.

Nelson, Ruben J. "Ruben J. Nelson Diary." Wisconsin Veterans Museum Library, Madison, Wisconsin, Mss. 2004.140.

Newhall, Richard Ager. Newhall's account of the Battle of Cantigny found in *Newhall and Williams College: Selected Papers of a History Teacher at a New England College, 1917–1973*. Reprinted with permission of the Williams College Archives and Special Collections, Williamstown, Mass.

Odle, Alva Sheridan. Alva's August 23, 1918, postcard provided to the author by Odle descendant Jo Ann McGhee. Also Alva Odle, ROQC.

Oliver, Clarence. Account of Company B at Cantigny from WWR 13: *Operations Reports, 28th Infantry*. George Rozelle's account of Oliver's death from Box 185, ABM.

Palmer, Frederick. His accounts of the size of the American army and the need for a draft from *Our Gallant Madness*. His descriptions of the Meuse-Argonne sector from *Collier's*, March 22, 1919, "America's Greatest Battle." His account of a conversation with a "kid lieutenant" in "America's Greatest Battle, Part II," *Collier's*, March 29, 1919.

Parker, Paul B. *The Battle of Cantigny*, MWW.

Parker, Samuel I. Parker's account of the Battle of Cantigny ran in the *Monroe (N.C.) Enquirer Journal*, July 15, 1918; for Parker's account of Soissons, see the *Bridgehead Sentinel*, Spring 1973; also *On Point: The Journal of Army History*, Spring 2007; and Paul R. Clancy, *Just a Country Lawyer*. Parker's account of the Argonne and the 28th Regiment's order for the October 2, 1918, patrol come from Box 188, ABM.

Peterson, Philip Danforth. Accounts of Peterson's heroism and death, ROQC.

Pol, Ralph. Biographical information on Pol comes from author interview with Durena Pol, wife of Ralph Pol's nephew and namesake, Ralph Pol. Also Ralph Pol, ROQC.

Pooler, John R. Account of Pooler's death, ROQC.

Purdy, Robert O. Account of Purdy's death from Snowden Yates and H. G. Cutler, *History of South Carolina*.

Redwood, George Buchanan. Accounts of Redwood's night patrol and death can be found in the George B. Redwood Papers, 1917–1918, Mss. 1530.3, Maryland Historical Society, Baltimore, Maryland. Used with permission.

Roosevelt, Theodore, Jr. Roosevelt's account of gas warnings appears in his *Average Americans*.

Rozelle, George F. Rozelle's account of the Battle of Soissons found in Box 185, ABM. Also, George F. Rozelle obituary in the *Boerne (Tex.) Star*, June 7, 1962; additional biographical material from the United States Military Academy Library, West Point, New York; Rozelle's report on the Battle of Cantigny and John Church night patrol from WWR 13: *Operations Reports 28th Infantry Regiment*.

Sachs, Abe. Interview with Sachs ran in the *Chicago Tribune*, August 25, 1918.

Sargent, Daniel. Sargent's account of the Battle of Cantigny found in *The World War I Veterans Survey Collection*, U.S. Army Military History Institute, Carlisle, Pennsylvania.

Scarborough, Milton. Account of Scarborough's death, ROQC.

Schindler, William. Schindler's account of the Battle of Cantigny from the *Janesville (Wisc.) Daily Gazette*, July 17, 1918.

Senay, Charles T. Senay's unpublished memoir, "From Shavetail to Captain," was graciously provided to the author by Charles Senay's son, David, and grandson, Tim Senay. Also, August 1964 letter from Senay to his daughter titled "Country Boy," also provided by Tim Senay. Senay's postwar writings on the St. Mihiel offensive come from two sources: *Operations of First Battalion, 28th Infantry in Reduction of St. Mihiel Salient, September 12 and 13th, 1918*, WWR; and the undated papers "An Unlimited Objective Attack in the Reduction of the St. Mihiel Salient 12 Sept. 1918" and "Operations of the 28th Infantry 18–23 July, 1918," found at the Combined Arms Research Library, Fort Leavenworth, Kansas. Also WWR 13: *Operations Reports 28th Infantry Regiment* and Box 185, ABM.

Slinker, Thomas Dewey. Correspondence from and about Thomas Dewey Slinker found in Records of the Bureau of Indian Affairs, RG 75, Entry 1327, File 455, *Carlisle Indian School Student Records, 1879–1918*, U.S. National Archives, Washington, D.C. George Butler's description of Slinker as the best bugler in the 28th Regiment from Emery Kurtchka, comp., *The American Indian in the World War*, Book 5, Mathers Museum of World Cultures, Bloomington, Indiana.

Sorensen, Soren C. Material on Sorensen's earlier army career comes from Records of the Adjutant General's Office, 1780s–1917, RG 94, *Register of Enlistments in the U.S. Army, 1798–1914*, Microfilm Publication M233, Entry 91, Roll #68, p. 157; and Records of the Adjutant General's Office, 1780s–1917, *General Correspondence of the Adjutant General, 1890–1917*, RG 94, Entry 25, File #1580753, U.S. National Archives, Washington, D.C. Request for transfer to military police from RG 120, Entry 1241, Box 161, *First Division Document File*, U.S. National Archives, College Park, Maryland. Other material found in the *Lincoln (Neb.). Evening State Journal*, September 14, 1918; the *Lead (S.D.) Daily Call*, June 1, 1917; the *Deadwood (S.D.) Daily Telegram*, June 8, 1917; account of Sorensen's death from *The Amaroc News*, June 3, 1919, and *Grand Island (Neb.) Independent*, June 23, 1919; Laura Evelyn Sorensen's letters found in Sorensen ROQC; biographical information regarding Laura Evelyn provided by the Stuhr Museum of the Prairie Pioneer, Grand Island, Nebraska. Sorensen's account of the Battle of Cantigny found in WWR 13: *Operations Reports 28th Infantry Regiment*. Sorensen letter to Robert Livick from the Rollin Livick Papers.

Stainton, Marvin Everett. Newspaper articles and correspondence from, to, and about Marvin Stainton are contained in the Marvin Stainton Papers, use of which was graciously provided to the author by Hubert M. Stainton Jr. Used with permission. Accounts of his death and disinterment also from ROQC, which contains the March 25, 1921, *Washington (D.C.) Herald* article, "Girl Shaken by Note From 'Dead' Yank."

Stainton, Sam Dave. Sam's letters from the Marvin Stainton Papers.

Stamm, Gerald V. Stamm's account of Soissons comes from "No Medals," in Edward S. Johnson et al., *Americans vs. Germans: The First AEF in Action.*

Storms, Willard Sidney. Accounts of Storms's induction into the army were found in the *Dwight (Kan.) Signal* in May and June 1917. Letters marking his arrival in France ran in the *Signal*, December 6, 1917; Storms's descriptions of the front lines ran in the *Weekly Guard and Dwight Signal*, June 28, 1918; his account of the assault on Berzy-le-Sec ran in the *Weekly Guard and Dwight Register*, September 20, 1918. The account of Willard Storms in No Man's Land is from an August 28, 1935, letter from George Butler to Storms's daughter, Jessie Stocks; that letter, other letters written by Willard Storms, and biographical information were provided to the author by Storms's granddaughter, Diane Williamson. Storms's postwar correspondence with the Graves Registration Service found in the burial files for Rufus Durham and George Dust, ROQC. Storms's obituary from the *Riverside (Calif.) Enterprise*, December 14, 1934.

Suchocki, Boleslaw. Suchocki's account of the Battle of Cantigny found in WWR 14: *Operations Reports First Engineers.*

Swanson, Otto B. Information on the discovery of Swanson's grave comes from ROQC.

Teeple, Jay. An account of Teeple's actions during the Battle of Soissons ran in the *Fort Wayne (Ind.) News and Sentinel*, January 11, 1919.

Tenbroeck, Howard. Tenbroeck's letter from the hospital from the *Middletown (N.Y.) Times-Press*, July 6, 1918.

Terman, Sam. The account of Terman's death is from ROQC; also RG 391, Entry 2133, *Records of Regular Army Mobile Units, 28th Infantry Regiment*, U.S. National Archives, College Park, Maryland.

Thompson, Nelson H. Thompson's account of Soissons comes from the *Fort Wayne (Ind.) News and Sentinel*, February 26, 1919.

Tippman, Bert. Tippman's account of his experiences in the Battle of Soissons are spread across two letters that ran in the *La Crosse (Wisc.) Tribune and Leader-Press*, September 29 and October 20, 1918. Tippman's account of his entry into the lines at Cantigny from the *Tribune and Leader-Press*, October 20, 1918.

Tyler, Gerald R. Tyler's account of the Battle of Cantigny found in Box 184, ABM.

Underwood, Arza. Account of Underwood's death found in the *Doddridge County (W.Va.) Republican*, September 17, 1931. Also author interview with Underwood's daughter, Thelma Leasure.

Usher, Ellis B. Usher's article ran in the *Janesville (Wisc.) Daily Gazette*, April 7, 1918.

Van Natter, Francis M. In the Battle of Cantigny, WWR 13: *Operations Reports 28th Infantry Regiment*. The account of Van Natter at Soissons in letter Herman Dacus to Ed Burke, August 1984. See entry for Herman Dacus.

Vedral, Anthony. Vedral's descriptions of the front lines, the death of Marvin Stainton, and postwar duty in Germany found in the Marvin Stainton Papers.

Vogel, Paul. Vogel's account of the assault of the 1st Battalion, 28th Infantry, on July 19, 1918, ran in the *Janesville (Wisc.) Daily Gazette* on December 28, 1918.

Waltz, Welcome P. Waltz's description of Cantigny was found in *Operations of Company C, 3d Machine Gun Battalion at Cantigny*, MWW.

Warren, William Dwight. Warren's letters are found in Dorothy Rinaldo, *An Imperfect Genealogy*. Used with permission. Warren's recollections of the assault on Berzy-le-Sec from Box 185, ABM.

Warren, John G. Accounts of Warren's death, ROQC.

Weil, Edward. Account of Weil's death, ROQC.

White, Elmer E. White's account of the Battle of Soissons comes from the *Syracuse (N.Y.) Herald*, September 10, 1918.

Wilder, Stuart G. Wilder's postwar monograph *Operations of Co "M" 16th Infantry (1st Division) in the Cantigny Operations*, MWW.

Wilson, Leigh Ellsworth. Biographical information on the Wilson family from *Genealogy of the Family of Hannah Allen and Abraham Willis*, Waseca County (Minn.) Historical Society. Also author interviews with Anna Wilson's granddaughters, Dorothy Geduldig and Beverly Fuque; Anna's search for Leigh comes from *Janesville (Minn.) Argus*, March 5, 1919, and April 23, 1919; also Leigh Wilson, ROQC.

Yuill, Charles W. *Operations of Co B 3d MG Bn (First Division) in the Aisne-Marne Offensive, July 16–July 23, 1918*, MWW.

Zerwes, Joseph. Biographical material on Joseph Zerwes graciously provided to the author by Marjorie Ulseth, Zerwes's niece. Used with permission. Zerwes's military service record provided by the Waukesha County (Wisc.) Historical Society and Museum. Also RG 391, Entry 2133, Box 85, *Records of Regular Army Mobile Units, 28th Infantry Regiment*.

BIBLIOGRAPHY

Adams, Myron E., and Girton, Fred. *The History and Achievements of the Fort Sheridan Officers' Training Camps.* Ft. Sheridan, Ill. Fort Sheridan Association, 1920.

American Battle Monuments Commission. *American Armies and Battlefields in Europe.* Washington, D.C.: Government Printing Office, 1938.

———. *1st Division, Summary of Operations in the World War.* Washington, D.C.: Government Printing Office, 1944.

Berry, Henry. *Make the Kaiser Dance: The American Experience in World War I.* New York: Doubleday, 1978.

Bogert, George D. *"Let's Go!" 10 Years' Retrospect of the World War.* San Francisco: H. S. Crocker Co., 1927.

Boot, Max. *The Savage Wars of Peace: Small Wars and the Rise of American Power.* New York: Basic Books, 2002.

Bostert, Russell H., ed., *Newhall and Williams College: Selected Papers of a History Teacher at a New England College, 1917–1973.* New York: Peter Lang, 1989.

Bowman, Stephen L. *A Century of Valor: The First One Hundred Years of the Twenty-Eighth United States Infantry Regiment (Black Lions).* Wheaton, Ill.: Cantigny First Division Foundation, 2004.

Braim, Paul F. *The Test of Battle: The American Expeditionary Forces in the Meuse-Argonne Campaign.* Cranbury, N.J.: Associated University Presses, 1987.

———. *Brodhead's Tribute to Her Men in Service, 1914–1918.* Madison, Wisc.: Cantwell Printing Co., 1921.

Brown, G. Waldo, and Rosecrans, W. Pillsbury. *The American Army in the World War: A Divisional Record of the American Expeditionary Forces in Europe.* Manchester, N.H.: Overseas Book Company, 1921.

Buck, Beaumont B. *Memories of Peace and War.* San Antonio: Naylor, 1935.

Bullard, Robert Lee. *American Soldiers Also Fought.* New York, Toronto; Longmans, Green and Co. 1936.

———. *Personalities and Reminiscences of the War.* Garden City, N.Y.: Doubleday & Page, 1925.

Butler, Charles E. *The Yanks Are Coming!* New York: Vantage Press, 1963.

Clancy, Paul R. *Just a Country Lawyer: A Biography of Senator Sam Ervin.* Bloomington: Indiana University Press, 1974.

Clay, Steven E. *Blood and Sacrifice: The History of the 16th Infantry Regiment from the Civil War Through the Gulf War.* Chicago and Maryland: Cantigny First Division Foundation, 16th Infantry Regiment Association, 2001.

Cochrane, Rexmond C. *Gas Warfare in World War I, Study Number 9.* Maryland, U.S. Army Chemical Corps Historical Office, 1958.

Coffman, Edward M. *The War to End All Wars: The American Military Experience in World War I.* New York: Oxford University Press, 1968.

Crozier, Emmet. *American Reporters on the Western Front, 1914–1918.* New York: Oxford University Press, 1959.

Dorr, Rheta Childe. *A Soldier's Mother in France.* Indianapolis: Bobbs-Merrill, 1918.

Eisenhower, John S. D., and Eisenhower, Joanne Thompson. *Yanks: The Epic Story of the American Army in World War I.* New York: Free Press, 2001.

Evarts, Jeremiah M. *Cantigny: A Corner of the War.* New York: Scribner Press, 1938.

Fredericks, Pierce G. *The Yanks Are Coming.* New York: Bantam Books, 1964.

Garey, E. B.; Ellis, O. O.; Magoffin, R. V. D. *The American Guide Book to France and Its Battlefields.* New York: Macmillan, 1920.

Gilbert, Martin. *The First World War: A Complete History.* New York: Henry Holt, 1994.

Gowenlock, Thomas R., and Murchie, Guy, Jr. *Soldiers of Darkness.* Garden City, N.Y.: Doubleday, Doran, 1937.

Hallas, James H., ed. *Doughboy War: The American Expeditionary Force in World War I.* Boulder, Colo.: Lynne Rienner Publishers, 2000.

Hamilton, Craig, and Corbin, Louise, eds. *Echoes From Over There.* New York: Soldiers' Publishing Company, 1919.

Hanson, Neil. *Unknown Soldier: The Story of the Missing of the First World War.* New York, Vintage Books, 2005.

Harbord, James G. *The American Army in France, 1917–1919.* Boston: Little, Brown, 1936.

Harries, Meirion and Susie. *The Last Days of Innocence: America at War, 1917–1918.* New York: Vintage Books, 1997.

Haulsee, W. M.; Howe, F. G.; and Doyle, A. C., comp. *Soldiers of the Great War.* 3 vol. Washington, D.C.: Soldiers Record Publishing Association, 1920.

Heller, Charles E., and Stofft, William A., eds. *America's First Battles, 1776–1965.* Lawrence: University Press of Kansas, 1986.

Hoehling, A. A. *The Fierce Lambs.* Boston and Toronto: Little, Brown, 1960.

Howe, M. A. DeWolfe. *Memoirs of the Harvard Dead in the War Against Germany,* vol. 3. Cambridge, Mass.: Harvard University Press, 1922.

Huelfer, Evan Andrew. *The "Casualty Issue" in American Military Practice: The Impact of World War I.* Westport, Conn.: Praeger, 2003.

Johnson, Douglas V., and Hillman, Rolfe L., Jr. *Soissons, 1918.* College Station: Texas A&M University Press, 1999.

Johnson, Harry. *A History of Anderson County, Kansas.* Garnett, Kan.: Garnett Review Company, 1938.

Johnston, Edward S., et al. *Americans vs. Germans: The First AEF in Action.* New York: Penguin Books: Washington: Infantry Journal, 1942.

Keegan, John. *The Face of Battle.* London: Penguin Group, 1978.

Keene, Jennifer D. *Doughboys, the Great War, and the Remaking of America.* Baltimore and London: Johns Hopkins University Press, 2001.

Kennedy, David M. *Over Here: The First World War and American Society.* New York: Oxford University Press, 1982.

Knapp, Virginia. *Remembering Rusk County.* Dallas: Curtis Media Corp., 1992.

Lengel, Edward G. *To Conquer Hell: The Meuse-Argonne, 1918.* New York: Henry Holt, 2008.

Lickteig, Dorothy Kipper. *Early Gleanings of Anderson County,* vol. 3. Garnett, Kan.: Anderson County, Kansas, Historical Society, n.d.

March, William. *Company K.* New York: American Mercury, Inc., 1931.

Marshall, George C. *Memoirs of My Services in the World War, 1917–1918.* Boston: Houghton Mifflin, 1976.

Maverick, Maury. *A Maverick American.* New York: J. J. Little and Ives Company, 1937.

McGlachlin, E. F., Jr. *Brief History of Operations of 1st Division.* Montabaur, Germany: Printing Office of G. Sauerborn, 1918.

Mead, Gary. *The Doughboys: America and the First World War.* Woodstock, N.Y.: Overlook Press, Peter Mayer, Publishers, 2000.

Miller, Henry Russell. *The First Division.* Pittsburgh: Crescent Press, 1920.

North, Sterling. *Rascal: A Memoir of a Better Era.* New York; Puffin Books, 1990.

Palmer, Frederick. *Our Gallant Madness.* Garden City, N.Y.: Doubleday, Doran, 1937.

Pershing, John J. *My Experiences in the World War.* 2 vols. New York: Frederick A. Stokes Company, 1931.

Persico, Joseph E. *Eleventh Month, Eleventh Day, Eleventh Hour: Armistice Day, World War I and Its Violent Climax.* New York: Random House, 2005.

Piehler, G. Kurt. *Remembering War the American Way.* Washington, D.C.: Smithsonian Books, 1995.

Pugh, Irving Edwin, and Thayer, William F. *Forgotten Fights of the A.E.F.* Boston: Roxburgh Publishing Company, 1921.

Quiner, Edwin Bentley. *The Military History of Wisconsin: A Record of the Civil and Military Patriotism of the State in the War for the Union.* Chicago; Clarke & Co., 1866.

Rinaldo, Dorothy Warren. *An Imperfect Genealogy: Tates, Hastings, Warrens.* Ithaca, N.Y.: Dorpete Press, 2005.

Roosevelt, Theodore, Jr. *Average Americans.* New York and London, G. P. Putnam's Sons, Knickerbocker Press, 1919.

Smythe, Donald. *Pershing: General of the Armies.* Bloomington: Indiana University Press, 1986.

Society of the First Division. *History of the First Division During the World War, 1917–1919.* Philadelphia: Winston, 1931.

Stallings, Laurence. *The Doughboys: The Story of the AEF, 1917–1919.* New York: Popular Library, 1964.

Summerall, C. P. *The Story of the Twenty-Eighth Infantry in the Great War.* American Expeditionary Forces, 1919.

Thomas, Shipley. *The History of the A.E.F.* New York: George H. Doran Company, 1920.

Toland, John. *No Man's Land: 1918, the Last Year of the Great War.* Garden City, N.Y.: Doubleday, 1980.

United States. Adjutant General's Office. *Congressional Medal of Honor, the Distinguished Service Cross, and the Distinguished Service Medal Issued by the War Department Since April 6, 1917.* Washington: Government Printing Office, 1920.

United States. Army Division, 1st. *World War Records, Base Maps and Overlays / First Division, A.E.F. Regular,* vol. 1. Washington, D.C.: s.n., 1928–1930. 23 vols.

Votaw, John F. *The American Expeditionary Forces in World War I.* Oxford, United Kingdom and New York: Osprey Publishing, 2005.

Wise, Jennings C. *The Turn of the Tide.* New York: Henry Holt, 1920.

Yates, Snowden, and Cutler, H. G. *History of South Carolina,* 3 vols. Chicago and New York: Lewis Publishing Company, 1920.

Additional Archival Records

United States National Archives

Record Group 92, Entry 2061. *Office of the Quartermaster General Army Transport Service*

RG 94, Entry 25, Records of the Adjutant General's Office, 1780–1916. *General Correspondence of the Adjutant General, 1780s–1917*

Record Group 391, Entry 2133, *Records of Regular Army Mobile Units, Company L, 344th Infantry Regiment*

Record Group 407-A, Records of the Adjutant General's Office, *Commissions of Officers in the Regular Army, National Guard, and Officer Reserve Corps, 1917–1940*

National Personnel Records Center, St. Louis, Missouri: *Morning Reports, Company D, First Battalion, 28th Infantry Regiment, United States First Division, February, 1918–November, 1918*

Robert R. McCormick Research Center Muster rolls, Co. D, 28th Infantry, United States 1st Division, December, 1917–September, 1919

Additional Interviews

Robert L. Beard	Charles L. Gunn
Margaret Brackett	Robert Hoyle
Norma Carns	Thelma Leasure
Robert Cibulka	Philip H. Peterson
Tom Conzatti	Paul Proulx
Carol Corby	Dorothy Rinaldo
Simon Dean	Roger Shell
George Gahring	Marjorie Ulseth
Dean Gunderson	Edwin Wilber

Newspapers, ca. 1917–1991

Abilene (Tex.) Reporter-News

Altoona (Pa.) Mirror

Arkansas City (Kan.) Daily News

Arkansas City (Kan.) Daily Traveler

Boerne (Tex.) Star

Brockton (Mass.) Daily Enterprise

Brodhead (Wisc.) News

Brodhead (Wisc.) Independent-Register

Chicago Daily News

Chicago Tribune

Columbia City (Ind.) Post

The Deadwood (S.D.) Daily Telegram

Deadwood (S.D.) Daily Pioneer Times

Door County (Wisc.) Advocate

Dwight (Kan.) Signal and *The Weekly Guard and Dwight Signal*

Ellenville (N.Y.) Journal

Emporia (Kan.) Weekly Gazette

Flushing (N.Y.) Daily Times

Fort Wayne (Ind.) Journal-Gazette

Fort Wayne (Ind.) News and Sentinel

Garnett (Kan.) Review

Grand Island (Neb.) Independent

Green County (Miss.) Herald

Hastings (Mich.) Banner

Indianapolis Star

Janesville (Wisc.) Daily Gazette

Janesville (Minn.) Argus

Kalamazoo (Mich.) Gazette

Kokomo (Ind.) Daily Tribune

La Crosse (Wisc.) Tribune and Leader-Press

Laurel (Miss.) Daily Leader

The Lead (S.D.) Daily Call

Lincoln (Neb.) Evening Star Journal

Martinsburg (W.Va.) Journal

McCammon (Ida.) News

Middletown (N.Y.) Times-Press

New York Tribune

Oakland (Cal.) Tribune

Omaha (Neb.) World Herald

Paragould (Ark.) Weekly Soliphone

Riverside (Calif.) Enterprise

San Antonio (Tex.) Light

Savanna (Ill.) Times-Journal

Shabbona (Ill.) Express

The Stars and Stripes

Syracuse (N.Y) Herald

Wakefield (Mich.) Advocate

Washington Herald

The Washington Post

Waukesha (Wisc.) Freeman

Waupaca County (Wisc.) Post

Wellsboro (Pa.) Agitator

Internet Resources

This book would not have been possible without the aid of several Internet resources, most notably www.ancestry.com, through which over the course of hundreds of hours I found draft-registration cards, state and federal censuses, family data, and other information vital to tracking Company D's soldiers and locating their descendants.

There are too many other Internet sources to list here, but the most important were www.infantry.army.mil/donovan (Donovan Research Library), www.nara.gov (United States National Archives), www.abmc.gov (American Battle Monuments Commission), www.carlisle.army.mil/ahec (U.S. Army Heritage and Education Center), www.history.navy.mil (Navy Historical Center), and www.newspaperarchive.com.

INDEX